Adobe® Flash® CS5

The Professional Portfolio

AGAINST THE CLOCK
mastering graphic technology

Managing Editor: Ellenn Behoriam
Cover & Interior Design: Erika Kendra
Copy Editor: Angelina Kendra

10 9 8 7 6 5 4 3 2 1   978-1-936201-05-1

mastering graphic technology

4710 28th Street North, Saint Petersburg, FL 33714
800-256-4ATC • www.againsttheclock.com

Acknowledgements

ABOUT AGAINST THE CLOCK

Against The Clock, long recognized as one of the nation's leaders in courseware development, has been publishing high-quality educational materials for the graphic and computer arts industries since 1990. The company has developed a solid and widely-respected approach to teaching people how to effectively utilize graphics applications, while maintaining a disciplined approach to real-world problems.

Having developed the *Against The Clock* and the *Essentials for Design* series with Prentice Hall/Pearson Education, ATC drew from years of professional experience and instructor feedback to develop *The Professional Portfolio Series*, focusing on the Adobe Creative Suite. These books feature step-by-step explanations, detailed foundational information, and advice and tips from industry professionals that offer practical solutions to technical issues.

Against The Clock works closely with all major software developers to create learning solutions that fulfill both the requirements of instructors and the needs of students. Thousands of graphic arts professionals — designers, illustrators, imaging specialists, prepress experts and production managers — began their educations with Against The Clock training books. These professionals studied at Baker College, Nossi College of Art, Virginia Tech, Appalachian State University, Keiser College, University of South Carolina, Gress Graphic Arts Institute, Hagerstown Community College, Kean University, Southern Polytechnic State University, Brenau University, and many other educational institutions.

ABOUT THE AUTHOR

Erika Kendra holds a BA in History and a BA in English Literature from the University of Pittsburgh. She began her career in the graphic communications industry as an editor at Graphic Arts Technical Foundation before moving to Los Angeles in 2000. Erika is the author or co-author of more than twenty books about Adobe graphic design software. She has also written several books about graphic design concepts such as color reproduction and preflighting, and dozens of articles for online and print journals in the graphics industry. Working with Against The Clock for more than ten years, Erika was a key partner in developing The Professional Portfolio Series of software training books.

CONTRIBUTING ARTISTS AND EDITORS

A big thank you to the people whose artwork, comments, and expertise contributed to the success of these books:

- **Pamela Harris**, University of North Texas Dallas
- **Carlos Miranda**, Tallahassee Community College
- **Colleen Bredahl**, United Tribes Technical College
- **Carol Atkinson**, University of Central Missouri
- **Robert Bunch**, Flash King Media
- **Burcu Arat Sup**, Mujka Design
- **Debbie Davidson**, Sweet Dreams Design
- **Dean Bagley**, Against The Clock, Inc.

Finally, thanks to **Angelina Kendra**, editor, for making sure that we all said what we meant to say.

Walk-Through

Project Goals
Each project begins with a clear description of the overall concepts that are explained in the project; these goals closely match the different "stages" of the project workflow.

The Project Meeting
Each project includes the client's initial comments, which provide valuable information about the job. The Project Art Director, a vital part of any design workflow, also provides fundamental advice and production requirements.

Project Objectives
Each Project Meeting includes a summary of the specific skills required to complete the project.

Real-World Workflow
Projects are broken into logical lessons or "stages" of the workflow. Brief introductions at the beginning of each stage provide vital foundational material required to complete the task.

Step-By-Step Exercises
Every stage of the workflow is broken into multiple hands-on, step-by-step exercises.

Visual Explanations
Wherever possible, screen shots are annotated so you can quickly identify important information.

Flash Foundations
Additional functionality, related tools, and underlying graphic design concepts are included throughout the book.

Advice and Warnings
Where appropriate, sidebars provide shortcuts, warnings, or tips about the topic at hand.

Project Review
After completing each project, you can complete these fill-in-the-blank and short-answer questions to test your understanding of the concepts in the project.

Portfolio Builder Projects
Each step-by-step project is accompanied by a freeform project, allowing you to practice skills and creativity, resulting in an extensive and diverse portfolio of work.

Visual Summary
Using an annotated version of the finished project, you can quickly identify the skills used to complete different aspects of the job.

Projects at a Glance

The Against The Clock *Portfolio Series* teaches graphic design software tools and techniques entirely within the framework of real-world projects; we introduce and explain skills where they would naturally fall into a real project workflow.

The project-based approach in *The Professional Portfolio Series* allows you to get in depth with the software beginning in Project 1 — you don't have to read several chapters of introductory material before you can start creating finished artwork.

Our approach also prevents "topic tedium" — in other words, we don't require you to read pages and pages of information about text (for example); instead, we explain text tools and options as part of a larger project (in this case, as static text in a solar system model and as dynamic text in a video playback module).

Clear, easy-to-read, step-by-step instructions walk you through every phase of each job, from creating a new file to saving the finished piece. Wherever logical, we also offer practical advice and tips about underlying concepts and graphic design practices that will benefit students as they enter the job market.

The projects in this book reflect a range of different types of Flash jobs, from animating creatures in the ocean to building a model of the solar system to programming an interactive game. When you finish the eight projects in this book (and the accompanying Portfolio Builder exercises), you will have a substantial body of work that should impress any potential employer.

The eight Flash CS5 projects are described briefly here; more detail is provided in the full table of contents (beginning on Page viii).

project 1 — *Corvette Artwork*

- ❏ Setting up the Workspace
- ❏ Drawing in Flash
- ❏ Painting and Coloring Objects

project 2 — *Talking Kiosk Interface*

- ❏ Working with Symbols
- ❏ Working with Sound
- ❏ Creating Frame Animations

project 3 — *Solar System Model*

- ❏ Modeling Complex Animations
- ❏ Creating Animated Movie Clips
- ❏ Working with Text
- ❏ Adding Movie Controls

project 4

Ocean Animation

- ❏ Importing Bitmaps and Symbols
- ❏ Animating Symbols
- ❏ Programming Basic Timeline Control

project 5

Gator Race Game

- ❏ Preparing for ActionScript
- ❏ Working with ActionScript 3
- ❏ Creating Custom Functions
- ❏ Working with Variables and Arrays
- ❏ Scripting Loops
- ❏ Adding Sound with ActionScript

project 6

Gopher Golf Game

- ❏ Preparing Game Artwork
- ❏ Programming Interactivity

project 7

Travel Video Module

- ❏ Encoding Video for Flash
- ❏ Working with Components

project 8

Seabreeze Web Site

- ❏ Building Site Navigation
- ❏ Loading External Content

Some experts claim most people use only a small fraction — maybe 10% — of their software's capabilities; this is likely because many people don't know what is available. As you complete the projects in this book, our goal is to familiarize you with the entire tool set so you can be more productive and more marketable in your career as a graphic designer.

It is important to keep in mind that Flash is an extremely versatile and powerful application. The sheer volume of available tools, panels, and features can seem intimidating when you first look at the software interface. Most of these tools, however, are fairly simple to use with a bit of background information and a little practice.

Wherever necessary, we explain the underlying concepts and terms that are required for understanding the software. We are confident that these projects provide the practice you need to be able to create sophisticated artwork by the end of the very first project.

Contents

ACKNOWLEDGEMENTS   **iii**

WALK-THROUGH   **iv**

PROJECTS AT A GLANCE   **vi**

GETTING STARTED   **xiv**

THE FLASH USER INTERFACE   **1**

Identifying and Accessing Tools in Flash 8
Create a Saved Workspace 9
Customizing Flash Behavior 11
Explore the Flash Document Window 12
Understanding the Flash View Options 14
Managing Multiple Documents 16

Project 1   **CORVETTE ARTWORK**   **17**

Stage 1   **Setting up the Workspace** 19
Create a New Document 19
Import a Raster Image 20
Raster Images vs. Vector Art 21
Change Document Properties 22
Create Layers for Organizing Artwork 24
Drawing Preferences 25

Stage 2   **Drawing in Flash** 26
Destructive vs. Non-Destructive Editing 27
Draw with the Line Tool 28
Adjust Lines with the Selection Tool 31
Anchor Point Basics 32
Draw with the Pen Tool 33
Adjust Bézier Curve Shapes 37
Use Destructive Editing to Create Shapes 39
Draw with the Oval Tool 43
Using Rulers, Guides, and Grids 43
Basic Shape Options 45
Using the Free Transform Tool 46
Draw with the Pencil Tool 47
Work with an Object Group 50

Stage 3   **Painting and Coloring Objects** 53
Apply Fill and Stroke Colors to Selected Shapes 53
Fill Artwork with the Paint Bucket Tool 54
Change Stroke Attributes with the Ink Bottle Tool 56
Adjust Alpha Transparency 58
Using the Eyedropper Tool 59
Convert Strokes to Softened Fills 60

Paint with the Brush Tool 61

Apply Linear and Radial Gradients 63

Transform Gradients 65

Locking Bitmap and Gradient Fills 67

Organize Finished Artwork Layers. 68

Export Artwork as an Image 69

Project Review 70

Portfolio Builder Project 71

Project 2   TALKING KIOSK INTERFACE   **73**

Stage 1   **Working with Symbols** 75

The Library Panel in Depth. 75

Import Adobe Illustrator Artwork 76

Illustrator File Import Preferences 80

Import Files to the Library 81

Convert Objects to Symbols 82

Create a Button Symbol 85

Define a Hit State 87

Edit Symbol Properties 88

Using Different Symbol Editing Modes. 89

Explore the Symbol Registration Point 90

Organize Your Library with Folders. 92

Stage 2   **Working with Sound** 94

Import Sound Files 95

Add Event Sound 96

Viewing Large Documents 97

Edit a Sound Envelope to Control Volume 98

Applying Built-In Sound Effects 100

Use the Start and Stop Sync Methods for Buttons 100

Edit a Sound Envelope to Control Duration 102

Stage 3   **Creating Frame Animation** 104

Add Streaming Sound 104

Prepare for Lip Syncing 107

Create Lip Sync Animation 108

Define Sound Compression Settings 111

Project Review 114

Portfolio Builder Project 115

Project 3   SOLAR SYSTEM MODEL   **117**

Stage 1   **Modeling Complex Animations** 119

Create the Basic Document. 119

Use Transparency to Blend Objects into the Background. 121

Import and Mask Planet Images 123

Create a Complex Mask Shape 126

Contents

Stage 2   Creating Animated Movie Clips 130
Create the Solar System Structure 130
Controlling Frame and Tween Properties. 133
Create Motion Paths to Animate the Planets' Orbits 134
Complete the Planets' Orbits. 139
Extending the Length of the Timeline 139
Organize the Library 140
Animate a Nested Movie Clip 141

Stage 3   Working with Text 144
Add Text to the Model. 144
Controlling Text Properties 147
Define Font Embedding 149

Stage 4   Adding Movie Controls 151
Prepare Instances for Button Control. 151
Add Start and Stop Buttons. 152
Assign Behaviors to Button Instances. 155
Export Movie File Types 158
Publish the Final Movie. 159
Understanding Publish Settings 160

Project Review 162

Portfolio Builder Project 163

Project 4   OCEAN ANIMATION   **165**

Stage 1   Importing Bitmaps and Symbols 167
Import Adobe Photoshop Artwork 167
Photoshop File Import Preferences 168
Copy Assets from External Libraries 170
Align Objects on the Stage 172
Transform Symbols and Instances 173
Understanding Transformation Options 175
Work with Layers in an Imported Movie Clip Symbol. 177
Use the Spray Brush 178
Organize Your Library with Folders. 180

Stage 2   Animating Symbols 182
Create a Basic Frame Animation in a Movie Clip Symbol 182
Create an Object-Based Animation 185
Using Onion Skins 188
Edit the Shape of the Motion Path 189
Controlling Animation Speed with Easing 190
Motion Tween Properties and Presets. 192
Copy and Paste Frames 193
Creating and Controlling Shape Tweens 194
Use the Motion Editor 196
The Motion Editor Panel in Depth 198

Graphics vs. Movie Clips 200
Animate Effects and Filters 201
Animate in 3D 204
Work with the Bone Tool 207
Animate the Bone Armature 209

Stage 3 Programming Basic Timeline Control 212
Convert a Motion Tween to a Movie Clip 212
Prepare Symbol Instances for ActionScript 216
Add Movie Clip Controls 217
Add Event Handlers to Buttons 221
Combine Multiple Event Handlers in a Button 224

Project Review 227

Portfolio Builder Project 228

Project 5 GATOR RACE GAME   231

Stage 1 Preparing for ActionScript 233
Review the File Structure 233
Define Instance Names 235
Add Motion to the Background 236
Move the Starter off the Stage 238
Planning Your Script 240

Stage 2 Working with ActionScript 3 240
Use Functions to Control Movie Clip Timelines 242
The Actions Panel in Depth 243
Getting Help in the Actions Panel 246
Use Functions to Loop Frame Animations 247
Use Scripting to Control Object Properties 251

Stage 3 Creating Custom Functions 254
Create an Event Listener 254
Define a Custom Function 256

Stage 4 Working with Variables and Arrays 259
Script with Variables and Random Numbers 260
Translating ActionScript to Plain English 263
Create an Array to Store Object Positions 264

Stage 5 Scripting Loops 266
Define a for...in Loop to Evaluate Array Elements 267
Translating ActionScript to Plain English, Part 2 270
Use an If Else Condition to Call Movie Clip Frames 271
Program the Restart Button Functionality 274
Test the Movie and Change Cursor Styles 277

Stage 6 Adding Sound with ActionScript 279
Create Access for Sound Files in the Library 279
Create Scripts to Call Sounds 281

Project Review 284

Portfolio Builder Project 285

Contents

Project 6   GOPHER GOLF GAME   **287**

Stage 1   Preparing Game Artwork 289
Import Provided Artwork 289
Define Symbols and Instances 291
Organize File Layers 294
Map Timeline Frames and Keyframes 297
Change Button States 300
Add Classic Dynamic Text Areas 301
Animate the Pop-up Gopher Movie Clip 303
Mask a Motion Tween 306

Stage 2   Programming Interactivity 310
Add Timeline Controls 310
Program Basic Game Functionality 312
Use the Trace Function and Code Comments 315
Change the Mouse Cursor to a Movie Clip 317
Animate the Golf Club Cursor 320
Track User Actions 323
Pass Values to the Parent Timeline 325
Program the Result 327
Using the Compiler Errors Panel 328
Project Review 329
Portfolio Builder Project 330

Project 7   TRAVEL VIDEO MODULE   **333**

Stage 1   Encoding Video for Flash 335
Create a Queue in the Adobe Media Encoder 335
Define Encoder Settings 337
Understanding Video Export Settings 338
Prepare the Container Flash File 341
Import Video into Flash 342

Stage 2   Working with Components 347
User Interface Components 347
Define FLVPlayback Component Parameters 348
FLVPlayback Component Parameters 349
TextArea Component Parameters 350
Use the TextArea Component for Captions 350
Add Thumbnail Navigation Objects 351

Add Content to the TileList Component. 352

Adjust TileList Parameters 354

TileList Component Parameters 355

Use a Change Event to Link Images, Movies, and Captions. 356

Edit an Interface Component Skin 359

Edit Component Text Styles 362

Text Properties in ActionScript 3 363

Export the Video Module for Upload 364

Project Review 365

Portfolio Builder Project 366

Project 8 SEABREEZE WEB SITE   369

Stage 1 **Building Site Navigation** 371

Add Frame Labels 371

Create Switch Case Navigation 374

Change Dynamic Text Using Switch Cases 377

Create a Dynamic Date Object 379

Stage 2 **Loading External Content** 382

Define a Loader Object for Image Files 382

Use the addChild Function to Add to the Display List 384

Changing Object Properties in ActionScript 386

Define a URLLoader Object for an External Text File 387

Create Custom Scroll Buttons 390

Use the UILoader Component for External SWF Files 392

Project Review 397

Portfolio Builder Project 398

Getting Started

PREREQUISITES

The entire Portfolio Series is based on the assumption that you have a basic understanding of how to use your computer. You should know how to use your mouse to point, click, and drag items around the screen. You should be able to resize and arrange windows on your desktop to maximize your available space. You should know how to access drop-down menus, and understand how check boxes and radio buttons work. It also doesn't hurt to have a good understanding of how your operating system organizes files and folders, and how to navigate your way around them. If you're familiar with these fundamental skills, then you know all that's necessary to use the Portfolio Series.

RESOURCE FILES

All of the files you need to complete the projects in this book — except, of course, the Flash application files — are on the Student Files Web page at www.againsttheclock.com. See the inside back cover of this book for access information.

Each archive (ZIP) file is named according to the related project (e.g., **FL5_RF_Project1.zip**). At the beginning of each project, you must download the archive file for that project and expand that archive to access the resource files that you need to complete the exercises. Detailed instructions for this process are included in the Interface chapter.

Files required for the related Portfolio Builder exercises at the end of each project are also available on the Student Files Web page; these archives are also named by project (e.g., **FL5_PB_Project1.zip**).

SYSTEM REQUIREMENTS

As software technology continues to mature, the differences in functionality from one platform to another continue to diminish. The Portfolio Series was designed to work on both Macintosh or Windows computers; where differences exist from one platform to another, we include specific instructions relative to each platform.

One issue that remains different from Macintosh to Windows is the use of different modifier keys (Control, Shift, etc.) to accomplish the same task. When we present key commands or other system-specific instructions, we always follow the same Macintosh/Windows format — Macintosh commands are listed first, then a slash, followed by the Windows command.

Minimum System Requirements for Adobe Flash CS5:

Windows
- Intel® Pentium® 4 or AMD Athlon® 64 processor
- Microsoft® Windows® XP with Service Pack 2 (Service Pack 3 recommended); Windows Vista® Home Premium, Business, Ultimate, or Enterprise with Service Pack 1; or Windows 7
- 1 GB of RAM
- 3.5 GB of available hard-disk space for installation; additional free space required during installation
- 1024×768 display (1280×800 recommended) with 16-bit video card
- DVD-ROM drive
- QuickTime 7.6.2 software required for multimedia features
- Broadband Internet connection required for online services

Macintosh
- Multicore Intel processor
- Mac OS X v10.5.7 or v10.6
- 1 GB of RAM
- 4 GB of available hard-disk space for installation; additional free space required during installation
- 1024×768 display (1280×800 recommended) with 16-bit video card
- DVD-ROM drive
- QuickTime 7.6.2 software required for multimedia features
- Broadband Internet connection required for online services

Adobe Flash is the industry-standard application for building animations and other interactive content. Mastering the tools and techniques of the application can significantly improve your potential career options.

Typical Flash work ranges from simply moving things around within a space to building fully interactive games and Web sites, complete with sound and video files. Flash is somewhat unique in the communications industry because these different types of work often require different sets of skills — specifically, a combination of both visual creativity and logical programming. Depending on the type of application you're building, you should have a basic understanding of both graphic design and ActionScript code.

Our goal in this book is to teach you how to use the available tools to create various types of work that you might encounter in your professional career. As you complete the projects, you explore the basic drawing techniques, and then move on to more advanced techniques such as adding animation and interactivity — two core functions that make multimedia one of the most popular elements of modern electronic communication.

The simple exercises in this introduction are designed to let you explore the Flash user interface. Whether you are new to the application or upgrading from a previous version, we highly recommend that you follow these steps to click around and become familiar with the basic workspace.

EXPLORE THE FLASH INTERFACE

The user interface (UI) is what you see when you launch Flash. The specific elements you see — including which panels are open and where — depend on what was done the last time the application was open. The first time you launch the application, you'll see the default workspace settings defined by Adobe. When you relaunch after you or another user has quit, the workspace defaults to the last-used settings — including specific open panels and the position of those panels on your screen.

We designed the following exercise so you can explore various ways of controlling Flash's panels. Because workspace preferences are largely a matter of personal taste, the projects in this book direct you to use specific panels, but you can choose where to place those elements within the interface.

1. **Create a new empty folder named WIP on any writable disk (where you plan to save your work).**

2. **Download the FL5_RF_Interface.zip archive from the Student Files Web page.**

3. **Macintosh users: Place the ZIP archive in your WIP folder, then double-click the file icon to expand it.**

Double-click the archive file icon to expand it.

Windows users: Double-click the ZIP archive file to open it. Click the folder inside the archive and drag it into your primary WIP folder.

Open the archive file...

...then drag the Interface folder from the archive to your WIP folder.

The resulting **Interface** folder contains all the files you need to complete this introduction.

4. In Flash, open the Window menu and choose Workspace>Essentials.

Saved workspaces, accessed in the Window>Workspace menu or in the Workspace switcher on the Application bar, provide one-click access to a defined group of tools that might otherwise take multiple clicks each time you need the same toolset.

Keyboard shortcuts (if available) are listed on the right side of the menu.

Many menu commands are toggles, which means they are either on or off. The checkmark indicates that an option is toggled on (visible or active).

Note:

When no file is open in Flash, only a few menus are available in the Menu bar. Others become available only when a file is open.

Note:

If a menu command is grayed out, it is unavailable for the current selection.

5. Choose Window>Workspace>Reset 'Essentials'.

Saved workspaces remember the last-used state; calling a workspace again restores the panels exactly as they were the last time you used it. For example, if you close a panel that is part of a saved workspace, the closed panel will not be reopened the next time you call the same workspace. To restore the saved state of the workspace, including opening closed panels or repositioning moved ones, you have to use the Reset option.

Steps 4 and 5 might not do anything, depending on what was done in Flash before you started this exercise. (If you or someone else changes anything and quits the application, those changes are remembered even when Flash is relaunched.) Because we can't be sure what your default settings show, by completing these steps you reset the interface to one of the built-in default workspaces so your screen will match our screen shots.

Menu bar

Application bar

Workspace switcher

When no file is open, six of the menus are not available.

Welcome Screen

Panel dock

Docked Tools panel

Docked panel groups

On Windows, the Menu bar and Application bar are the same.

The Welcome Screen appears by default when no file is open, unless you (or someone else) checked the Don't Show Again option. The Welcome Screen provides quick access to recently opened files, and links for creating a variety of new documents. If you don't see the Welcome Screen when no files are open, you can turn this feature back on by choosing Welcome Screen in the On Launch menu of the General pane of the Preferences dialog box. After you quit and relaunch the application, the Welcome Screen reappears.

6. **Move your mouse cursor over the top icon in the leftmost column of the panel dock.**

   Panels, whether docked or floating, can be collapsed to icons (called iconic or iconized panels) to save space in the document window. You can see what each icon symbolizes through the tool tip that appears when you hover over a specific icon.

7. **Click the left edge of the leftmost column of docked panels. Hold down the mouse button and drag left until the names of the panels are visible.**

   When panels are iconized, you can expand the icons to show the panel names. This is useful when you are not yet familiar with the icons. You can also drag the column edge to the right to hide the panel names.

   Click the edge of the column and drag left to show the panel names.

8. **Control/right-click the title bar above the docked panel icons. Make sure Auto-Collapse Icon Panels in the contextual menu is checked (toggled on).**

   As we explained in the Getting Started section, when commands are different for the Macintosh and Windows operating systems, we include the different commands in the Macintosh/Windows format. In this case, Macintosh users who do not have right-click mouse capability can press the Control key and click to access the contextual menu. You do not have to press Control *and* right-click to access the menus.

   If you're using a Macintosh and don't have a mouse with right-click capability, we highly recommend that you purchase one. Right-click mice are inexpensive, they're available in most retail stores, and they save you significant amounts of time when accessing contextual options.

   Control/right-clicking a dock title bar opens the dock contextual menu, where you can change the default panel behavior. If you toggle off the Auto-Collapse Icon Panels option (which is active by default), a panel remains open until you intentionally collapse it, or until you open a different panel in the same column of the dock.

   This option should be checked.

   The Auto-Collapse Icon Panels option is also available in the User Interface pane of the Preferences dialog box, which you can open directly from the dock contextual menu.

9. **Click the Color panel button in the column of iconized panels.**

Clicking a docked panel button opens the panel to the left of the panel dock.

Click this icon to intentionally collapse an expanded panel.

Note:

Press F4 to hide all open panels. If any panels are hidden, press F4 again to reshow the hidden panels.

10. **Click away from the expanded panel (in the main workspace area, above or below the Welcome Screen).**

By default, expanded panels close as soon as you click away from them.

11. **Double-click the header above the column of panel icons.**

Double-clicking the dock column header expands iconized panels (or vice versa).

Double-click the header bar over a collapsed dock column to expand that column.

Double-click the header bar over an expanded dock column to collapse that column.

Note:

You can create multiple columns of panels in the dock. Each column, technically considered a separate dock, can be expanded or iconized independently of other columns.

12. **Click the Transform panel tab in the middle panel group to make that panel active in the group.**

13. **Click the Info panel tab and drag left, away from the dock.**

Most panels are docked by default, but you can move any panel (or panel group) away from the dock so it will appear as a separate panel (called a **floating panel**). A panel does not need to be active before you move it around in the workspace.

Note:

When we say "click and drag", you should hold down the mouse button while dragging.

Each panel in a group has its own tab.

Click a tab and drag to move that panel.

When you release the mouse button, the dragged panel "floats" separate from the dock.

Note:

You don't need to move a panel out of the dock before placing it in a different position within the dock. We included Step 13 to show you how to float panels and panel groups.

14. **Click the Info panel tab again and drag back to the dock until a blue line appears below the docked Properties/Library panel group.**

You can move any panel or group to a specific position in the dock by dragging. The blue highlight indicates where the panel will be placed when you release the mouse button.

Drag the floating Info panel until you see a blue line below the docked Properties panel group.

When you release the mouse button, the dragged panel appears below the Properties panel in a separate group.

Note:

An individual panel can be dragged to different locations (including into different groups) by dragging the panel's tab. The target location — where the panel will be located when you release the mouse button — is identified by the blue highlight.

15. **In the leftmost dock column, click the drop zone behind the Align and Transform panels and drag right until a blue line appears between the two panel groups in the middle column.**

You can move entire panel groups by dragging from the group's drop zone.

Note:

Floating panel groups can be iconized just like columns in the dock. Simply click the floating panel group title bar to toggle between expanded and iconized mode.

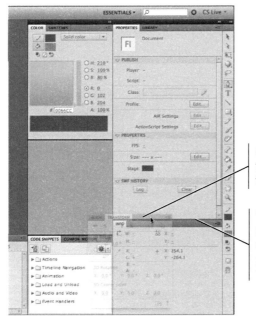

Click this area (called the **panel drop zone**) to move a panel group.

When you release the mouse button, the dragged panel group is placed at the location of the blue line.

Note:

Many screen shots in this book show floating panels so we can focus on the most important issue in a particular image. In our production workflow, however, we make heavy use of docked and iconized panels and take full advantage of saved custom workspaces.

16. Click the Color panel tab and drag down and right until a blue line appears around the entire Info panel.

When the blue line surrounds an existing panel (group), releasing the mouse button will group the moved panel with the existing panel (group).

Note:

You can also close individual panels by dragging them away from the dock or group, and then clicking the Close button of the floating panel (group).

17. Double-click the panel group drop zone behind the Info/Color panel tabs to collapse the group.

When a group is collapsed but not iconized, only the panel tabs are visible. Clicking a tab in a collapsed panel group expands the group and makes the selected panel active. You can also expand the group by again double-clicking the drop zone.

Double-click the panel group drop zone to collapse the group to show only the panel tabs.

Note:

When a file is open, you can access all panels from the Window menu.

If you choose a panel that's open but iconized, the panel expands to the left of its icon.

If you choose a panel that's open in an expanded group, that panel comes to the front of the group.

If you choose a panel that isn't currently open, it opens in the same position as when it was last closed.

18. Click the black line between the Properties and Transform panel groups and drag down to show as much of the Properties panel as possible.

You can drag the bottom edge of a docked panel group to vertically expand or shrink the panel; other panels in the same column expand or contract to fit the available space.

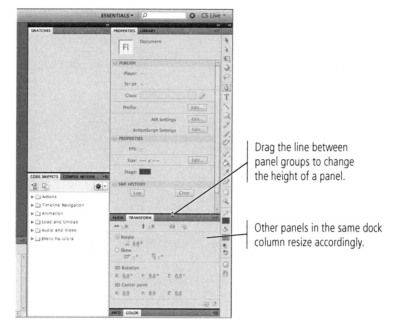

Drag the line between panel groups to change the height of a panel.

Other panels in the same dock column resize accordingly.

Note:

When docked, panel groups do not have their own Close buttons.

19. Control/right-click the Code Snippets tab in the left dock column. Choose Close Group from the contextual menu.

When panels are docked, the contextual menu is the only way to close a panel or panel group. (If the group is floating, you can use the panel or group's close button to put away those panels.)

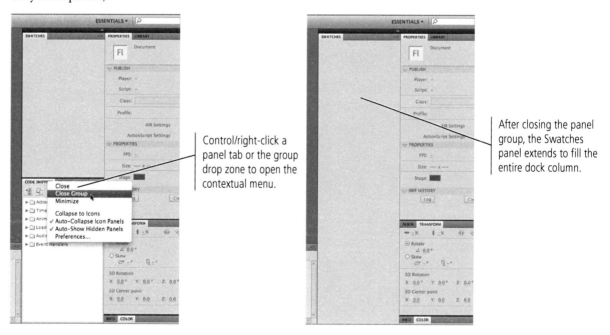

Control/right-click a panel tab or the group drop zone to open the contextual menu.

After closing the panel group, the Swatches panel extends to fill the entire dock column.

20. Control/right-click the Swatches panel tab and choose Close from the contextual menu.

FLASH FOUNDATIONS

In addition to a wide variety of panels, Flash CS5 includes 30 tools — a large number that indicates the power of the application. You can change the docked Tools panel to more than one column by dragging the right edge of the panel. When the Tools panel is floating, it defaults to show the various tools in rows.

You learn how to use these tools as you complete the projects in this book. For now, you should simply take the opportunity to identify the tools and their location on the Tools panel. The image to the right shows the icon, tool name, and keyboard shortcut (if any) that accesses each tool. Nested tools are shown indented and the names appear in italics.

Keyboard Shortcuts & Nested Tools

When you hover your mouse over a tool, the pop-up tool tip shows the name of the tool as well as a letter in parentheses. Pressing that letter activates the associated tool (unless you're working with type, in which case pressing a key adds that letter to your text). If you don't see tool tips, check the General pane of the Preferences dialog box; the Show Tooltips check box should be active.

When you hover the mouse cursor over the tool, a tool tip shows the name of the tool.

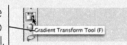

Any tool with an arrow in the bottom-right corner includes related tools nested below it. When you click a tool and hold down the mouse button, the nested tools appear in a pop-up menu. If you choose one of the nested tools, that variation becomes the default choice in the Tools panel.

This arrow means the tool has other nested tools.

Click and hold down the mouse button to show the nested tools.

Tool Options

In addition to the basic tool set, the bottom of the Tools panel includes options that control the fill and stroke colors, as well as options that change depending on the selected tool.

Stroke Color
Fill Color
Black and White
Swap Colors
Tool-specific options

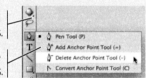

Customizing the Tools Panel

Flash offers a unique feature that makes it easy to customize the Tools panel (Flash>Customize Tools Panel on Macintosh or Edit>Customize Tools Panel on Windows).

If you click a tool icon in the left side of the dialog box, all tools nested in that space display in the Current Selection list. If you add a tool from the Available Tools list, it becomes nested under the selected tool. To remove a tool from the default Tools panel, select the tool name in the Current Selection list and click Remove.

➤	Selection tool (V)
➤	Subselection tool (A)
	Free Transform tool (Q)
	Gradient Transform tool (F)
	3D Rotation tool (W)
	3D Translation tool (G)
⌒	Lasso tool (L)
	Pen tool (P)
	Add Anchor Point tool (=)
	Delete Anchor Point tool (-)
	Convert Anchor Point tool (C)
T	Text tool (T)
＼	Line Segment tool (\)
	Rectangle tool (R)
	Oval tool (O)
	Rectangle Primitive tool
	Oval Primitive tool
	PolyStar tool
	Pencil tool (Y)
	Brush tool (B)
	Spray Brush tool
	Deco tool (U)
	Bone tool (M)
	Bind tool
	Paint Bucket tool (K)
	Ink Bottle tool (S)
	Eyedropper tool (I)
	Eraser tool (E)
	Hand tool (H)
	Zoom tool (Z)

21. **On the right side of the workspace, click the Tools panel title bar and drag away from the dock into the middle of the workspace.**

When docked, the Tools panel appears by default as a single column of tools.

When floating, the Tools panel defaults to a standard rectangular panel with the tools in several rows.

22. **Click the Tools panel title bar and drag left until a blue line appears on the left edge of the workspace.**

    This step docks the Tools panel on the left edge of the workspace.

This pop-up "drawer" indicates that you are adding a column to the panel dock (in this case, on the left edge of the workspace).

23. **Continue to the next exercise.**

CREATE A SAVED WORKSPACE

By now you should understand that you have extensive control over the appearance of your Flash workspace — you can determine what panels are visible, where and how they appear, and even the size of individual panels and panel groups. Rather than re-establishing every workspace element each time you return to Flash, you can save your custom workspace settings so you can recall them with a single click.

1. **Click the Workspace switcher in the Application/Menu bar and choose New Workspace.**

    Again, keep in mind that we list differing commands in the Macintosh/Windows format. On Macintosh, the Workspace switcher is in the Application bar; on Windows, it's in the Menu bar.

The Workspace switcher shows the name of the last-called workspace.

2. **In the New Workspace dialog box, type** `Portfolio` **as the Workspace name and click OK.**

After saving the current workspace, the Workspace switcher shows the name of the new saved workspace.

3. **Click the Library panel tab and drag down until a blue line appears between the Properties panel and the Align panel group.**

4. **Double-click the Align panel group drop zone to collapse the group.**

Note:

The Manage Workspaces option in the Workspace switcher opens a dialog box where you can choose a specific user-defined workspace to rename or delete. You can't rename or delete the default workspaces that come with the application.

5. **Click the Workspace switcher and choose Essentials from the list of available workspaces.**

Since you saved a different-named workspace after changing the Essentials arrangement, calling the workspace restores the saved state of that workspace.

6. Choose Portfolio from the Workspace switcher.

As we explained, calling a saved workspace restores the last-used state of the workspace. Even though you changed the panel arrangement after saving the Portfolio workspace, the adjusted arrangement is restored by calling the saved workspace.

Note:

If you move panels after calling a specific workspace, choosing Reset '[Workspace]' restores the active workspace to its saved settings.

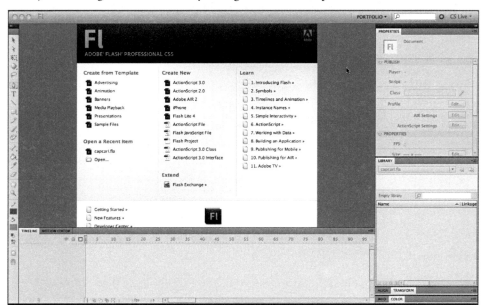

7. Continue to the next exercise.

Customizing Flash Behavior

FLASH FOUNDATIONS

Keyboard Shortcuts and Menus

Different people use Flash for various reasons, sometimes using a specific, limited set of tools to complete only one type of project. In addition to customizing the workspace and the Tools panel, you can also customize the various keyboard shortcuts used to access different commands (Flash>Keyboard Shortcuts on Macintosh or Edit>Keyboard Shortcuts on Windows). Once you have defined custom menus or shortcuts, you can save your choices as a set so you can access the same custom choices again without having to redo the work.

Application Preferences

You can also customize the way many of the program's tools and options function. The left side of the Preferences dialog box (Flash>Preferences on Macintosh or Edit>Preferences on Windows) allows you to display the various sets of preferences available in Flash. As you work your way through the projects in this book, you will learn not only what you can do with these collections of Preferences, but also why and when you might want to use them.

EXPLORE THE FLASH DOCUMENT WINDOW

There is far more to using Flash than arranging panels around the workspace. What you do with those panels — and even which panels you need — depends on the type of work you are doing in a particular file. In this exercise, you open a Flash file and explore the interface elements that you will use to create digital animations.

1. **In Flash, choose File>Open.**

2. **Navigate to your WIP>Interface folder and select capcarl.fla in the list of available files.**

   The Open dialog box is a system-standard navigation dialog. Press Shift to select and open multiple contiguous (consecutive) files in the list. Press Command/Control to select and open multiple non-contiguous files.

Note:

Press Command/Control-O to access the Open dialog box.

3. **Click Open.**

The Properties panel shows information about the selected object.

Open files are represented by tabs at the top of the document window.

Objects in the file appear on the Stage.

The Library panel stores various types of assets used in the file.

Placing each object in the file on its own layer simplifies and streamlines management of complex files.

The timeline contains frames, which are used to change what is visible at a given point in time.

4. **Above the top-right corner of the Stage, open the View Percentage menu and choose Fit in Window.**

5. **Click the bar that separates the Stage area from the Timeline panel. Drag up to enlarge the panel and show all the layers in the file.**

The Fit to Window command enlarges or reduces the view percentage to fill the available space in the document window.

Click here and drag up to show all the layers in the file.

6. **Review the Timeline panel.**

The Timeline panel is perhaps the most important panel in Flash. It represents the passage of time within your animation, and it enables you to control what happens to objects in your file, as well as when and where changes occur.

The playhead identifies the point in time that's currently active on the Stage.

The timeline includes frames, which represent fractions of a second in the resulting animation.

Keyframes identify the point in time at which something changes.

Layers can be used to organize elements of complex files.

New Layer button

New Folder button

Delete Layer button

Individual layers can be displayed as outlines by clicking in this column.

Individual layers can be locked or unlocked by clicking in this column.

Individual layer visibility can be toggled on or off by clicking in this column.

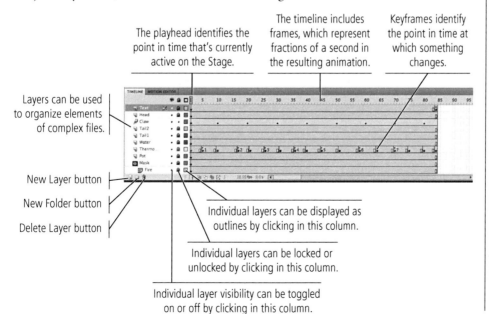

Note:

Different people prefer larger or smaller view percentages, depending on a number of factors (eyesight, monitor size, and so on). As you complete the projects in this book, you'll see our screen shots zoom in or out as necessary to show you the most relevant part of a particular file. In most cases we do not tell you what specific view percentage to use for a particular exercise, unless it's specifically required for the work being done.

Most Flash projects require some amount of zooming in and out, as well as navigating around the document within its window. As we show you how to complete different stages of the workflow, we usually won't tell you when to change your view percentage because that's largely a matter of personal preference. You should understand the different options for navigating around a Flash file, however, so you can easily and efficiently get to what you want, when you want to get there.

Zoom Tool

You can click with the Zoom tool to increase the view percentage in specific, predefined intervals (the same intervals you see in the View Percentage menu in the top-right corner of the document window). Pressing Option/Alt with the Zoom tool allows you to zoom out in the same predefined percentages. If you drag a marquee with the Zoom tool, you can zoom into a specific location; the area surrounded by the marquee fills the available space in the document window.

Click with the Zoom tool to zoom in.

Option/Alt-click with the Zoom tool to zoom out.

Draw a marquee with the Zoom tool...

...to fill the document window with the selected area.

View Menu

The View>Magnification menu also provides options for changing the view percentage, including their associated keyboard shortcuts. (The Zoom In and Zoom Out options step through the same predefined view percentages you see by clicking with the Zoom tool.)

Zoom In	Command/Control-equals (=)
Zoom Out	Command/Control-minus (–)
100%	Command/Control-1
Show Frame	Command/Control-2
Show All	Command/Control-3
400%	Command/Control-4
800%	Command/Control-8

View Percentage Field

In addition to the predefined view percentages in the menu, you can also type a specific percentage in the View Percentage field in the top-right corner of the document window.

Hand Tool

If scroll bars appear in the document window, you can use the Hand tool to drag the file around within the document window. The Hand tool changes the visible area in the document window; it has no effect on the actual content of the image.

7. Choose the Selection tool from the Tools panel and click the lobster's right claw on the Stage.

Although we will not discuss all 20+ Flash panels here, the Properties panel deserves mention. This important panel is **context sensitive**, which means it provides various options depending on what is selected on the Stage.

Selection tool

The outline shows the selected object.

The Properties panel shows options related to the object selected on the Stage.

8. Click the playhead above the timeline frames and drag right.

This technique of dragging the playhead above the timeline is called **scrubbing**.

As you drag right, the claw moves back and forth in a waving motion (based on objects on the Claw layer).

The mercury in the thermometer rises (based on objects on the Thermometer layer).

Drag the playhead to preview animation in the document window.

9. With nothing in the file selected, press Return/Enter.

If something is selected, click the emtpy gray area around the artwork to deselect.

One final reminder: throughout this book, we list differing commands in the Macintosh/Windows format. On Macintosh, you need to press the Return key; on Windows, press the Enter key. (We will not repeat this explanation every time different commands are required for the different operating systems.)

This keyboard shortcut plays the movie on the Stage from the current location of the playhead. If the playhead is already at the end of the frames, it moves back to Frame 1 and plays the entire movie.

Note:

When a movie is playing on the Stage, press the Escape key to stop the playback.

10. Press Command-Return/Control-Enter.

Instead of simply playing the movie on the Stage, you can preview the file to see what it will look like when exported. This keyboard shortcut, which is the same as choosing Test Movie in the Control menu, exports a SWF file from the existing FLA file so you can see what the final file will look like.

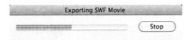

In the Flash Player window, you see some animated elements that did not appear when you played the movie on the Stage. This is a perfect example of why you should test actual animation files rather than relying only on what you see on the Stage. (This is especially true if you did not create the file, as in this case.)

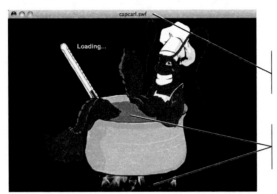

The exported SWF file appears in a Flash Player window and begins playing.

Some animation does not play on the Stage, but does play in the Player window.

Note:

The Controller panel (Window>Toolbars> Controller) enables you to control movie playback on the Flash Stage, using buttons similar to those on DVD players.

Step Back   Step Forward
Stop   One Frame   One Frame

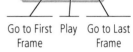

Go to First   Play   Go to Last
Frame   Frame

The Controller panel only affects the Flash Stage. It does not affect files open in the Flash Player window.

11. Close the Player window and return to Flash.

12. Click the Close button on the capcarl document tab. If asked, click Don't Save/No to close the file without saving.

Click here to close the file.

Clicking the Close button on the Application frame closes all open files and quits the application.

Application frame   Application frame
Close button (Macintosh)   Close button (Windows)

Managing Multiple Documents

FLASH FOUNDATIONS

When more than one document is open, each document is represented by a tab at the top of the document window. You can switch from one document to another by clicking a different tab. All open files are also listed at the bottom of the Window menu; you can use these menu options to navigate from one file to another.

If you want to look at more than one file at a time, you can separate a specific document into a floating window by dragging its tab away from the bar.

The active document tab is lighter than the rest.

Each document tab has its own Close button.

The active document is checked.

Dragging the pompano.fla tab away from the tab bar floats the document in its own document window.

Corvette Artwork

Your client is the main sponsor and event promoter of the annual Car Cruise and Music Festival at the Santa Monica Pier. You have been hired to create digital artwork for a number of elements that will be added to the event's Web site, including a game that he is going to develop with Flash programming functionality. The first step is to build a basic illustration that can later be used for the client's various purposes.

This project incorporates the following skills:

❏ Defining a movie file with appropriate settings for the job you're building

❏ Importing a scanned image provided by the creative director

❏ Using various drawing tools to develop a digital version of a rough sketch

❏ Understanding the different drawing modes that are available

❏ Changing fill and stroke colors using a variety of methods

❏ Adding depth using various shading techniques

client comments

I'm planning a number of different projects to promote this year's event. The American sportscar area is always a big draw at the event, so I'd like to feature Corvettes on all of the event collateral.

Most of the print work is going to use photos, but I'm planning some other projects where I want to use artwork instead of a picture — animations, Web banners, and I'm even thinking about an interactive game.

I'm a Flash programmer, but not an artist. If you can create the artwork directly in Flash, that would save me some time when I implement my other plans.

One final thing — I don't want it to look like a cartoon. Obviously, I don't want it to be a photo, but I do want it to be realistic looking.

art director comments

I sketched out a Corvette, and scanned the sketch for you. I want you to use that sketch as the basis for your finished piece. Start by tracing that drawing using a bright color that you can see against the gray lines in the sketch.

Once you've finished the basic artwork, try to make it seem more realistic than just a flat color conveys. Add some dimension and depth so it doesn't look too much like a cartoon.

Also, make sure you build the artwork using logical layers. That way, if we need to make changes later, or if the client decides to animate it, the document will be structured properly.

Since Flash produces vector artwork, we can use the artwork for just about anything once it's done. The important thing for now, however, is to create a static file that we can post on our Web site for the client's approval.

project objectives

To complete this project, you will:

- ❏ Set up the workspace to match the requirements of the project
- ❏ Import the scan of the sketched Corvette
- ❏ Create a set of logical layers to hold the various components that you will create
- ❏ Understand the difference between standard- and object-drawing modes
- ❏ Use the basic shape and line tools to develop the components of the drawing
- ❏ Draw precise Bézier curves with the Pen tool
- ❏ Use the Pencil tool to draw freehand shapes
- ❏ Apply color with the Paint Bucket, Ink Bottle, and Brush tools
- ❏ Use object groups to combine and protect drawing objects
- ❏ Apply and edit color gradients
- ❏ Export a static image for online review

Stage 1 Setting up the Workspace

CREATE A NEW DOCUMENT

1. Download **FL5_RF_Project1.zip** from the Student Files Web page.

2. Expand the ZIP archive in your WIP folder (Macintosh) or copy the archive contents into your WIP folder (Windows).

   This results in a folder named **Car**, which contains all of the files you need for this project. You should also use this folder to save the files you create in this project.

   If necessary, refer to Page 1 of the Interface chapter for specific information on expanding or accessing the required resource files.

3. In Flash, choose File>New.

Note:

You can click the Templates tab to access pre-defined templates in many different styles.

4. In the General tab, make sure the first option — ActionScript 3.0 — is selected in the list, and then click OK.

   In this case, you are using the Flash Stage as a drawing board (literally); the version of ActionScript does not matter for this project. In later projects, you will learn about the differences between the two versions, and when one version is preferred over another.

   When you create a new file, the white Stage is automatically centered in the document window. The Stage is essentially the workspace, or the digital "page" area; anything outside the Stage area will not be visible in the exported movie.

Note:

Although there are slight differences in appearance between the Macintosh (shown here) and Windows dialog boxes, the options are the same.

Note:

We have arranged our workspace to make the best possible use of space in our screen shots, including two docked and collapsed panels that we will expand when necessary. Feel free to arrange the panels however you prefer; for this project, you will be using the Tools, Properties, Align, Timeline, and Color panels.

5. **Choose File>Save As.**

6. **In the resulting dialog box, navigate to your WIP>Car folder.**

7. **Change the file name to corvette.fla. Make sure Flash CS5 Document is selected in the Format/Save As Type menu and click Save.**

   Native Flash files use the FLA extension. By default, the extension is included in the Save As/File Name field. You don't need to type it again if you don't delete the default extension from the field.

If necessary, you can use this menu to save a file to be compatible with the previous version of Flash.

8. **Continue to the next exercise.**

 ## IMPORT A RASTER IMAGE

As we discussed during the production meeting for this assignment, you will base your work on a scanned sketch. Flash can import a range of file formats, including JPG, GIF, PNG, TIF, EPS (Encapsulated PostScript), and native Illustrator and Photoshop files.

1. **With corvette.fla open, choose File>Import>Import to Stage.**

   Four options are available when you choose the Import command:

   - **Import to Stage** simply brings an external image onto the current Stage. (The image is also added to the file Library panel.)

   - **Import to Library** automatically places graphics into the Flash Library panel.

   - **Open External Library** is commonly used to incorporate graphics from one project into another project.

   - **Import Video** allows you to bring digital video into a Flash file.

2. **Navigate to your WIP>Car folder, select corvette.jpg, and click Open/Import.**

   The imported file is placed on the Stage, aligned to the left edge and centered vertically to the Stage area. As you can see, the placed image does not fit in the default Stage area.

3. **Note the placed image's width and height in the Properties panel.**

Because the imported image is still selected, the Properties panel shows information about the image — most importantly for this exercise, the image's physical dimensions.

The Properties panel shows that the selected object is a bitmap file.

The object's position and size are clearly listed in the panel.

The placed file is aligned to the left edge and centered vertically on the Stage.

The placed file is wider than the current Stage area.

4. **Save the file and continue to the next exercise.**

There are two kinds of computer images. The first, known as a **raster image** or **bitmap**, is composed of simple pixels. Each pixel has a specific value, and that value determines the color, intensity, and brightness of that pixel. The number of pixels that make up a raster image is fixed at the time of the scan or photograph. If you blow up (enlarge) a raster image, it becomes grainy and loses quality; in fact, you can see the individual pixels in an enlarged raster image.

Flash is a vector-based program. **Vector art** is not based on pixels; instead, it is based on mathematical values. Vector art is essentially a tiny program that tells the printer or monitor to "draw a line from Point A to Point B, bending X degrees coming out of Point A and entering Point B from an angle of Z." Although this might sound confusing, you don't have to write any complicated code to make vectors work properly; you can simply draw with the Flash tools and the vectors are created for you.

An example of the difference between a raster image and vector art is shown below. At 100% size, both the raster image and the type (composed of vector objects) are crisp. If you zoom in close enough, however, the individual pixels in the photograph start to show, and the image breaks down — but the type remains perfectly crisp and clear.

At actual size, both the type in this image and the photograph appear perfectly crisp and clear.

The detail on the tree breaks down if you look closely enough.

The type object, which is a vector object, remains clear even when enlarged

CHANGE DOCUMENT PROPERTIES

The imported artwork is larger than the defined Stage size. Because you're going to trace the imported sketch, you need to make the Stage area large enough to hold the entire sketch (and ultimately, the finished artwork).

1. **With corvette.fla open, choose the Selection tool at the top of the Tools panel.**

2. **Click away from the imported raster image to make sure nothing is selected.**

   When nothing is selected in the file, you can use the Properties panel to access a number of options that affect the entire document — including the file's physical dimensions.

When nothing is selected, the Properties panel shows options related to the overall file.

3. **In the Properties panel, click the Edit button to the right of the document size.**

   This command opens the Document Settings dialog box. Changes made here affect the Stage (including all scenes contained within the movie). These changes do not, however, affect the objects contained in the movie.

Note:

You can also choose Modify>Document to open the Document Settings dialog box.

4. **Change the Width field to 850 px, change the Height to 450 px, and click OK to apply the change.**

5. **If you can't see the entire Stage area, use the Hand tool to drag the Stage until you can see the entire Stage. If the entire Stage does not fit into your document window, choose Fit In Window in the View Percentage menu.**

If necessary, use this menu to fit the entire Stage area in the document window.

The placed file's position relative to the Stage is not affected. The top-left corner is in the same spot as before you changed the Stage size.

6. **At the bottom of the Align panel, check the Align To Stage box.**

When this option is active, you can use the Align panel to precisely position one or more objects relative to the defined Stage area in your file. (The Align panel remembers the last-used state of the Align To Stage option, so it might already be checked.)

Note:

Remember: all Flash panels can be accessed in the Window menu.

Note:

Press Command/Control-K to show or hide the Align panel.

Button icons indicate which edge will be aligned or distributed.

Check this option

Align options move selected objects based on the defined edge or center.

Distribute options average the spacing between the selected edge or center of objects.

Space options can be used to create uniform space between selected objects.

Match Size options can be used to force objects to the same height, width, or both.

7. **Click the sketch with the Selection tool to select it, and then click the Align Horizontal Center and Align Vertical Center buttons in the Align panel.**

Align Horizontal Center

Align Vertical Center

8. **Save the file and continue to the next exercise.**

CREATE LAYERS FOR ORGANIZING ARTWORK

The Timeline panel allows you to easily create, arrange, and manage multiple layers in order to better organize your work. Layers can help you organize complex drawings and animations into a logical, easy-to-understand structure, while keeping all the components separate. You will use the Timeline layers extensively as you complete the projects in this book.

1. **With corvette.fla open, review the timeline panel.**

   Layers are listed on the left side of the timeline; the order in which the layers are stacked (from top to bottom) is referred to as the layer **stacking order**. Objects on higher layers in the stack will obscure objects on layers that are lower in the stack. You can easily change the stacking order by dragging a layer to a new position in the stack.

   Every file includes a default layer, named Layer 1. The icons to the right of the layer name provide a number of options, as well as some useful information.

2. **Double-click the name of the layer to highlight the name. Type Sketch to rename the layer, and then press Return/Enter to apply the change.**

3. **Below the list of layers, click the New Layer button to add another layer on top of the first layer.**

   The new layer is automatically added immediately above the previously selected layer. New layers (and layer folders) are created in the same nesting level as the currently selected layer. In this case there is only one level of layers, so all new layers will be placed at the primary level.

4. **Using the same technique from Step 2, rename the new layer Window and press Return/Enter to apply the change.**

5. **Repeat Steps 3–4 to create four more layers: Body, Wheels, Door, and Accents.**

6. **If you can't see all six layer names, click the bar above the docked Timeline panel and drag up to expand the panel.**

Drag this bar up or down to change the height of the Timeline panel.

Note:

If your Timeline panel is not docked, click the bottom edge of the floating panel and drag down to expand the panel.

7. **If you can't see the full layer names, click the bar to the right of the Outline icons and drag right.**

Drag this bar right to widen the area where layer names are listed.

8. **Lock the Sketch layer by clicking the small dot below the Lock icon.**

Locking the layer prevents you from accidentally deleting or otherwise modifying the sketch, which will be the basis for developing the actual drawing.

Click the dot to lock the layer.

Click the lock icon to unlock the layer.

Note:

If a layer is selected but locked, the pencil is covered with a slash, indicating that you can't change objects on the layer or add objects to the layer.

9. **Save the file and continue to the next stage of the project.**

Drawing Preferences

FLASH FOUNDATIONS

You can control a number of drawing options using the Drawing pane of the Preferences dialog box (accessed in the Flash menu on Macintosh, or in the Edit menu on Windows).

Each time you click with the Pen tool, you add an anchor point; successive anchor points are connected by lines. If the **Show Pen Preview** option is checked, a preview line follows the cursor to show the line that will be created when you add a new anchor point.

When the **Show Solid Points** check box is active, selecting an anchor point with the Subselection tool shows the selected point as solid instead of hollow.

You can change the Pen tool cursor ( ) to a precise crosshair (×) by activating the **Show Precise Cursors** check box.

The **Connect Lines** options (Must Be Close, Normal, and Can Be Distant) determine how close lines or points must be before Flash automatically connects them.

The **Smooth Curves** options (Off, Rough, Normal, and Smooth) determine how many points will be used to create a line when you're drawing with the Pencil tool with the Smooth or Straighten options turned on. The Rough option results in more points and a jagged line; the Smooth option results in fewer points and a smoother line.

The **Recognize Lines** options (Off, Strict, Normal, and Tolerant) determine how close to straight a line drawn with the Pencil tool must be before Flash recognizes it as straight.

The **Recognize Shapes** options (Off, Strict, Normal, and Tolerant) determine how close to the shape an oval or square drawn with the Pencil tool must be before Flash recognizes it as the actual shape and makes the necessary adjustment.

The **Click Accuracy** options (Strict, Normal, and Tolerant) determine how close to an object you must place the cursor to select the object.

Stage 2 **Drawing in Flash**

Most drawing objects display two primary attributes: a fill and a stroke. The **fill** is the color contained within a shape, and the **stroke** is the line that defines the outside border of a shape. To change the fill and stroke of an object, use the pop-up Swatches panel that appears when you click and hold the Stroke or Fill swatch at the bottom of the Tools panel.

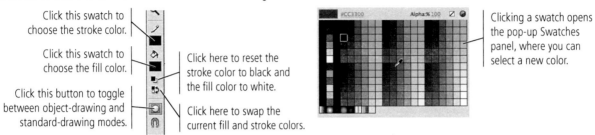

Click this swatch to choose the stroke color.

Click this swatch to choose the fill color.

Click this button to toggle between object-drawing and standard-drawing modes.

Click here to reset the stroke color to black and the fill color to white.

Click here to swap the current fill and stroke colors.

Clicking a swatch opens the pop-up Swatches panel, where you can select a new color.

There are two modes for drawing in Flash: standard drawing and object drawing. When you draw with the basic shape tools, or with the Pen, Line, Pencil, or Brush tool, a toggle near the bottom of the Tools panel determines which type of drawing you will create.

When object-drawing mode is active, the toggle is highlighted.

When object-drawing mode is inactive, the toggle is not highlighted; this is called standard-drawing mode.

When you create an object in **standard-drawing mode**, the fill and stroke are treated as separate entities. You can individually select each part with the Selection (solid arrow) tool, and you can move or modify each part without affecting the other.

Oval drawn in standard-drawing mode. It has a blue fill and a green stroke.

The fill was selected with the Selection tool and dragged away from the stroke; the tiny cross-hatch pattern indicates the selected area.

Standard-drawing mode has some advantages over object-drawing mode; specifically, you can select a part of a shape by dragging a marquee with the Selection tool.

Drag a selection marquee to select part of a shape.

The selected area can be deleted without affecting the rest of the shape.

You can prevent this type of editing by grouping the components of the object. Simply drag a selection around the entire object and choose Modify>Group. When a standard object is grouped, you see only the group **bounding box** (the blue border) when you select the object on the Stage.

Bounding box

After grouping the fill and stroke, you can't select the individual components. The bounding box indicates the boundary of the group.

Note:

An object's bounding box and handles are the same color as the layer color (in the Timeline panel).

Even when standard objects are grouped, you can access the individual pixel components by double-clicking them on the Stage. This opens a secondary Stage — called **Edit mode** — where you can access and edit the individual components. The Edit bar above the Stage shows that you are no longer on the main Stage (Scene 1), but editing a group.

Edit bar

Double-clicking a group enters Edit mode for that group, where you can access the individual components of the group.

Of course, standard-drawing objects have drawbacks as well; you could easily move or change an object that you don't want to change — such as dragging a fill away from its stroke and not realizing it until 15 steps later when it's too late to easily undo the error.

To solve this problem, you can draw in **object-drawing mode** by toggling on the switch at the bottom of the Tools panel. When you create a shape or line in object-drawing mode, it automatically displays the bounding box as soon as you create it, and you can't select the fill and stroke independently — at least not on the main Stage.

For a shape created in standard-drawing mode, you can use the Selection tool to independently select the shape's fill and stroke.

For a shape created in object-drawing mode, you can use the Selection tool to reveal the shape's bounding box. You can't independently select the object's fill or stroke.

If you want to access the individual components of an object created in object-drawing mode, simply double-click the object. Double-clicking activates Edit mode; the Edit bar shows that you are "inside" (editing) a drawing object.

In Edit mode, you can access the individual drawing objects that make up a shape created in object-drawing mode.

Destructive vs. Non-Destructive Editing

When you drag one standard-drawing object onto another on the same layer, the topmost object removes whatever portion of the lower shape it covers. In the image to the right, the second column shows that we moved the orange circle on top of the blue circle. In the third column, you see the result of deselecting the orange circle, and then reselecting it and pulling it away from the blue circle. (This type of destructive interaction does not occur until you deselect the topmost object, which gives you a chance to "finalize" the edit. As long as you still see the crosshatch pattern on the object you're dragging, the underlying objects have not yet been changed.)

This type of interaction does not occur with objects created in object-drawing mode or when you're working with grouped objects. If you select something with the Selection tool and see a bounding box instead of the crosshatch pattern, underlying objects will not be affected. Only you can tell when an object needs to be protected from destructive interaction with other objects or, conversely, when you want one object to interact another object.

DRAW WITH THE LINE TOOL

The Line tool creates straight lines, which are simply strokes with no fills. You can combine lines with other shapes to develop custom objects. In this exercise, you draw several lines to complete the shape of the car's window.

1. **With corvette.fla open, click the Window layer (in the Timeline panel) to make it the active one.**

   Any objects you draw will be placed on the active layer. It's important to check which layer you're working on whenever you start to create new artwork.

2. **Select the Line tool in the Tools panel. At the bottom of the Tools panel, make sure the object-drawing option is turned off.**

   The Object Drawing toggle is dark gray when active.
   The Object Drawing toggle is not highlighted when inactive.

3. **Using either the Properties panel or the Tools panel, click the Stroke Color swatch to open the pop-up Swatches panel.**

   When you select a drawing tool, the Properties panel provides a number of options that are relevant to the selected tool. These options remember the last-used settings, so some might already reflect the settings we define in the following steps.

   The Stroke Color swatch in the Properties panel is the same as the Stroke Color swatch in the Tools panel. Changing either swatch reflects the same color in the other one.

   When you use the Line tool, the Fill Color swatch in the Properties panel is always set to None. By definition, a line has no fill; you can't change the fill color of a line. The Fill Color swatch in the Tools panel, on the other hand, retains the last-used fill option. When you switch to a tool that creates filled shapes, the swatch in the Tools panel becomes the default fill color.

   Note:

   The Line tool does not create filled shapes, so the fill color is not relevant for this exercise.

4. **Choose a bright green color as the stroke color.**

   You can use any color you prefer; we are using green so it is easily visible against the gray lines in the sketch. Later in this project, you will change the stroke and fill colors of the various pieces to create the finished artwork.

   Line tool

   Click the swatch to open the Swatches panel.

   We are using this green color for the strokes.

   Object-drawing mode is toggled off (not active).

   The Window layer is active.

5. **In the Properties panel, set the stroke weight (thickness) to 2 and choose Solid in the Style menu.**

   You can type a specific stroke weight in the Stroke Weight field, or you can drag the associated slider for a live preview of the size you drag to (between 0.25 and 200 points).

   Flash includes a number of built-in line styles, including dashed, dotted, ragged, stippled, and hatched. You can also edit the selected stroke style by clicking the pencil icon to the right of the Style menu.

Note:

The Scale menu defines how strokes are affected by scaling a symbol in which the line exists. (This option only affects strokes that are part of a symbol, which you will learn about starting in Project 2.)

6. **Open the Cap menu and make sure the Round option is active.**

   The Cap options define the appearance of a stroke beyond the endpoint of the line.

None end cap style

Round end cap style

Square end cap style

Note:

The Hinting check box helps when you draw straight lines that are connected to smooth curves. When this option is not checked, the curves might seem to be disconnected from the straight lines.

7. **Open the Join menu and make sure the Round option is selected.**

   The Join options define the appearance of corners where two lines meet. When Miter is selected, you can define a miter limit in the Miter field. (This option is not relevant for Round or Bevel joins.) A miter limit controls when the corner switches from a pointed joint to a beveled joint, as a factor of the stroke weight. If you define a miter limit of 2 for a 2-point line, the corner is beveled if the pointed corner extends beyond 4 points (2 × 2).

Miter join results in pointed corners.

Round join applies a circular edge to the corners.

Bevel join cuts off the points of the corners.

8. **Zoom in to the window on the sketch.**

   As a general rule, we don't tell you the specific view percentage to use because every user's monitor and personal preference determine a comfortable working environment. We do, however, tell you where to focus your attention.

9. **Choose View>Snapping>Snap to Objects. If this option is already checked (toggled on), move the mouse cursor away from the menu and click to dismiss the menu.**

   As you draw different line segments with the Line tool, you want the ends of individual segments to align with each other. This is much easier when the Snap to Objects option is toggled on.

10. **Click the top-left corner of the window, hold down the mouse button, drag down and right past the bottom-left corner, and then release the mouse button. When you release the mouse button, do not move the mouse cursor.**

Click here...
...and drag to here.

When you release the mouse button, a line appears with the defined stroke properties.

11. **With the cursor in the same position as when you finished the previous step, click and drag down and right to create the lower-left corner of the window shape (use the following image as a guide).**

Because the Snap to Objects option is toggled on, when you first click you should see a small circle connecting to the end of the line you drew in the previous step. This indicates that the new line is connecting to that open endpoint.

A small circle indicates that you are connecting to the open endpoint of an existing line.

Click and drag to create the second line in the shape.

12. **With the cursor in the exact position as at the end of Step 11, click and drag right to create the bottom edge of the window.**

13. **With the cursor in the exact position as at the end of Step 12, click and drag up and left until you see a small circle over the end of the first line you created, then release the mouse button.**

Again, the circle icon indicates that you are connecting to the open endpoint of an existing line — in this case, you are closing the shape.

The circle indicates that you are connecting to the open endpoint, effectively closing the shape.

14. **Save the file and continue to the next exercise.**

ADJUST LINES WITH THE SELECTION TOOL

As the name suggests, the Selection tool is used to select objects. It can also be used to push or pull drawing objects into different shapes, almost as if you were pushing a string with your finger. In this exercise you will use this capability to bend the lines you just created into the correct shape for the car's window.

1. With **corvette.fla** open, choose the Selection tool in the Tools panel.

2. **Review the positions of the window corners. If any do not line up with the sketch, move the Selection tool cursor near the corner until a small corner shape appears in the tool icon. Click and drag to reposition the corner point.**

The corner in the cursor icon indicates that you can click to drag the corner.

3. **Move the cursor near the diagonal line that makes up the top of the window shape until you see a curved line in the cursor icon.**

The curved line in the cursor icon indicates that you can click and drag to bend the line.

Note:

If an object is already selected, you have to first deselect it before you can use the Selection tool to bend the lines into different shapes.

4. **Click and drag up to push the line into a curved shape that matches the sketch.**

One unique aspect of drawing with Flash is using the Selection tool to pull or push a line into a different shape. When you release the mouse button, the line is reshaped.

Click and drag up to push the line into a curve that matches the sketch.

Note:

This type of "bending" works for objects created in standard-drawing or object-drawing mode.

5. **Repeat this process to slightly bend the diagonal line in the bottom-left corner of the window shape.**

6. **Save the file and continue to the next exercise.**

Using the Subselection tool. When you click a line with the Subselection tool, you can see the object's anchor points. In the image to the right, both objects were selected by surrounding them with a selection rectangle; you can see all the objects' points and curves.

Paths selected with the Subselection tool show the anchor points.

Subselection tool cursor

Selecting entire objects or single points. As you move the Subselection tool near a stroke, a small, solid black square appears at the bottom right of the icon. If you move the Subselection tool directly over a single anchor point, a hollow square in the icon indicates that clicking will select only that point.

A solid square in the Subselection tool cursor indicates you are selecting the path.

A hollow square cursor indicates you are selecting the anchor point.

Moving points. To move an anchor point, select the point with the Subselection tool and move it to the desired location. You can also **nudge** (move just a little bit at a time) a point by selecting it and then pressing the Up/Down/Left/Right Arrow keys on your keyboard.

Reshaping a curve using its handles. To reshape a curve, first select it with the Subselection tool, and then drag the related handles. (Handles will appear from each smooth anchor point that is connected to the curve.)

As you drag the handle up and out to the right, the shape of the curve changes accordingly.

Converting corner points to curves. To change a corner point into a smooth curve, first select the point you want to convert with the Subselection tool, then press the Option/Alt key and drag the point; handles appear, and the corner becomes a curve. You can then adjust the shape of the curve by adjusting the handles.

First, use the Subselection tool to select the point you want to convert, then Option/Alt-drag to pull out handles.

Converting curves to corner points. If you need to convert a curve to a corner point, place the Pen tool over the curve point, press the Option/Alt key, and click to change the point to a sharp corner. (Alternatively, use the Convert Anchor Point tool.)

Press Option/Alt to access the Convert Anchor Point option.

Clicking changes a curve point to a corner point.

Adding anchor points. To add an anchor point, first select the path with the Subselection tool. Using the Pen tool, place the cursor near the path but not over an existing anchor point until you see a plus sign (+) in the tool cursor. Click the path to add a new point to the line. (Alternatively, use the Add Anchor Point tool.)

A plus sign (+) in the Pen tool cursor means clicking will add a point to the selected line.

Clicking adds a new point to the existing line.

Deleting anchor points. To delete an anchor point, first select the path with the Subselection tool. Using the Pen tool, place the cursor near an existing point until you see a minus sign (-) in the tool cursor. (Alternatively, use the Delete Anchor Point tool.)

A minus sign (-) in the Pen tool cursor means clicking will remove a point from the selected line.

Clicking removes the point from the line.

DRAW WITH THE PEN TOOL

The Pen tool draws curved lines, known as **Bézier curves**, that are shaped based on the position of anchor points and their connected direction handles. This type of drawing creates very precise shapes, but can be difficult to master. In this exercise, you will draw the shape of the car body. While you work through the steps, you should try to get a feeling for how clicking and dragging affects the shape you create. The best way to master the Pen tool is to practice; as you gain more experience using the Pen tool, you will be better able to understand and predict exactly where you should click to create the shape you want.

1. **With `corvette.fla` open, select the Body layer to select it as the active layer. Zoom out so you can see the entire car shape.**

   Remember, to zoom out you can use press Option/Alt and click with the Zoom tool, or press Command/Control-minus (–).

2. **Choose the Pen tool in the Tools panel, and toggle on the Object-Drawing mode option.**

3. **Click the Fill Color swatch in the Tools panel and choose the None swatch in the top-right corner of the pop-up Swatches panel.**

   Because you want to be able to see the sketch through the shapes you create in this stage of the project, you are setting the fill to none.

   Click the Fill Color swatch and choose the None option.

4. **Using the Properties panel, make sure you are using the same color and size stroke that you used to create the window shape.**

   When you choose a new drawing tool, the object-drawing mode toggle, stroke, and fill properties retain the last-used options. If you took a break from this project after the previous exercise, make sure your drawing options are correct.

   Pen tool

   Pen tool cursor

   Make sure the stroke color, size, and style are the same as you used earlier.

   Object-drawing mode is toggled on.

   The Body layer is active.

5. **Click once at the top-left corner of the car shape.**

   Clicking with the Pen tool places an anchor point with no direction handles. (You might have to look very closely to see the anchor point.)

Click here without dragging to place an anchor point with no direction handles.

6. **Move to the right until you are above the back edge of the rear wheel. Click and drag to the right to place an anchor point with symmetrical direction handles.**

   When you click and drag with the Pen tool, you create a smooth anchor point with symmetrical direction handles (the handles on both sides of the point are the same length, exactly opposite one another). The length and angle of the direction handles define the shape of the segment that connects the two anchor points.

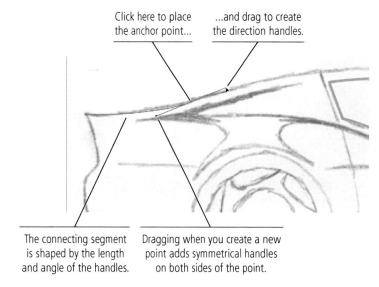

Click here to place the anchor point...   ...and drag to create the direction handles.

The connecting segment is shaped by the length and angle of the handles.   Dragging when you create a new point adds symmetrical handles on both sides of the point.

Note:

Pressing Command/Control while using the Pen tool temporarily switches to the Subselection tool. When you release the key, the Pen tool is again active.

7. **Click and drag right again where the back of the door intersects the top of the car.**

   As you drag, notice how the position of the direction handles affects the shape of the connecting line segment. Experiment with dragging up, down, left, and right to see the effect on the curve shape.

8. **Click and drag again where the top of the car meets the hood.**

You can drag handles past the edge of the document window if necessary.

9. **Place the cursor over the point you just created and click to remove the handle from the outside of the open point.**

While you are drawing, clicking a symmetrical point again removes the direction handle from the outside of the point — converting the point to a corner point. The handle on the inside of the point remains because it is required to define the existing curve shape between the converted point and the previous one.

The upside-down v in the cursor icon indicates that clicking will convert this point to a corner point.

The inner handle is required to create the shape of the previous segment, so it is not removed from the new corner point.

Clicking removes the handle from the outside of the point.

10. **Click and drag again near the corner of the front bumper.**

Do not click the actual corner in the sketch. Because the bumper's edge is actually rounded, it's better to place anchor points on both sides of the curve rather than in the exact center of the curve.

Don't worry about matching the sketched hood shape; you'll fix this in the next exercise.

11. **Click on the front side of the bumper, just below the curve, and drag short handles along the path of the bumper's front edge.**

As you can see in our example, symmetrical points often result in incorrect paths. You will learn how to fix this type of problem in the next exercise.

The handle from the symmetrical point makes the connecting curve shape incorrect.

12. **Click just before the bottom curve of the bumper shape and drag slightly along the path of the bumper's front edge.**

The point here is to create a smooth point with handles on both sides, without significantly affecting the shape of the connecting curve. Dragging a very small distance accomplishes this goal.

13. **Click and drag slightly along on the bottom edge of the car, just past the bottom-front corner.**

Short direction handles can be used to create smooth points with very tight connecting curves.

14. **Continue drawing the rest of the car shape by clicking and dragging to place anchor points with handles. For the bottom edge, simply extend the bottom-edge line over the wheel shapes.**

15. **When you get to the end of the shape, place the cursor over the original starting point and click to close the shape.**

When you hover the cursor over the original starting point, the cursor shows a hollow circle in the icon, indicating that you can click to close the shape.

The circle in the cursor icon indicates that clicking will connect to the open endpoint and close the shape.

16. **Save the file and continue to the next exercise.**

ADJUST BÉZIER CURVE SHAPES

From the previous exercise, you might have guessed that many of the lines that you draw with the Pen tool will not be perfect when you first create them. Fortunately, the Subselection tool makes it easy to edit the position of individual anchor points, as well as the length and angle of the direction handles that define connecting line segments.

Note:

The Selection tool selects entire paths, but the Subselection tool selects individual anchor points. You use the Subselection tool to select and edit anchor points, or adjust curves using the handles that radiate from anchor points.

1. **With corvette.fla open, zoom into the front end of the car.**

2. **Choose the Subselection tool in the Tools panel.**

   You can use the Subselection tool to access and adjust the anchor points that make up a line. You can also use this tool to adjust the direction handles that define the shapes of curves that connect two anchor points.

3. **Click the green line on the hood to select the shape, then click the anchor point on the front edge of the car hood to select it.**

   Clicking a line with the Subselection tool reveals the shape's anchor points.

Click a line to reveal the shape's anchor points.

Click a point to reveal its direction handles.

4. **Click the outer direction handle and drag up and left to reshape the curve on the top corner of the bumper.**

   When you drag one direction handle, the point remains smooth but it is no longer symmetrical; changing the length, but not the angle, of a direction handle affects only the segment on the same side of the point as the handle that you change.

   Because this is still a smooth point, however, dragging one handle to a different angle would also affect the point's other handle — affecting the shapes of both segments that are connected to the anchor point.

Note:

If you drag toward or away from the anchor point without changing the angle, you are changing the arc of the segment that is related to the changed handle.

Drag the handle along the existing line position to shorten the handle without changing its angle.

Changing the handle's length without changing its angle affects the shape of the connected segment.

5. **Choose the Add Anchor Point tool (nested under the Pen tool), then click the existing line midway along the hood to add a new anchor point.**

You can also add a point by moving the Pen tool cursor over an existing line segment.

Add Anchor Point tool

Click this line to add an anchor point near the middle of the hood.

Handles are created as necessary to keep the same curve.

Existing handles are adjusted to maintain the same curve.

6. **Using the Subselection tool, click the new point and drag until the path more closely resembles the line in the sketch.**

When you move a point, the length and angle of the related handles are not affected. In many cases, you might need to move a point and then adjust the handles to achieve the effect you want.

7. **Review the position of each anchor point and line segment in the car shape. Make any necessary adjustments until you are satisfied with your drawing.**

Keep the following points in mind as you fine-tune your shape:

- To move a point, click and drag with the Subselection tool.
- To add an anchor point, click an existing segment with the Pen tool (or use the Add Anchor Point tool that is nested under the Pen tool).
- To remove a point, click an existing point with the Pen tool (or use the Delete Anchor Point tool that is nested under the Pen tool).
- To convert a smooth point to a corner point, Option/Alt click the point with the Pen tool (or use the Convert Anchor Point tool).
- To convert a corner point to a smooth point, Option/Alt click the point with the Pen tool and drag to create symmetrical direction handles for the point (or use the Convert Anchor Point tool).

8. **In the Timeline panel, click the dot under the Eye icon for the Sketch layer. Review your progress.**

   Any time you are working from a sketch, it can be helpful to hide the sketch so you can better see exactly what you have created.

Click in this column to hide the Sketch layer.

9. **Click the red X for the Sketch layer to show that layer again.**

   Feel free to repeat this process throughout this project — we won't include this step again.

10. **Save the file and continue to the next exercise.**

 ## Use Destructive Editing to Create Shapes

When you work on a standard-drawing object (in other words, one created without object-drawing mode toggled on), you can use the Selection tool to select specific pieces of objects:

- Clicking a stroke selects the line segment between the nearest two anchor points.

- Clicking a fill selects the entire area of the color you click.

- Clicking and dragging a marquee selects only the pixels inside the marquee area.

This behavior enables a type of **destructive editing** that is unique to Flash drawing tools. You can select and move or delete certain pieces of an object without affecting other pieces of the same object.

1. **With `corvette.fla` open, click the Body layer icon in the Timeline panel to select the layer.**

   When you select a layer, all objects on the layer become selected. In this case, the layer only contains one object — the shape of the car's body. You created this shape in object-drawing mode, so a bounding box identifies the selected object.

Clicking a layer icon in the Timeline panel selects all objects on that layer.

2. **Using the Selection tool, double-click any line of the car body shape to enter into the drawing object.**

   Double-clicking an object on the Stage switches into Edit mode for the object (often referred to as "entering" the object). While in Edit mode for a particular object, you can see but not access other objects on the Stage.

The Edit bar shows the path to the object you are currently editing.

Other objects are visible, but cannot be selected or edited.

3. **Choose the Line tool in the Tools panel. At the bottom of the Tools panel, make sure Object-Drawing mode is toggled on.**

4. **Draw a straight line where the back of the door is indicated in the sketch. Extend the line above and below the car body shape.**

Note:

While drawing, press Command/Control to temporarily access the Selection tool; when you release the modifier key, you return to the last-selected tool.

The easiest way to deselect everything is to press Command/Control, and then click away from any object on the Stage.

5. **Choose the Selection tool. Click away from the line to deselect it, and then use the Selection tool to bend the line into shape.**

6. **Click the line to select it again, and then choose Modify>Break Apart.**

   This command converts objects in object-drawing mode to standard-drawing mode so you can use the destructive editing capabilities of the Selection tool.

Before breaking apart, selecting the line with the Selection tool reveals the object's bounding box.

After breaking apart, the line is a standard-drawing object; you can select the object's pixels with the Selection tool.

7. **Choose the Subselection tool in the Tools panel, and click any of the lines that make up the car body shape.**

All lines you create in Flash are vectors, which means their position and shape are defined mathematically based on the anchor points that make up the shape. Flash automatically creates whatever anchor points are necessary to reproduce the line you draw — including points wherever two lines overlap, as you can see where the vertical curved line intersects the car body shape.

8. **Click away from the lines to deselect everything, then use the Selection tool to click the overhanging line above the car.**

The selected area displays a small cross-hatch pattern.

9. **Press Shift and click the overhanging line below the car.**

Pressing Shift allows you to select multiple objects at once; each item you Shift-click is added to the previous selection.

Both overhanging lines should be selected.

10. **Press Delete/Backspace to remove both elements from the drawing.**

11. Repeat Steps 3–10 to create the line that marks the front of the door.

Later in this project, you need to be able to work with the car body shape as a single piece. If you left the door lines on the Body layer, the car shape would be effectively split into three pieces by the door-edge lines. To solve this potential problem, you are now going to move the door lines onto their own layer so they do not cut the car shape into pieces.

12. Click one of the door edges to select it, then Shift-click to select the other.

13. With both lines selected, choose Edit>Cut.

When you cut an object, it is removed from its original position and temporarily stored on the Clipboard — a reserved area of memory that allows you to temporarily hold objects until you need to use them again somewhere else. This is not the same as deleting (as you did in Step 10); when you delete a selection, it is not stored on the Clipboard.

14. In the Edit bar, click Scene 1 to return to the main Stage.

15. Select the Door layer as the target layer and then choose Edit>Paste in Place.

The Paste in Place command puts the cut objects in the exact position as they were cut from, but on the now-selected Door layer instead of the original Body layer.

The lines are pasted in the exact position...

...but on the now-selected Door layer.

16. Save the file and continue to the next exercise.

DRAW WITH THE OVAL TOOL

Many otherwise complex objects are, in fact, simply a collection of primitive shapes. In the case of this car, you should recognize that the car's wheels are actually made up of three concentric circles. The basic shape tools — including the Oval tool — make it very easy to create this type of object.

1. **With corvette.fla open, select the Wheels layer (in the Timeline panel) as the active layer. Zoom into the rear wheel in the sketch.**

2. **Choose View>Rulers to show the Stage rulers at the top and left edges of the document window.**

3. **Click the horizontal ruler, hold down the mouse button, and drag down to place a horizontal guide in the center of the sketched wheel.**

Rulers appear at the top and left edges of the document window.

Click the top ruler and drag down to place a horizontal guide.

Using Rulers, Guides, and Grids

FLASH FOUNDATIONS

Flash rulers, guides, and grids can dramatically improve accuracy and reduce development time. All three can be accessed and controlled in the View menu.

Rulers can be toggled on and off by choosing View>Rulers. Rulers normally measure in pixels, but you can use the General pane of the Preferences dialog box to change this setting to any measurement system you prefer.

The grid is a pattern of horizontal and vertical lines that also aid in the development/alignment process. The View>Grid submenu includes options for toggling the grid visibility (Show Grid), as well as editing the appearance and behavior of the grid (Edit Grid).

Guides are user-defined lines that you place on the Stage to mark a specific location; they are for development purposes only, and do not appear in the final output. The View>Guides submenu includes options for toggling guide visibility (Show Guides), preventing guides from being moved (Lock Guides), modifying the appearance and behavior of guides (Edit Guides), and removing all guides from the file (Clear Guides).

The View>Snapping submenu includes options for making guides (Snap to Guides) and the grid (Snap to Grid) act like magnets when objects are dragged near.

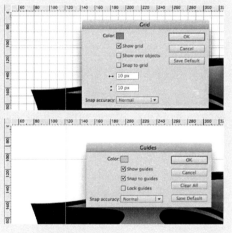

4. **Click the vertical ruler, hold down the mouse button, and drag right to place a vertical guide in the center of the wheel.**

    You will perform a number of steps in this and the next exercise that will depend on an exact center point — where these two guides intersect.

Note:

Because this is a hand-drawn sketch, the wheels aren't exactly circular. It's okay if your circle doesn't exactly match the sketch.

Click the left ruler and drag right to place a vertical guide.

5. **Choose the Oval tool (nested under the Rectangle tool) in the Tools panel. Make sure object-drawing mode is toggled on.**

6. **In the Properties panel, make sure the fill and stroke settings match what you used in earlier exercises. In the Oval Options section, set all three sliders to 0.**

    The Oval tool shares many of the same properties as the Pen tool. You can define the fill and stroke color, as well as the stroke style, cap, and join.

Oval tool

Object-drawing mode is toggled on.

The Wheels layer is selected.

7. **Click at the intersection of the two guides, hold down the mouse button, press Option/Alt-Shift, and drag until the shape approximately matches the outer circle of the sketched wheel.**

    You can create a basic shape by simply clicking and dragging; the shape is anchored where you first click. Holding down the Option/Alt key as you drag draws the shape from the center out. Holding down the Shift key while dragging constrains the shape to equal height and width.

Note:

Whenever we say "click and drag", you should hold down the mouse button as you drag. We will not repeat the instruction to hold down the mouse button unless it differs in some way from the normal click-and-drag procedure.

Click at the exact intersection of the guides, press Option/Alt-Shift...

...and drag to create a circle from the center out.

8. **With the new circle selected, choose Edit>Copy.**

   Copying stores the selected object in the Clipboard.

9. **Choose Edit>Paste in Place.**

   Pasting places a copy of the Clipboard contents onto the selected layer. The Paste in Place command puts the copy in the exact position as the original. You can also choose Paste in Center to place the copy in the exact center of the document window.

10. **Choose the Free Transform tool in the Tools panel.**

    When you select an object with the Free Transform tool, the object is bounded by eight transformation handles. You can use these handles to scale, stretch, skew, or rotate the selection. The hollow white circle in the center of the bounding box is the **transformation registration point**, which identifies the origin point around which the transformation will occur.

Note:

To copy an object, select the object and press Command/Control-C.

To cut an object, select the object and press Command/Control-X.

To paste an object, select the object and press Command/Control-V.

To paste an object in place, select the object and press Command/Control-Shift-V.

Free Transform tool

Transformation handles

Transformation registration point

Basic Shape Options

FLASH FOUNDATIONS

When you draw a basic shape, the Properties panel also includes options for defining the shape that will be created.

When you use the Oval tool, you can define the **Start Angle** and **End Angle** to create a shape with a defined wedge removed (such as you might see in a pie chart). You can also use the **Inner Radius** option to remove a circle from inside the circle; the defined value refers to the radius of the inner circle (the part that is removed). The **Close Path** option, which is checked by default, can be unchecked to create an open path rather than a closed shape.

When Close Path is not checked, the result is one or more open paths.

When you use the Rectangle tool, you can easily create a shape with rounded corners. The Options area in the Properties panel defines the **Corner Radius**; by default, all four corners are linked, but you can click the chain icon to define a different radius for each corner. (To understand the concept of corner radius, think of an imaginary circle at the corner of the shape; the radius of that circle is the corner radius, as shown in the following image.)

Corner radius

Free Transform mode allows you to change an object (or group) on the Stage by simply dragging. You can enter Free Transform mode by selecting an object with the Free Transform tool, by pressing Q (the keyboard shortcut for the tool), or by choosing Modify>Transform>Free Transform.

In Free Transform mode, the selected object is surrounded by a black bounding box with heavy black handles. A hollow circle in the center indicates the object's registration point. Depending on where you place the cursor, you can apply different kinds of transformations. The cursor icon changes to reflect the change you will make by dragging.

Click a side handle and drag to resize the object's height (left) or width (right).

Click outside a corner handle and drag to rotate the object.

Click and drag between handles on the top or side to skew the object.

Click a corner handle and drag to resize both height and width at once.

Press **Shift** while dragging a corner handle to maintain the original height-to-width ratio in the resized object (called "constraining").

Press **Option/Alt** while dragging a handle to apply a change around the transformation registration point. (In this example, Option/Alt-dragging the bottom handle also moves the top handle.)

Press **Command/Control** while dragging a corner handle to distort the object shape.

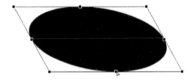

Press **Command/Control** while dragging a side handle to skew and resize an object at the same time.

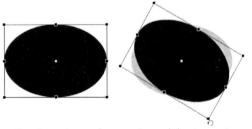

Transformations such as rotation and skewing apply around the transformation registration point, which defaults to the center of the object.

Moving the transformation registration point (left) changes the fixed point around which the rotation applies (right).

11. **Press Option/Alt-Shift, click the bottom-right bounding box handle, and drag up and left to shrink the circle around the center point.**

Here pressing Option/Alt applies the transformation around the transformation registration point, which defaults to the center of the selected shape. Adding Shift constrains the transformation so the object's height-to-width ratio remains the same as the original shape.

Option/Alt-Shift drag the corner handle to resize the circle around the transformation registration point.

12. **Repeat Steps 8–11 to create the third circle in the wheel shape.**

13. **Save the file and continue to the next exercise.**

DRAW WITH THE PENCIL TOOL

The Pencil tool provides another way to develop curved artwork. Drawing with the Pencil tool is easy; simply drag a line or shape, and the stroke — in whatever color is currently set in the Tools panel — follows the cursor.

With the proper equipment — notably a pressure-sensitive drawing tablet — the Pencil tool might very well be the most important tool Flash offers. This notion is particularly true for artists skilled at sketching or drawing with natural media such as pen and ink, pencils, and pastel chalks. Other people find the Pencil tool difficult to use, preferring the Pen tool, Bézier curves, primitive shapes, freeform shapes, and combinations thereof.

1. **With `corvette.fla` open, make sure the Wheels layer is active. Hide the Body layer so the lines do not interfere with the area where you are working.**

2. **Choose the Pencil tool in the Tools panel. At the bottom of the Tools panel, make sure Object Drawing is toggled on.**

Pencil tool

Object-drawing mode is toggled on.

Click here to access the Pencil modes.

The Wheels layer is selected.

Note:

In the Properties panel, options for the Pencil tool are the same as those for the Pen tool.

3. **Click the mode button in the Tools panel and choose the Smooth option.**

The Pencil tool offers three possible modes:

- Straighten mode favors straight lines and corner points.
- Smooth mode favors curves and smooth anchor points in the resulting paths. This option allows greater tolerance for slightly jerky movement as you drag, which can be very useful if you are using a mouse instead of a drawing tablet.
- Ink mode closely follows the path that you draw, placing a large number of anchor points to capture very small movements of the cursor; this mode often results in a very jagged path, especially if you are using a mouse instead of a drawing tablet.

4. **Click and drag to create one of the inset shapes on the wheel. Make sure you overlap the line ends with the second circle, as shown in the following image.**

When you release the mouse button, the Smooth mode should result in a fairly rounded inset shape.

Click and drag to draw this shape.

When you release the mouse button, the path smoothes out.

5. **With the new shape selected, click the Free Transform tool to reveal the transformation handles.**

6. **Click the transformation registration point and drag to the intersection of the two ruler guides.**

   You are going to copy and rotate this object around the wheel's center point to create the six inset shapes. The ruler guides that you placed mark the center of the wheel, which you used when you Option/Alt dragged from the guide intersection to create the circles. To rotate the inset shape around the same center, you are now moving the first shape's transformation registration point to the same center point as the overall wheel shape.

The Free Transform tool is selected.

Drag the transformation registration point from the center of the shape to the intersection of the guides.

7. **With the object selected, choose Edit>Copy.**

8. **Immediately choose Edit>Paste in Place.**

   Because you moved the transformation registration point before copying and pasting the object, the pasted copy also has the same relocated registration point.

9. **Move the cursor outside one of the object's corner handles until you see the rotation icon in the tool cursor.**

10. **Click and drag left to rotate the copy, approximating the position of the second inset.**

    As you drag, you should recognize that the object is rotating around the repositioned transformation registration point; in other words, it's rotating around the wheel center.

Place the cursor near a corner point until you see the rotation icon.

Click and drag to rotate the object around the defined registration point.

11. **Repeat Steps 7–10 four more times to create the six wheel insets.**

    In this case, don't worry about perfectly matching the sketch. The important point is to have six inset shapes, spaced approximately evenly around the wheel shape.

12. **Choose View>Guides>Clear Guides.**

You no longer need the wheel's center-point reference now that all of the necessary shapes are in place, so you can delete the ruler guides.

Note that this menu also includes options for showing or hiding guides, locking guides, and numerically editing the position of a guide. These options are all useful at some point, depending on the purpose of a particular guide.

13. **Save the file and continue to the next exercise.**

WORK WITH AN OBJECT GROUP

You want to be able to access the individual shapes that make up the wheel, but you also want to be able to treat the wheel as a single unit on the main Stage. A **group** is a collection of shapes that is combined so it can be treated as a single object.

1. **With corvette.fla open, hide the Sketch layer to make the wheel shapes more prominent.**

2. **Use the Selection tool to draw a marquee around all the shapes that make up the wheel artwork.**

Because you created these objects in object-drawing mode, you can see a bounding box surrounding each shape. To prevent moving one of these components independently of the others, you can group them into a single unit.

Note:

Press Command/ Control-A to select all objects (on all layers) that are not locked.

You can also click the layer icon to select all objects on the layer.

3. Choose Modify>Group.

When you group objects, the bounding box displays around the entire group. By manipulating the bounding box, you can resize, move, and otherwise modify a group as you would a single object. Grouped objects are isolated from other elements on the same layer, so you can place grouped objects on top of one another with no worries of damaging the underlying objects.

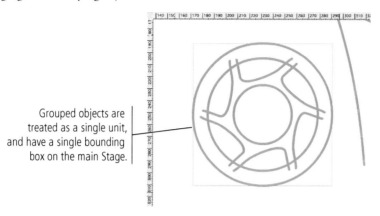

Grouped objects are treated as a single unit, and have a single bounding box on the main Stage.

Note:

You can group objects by pressing Command/ Control-G.

To ungroup objects, select the group and choose Modify>Ungroup or press Command/Control- Shift-G.

4. Double-click the group to enter into it (view the group in Edit mode).

Even though the objects are grouped on the main Stage, you can still access the individual components in Edit mode.

Because you drew these shapes in object-drawing mode, you can't access the pixels of the lines. You can't select and delete parts of the lines with the Selection tool, which you need to do.

The Edit bar shows that you are working inside the group.

In Edit mode, you can access the individual components of the group.

5. With all objects in the group selected, choose Modify>Break Apart.

After breaking apart the drawing objects, you can use the Selection tool to select specific pixels, or segments between anchor points.

6. Click away from the lines to deselect everything.

7. **Click to select one of the overhanging lines between the outer and middle circles, then press Delete/Backspace.**

   Remember from the earlier discussion on destructive editing that when you're editing a drawing object, Flash recognizes and separates overlapping elements.

8. **Repeat Step 7 to remove all of the extraneous line segments.**

9. **In the Edit bar, click Scene 1 to return to the main Stage.**

   Because these objects started as a group, and you made all the edits inside the group, the selection on the main Stage is still treated a single unit; the bounding box surrounds the outer edge of all the objects in the group.

10. **Show the Body and Sketch layers.**

Note:

It's always a good idea to look for ways to avoid duplicating work. You will create the second wheel by duplicating the first wheel after you fill it with color.

11. **Save the file and continue to the next stage of the project.**

Stage 3 Painting and Coloring Objects

You now have all of the primary shapes you need for this project, clearly organized on separate layers. (You will create the front wheel later by duplicating the finished back wheel.) You drew all of these shapes as unfilled objects so you could see the underlying sketch; now you can apply fill colors to the various shapes. You can use a wide variety of methods to paint the car; you will explore these options in this stage of the project.

APPLY FILL AND STROKE COLORS TO SELECTED SHAPES

The most basic way to change an object's color attributes is simply to select the object and then define the appropriate colors — which you will do in this exercise.

1. **With corvette.fla open, click the Body layer icon in the Timeline panel.**

   Remember, clicking a layer icon selects all objects on that layer.

2. **Click the Fill Color swatch in the Tools panel and choose a dark red color from the pop-up Swatches panel.**

   When you change the fill or stroke color when an object is already selected, you affect the relevant attributes of the selected object.

Choosing a new color changes the attribute of all selected objects.

Click the swatch to open the Swatches panel.

3. **With the car shape still selected, click the Stroke Color swatch in the Tools panel and choose the None swatch.**

   This removes the green lines which were only necessary for the original drawing process.

4. **Review the layers in the Timeline panel.**

   The layer stacking order shows that the window is below the car body. Because the car shape now has a solid fill, you can no longer see the window shape.

5. **Click the Window layer in the Timeline panel and drag up. When a line appears above the Body layer, release the mouse button.**

   Rearranging the layer stacking order is as simple as clicking and dragging. When the Window layer is above the Body layer, you can again see the window shape.

6. **Save the file and continue to the next exercise.**

FILL ARTWORK WITH THE PAINT BUCKET TOOL

The Paint Bucket tool provides an easy way to change objects' fill colors without first selecting the target objects. In this exercise you will use the Paint Bucket tool to change the fill colors of the window and the wheel.

1. **With corvette.fla open, make sure nothing is selected on the Stage.**

   If you change the Fill or Swatch color when an object it selected, the new color will affect the selected object.

2. **Choose the Paint Bucket tool in the Tools panel.**

3. **Use the Fill Color swatch in either the Tools panel or the Properties panel to change the Fill color to Black.**

4. **Click the Gap Size button at the bottom of the Tools panel and choose Close Large Gaps.**

   The Gap Size menu allows Flash to overlook slight openings between line segments, which is a common occurrence when you draw with tools such as the Pencil or Line tool. Because you want all of these objects to be solid fills, you are using the largest setting to allow the application to fill the areas that you have defined.

5. Click the line that identifies the window shape to fill the shape with the defined fill color.

Because the object doesn't yet have a fill color, you have to click exactly on the existing line to fill the closed shape. If you clicked inside the shape, the tool would recognize the fill color of the body shape and change its fill to black.

Click exactly on the shape's stroke to fill it with the defined Paint Bucket fill color.

6. Using the Selection tool, double-click the wheel group to enter into the group.

You have to enter into the group to edit the properties of individual group components.

7. Choose the Paint Bucket tool again.

8. Click between the outer and middle circles of the wheel shape to change the fill color to black.

In this case, you are editing only the group. There are no other objects on the group's Stage, so the Paint Bucket tool recognizes the closed area between the two circles and adds the black fill color.

The Edit bar verifies that you are editing the group.

When inside the group, you can click between the two lines to fill the closed area.

9. Click inside the center circle, and then click inside each of the inset shapes to change all of those fills to black (as shown in the image after Step 10).

10. Change the fill color to medium gray, and then click inside the remaining shape (around the wheel insets) to fill that area with gray.

11. Click Scene 1 in the Edit bar to return to the main Stage.

12. Save the file and continue to the next exercise.

CHANGE STROKE ATTRIBUTES WITH THE INK BOTTLE TOOL

The Ink Bottle tool allows you to change the color of strokes without first selecting a specific object. Any stroke you click will be affected by the defined tool settings. In this exercise you will change the bright green strokes that you used during development to something that more accurately suits the desired artwork.

1. **With corvette.fla open, choose Edit>Deselect All to deselect everything.**

2. **Choose the Ink Bottle tool (under the Paint Bucket tool), change the stroke color to black, and change the stroke weight to 1 pt.**

   Once you select the Ink Bottle tool, you can use the Properties panel to predetermine the weight, color, stroke style, and other features before you use the tool. The current settings in the Properties panel will be applied to any shape you click with the Ink Bottle tool, and will remain in effect until you change them.

3. **Click inside the Window shape to change the object's stroke color to black.**

   The stroke instantly changes to the new color; it doesn't matter if you select the layer or not. Since all objects are on unlocked layers, the Ink Bottle tool "knows" which objects it's touching.

Note:

When either selection tool is active, you can also simply click an empty area of the Stage to deselect everything in the file.

Ink Bottle tool

You can click the Ink Bottle tool inside a filled shape to change the object's stroke attributes.

4. **With the Ink Bottle tool still selected, click directly on each line that marks the front and back of the car door.**

   When an object has an existing fill, you can click with the Ink Bottle tool anywhere in the object's fill to change the stroke attributes. If an object has no defined fill, you have to click on the existing stroke to change its attributes.

   To accomplish this step, it might help to zoom into the lines you want to change.

Note:

You don't need to select the objects before clicking with the Ink Bottle tool to change the stroke color.

Click when the end of the "drip" touches the line you want to paint.

Because these are open lines with no fill, you have to click directly on the lines to change their attributes.

5. **Using the Selection tool, double-click the wheel group to enter into the group.**

6. **Choose the Ink Bottle tool again and change the stroke color to medium gray.**

7. Click exactly on the edge of the middle circle.

When you used the destructive editing functionality to create the inset shapes, a number of anchor points were added to the circle shape to create the inset pieces. You need click the circle edge between and within every inset piece to change the entire stroke to gray.

8. Continue clicking around the circle until the entire middle circle has a 1-pt gray stroke.

9. Change the stroke color to black and then click all of the remaining green strokes in the wheel to change them to black.

In this case, you have to click the actual strokes. If you clicked the fills, you might inadvertently change the gray stroke of the middle circle back to black.

10. **Click Scene 1 in the Edit bar to return to the main Stage.**

11. **Using the Selection tool, click the wheel group, press Option/Alt, and drag right until the duplicate wheel aligns with the front wheel.**

    Pressing Option/Alt while dragging **clones** (makes a copy of) the object you drag.

Option/Alt-dragging an object makes an exact copy (called cloning).

Note:

Be careful while making copies of any object. Do not release the Option/Alt key before releasing the mouse. Doing so might move the original object instead of making a copy.

12. **Save the file and continue to the next exercise.**

ADJUST ALPHA TRANSPARENCY

The Alpha property defines the degree of transparency of an object; in other words, it determines how much you can see underlying objects through another object. This can be useful for creating special effects, including the appearance of depth. In this exercise you will adjust alpha values to create the appearance of reflections on the car's surface.

1. **With corvette.fla open, click the Outline button for the Body layer so you can see the underlying sketch. Select the Accents layer as the active one.**

    Outline mode allows you to see through filled artwork without changing the objects' fill properties. All objects on outlined layers appear as simple lines that match that layer's defined color swatch; defined fill and stroke attributes are not visible.

Click this button to display the layer as only outlines.

2. **Use any tool you prefer (with object-drawing mode toggled on) to create the two curved shapes that represent reflections on the car's upper body.**

3. **In the Timeline panel, click the Outline button for the Body layer to restore the layer to the regular view.**

4. **Select both of the accent shapes and apply a white fill and no stroke.**

5. **In the Color panel, click the Fill Color swatch to open the color palette.**

   Remember, all panels can be accessed in the Window menu.

6. **Place the cursor over the Alpha value (in the top-right corner of the palette) until you see a two-headed arrow in the hand icon.**

   When you see this cursor, you can click and drag left or right to change the associated value (called "scrubbing").

7. **Click and drag left to reduce the Alpha value to 50%.**

   After reducing the Alpha value, you can see some of the red color through the white-filled shapes.

8. **Save the file and continue to the next exercise.**

Using the Eyedropper Tool

The Eyedropper tool makes it very easy to choose colors from existing objects on the Stage (called **sampling**). Clicking with the tool cursor pulls the color where you click.

If you sample color from the fill of an object or from a raster image, the tool automatically switches to the Paint Bucket tool loaded with the sampled color.

If you sample color from an existing object's stroke, the tool automatically switches to the Ink Bottle tool loaded with the sampled color.

You can also Command/Control-Option click to change both the fill and stroke color to the sampled color. In this case, the Eyedropper tool remains selected; you need to choose another tool to apply those colors.

Eyedropper tool

Click to sample a fill color from an object or image.

The Paint Bucket tool is automatically loaded with the sampled color.

CONVERT STROKES TO SOFTENED FILLS

The sketch in this project shows three lines that seem to bisect the car, creating an edge that catches the reflection of light. In this exercise, you will create these lines and then adjust them to add depth and texture to the artwork.

1. **With corvette.fla open, click the Outline icon for the Body layer. Make sure the Accents layer is the active one.**

2. **Choose the Line tool in the Tools panel and activate object-drawing mode. Change stroke color to white with a 50% Alpha value, and set the stroke weight to 1 pt.**

3. **Draw the three lines on the car that seem to bisect the car horizontally. Use the Selection tool to position and bend the lines as necessary.**

4. **Click the Outline button for the Body layer to restore it to the normal view.**

These are the lines to draw.

5. **Using the Selection tool, Shift-click to select all three lines.**

6. **Choose Modify>Shape>Convert Lines to Fills.**

   These hard-edged lines appear rather harsh; you are going to modify these lines to more smoothly blend into the underlying shape. To do this, you first need to convert the strokes to filled shapes. The fill of the new shapes adopts the stroke color that was applied to the original line.

7. **With the three lines still selected, choose Modify>Shape>Soften Fill Edges.**

8. **In the resulting dialog box, set the Distance field to 2 px and set the Number of Steps field to 4. Choose the Expand option.**

9. Click OK to apply the change.

Each edge of the shape is now extended by 2 pixels, moving in four steps from the original alpha value (50%) to 0%, or entirely transparent.

Before converting to a fill   After converting to a fill   After softening edges

10. Save the file and continue to the next exercise.

 ## PAINT WITH THE BRUSH TOOL

The Brush tool, as you might expect, is used to paint areas of color. This tool offers a number of modes that allow you to paint in only specific areas, as you will do in this exercise to create a shadow underneath the car.

1. With **corvette.fla** open, select the Body layer as the active one.

2. Click away from the artwork on the Stage to deselect everything.

3. Choose the Brush tool, change the fill color to a medium gray, and set the Alpha value to 100%.

4. At the bottom of the Tools panel, click the Brush Mode menu and choose Paint Behind.

Note:

The tool options remember the last-used settings, so some of these might already be set to the options we use in this exercise.

The Brush tool has five modes:

Brush tool

- **Paint Normal** is exactly that: it paints on top of anything already on the Stage.

- Using the **Paint Fills** mode, you paint over the background and any object fills, but you leave object strokes unaffected.

- **Paint Behind** allows you to paint only the background; any area with a fill remains unaffected by the brush stroke.

Lock Fill toggle
Brush Mode menu
Brush Size menu
Brush Shape menu

- **Paint Selection** applies your brush strokes to currently selected fill areas only.

- **Paint Inside** applies the brush stroke within the boundaries of the fill where you first click.

5. Click the Brush Size button and choose the largest available brush.

6. Click the Brush Shape button and choose the full round option.

7. **Using the sketch as a rough guide, click and drag to paint a shadow shape underneath the car.**

Don't worry about overlapping the car body shape while you're painting the shadow; although it appears to be on top of (and obscuring) the car shape, the shadow assumes its proper place behind the body when you release the mouse button.

Brush tool cursor

While you're painting, the brush strokes appear to be on top of the existing shape.

The Body layer should be active.

Using the Paint Behind option, the overlapping paint disappears when you release the mouse button.

8. **Using the Selection tool, select the shadow shape and then choose Edit>Cut.**

9. **In the Timeline panel, click the New Layer button. Name the new layer Shadow.**

As we explained previously, new layers are always added immediately above the previously selected layer.

10. **With the Shadow layer selected, choose Edit>Paste in Place.**

Even though you couldn't see the entire brush stroke after releasing the mouse button, the shape exactly matches the area that you painted. When moved to a higher layer in the stack, the entire area becomes visible — obscuring some of the car body.

With the Shadow layer above the Body layer, the entire painted shape is visible.

11. **Click the Shadow layer in the Timeline panel and drag it below the Body layer.**

Rearranging the layer stacking order hides the shadow edge behind the car body.

12. **Save the file and continue to the next exercise.**

APPLY LINEAR AND RADIAL GRADIENTS

At this point your artwork is a technically complete piece of artwork; all of the shapes are in place, with the necessary solid fills and strokes to clearly portray a digital Corvette. To add greater depth and dimension, however, you are going to apply gradients to the car's body and window.

Note:

*Artwork that contains only solid fills is referred to as **flat art**.*

1. **With corvette.fla open, click the window shape with the Selection tool.**

2. **Using either the Properties or Tools panel, open the Fill Color palette and choose the white-to-black radial gradient swatch.**

Note:

The terms "gradient" and "blend" are used interchangeably. Flash documentation uses both gradient and blend; both terms mean a smooth transition from one color to another.

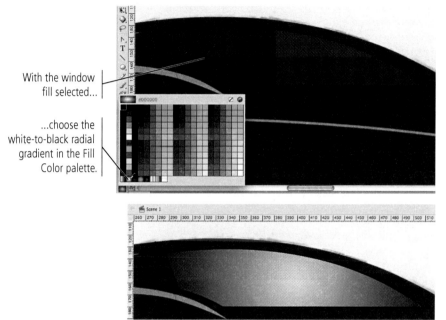

With the window fill selected...

...choose the white-to-black radial gradient in the Fill Color palette.

3. **In the Color panel, click below the gradient ramp near the middle to add a new color stop to the gradient.**

   Clicking below the ramp adds a new stop, which defaults to the color of the location where you first click.

Note:

You can define up to 15 color stops in a single gradient.

Click below the ramp to add a stop to the gradient.

4. **Drag the new stop left, to approximately one-fourth of the way across the ramp.**

The selected shape adopts the new distribution of color.

Click the stop and drag to move that color to a different position along the gradient.

5. **Click the car body shape with the Selection tool.**

6. **In the Color panel, click the Fill Color icon to activate that attribute.**

7. **In the Color Type menu, choose Linear Gradient.**

   The gradient ramp remembers the last-used gradient, so the adjusted white-to-black gradient from the window is applied to the selected shape (the car body).

Click here to make sure the Fill icon is active.

Choose from this menu to apply a linear gradient to the selected object.

The last-used gradient is automatically applied.

8. **At the bottom of the Color panel, click the color stop in the middle of the gradient ramp and drag down away from the ramp.**

   You can remove any stop from a gradient by simply dragging it away from the ramp.

9. **Double-click the color stop at the left end of the gradient ramp. Choose the dark red color swatch from the pop-up palette.**

Double-click a gradient stop to open the color palette for that stop.

10. **Double-click the right color stop and choose the same dark red color that you applied to the left stop.**

11. **With the right stop still selected, drag the Brightness slider in the Color panel down until the B% option (in the HSB group) shows 10%.**

This is the value you are affecting by dragging the slider.

Drag here to change the stop's brightness value.

12. **Save the file and continue to the next exercise.**

TRANSFORM GRADIENTS

As you saw in the previous exercise, it is fairly easy to apply gradients to any drawing object, and to change the colors that are used in those gradients. Of course, the left-to-right gradient on the car's body does not create the realistic effect that you want. You now need to transform the applied gradients to finish the piece.

1. **With corvette.fla open, choose the Gradient Transform tool (under the Free Transform tool).**

2. **Click the window shape to select it.**

   The Gradient Transform tool enables you to adjust the size, direction, and center point of a gradient fill. When you click an object filled with a gradient, a special bounding box shows the gradient-editing handles.

3. **Click the center point of the gradient and drag to the top-left corner of the window shape.**

   Dragging the center-point handle moves the center of the gradient to a new location.

4. **Click the gradient-width handle and drag in about halfway to flatten the gradient.**

   Dragging the width handle of a radial gradient makes the gradient narrower or wider in one direction, essentially creating a skewed effect.

5. Click the gradient-rotation handle and drag left to change the angle of the gradient.

Dragging the rotation handle rotates the gradient around its center point.

6. Click the gradient-size handle and drag out to enlarge the adjusted gradient.

Dragging the size handle makes the overall gradient larger or smaller in both directions (without affecting the gradient's aspect ratio).

7. Still using the Gradient Transform tool, click the car body shape to select it and access the gradient transformation handles.

Center-point handle
Rotation handle
Width handle

8. Click the gradient-rotation handle and drag down and left to rotate the gradient approximately 90°, with the dark part of the gradient toward the bottom edge of the car.

Because you did not yet change the gradient width, the rotated gradient transformation handles will be well below the Stage edge. If necessary, zoom out so you can see all the gradient transformation handles.

Note:

You can use the rotation handle to reverse a gradient. Simply drag all the way around (180°) until the gradient colors are reversed.

The gradient transformation handles are below the Stage edge because you have not yet changed the gradient width.

9. **Click the gradient-width handle and drag up until the gradient is just slightly larger than the height of your artwork.**

For a linear gradient, dragging the width handle makes the gradient narrower or wider.

10. **Click the center point of the gradient and drag down, about one-third of the way closer to the bottom of the car body.**

11. **Save the file and continue to the next exercise.**

Locking Bitmap and Gradient Fills

You can use a bitmap (raster) image as the fill of an object by choosing Bitmap Fill in the Fill Type menu of the Color panel. All available bitmap files appear as tiles in the lower half of the panel; if none are avilable, choosing Bitmap Fill in the menu opens a dialog box, where you can import the file you want to use.

You can use the Paint Bucket tool to fill an existing object with a bitmap, or you can use the Brush tool to paint the bitmap onto the Stage. The **Lock Fill** modifier at the bottom of the Tools panel determines how the fill will be added.

Choose Bitmap Fill in this menu.

Click Import to add bitmaps to the file.

Click any available tile to select that bitmap as the fill.

- When toggled on, the selected bitmap image is tiled inside the shape.
- When toggled off, the selected bitmap image is basically pasted to the Stage. The filled area essentially "reveals" the area of the selected bitmap image. (If a bitmap-fill image is too small to fill the Stage, the image is tiled as necessary)

Lock Fill modifier

If you select a bitmap-filled object with the Gradient Transform tool, you can edit the size, skew, rotation, and position of the fill image.

Turned on, the bitmap image is tiled inside the filled shape

Turned off, the shape reveals the relevant area of the bitmap.

Similar Lock Fill options are available when you work with gradients. When this option is toggled on, the gradient is applied relative to the overall Stage; filled areas reveal the relevant area of the gradient. If the option is turned off, the gradient is applied to each object independently.

With the Lock Fill modifier, the same gradient extends across all four squares.

Without the Lock Fill modifier, the gradient is applied individually to each square.

ORGANIZE FINISHED ARTWORK LAYERS

A Flash project can contain dozens of layers representing the various components of the animation or movie. To organize all of these layers into logical groups or categories, you can use layer folders.

1. **With corvette.fla open, select the top layer (Accents) in the Timeline panel.**

2. **Click the New Folder button at the bottom of the Timeline panel.**

New Folder button

3. **Double-click the new folder name. Type Car Parts as the new folder name and press Return/Enter to finalize the new name.**

   You change the name of a layer folder the same way you change the name of a layer; simply double-click the folder name and type in the new name.

4. **Click the Accents layer to select it, then Shift-click the Shadow layer to add it and all contiguous layers to the selection.**

5. **Click any of the selected layers and drag them into the Car Parts folder.**

   The dragged layers now reside inside the layer folder, which makes it easier to treat the entire group of layers as a single object. This will be helpful later when the artwork is used in programming and interactive development.

Note:

You can rename layer folders in the same way you rename layers, and you can reorder layer folders (and their contents) by dragging the folders into new positions in the layer stack.

Shift-click to select multiple adjacent items.

The indented line shows that the selected layers will be placed inside the Car Parts folder.

6. **Click the Lock column for the Car Parts folder.**

   By locking the layer folder, you have effectively locked each layer inside the folder (although you can unlock individual layers in the folder by clicking that layer's Lock icon). The same concept is true of the Visibility and Outline buttons for the layer folder.

Note:

Press Shift to select contiguous layers — that is, layers directly on top of or below one another. To select layers that aren't next to each other, press the Command/Control key while clicking the individual (non-contiguous) layers.

Locking a folder locks all layers inside that folder.

7. **Click the arrow to the left of the Car Parts folder to collapse it.**

   Once collapsed, only the layer folder is visible. This makes it easier to navigate through the Timeline panel, which can grow very large for complex projects.

8. **Select the Sketch layer and click the panel's Delete button.**

Note:

When you use layer folders, you can lock and hide all the contents in the folder by locking and hiding the entire folder.

Click here to collapse the Car Parts folder.

Select the Sketch layer and click here to delete it.

9. **Save the file and continue to the final exercise.**

EXPORT ARTWORK AS AN IMAGE

Instead of sending the Flash file to your client, you are going to export a static image that can be easily reviewed by anyone with a Web browser. Flash includes the ability to export a number of different static image formats, including JPEG, GIF, Adobe FXG (Flash XML Graphics), PNG, and BMP (Windows only).

1. **With `corvette.fla` open, choose File>Export>Export Image. Navigate to your WIP>Car folder as the target location.**

2. **Add `_drawing` to the end of the existing file name (before the file extension).**

3. **Choose JPEG Image in the Format/Save As Type menu, then click Save.**

The original file name is automatically based on the file name of your native Flash file

Add the second half of the file name to distinguish this file from the sketch.

The extension automatically changes to match what you select in the Format/Save As Type menu.

4. **In the resulting Export JPEG dialog box, make sure the Resolution option is set to 72 dpi.**

   You are creating this image for on-screen review, so 72 dpi is fine. If you needed the artwork for high-quality printing, you should use a higher resolution (i.e., 300 dpi).

5. **Choose Full Document Size in the Include menu.**

   If you choose Minimum Image Area, the exported image will be only and exactly as large as the outermost edges of the artwork. The Full Document Size option creates a file that matches the defined Stage size.

6. **Change the Quality value to 100%.**

   Reducing the Quality value will result in a smaller file size, but can significantly decrease the resulting image quality (especially in complex artwork). For review purposes, the highest possible quality setting is a better option.

7. **Click OK to export the JPEG file.**

8. **Close the `corvette.fla` file.**

Note:

Flash should generally not be used for developing artwork for high-quality commercial print applications.

Note:

You can click the Match Screen button to restore the size and resolution fields to match what you see on your monitor.

Note:

If the Progressive Display option is checked, the image will appear in progressive degrees of detail as it downloads.

fill in the blank

1. The _____ can be used to change the size of the Stage.

2. _____ in the timeline can be used to manage the top-to-bottom order of objects on the Stage.

3. When created in _____, the fill and stroke are treated as separate entities; you can individually select each part, and move or modify each part without affecting the other.

4. When you create a shape in _____, it automatically displays the bounding box as soon as you create it; you can't select the fill and stroke independently on the main Stage.

5. A(n) _____ allows multiple objects to be treated as a single entity on the Stage.

6. The _____ tool can be used to select areas of a standard-drawing object, or to bend lines created in either drawing mode.

7. The _____ tool can be used to select individual anchor points and handles that make up a shape.

8. The _____ tool is used to create precise Bézier curves.

9. The _____ tool is used to change the fill color of closed shapes.

10. The _____ tool is used to change the stroke color of any object.

short answer

1. Briefly explain how anchor points and handles control the lines in a vector shape.

2. Briefly explain the difference between the Selection tool and the Subselection tool.

3. Briefly explain what is meant by "destructive editing."

Use what you learned in this project to complete the following freeform exercise.
Carefully read the art director and client comments, then create your own design to meet the needs of the project.
Use the space below to sketch ideas; when finished, write a brief explanation of your reasoning behind your final design.

art director comments

Your client is happy with the Corvette, and asked you to create two more illustrations that he can use in different digital projects.

To complete this project, you should:

❏ Search the Internet for photos that you can use as templates for creating the other new illustrations.

❏ Create each illustration in a separate file.

❏ Carefully consider the best approach for each icon and use whichever tool (or tools) are most appropriate to create the icon artwork.

client comments

The cars are a big part of the annual event, but it isn't limited to only cars. Really, the show includes categories for just about anything with a motor. Aside from the American Heavy Metal sports cars, the two most popular parts of the show are Early Antiques and Motorcycles.

I'd like you to create illustrations for both of those categories. For the Early Antiques, the Model T Ford of the 1910s will be a perfect icon for the class. For motorcycles, a 1940s Indian would be ideal for the different projects I want to create.

I really like the Corvette artwork, so I want the two new illustrations to have a similar style. When I look at the three pieces together, I'd like it to be clear that all three were created by the same artist.

project justification

_____
_____
_____
_____
_____
_____
_____
_____
_____
_____
_____
_____
_____

Although Flash is known as an animation program, you can see from this project that the application offers a considerable array of drawing and painting tools. You learned how to import a sketch, control the size of the Flash Stage, and align objects to the Stage. These skills set the groundwork for any type of assignment. You also developed an understanding of layers and how they positively affect the construction of complex drawings and artwork.

Flash includes a range of drawing tools — from the basic shape tools, the Line tool for simple lines, and the Pen and Pencil tools for more complex curves. Those tools, combined with the two Flash drawing modes and the unique destructive editing capabilities that are part of the Flash toolset, make it possible to create complex artwork directly on the Stage.

Use the Pencil tool to create custom shapes

Create and edit basic shapes

Use the Pen tool to create precise curves

Control object fill and stroke attributes

Use alpha transparency to soften fills

Use destructive pixel editing to remove drawing elements

Work in both standard- and object-drawing modes

Convert lines to filled shapes

Paint shapes with different brush modes

Use layers to control object visibility

Create the appearance of depth with gradients

Talking Kiosk Interface

You were hired to create an animated introduction for a shopping mall information kiosk. The Flash-based animation must feature a character that offers shoppers assistance in finding various facilities. Each button should also offer audio instructions that explain the link's purpose. As part of the Flash development team, your job is to prepare the interface artwork that will be handed off to the programmer, who will script the interactivity.

This project incorporates the following skills:

❑ Importing and managing artwork from Adobe Illustrator

❑ Using the Library panel to manage a complex file

❑ Building a frame-by-frame animation

❑ Editing various button states

❑ Importing sound files into Flash

❑ Adding event and stream sounds to the Flash timeline

❑ Controlling volume and duration of sound

❑ Applying built-in sound effects

❑ Synchronizing sound to animation

❑ Defining sound compression settings

Project Meeting

client comments

Throughout the facility grounds, we are replacing all of the static "You Are Here" maps with interactive kiosks that will help users more quickly find the shops they are looking for.

I'd like the interface to be personal — a person actually talking to the user. We thought about the video route, but I'm convinced an animated character would be better (plus we won't have to pay an actor to use her image).

The interface should provide a link to four different categories of shops: Shoes & Apparel, Home Furnishings, Music & Electronics, and Casual & Fine Dining. We might break it down into more specific categories later, but the important point for now is to get the first version of this thing into use quickly.

art director comments

I already had all of the kiosk components created. I need you to assemble everything in Flash and prepare the various elements for the programmer, who will create all of the necessary code and links.

The artwork was created in Adobe Illustrator. Our illustrator is fairly knowledgeable about Flash requirements, so you should be able to import the artwork without too many problems. He even created the basic appearance of the navigation buttons, so you'll just need to modify those rather than create them from scratch.

When I reviewed the sound files, it seemed like the background music was very loud compared to the spoken intro. You should fix the music so the talking is audible above the background (especially in a noisy mall).

The lip-syncing part of the interface requires some careful attention to detail, but overall, it isn't a difficult job. Just take your time and try to make the mouths follow the words.

project objectives

To complete this project, you will:

- ❑ Create symbols from imported Illustrator files
- ❑ Place and manage instances of symbols on the Stage
- ❑ Control timing using keyframes
- ❑ Add visual interactivity to button symbols
- ❑ Import sound files into Flash
- ❑ Add event and stream sounds to a movie
- ❑ Use the start and stop sync methods for button sounds
- ❑ Edit a sound envelope to control volume and duration
- ❑ Swap graphics at precise moments in time
- ❑ Define sound compression settings

Stage 1 Working with Symbols

Although Flash can be used to create extraordinary interactive content, the program can also create extremely large files that take a very long time to download. (The size of a file is often referred to as a file's **weight**.) Users will not wait for more than a few seconds to download a file, so you should always try to keep file weight to a minimum — and that's where symbols come into play.

Symbols are objects that can be used repeatedly without increasing file size. The original symbol resides in the Library panel; **symbol instances** are copies of the symbol that you place onto the Stage. Although a regular graphic object adds to the overall file weight every time you use it on the Stage, a symbol counts only once no matter how many times you use it — which can mean dramatically smaller file size.

As another benefit, changes made to the content of an original symbol reflect in every placed instance of that symbol. For example, if you have placed 40 instances of a bird symbol, you can simultaneously change all 40 birds from blue jays to cardinals by changing the primary symbol in the Library panel.

A third benefit of symbols is that you can name placed instances, which means those instances can be targeted and affected by programming — one of the keys to animation and interactive development.

Note:

There are three primary types of symbols — graphic, movie clip, and button — and a number of other types of assets, such as audio and video files. In Flash, all of these assets are automatically stored in the Library panel.

The Library Panel in Depth

FLASH FOUNDATIONS

Assets in Flash are stored in the Library panel. Additional information about each asset is listed on the right side of the panel, including files that are required by the asset (Linkage), the number of instances in the current file (Use Count), the date the asset was last modified (Date Modified), and the type of asset (Type). If the panel is too narrow to show the additional information, you can either make the panel wider or use the scroll bar at the bottom of the panel to find this additional asset information. In addition to storing and organizing assets, the Library panel has a number of other uses:

- Each type of asset is identified by a unique icon. Double-clicking a symbol icon enters into Symbol-Editing mode, where you can modify the symbol on its own Stage.

- You can use the Library menu to switch between the libraries of currently open files.

- The Preview pane shows the selected asset. If the asset includes animation, video, or sound, you can use the Play and Stop buttons to preview the file in the panel. (The background color of the Stage appears in the Preview pane behind the selected symbol; if you have a dark background and can't see the Play button, move your mouse over the area of the button to reveal it.)

- If a file has a large number of assets (which is common), you can use the Search field to find assets by name.

- Clicking the Pin button to the right of the Library menu attaches the current library to the open Flash file.

- Clicking the New Library Panel button opens a new version of the Library panel, which allows you to view multiple libraries at one time.

- Clicking the New Symbol button opens the Create New Symbol dialog box, where you can define the name and type of the new symbol you want to create.

- Clicking the New Folder button adds a new folder in the current file's library.

- Clicking the Properties button opens a dialog box that shows information about the selected library asset.

- Clicking Delete removes an asset from the library. Placed instances of that symbol are deleted from the file.

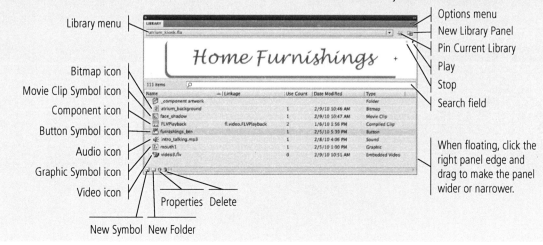

Library menu · Bitmap icon · Movie Clip Symbol icon · Component icon · Button Symbol icon · Audio icon · Graphic Symbol icon · Video icon · Properties · Delete · New Symbol · New Folder · Options menu · New Library Panel · Pin Current Library · Play · Stop · Search field · When floating, click the right panel edge and drag to make the panel wider or narrower.

IMPORT ADOBE ILLUSTRATOR ARTWORK

As you learned in Project 1, you can use the built-in Flash tools to draw complex custom artwork. In many cases, however, your work in Flash will incorporate files that were created in other applications. For example, illustrations and other vector graphics for animation are typically created in Adobe Illustrator. This project incorporates a number of external files, which you need to import into your Flash file.

1. **Download FL5_RF_Project2.zip from the Student Files Web page.**

2. **Expand the ZIP archive in your WIP folder (Macintosh) or copy the archive contents into your WIP folder (Windows).**

   This results in a folder named **Atrium**, which contains the files you need for this project. You should also use this folder to save the files you create in this project.

3. **In Flash, create a new Flash document for ActionScript 3.0.**

   You can choose File>New, or use the Create New ActionScript 3.0 option in the Welcome Screen.

4. **Choose File>Save. Save the file in your WIP>Atrium folder as a Flash document named atrium_kiosk.fla.**

   In this project, you will use the Tools, Properties, Library, Align, and Timeline panels. You should arrange your workspace to best suit your personal preferences.

5. **Review the Properties and Library panels.**

The Stage defaults to 550 x 400 pixels.

The new file has a single layer, named Layer 1 by default.

The new file has an empty library.

6. **Choose File>Import>Import to Stage. Navigate to the file interface.ai in the WIP>Atrium folder and click Import/Open.**

7. In the top-left section of the resulting dialog box, review the contents of the file that you are importing.

The list of imported elements will make more sense if you're familiar with Adobe Illustrator. If you're not, the best choice is usually to import everything and review it carefully once it is in the Flash file.

If the Illustrator file has more than one artboard, access them here.

Layers in the file are the first-level listings.

Groups on the individual layers are listed under the appropriate layers.

Items that make up a group are listed below the appropriate groups.

By default, all items are checked, which means all items will be imported.

This icon identifies a graphic symbol, which can be created in Adobe Illustrator.

Some Illustrator objects can't be reproduced by the Flash drawing model.

8. Click the path with the warning icon in the list, and review the information on the right side of the dialog box.

Many objects created in Illustrator are fully compatible with Flash drawing capabilities, so they are imported as regular drawing objects. Any objects that don't fit into the Flash drawing model — primarily, ones with some type of applied transparency — are imported in a way that allows Flash to maintain the integrity of the overall artwork. Effects that cannot be reproduced by Flash display a warning icon in the list of elements.

Note:

*Learn more about Adobe Illustrator in the companion book of this series, **Adobe Illustrator CS5: The Professional Portfolio**.*

Select an item in the list to review the options for that object.

By default, objects that can be reproduced with the Flash drawing model are imported as editable paths.

The message shows that the selected object can't be reproduced accurately using the Flash drawing model.

Click the warning icon to see exactly what drawing elements are not compatible with Flash.

9. **With the incompatible path selected, choose the Bitmap radio button in the Import As area.**

Importing the object as a bitmap preserves its appearance, but you won't be able to edit the vector paths that make up the shape.

Bitmaps are typically larger files than vector graphics, which means that bitmaps require more time to download. Be careful when you use bitmaps in a Flash movie, especially one that will be downloaded over the Internet; very large bitmap files in the library can still affect the file's overall download time. (Because this project will be placed on a kiosk rather than downloaded over the Internet, file size is not a significant issue.)

Importing the object as a bitmap preserves the appearance of effects that can't be reproduced by the Flash drawing model.

This icon identifies a bitmap.

10. **Click the arrow to the left of the Buttons layer name to collapse that layer. Review the rest of the items in the list.**

We prepared this Adobe Illustrator file very carefully to meet the requirements of this Flash project, including assigning descriptive names to all layers and groups. Many illustrators will not provide this level of detail in their files.

Illustrator objects that do not directly correlate to Flash drawing objects, such as shapes with applied transparency settings, are automatically converted to movie clip symbols when imported to Flash.

Use these arrows to collapse or expand layers and sublayers.

This icon identifies a movie clip symbol.

These paths will be imported as movie clips because they include transparent effects.

11. **At the bottom of the dialog box, choose Flash Layers in the Convert Layers To menu.**

This option maintains the existing layers from the original artwork; each Illustrator layer becomes a layer in the Flash file. This is useful if you aren't sure about what you're importing; you can always change or delete imported layers if you don't need them.

You can also choose Single Flash Layer, which flattens all objects onto a single layer (named according to the imported file name), or choose Keyframes to add each layer as a keyframe on the default Layer 1.

Note:

You will learn about keyframes in Stage 2 of this project.

12. Check the Place Objects at Original Position option.

Using this option places the imported artwork at the same relative position where it appeared on the Illustrator artboard (the "page" or drawing space). For example, if a square is placed 1 inch from the top and left edges of the artboard, it will be placed 1 inch from the top and left edges of the Stage. When this option is not checked, the imported artwork is centered in the document window, regardless of the position of the Flash Stage.

It is important to note that the relative position of imported artwork is maintained, regardless of your selection here. In other words, all imported objects appear in the same place (relative to each other) as in the Illustrator file. The import process treats all objects in the import as a single group for the purposes of the import only; this option simply controls the imported artwork's position relative to the Stage.

13. Check the Set Stage to Same Size as Illustrator Artboard option.

The Illustrator artboard is the area that defines the physical dimensions of the file, just as the Stage defines the physical size of a Flash file. This option shows the dimensions of the imported file's artboard; if you know the Illustrator file was created to the correct dimensions — as it was in this case — you can use this option to automatically change the Stage size to match the imported artwork.

14. Uncheck the Import Unused Symbols option.

Illustrator can be used to create graphic and movie clip symbols (but not buttons), which are stored in a file's Symbols panel. This can include symbols that are not placed in the file, but which might be necessary for the overall project.

If you don't know what a file contains, you can check this option to be sure all of the necessary bits are imported; you can always delete unwanted symbols once they have been imported. For this project, we are telling you that all required symbols in the imported artwork are placed on the artboard.

15. Uncheck the Import as a Single Bitmap Image option.

If this option is checked, the entire file is flattened and converted to a bitmap image; you would not be able to access any of the components of the imported artwork.

16. Click OK to import the Illustrator artwork.

17. Click away from all objects on the Stage to deselect them.

All objects are automatically selected after being imported to the Stage. Deselecting them allows you to review the Flash file's properties.

Convert layers to: Flash Layers
☑ Place objects at original position
☑ Set stage size to same size as Illustrator artboard (1024 x 768)
☐ Import unused symbols
☐ Import as a single bitmap image

Note:

The options at the bottom of the dialog box remember the last-used settings. Some of the choices we define in Steps 11–15 might already be set on your computer.

The imported artwork is aligned to the top-left corner of the Stage, matching its relative position on the original Illustrator artboard.

With nothing selected, the Properties panel shows the adjusted Stage size.

A folder (named the same as the imported file) is added to the library, containing all the pieces necessary for the imported artwork.

Five layers are added to the Timeline panel, named the same as the layers in the original Illustrator file.

18. **In the Library panel, click the arrow to the left of the interface.ai folder to expand it, and then click the arrows to expand all but the Girl folder.**

Imported assets are sorted by layer; folder names match the imported layer names to help you understand where different pieces are required. A separate folder for Illustrator Symbols is included.

Click the arrows to expand or collapse folders.

Bitmap icon

Graphic symbol icon

Movie clip symbol icon

This bitmap image was placed on the Background layer in Illustrator.

This bitmap image was created by the Import process to solve incompatibility problems.

These graphic symbols were created in the Illustrator file.

These movie clips were created by the Import process to maintain the appearance of transparent effects.

Note:

The Girl folder includes a long list of paths and groups that were imported as movie clips to preserve transparency effects that were applied in the Illustrator file. We did not include that folder in this instruction simply because the list is so long.

19. **Save the file and continue to the next exercise.**

Illustrator File Import Preferences

FLASH FOUNDATIONS

You can define the default options for importing native Illustrator files in the AI File Importer pane of the Preferences dialog box. (Remember, preferences are accessed in the Flash menu on Macintosh and in the Edit menu on Windows.) Most of these options will become clearer as you work through this project and learn more about the different types of symbols. In some cases, the options refer to specific features in the native application.

- **Show Import Dialog Box** is checked by default. If you uncheck this option, Illustrator files will import using the default options defined here (without showing the Import dialog box).

- If **Exclude Objects Outside Artboard** is checked, objects outside the artboard (Illustrator's "page") are unchecked by default in the Import dialog box.

- If **Import Hidden Layers** is checked, all layers in the file (including ones that are not visible) are listed in the Import dialog box.

- The **Import Text As** options define how text objects in the Illustrator file import into the Flash file. Editable Text, selected by default, imports text objects that you can edit using the Flash Text tool. If you choose Vector Outlines, text objects import as a group of vector shapes; you cannot edit the text in these objects (other than manipulating the vector paths). If you choose Bitmaps, text objects import as raster objects that cannot be edited with either the Text tool or the Subselection tool.

- The **Import Paths As** options determine the default behavior for how vector paths in the Illustrator file are added to the Flash file. Editable Paths means you can use the Flash Subselection tool to manipulate the anchor points and handles on the imported paths; if you select the Bitmaps option, you will not be able to edit the vector paths within Flash.

- **Images** placed in an Illustrator file are maintained when the file imports into Flash; if you select an image in the Import dialog box, you can choose to flatten the bitmap file or automatically create a movie clip. You can use the Images preference options to automatically check the related boxes in the Import dialog box.

- **Groups** and **Layers** from the Illustrator file are listed separately in the Import dialog box. You can use the Groups and Layers preference options to automatically check the Import as Bitmap and Create Movie Clip options in the Import dialog box.

- **Movie Clip Registration** defines the default registration options for any objects you import as movie clip symbols.

IMPORT FILES TO THE LIBRARY

In addition to importing files to the Flash Stage, you can also import external files directly into the Flash file's Library panel. This option is particularly useful when certain objects aren't going to be placed on the main Stage, or if you don't yet know how you will use a particular object.

1. **With atrium_kiosk.fla open, choose File>Import>Import to Library. Navigate to the file mouths.ai in the WIP>Atrium folder and click Import to Library/Open.**

   When you import an Illustrator file directly to the Library panel, most of the options are the same as for importing to the Stage. The Place Objects at Original Position and Set Stage Size to Same Size as Illustrator Artboard options are not available because they do not apply to files that only exist (for now) in the file's library.

Note:

Flash defaults to the last-used folder, so you might not have to navigate to the folder you used in the previous exercise.

2. **Click OK to import the artwork to the library.**

   The Library panel shows that the resulting object was imported as a graphic symbol. Nothing is added to the Stage or the timeline.

3. **In the Library panel, click the mouths.ai item to select it.**

   The top portion of the panel shows a preview of the selected item.

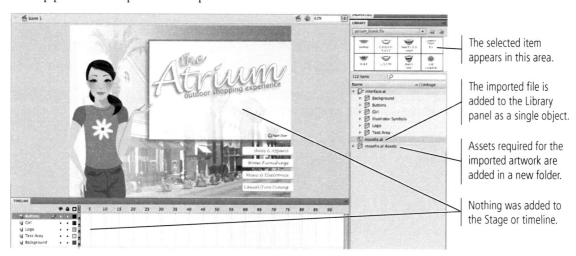

The selected item appears in this area.

The imported file is added to the Library panel as a single object.

Assets required for the imported artwork are added in a new folder.

Nothing was added to the Stage or timeline.

4. **Save the file and continue to the next exercise.**

CONVERT OBJECTS TO SYMBOLS

You now have a number of assets in your file's Library panel. The mouths.ai graphic contains eight groups of graphics — the different mouth shapes that you will use later in this project to synchronize the character to a sound file. For the process to work, you need to separate each mouth shape into a distinct symbol so the correct artwork can be placed at the appropriate point in the file.

1. **With atrium_kiosk.fla open, double-click the mouths.ai symbol icon to enter into the symbol's Stage.**

   Every symbol has its own Stage, which is theoretically infinite and separate from the main Stage of the base file. When you double-click the symbol icon in the Library panel, you enter **Symbol-Editing mode** for that symbol; other elements of the base file are not visible on the Stage.

The Edit bar shows that you are now working on the mouths.ai Stage (called **Symbol-Editing mode**).

When you first enter into the symbol, all artwork in the symbol is selected.

2. **Click away from the artwork to deselect everything, then click the top-left mouth shape to select that group (but not the word "resting").**

   Grouping in the original artwork is maintained in the imported artwork.

3. **Control/right-click the selected artwork and choose Convert to Symbol from the contextual menu.**

Note:

You can also drag an object onto the Library panel to open the Convert to Symbol dialog box for that object.

4. **In the resulting dialog box, type mouth1 in the Name field and choose Graphic in the Type menu.**

   A graphic symbol is the most basic type of symbol. It is typically used for objects that will simply be placed on the Stage. (A graphic symbol can include animation; you will explore these options in Project 4.)

5. Select the center point in the registration proxy icon.

The registration grid affects the placement of the symbol's registration point. (This will make more sense shortly when you begin editing symbols on their own Stages.)

6. Click OK to create the new symbol.

The Properties panel now shows that the selected object is an instance of the mouth1 symbol, which has been added to the Library panel.

The Properties panel shows that the selected artwork is now an instance of the mouth1 symbol.

The new symbol is added to the file's Library panel.

7. Click the second mouth shape (to the right) to select it. Control/right-click the group and choose Convert to Symbol.

The Convert to Symbol dialog box remembers the last-used settings. The Type menu is already set to Graphic, and the center registration point is already selected.

8. Type mouth2 in the Name field and click OK.

9. Repeat Steps 7–8 to convert the rest of the mouth shapes into symbols, working from left to right across the top row and then left to right across the bottom row.

10. **Click Scene 1 in the Edit bar to return to the main Stage.**

11. **Click the mouth shape on the Stage to select it.**

The selected object is a group. It is not an instance of any symbol.

12. **In the Timeline panel, add a new layer immediately above the Girl layer. Name the new layer Mouths.**

    When you selected the mouth shape in Step 11, the layer containing the object (Girl) automatically became the active layer. When you click the New Layer button in this step, the new layer is automatically added above the previously selected layer.

13. **Click mouth1 in the Library panel and drag an instance onto the Stage.**

14. **Use the Selection tool to drag the placed instance to the same position as the mouth group on the underlying Girl layer.**

15. **Hide the Mouths layer, select the mouth group on the Girl layer and delete it, and then show the Mouths layer again.**

The X and Y fields show the position of the instance's registration point.

Drag the symbol from the Library panel to the Stage to place an instance on the active layer.

16. **Save the file and continue to the next exercise.**

CREATE A BUTTON SYMBOL

Buttons, one of the three main symbol types in Flash, are interactive assets that change when a user interacts with them. A button can be in one of four "states" at any particular time.

- A button's **Up state** (also referred to as the idle or default state) is the basic appearance of a button when a user first loads a file.

- The **Over state** occurs when a mouse pointer rolls over a button. (When a user places a mouse cursor over a rollover area, the cursor often turns into a pointing finger or some other custom shape.)

- The **Down state** occurs when a user clicks a button.

- The **Hit state** controls the size of a rollover area (**hot spot**) of a button.

Note:

Buttons can be both animated and idle at the same time; idle simply means that no one has passed over or clicked the button with the mouse pointer.

This file includes five buttons. Four were created as symbols in the Illustrator artwork, and one was imported onto the Stage as a group.

1. **With `atrium_kiosk.fla` open, use the Selection tool to select the group containing the words "Start Over".**

2. **Control/right-click the selected group and choose Convert to Symbol in the contextual menu.**

3. **In the resulting dialog box, type `start_over` in the name field and choose Button in the Type menu.**

4. **Click OK to create the new symbol.**

Because you created the symbol from objects on the Stage, the Properties panel shows that the selection is automatically an instance of the new symbol.

This group is now an instance of the new start_over button symbol.

This icon identifies a button symbol.

5. **Double-click the Start Over button on the Stage to enter into the symbol.**

This method of editing a symbol is called **editing in place**. Other objects on the Stage are still visible, but they are screened back and cannot be accessed.

As we explained earlier, a button is a special type of symbol with four distinct states. Each possible state is represented as a frame in the special Button symbol timeline.

The Edit bar shows that you are editing on the start_over button symbol Stage.

Editing a symbol in place means you can see — but not access — the other objects on the Stage.

6. **In the Timeline panel, Control/right-click the Over frame of Layer 1 and choose Insert Keyframe from the contextual menu.**

A **keyframe** defines a point where something changes. If you want to make something appear different from one frame to the next — whether inside a symbol or on the main Stage — you need to place a keyframe at the point where the change should occur.

Note:

You can also insert a keyframe by choosing Insert>Timeline> Keyframe, or pressing F6.

Control/right-click the Over frame for Layer 1.

7. **Make sure the Over frame is selected in the Timeline panel, then double-click the words "Start Over" in the graphic to enter into that group.**

The contents of the Over frame will appear when the user's mouse moves over the button area. You are going to change the color of the letters in this button.

8. **Double-click any letter in the group to access the individual letters that make up the group.**

Remember, Flash remembers the groupings from the original Illustrator file. Depending on how a file was created, you might have to enter into a number of nested groups before you get to the level you need.

9. **With the individual letter shapes selected, use the Fill Color swatch in the Tools or Properties panel to change the fill color to a medium blue.**

You have to drill down into two levels of grouping to access the individual letter shapes.

You are editing only the Over frame.

Note:

Even if you have drilled into multiple levels of Symbol-Editing mode, you can return to the main Stage with a single click on the Edit bar.

10. **Click Scene 1 in the Edit bar to return to the main Stage.**

11. **Save the file and continue to the next exercise.**

DEFINE A HIT STATE

In the previous exercise, you changed the color of button text in the Over frame. However, there is still a problem — the button currently works only if the mouse pointer touches the icon or one of the letter shapes. If the pointer lies between two letters, for example, the button fails to activate.

All spaces within the button should be active. Moving the pointer close to or on top of the button should trigger the desired action. To resolve the problem, you need to use the Hit frame, which determines where a user can click to activate the button.

1. **With atrium_kiosk.fla open, choose Control>Enable Simple Buttons to toggle that option on.**

   This command allows you to test button states directly on the Flash Stage.

2. **Check the current condition of the Start Over button by positioning the pointer between the two words in the button.**

   There are "dead" areas within the button that don't cause the color change to occur. (You might need to zoom in to verify this problem.)

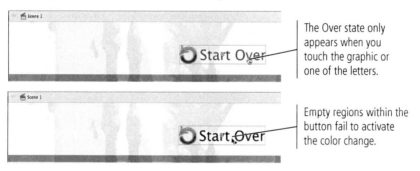

The Over state only appears when you touch the graphic or one of the letters.

Empty regions within the button fail to activate the color change.

3. **Choose Control>Enable Simple Buttons to toggle that option off.**

   When this option is active, you can't select a button instance on the Stage — which means you can't double-click the button to edit the symbol in place.

4. **Double-click the Start Over button on the Stage to edit the symbol in place.**

5. **Control/right-click the Hit frame and choose Insert Keyframe from the contextual menu.**

   The **Hit frame** defines the live area of the button, or the area where a user can click to activate the button. Objects on this state do not appear in the movie; you only need to define the general shapes.

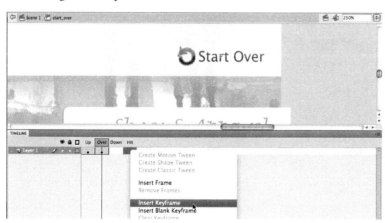

Note:

Using a button symbol mimics a four-frame Flash animation; it is the basic concept behind all Flash buttons. You add keyframes, you modify the content of each frame, and then Flash displays the appropriate frame when the user hovers over the object, clicks the object, or — in the case of the Hit frame — approaches the object.

6. **Choose the Rectangle tool from the Tools panel and draw a rectangle that covers the entire contents of the button.**

   We used the default fill color, but any color will work because the Hit frame doesn't appear on the Stage when you play the movie.

7. **Click Scene 1 in the Edit bar to return to the main Stage.**

8. **Choose Control>Enable Simple Buttons to toggle the option back on.**

9. **Place the mouse cursor between the words in the button.**

   Now the button works even if you hover over the white areas or between the letters. The Hit frame rectangle determines the live (hit) area of the button.

Now the button works even if you hover between the words.

10. **Save the file and continue to the next exercise.**

EDIT SYMBOL PROPERTIES

The control buttons, which you imported as graphic symbols from the external file library, are the final pieces of artwork for your Flash movie. Illustrator, however, does not create button symbols; you now need to convert the imported graphic symbols into the necessary button symbols.

1. **With `atrium_kiosk.fla` open, choose Control>Enable Simple Buttons. Make sure that option is toggled off.**

   Remember, you can't select a button on the Stage if this control is toggled on.

2. **In the Library panel, expand the Illustrator Symbols folder. Control/right-click the shoes_btn symbol icon in the Library panel and choose Properties from the contextual menu.**

FLASH FOUNDATIONS

You can edit symbols in three different ways: in Symbol-Editing mode, in place on the Stage, or in a separate window.

You're already familiar with Symbol-Editing mode, the discrete Stage that appears when you double-click a symbol in the Library panel; the name of the symbol appears to the right of the Scene name in the timeline, indicating that you're working on the symbol instead of the main scene. You can also access this option by Control/right-clicking a placed instance on the Stage and choosing Edit.

In basic Symbol-Editing mode, the name of the symbol appears above the Stage in the Edit bar.

When editing a symbol on its own Stage, other placed objects are not visible.

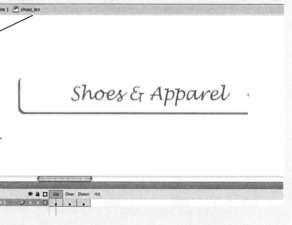

The second option, editing in place, means you can edit a symbol while still seeing other objects on the Stage. If you double-click a symbol on the Stage, you can edit the symbol in the context of the larger movie (as shown by the symbol name in the Edit bar). You can also access this option by Control/right-clicking a placed symbol instance and choosing Edit in Place.

Editing in place is a variant of Symbol-Editing mode, so the name of the symbol appears above the Stage.

When editing a symbol in place, other placed objects remain visible but screened back.

The third option, editing in a separate window, opens the symbol in its own document window (not as a separate tab in the existing window). Only the symbol name appears above the Stage; there is no preceding scene. You can access this option by Control/right-clicking an instance on the Stage and choosing Edit in New Window in the contextual menu.

When editing the symbol in a new window, there is no associated scene; only the symbol name appears above the Stage.

The document tabs show that you are editing in a second instance of the file containing the symbol.

3. **In the Symbol Properties dialog box, choose Button in the Type menu, and then click OK.**

4. **Using the Selection tool, click the Shoes & Apparel button on the Stage to select it.**

5. **In the Properties panel, open the top menu and choose Button.**

Unlike changing the content of a symbol, changes to the symbol type do not reflect in placed instances. When you change the type of a symbol that has already been placed on the Stage, you also have to change the instance type in the Properties panel.

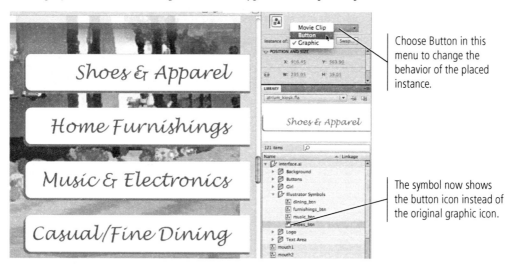

Choose Button in this menu to change the behavior of the placed instance.

The symbol now shows the button icon instead of the original graphic icon.

6. **Repeat Steps 2–5 to convert the remaining three graphic symbols to buttons.**

7. **Save the file and continue to the next exercise.**

 EXPLORE THE SYMBOL REGISTRATION POINT

Now that the buttons are symbols rather than graphics, you can define the various states of the buttons. You are going to edit the artwork so the buttons seem to move when the mouse cursor rolls over the hit area.

1. **With atrium_kiosk.fla open, double-click the Shoes & Apparel button instance to edit the symbol in place.**

The crosshairs in the middle of the symbol artwork identify the **symbol registration point**; all measurements for placed instances begin at this location.

When editing the symbol, the X and Y fields show the position of the top-left corner relative to the symbol's registration point.

Symbol registration point

2. **In the Align panel, make sure the Align To Stage option is active and then click the Align Right Edge button.**

   The right edge of the symbol artwork is now aligned to the symbol registration point. Because you are editing the symbol in place, you can see the effect of the new alignment relative to the overall file artwork.

Note:

Use the Align panel with the Align To Stage option active to align the placed object to the symbol Stage's registration point.

3. **Click Scene 1 in the Edit bar to return to the main Stage.**

4. **With the Shoes & Apparel button selected, click the current X value in the Properties panel to access the field.**

5. **Type 1034 in the highlighted X field and press Return/Enter to apply the change.**

   As we explained earlier, the symbol registration point is the origin of measurements for placed instances. When you change the X position, you are defining the location of the symbol registration point for the selected instance.

   The Stage for this file is 1024 pixels wide (as defined by the imported Illustrator artboard); you are placing the right edge of the button 10 pixels past the Stage edge.

On the main Stage, the X and Y fields define the position of the registration point for the instance.

6. **Double-click the Shoes & Apparel button again to enter back into the symbol Stage.**

7. **Insert a new keyframe on the button's Over frame. With the Over keyframe selected, click the button artwork to select it.**

   The object must be selected to change its properties. Selecting the frame in the timeline also selects the object on that frame.

8. **In the Properties panel, click the current X value in the Properties panel to access the field.**

Click the field to access the current value.

You should be working on the Over keyframe.

9. **Place the insertion point after the existing value and type -10. Press Enter to move the selected object.**

Using mathematical operators makes it easy to move an object a specific distance without manually calculating the change:

- Subtract from the X position to move an object left.
- Add to the X position to move an object right.
- Subtract from the Y position to move an object up.
- Add to the Y position to move an object down.

Type **−10** after the current value.

The new X value moves the artwork 10 pixels to the left.

10. **Click Scene 1 in the Edit bar to return to the main Stage.**

11. **Repeat Steps 1–10 for the three remaining buttons.**

12. **Choose Control>Enable Simple Buttons to toggle the option back on. Move your mouse cursor over the buttons to test the Over state functionality.**

13. **Save the file and continue to the next exercise.**

Note:

Because this button artwork includes a solid-filled white rectangle, you don't need to define a separate hit frame. The artwork itself is sufficient to trigger the button.

ORGANIZE YOUR LIBRARY WITH FOLDERS

Library folders work the same as layer folders; they help you organize and structure complex files. Movies often contain dozens or even hundreds of assets — and the more complex a movie becomes, the more useful it is to clearly organize those assets. Although this step isn't strictly necessary, it is always a good idea to organize your work so you can more easily organize your thoughts and processes going forward.

1. **With atrium_kiosk.fla open, expand the interface.ai folder in the Library panel.**

2. **Click the Illustrator Symbols folder and drag down to the empty area at the bottom of the panel.**

This moves the Illustrator Symbols folder to the first level of the library. The symbols, which are placed on the Stage, are not affected by the move.

Drag the Illustrator Symbols folder to the empty area at the bottom of the panel to move it out of the interface.ai folder.

The highlight shows that the folder will be moved to the first level of the panel.

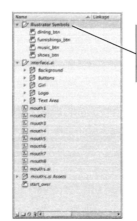

Click a column heading to sort library items by that category.

Note:

If your Library panel is too short to show an empty area below the current assets, Control/right-click any of the existing first-level assets and choose Paste. The pasted symbols are pasted at the same level as the asset where you Control/right-click.

3. **Double-click the Illustrator Symbols folder name to highlight the name. Type buttons to change the folder name.**

4. **Click the start_over button symbol icon and drag it into the Buttons folder.**

5. **Double-click the interface.ai folder name to highlight the name. Type component artwork to change the folder name.**

6. **Click the mouths.ai Assets folder and drag it into the Component Artwork folder.**

7. **Click the empty area at the bottom of the panel to deselect all assets and folders.**

8. **Click the New Folder button at the bottom of the Library panel. Type mouth graphics as the new folder name.**

   The new folder is added at the main level of the library, alphabetized with other items at the same level. If you didn't deselect in Step 7, the new folder would have been created at the same nesting level as the selected item.

New Folder button

9. **Click the mouth1 symbol to select it, then Shift-click the mouth8 symbol to select it and all files in between.**

   Press Shift to select multiple contiguous items in the panel, or press Command/Control to select multiple, non-contiguous items.

10. **Click the icon of any selected file and drag into the mouth graphics folder.**

All eight of these files are selected.

11. **Click the mouths.ai graphic symbol and click the panel's Delete button.**

Although you used this artwork to create the individual mouth symbols, this symbol is not used in the file, so it can be safely deleted from the library. If you delete a symbol that is used in the file, the placed instances will also be deleted from the file.

Delete button

12. **Collapse all library folders, then save the file and continue to the next stage of the project.**

Stage 2 Working with Sound

Sound files can be categorized into three basic types: uncompressed, compressed (lossless), and compressed (lossy). **Uncompressed sound files** encode all sounds with the same number of bits per unit of time. In an uncompressed format, two sound files of the same duration — whether a symphony or a simple beep — have the same size (which is typically very large). Such files are commonly used for archiving or other situations where file size is not an issue.

Lossless compression sound files lose no data during compression; these files are smaller than uncompressed files, but not as small as lossy compression file formats. **Lossy compression sound files** lose some data but retain good sound quality; a large number of these files can be stored in relatively small amounts of space.

Flash handles most major audio formats, including the ones most commonly used today:

Note:

Compression is the process of removing data to reduce file size.

- The **MP3** format (also known as **MPEG**) is the most commonly used audio format. This format compresses a music file in the most efficient manner, so file size is reduced without compromising quality.

- The **WAV** format is an uncompressed format with very high quality. This file type can be used in Flash animations for desktop applications, but should be avoided for Web-based movies because the files are huge and take a long time to download.

- The **AIFF** format (Audio Interchange File Format) is common on Macintosh computers. This format is generally uncompressed, so file sizes are large compared to the MP3 format. AIFF files are suitable for applications specifically targeted for Macintosh computers.

- The **Audio** (AU) file format, developed by Sun Microsystems, transmits sound files over the Internet and can be played in Java programs. These files are smaller than AIFF and WAV formats, but the quality of sound is not as good as regular WAV files.

- The **QuickTime** (MOV) format is technically a video format, but it can also include audio.

IMPORT SOUND FILES

In general, there are three methods for incorporating sound into a Flash movie. Sounds in a file's library can be placed directly on the timeline, or you can use code to call a library sound based on a particular event. You can also use code to load and play external sound files (those that don't exist in the Flash library).

In this project, you will use the timeline method to add the various sounds that are needed for the kiosk to function properly. The first step is to import the necessary sound files into the Flash library.

1. **With atrium_kiosk.fla open, choose File>Import>Import to Stage.**

2. **In the resulting dialog box, navigate to the WIP>Atrium>Audio folder.**

3. **Select all files in the folder and click Import/Open.**

4. **Open the Library panel and review the contents.**

    Sound files do not exist on the Stage. Even though you chose Import to Stage, the sound files are automatically imported into the file's Library panel.

5. **Click the New Folder button at the bottom of the Library panel. Rename the new folder audio.**

6. **Command/Control-click all six imported audio files and drag them into the audio folder.**

7. **Expand the audio folder so you can see the available files.**

8. **Save the file and continue to the next exercise.**

Note:

It's always a good idea to keep your library well organized while developing a file with numerous assets.

ADD EVENT SOUND

Event sounds are downloaded completely and stored in the user computer's memory before they play. This means they can be played repeatedly — including continuously looping — without having to redownload the file. This type of sound is typically used for short sounds or looped sounds that play continuously. They play from start to finish, and cannot be turned off midstream.

1. **With the file atrium_kiosk.fla open, click to select the atrium_jazz.mp3 file in the Library panel.**

    This file will be the background music for the entire file. It will play in an infinite loop as long as the kiosk file is open.

2. **Click the Play button in the top-right corner of the Preview area.**

    You can use the Library panel to hear imported sounds before they are used on the Stage.

Click the Play button to hear the selected file.

This waveform is a visual representation of the sound file.

3. **Select the Frame 1 keyframe on the Background layer.**

4. **In the Sound section of the Properties panel, choose atrium_jazz.mp3 in the Name menu.**

This menu lists all sound files that are available in the library.

Click Frame 1 of the Background layer to select it.

5. **In the Sync menu, choose Event.**

    Event sounds default to the Repeat 1 method, which means the sound plays one time. You can change the number in the Repeat field to play the sound a specific number of times.

Choose Event in this menu.

A small line, which is actually part of the sound waveform, crosses the selected frame.

6. Choose Control>Test Movie>In Flash Professional.

This command opens the file in a separate Flash Player window. (You will use this command frequently as you develop this and most Flash projects.) Although the sound waveform only appears on Frame 1 of the Background layer, the entire sound plays from start to finish when you test the movie file.

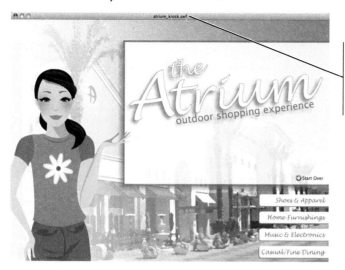

The Test Movie command opens the file in a Flash Player window, showing what the exported movie would look — and sound — like.

Note:

Press Command-Return/ Control-Enter to test the movie in a Flash Player window.

7. Close the Player window and return to Flash.

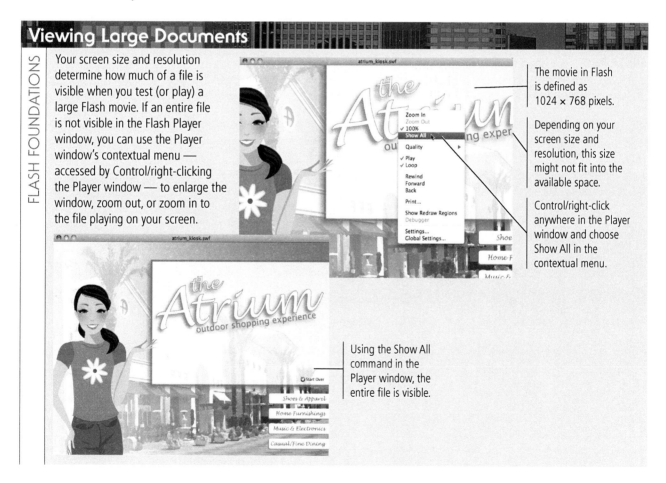

Viewing Large Documents

FLASH FOUNDATIONS

Your screen size and resolution determine how much of a file is visible when you test (or play) a large Flash movie. If an entire file is not visible in the Flash Player window, you can use the Player window's contextual menu — accessed by Control/right-clicking the Player window — to enlarge the window, zoom out, or zoom in to the file playing on your screen.

The movie in Flash is defined as 1024 × 768 pixels.

Depending on your screen size and resolution, this size might not fit into the available space.

Control/right-click anywhere in the Player window and choose Show All in the contextual menu.

Using the Show All command in the Player window, the entire file is visible.

8. **With Frame 1 of the Background layer selected, choose Loop in the menu under the Sync menu (in the Sound area of the Properties panel).**

   Using the Loop method, the event sound plays continuously as long as the movie remains open.

9. **Press Command-Return/Control-Enter to test the movie again.**

   The background sound now plays from start to finish, and then repeats to create a continuous background sound track.

10. **Close the Player window and return to Flash.**

11. **Save the file and continue to the next exercise.**

EDIT A SOUND ENVELOPE TO CONTROL VOLUME

Although Flash is not intended to be a sound-editing application, you can apply a limited number of effects to control the volume and length of sounds on the Flash timeline. These options are available in the Effect menu of the Properties panel when a sound is attached to a keyframe.

1. **With atrium_kiosk.fla open, click Frame 1 of the Background layer to select the frame where you attached the sound in the previous exercise.**

2. **In the Properties panel, open the Effect menu and choose Custom to open the Edit Envelope dialog box.**

Clicking the Edit Sound Envelope button has the same result as choosing Custom in the Effect menu.

Frame 1 of the Background layer must be selected to acccess the sound settings.

The Edit Envelope dialog box shows the waveforms for each channel in a sound file. (In many cases, both channels have the same waveform.) You can view the sound waves by seconds or frames, and you can zoom in or out to show various portions of the sound.

The left and right channels refer to sound output systems that have more than one speaker — one on the left and one on the right. You can apply different settings to individual channels to create an effect of aural depth. For example, fading a car sound out for the left channel and in for the right channel helps to reinforce a visual that moves the car from left to right across the Stage.

3. **Click the Frames button to show the sound based on frames (if this isn't already active).**

4. **Click the Zoom Out button until you can see the entire waveform.**

5. **In the left channel area (the top waveform), click the handle on the right end of the waveform, and drag down to below the existing waveform.**

Click the envelope handle and drag down to this point.

Note:

Click the envelope line to add a new handle to the envelope. Click an existing handle and drag it away from the window to remove a point from the envelope.

6. **Repeat Step 5 for the right channel (the bottom waveform).**

By lowering the envelope handles, you reduced the volume of the sound file.

7. **Click OK to close the Edit Envelope dialog box and apply the change.**

8. **Save the file and continue to the next exercise.**

Applying Built-In Sound Effects

The Effect menu in the Properties panel lists a number of common sound envelope effects built into Flash. These sound effects do not alter the sound in the files; they simply control how the sound data plays.

- **Left Channel** plays only the left channel of the sound.
- **Right Channel** plays only the right channel of the sound.
- **Fade to Right** gradually lowers the sound level of the left channel, and then gradually raises the sound level of the right channel.
- **Fade to Left** gradually lowers the sound level of the right channel, and then gradually raises the sound level of the left channel.

- **Fade In** gradually raises the sound level at the beginning of the sound file.
- **Fade Out** gradually lowers the sound level at the end of the sound file.
- **Custom** opens the Edit Envelope dialog box, where you can define your own sound effects.

USE THE START AND STOP SYNC METHODS FOR BUTTONS

The four category buttons will link to different screens in the kiosk. Each button needs to trigger a sound that plays when the user's mouse rolls over the button. To achieve this result, you can attach the relevant sound to each button using the same technique you applied in the previous exercise. Because of the four-frame nature of button symbols, however, a few extra steps are required to make the sounds play only when you want them to play.

1. **With atrium_kiosk.fla open, choose Control>Enable Simple Buttons to make sure that option is toggled on.**

2. **In the Library panel, double-click the shoes_btn symbol icon to enter Symbol-Editing mode for that symbol.**

   Remember, you can edit a symbol by double-clicking the symbol icon. This is especially useful when the Enable Simple Buttons feature is toggled on, because you can't select buttons on the Stage in that mode.

3. **Select the Over frame of Layer 1. In the Properties panel, choose shoes.mp3 in the Sound menu and set the Sync menu to Event.**

You are attaching the sound to the button's Over frame.

4. **Click Scene 1 in the Edit bar to return to the main Stage.**

5. **Move your mouse cursor over the Shoes & Apparel button to hear the attached sound.**

Moving the mouse over the button triggers the Over state, including the attached sound file.

6. **Move your mouse cursor away, and then move back over the Shoes & Apparel button to trigger the sound again.**

When the mouse re-enters the button area — triggering the Over frame — the message plays again. (Because the sound is very short, this might not be apparent unless you move the mouse back into the button area very quickly.)

7. **Double-click the shoes_btn symbol icon to enter back into the button Stage. Select the Over frame, then change the Sound Sync menu to Start.**

The Start sync option is similar to the Event method. The difference is that the Start method allows only one instance of the same sound to play at a time; this prevents the overlap problem caused by the Event method.

Apply the Start sync method to the Over frame.

8. **Control/right-click the Down frame and choose Insert Keyframe from the contextual menu.**

9. **In the Properties panel, choose shoes.mp3 in the Sound menu and choose Stop in the Sync menu.**

The Stop option stops all instances of the selected sound from playing. When a user clicks the Shoes & Apparel button, the sound triggered on the Over frame will stop playing.

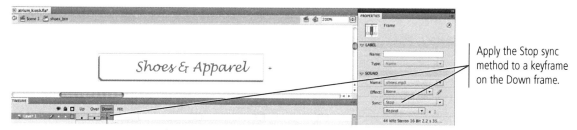

Apply the Stop sync method to a keyframe on the Down frame.

10. **Click Scene 1 to return to the main Stage.**

11. **Repeat the same basic process to add the appropriate event sounds to the other three navigation buttons:**
    - Double-click the button symbol icon to enter the symbol's Stage.
    - Select the Over frame and attach the appropriate sound file using the Start sync option.
        - For the Home Furnishings button, use the furnishings.mp3 sound file.
        - For the Music & Electronics button, use the music.mp3 sound file.
        - For the Casual/Fine Dining button, use the dining.mp3 sound file.
    - Add a keyframe to the Down frame.
    - Attach the same sound you used for the Over frame, and apply the Stop sync option.

12. **If you haven't done so already, click Scene 1 in the Edit bar to return to the main Stage.**

13. **Roll your mouse cursor over the four buttons to test all four sounds. Click each to make sure the sounds stop when they're supposed to.**

14. **Save the file and continue to the next exercise.**

EDIT A SOUND ENVELOPE TO CONTROL DURATION

In addition to controlling the volume of a sound file, you can also use the Edit Envelope dialog box to determine which part of a sound file plays in the movie. Although it is usually a better idea to edit sound files in a true sound-editing application, the controls in Flash are perfectly suitable for shortening the duration of a sound file.

1. **With atrium_kiosk.fla open, click the shoes.mp3 file in the Library panel. Make sure the Enable Simple Buttons option is toggled on.**

   When you tested the buttons in the previous exercise, you might have noticed a lag between the time the mouse triggered the Over state and when the sound actually played. The waveform preview, which you can see at the top of the Library panel, shows a long flat area before the speaking begins. To eliminate this lag, you are going to change the starting point of the sound.

2. **Double-click the shoes_btn symbol icon in the Library panel to enter into the symbol Stage.**

   Remember, because Enable Simple Buttons is toggled on, you can't double-click the button instance to edit the symbol. You have to click the symbol icon in the Library panel to enter into Symbol-Editing mode.

3. **Select the button's Over keyframe (in the Timeline panel), and then click the Edit Sound Envelope button in the Properties panel.**

You are editing on the shoes_btn symbol Stage.

Click this button to edit the sound envelope.

The Over frame, which triggers the sound, is selected.

4. **Click the Zoom Out button until you can see the entire waveform.**

These small fluctuations are common at the beginning or end of spoken words.

Time In Control bar

Note:

The small resonance in the waveform is common at the beginning and end of spoken words.

5. **Click the Play button in the bottom-left corner of the dialog box and listen to the sound file.**

   Waveforms typically spike for louder or more distinct sounds. In the case of speech, the waveform spikes represent different words in the spoken message. The long flat area before the first spike is the lag you heard when you applied this sound to the button.

6. **Click the Time In Control bar and drag to the point just before the first major spike in the waveform.**

    The sound file is now set to begin at the new Time In position. This is an easy way to edit the portion of the sound included in a movie.

Drag the Time In Control bar to just before the first spike in the waveform.

Parts of the waveform to the left of the Time In Control bar will not be included in the movie.

7. **Click the Play button.**

    The sound should now begin almost immediately, without the lag at the beginning.

8. **If necessary, scroll to the right so you can see the right end of the waveform.**

9. **Click the Time Out Control bar and drag left, so the small fluctuations at the end of the waveform are removed.**

Time Out Control bar

Use the scroll bar to find the end of the waveform.

10. **Click OK to apply the change to the edited sound file.**

11. **Click Scene 1 in the Edit bar to return to the main Stage, then roll your mouse over the Shoes & Apparel button on the Stage to test the sound.**

    The message now begins almost immediately when the button's Over state is triggered.

12. **Save the file and continue to the next stage of the project.**

Stage 3 Creating Frame Animations

The basic underlying premise of animation is that objects change over time — from complex transitions in color, shape, and opacity to moving a character to a new position. The most basic type of animation is to simply replace one object with another at specific points in time; you will create this type of animation in this stage of the kiosk project to make it seem like the girl is talking.

Repositioning or replacing objects on successive frames results in the appearance of movement when you watch an animation; in reality, your brain is being fooled — you're simply seeing a series of images flash before your eyes (hence the application's name). Your brain thinks it's seeing movement, when in fact it's simply processing a series of still images displayed in rapid succession.

To make an animation appear to run continuously, you can **loop** it so it starts over at Frame 1 after reaching the last frame. (In fact, as you will see, looping is the default state of an animation; you have to use code to prevent the timeline from automatically looping in the exported file.)

To create animation, you need to understand several terms and concepts:

- The Flash timeline shows a visual depiction of the passage of time. Each fraction of a second is represented by a frame (the rectangles to the right of the layer names). The **playhead** indicates the current point in time, or the frame that is visible on the Stage.

- The number of frames in one second (called **frames per second**, **FPS**, or **frame rate**) determines the length and quality of the overall animation. Most film movies are captured and replayed at 24 fps, but HD (high definition) format can range as high as 60 fps; animations for the Web are commonly developed at 12 or 15 fps.

- A **keyframe** indicates the point in time at which something changes. If you want to change something, you need to insert a keyframe at the appropriate moment on the timeline.

- Regular frames between keyframes have the same content as the preceding keyframe.

Note:

*The term **playhead** is a throwback to the days when animation and video were shown on physical tape-reading machines. The playhead is the component under which the tape moves, and the tape is read by the player. By sliding the tape back and forth underneath the playhead, an animator could make a movie run forward and backward.*

ADD STREAMING SOUND

Unlike the event sounds that you used in the previous exercises, **stream sounds** play as soon as enough data is downloaded (called **progressive downloading**) to the user's computer; stream sounds cannot be saved on a user's computer; the sound file must be redownloaded every time it is played. Stream sounds are linked to the movie timeline, which means they can be switched off midstream.

Note:

Because stream sounds are typically larger files (longer sounds equal more data and larger file size), the quality of these sounds might be poor for users who have slow Internet connections.

1. **With atrium_kiosk.fla open, add a new layer named Talking immediately above the Mouths layer.**

The empty circle indicates that no content currently resides on the keyframe.

The filled circle indicates that some content exists on the keyframe.

By default, the first frame of every layer is a keyframe.

2. **Select the Frame 1 keyframe of the Talking layer.**

3. **In the Properties panel, choose intro_talking.mp3 from the Sound menu and choose Stream in the Sync menu.**

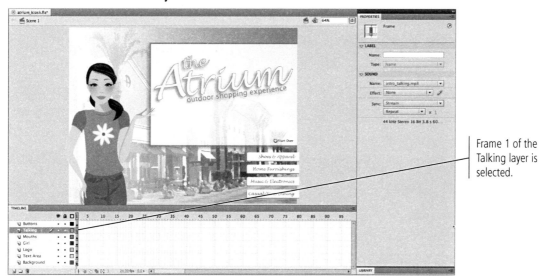

Frame 1 of the Talking layer is selected.

4. **Press Command-Return/Control-Enter to test the movie.**

   The background sound plays as expected, but the intro_talking sound does not. Using the Stream sync option, the sound file is related to the position of the playhead on the timeline. Because this file currently has only one frame, only one frame of the stream sound can play (in other words, virtually nothing) in the Player window.

5. **Close the Player window and return to Flash.**

6. **In the timeline, Control/right-click Frame 95 of the Talking layer and choose Insert Frame from the contextual menu.**

Frame numbers appear at the top of the timeline.

Control/right-click Frame 95 of the Talking layer to open the contextual menu.

   When you add a new frame, you extend the layer's timeline to the point where you place the new frame. The red playhead above the timeline shows the currently active frame.

   You can now see the entire waveform of the sound that is attached to Frame 1 of the Talking layer. As you can see, however, none of the graphics are visible on the Stage, because you have not added frames to the other layers. In other words, objects on those layers don't yet exist at Frame 95.

Other layers are not yet extended to Frame 95, so the graphics on those layers are not visible.

The playhead shows the currently active frame.

Adding a frame extends the layer's timeline.

The waveform on the Talking layer, which extends to Frame 91, is now entirely visible.

7. **Click Frame 95 of the Buttons layer to select it, then press F5.**

This keyboard shortcut inserts a new frame at the selected location on the timeline; it is the same as choosing Insert Frame from the contextual menu.

After adding the new frame to the Buttons layer, objects on that layer are now visible at Frame 95. The other graphics are still not visible because those layers do not yet have frames at Frame 95.

Objects on the Buttons layer are visible once that layer has been extended to Frame 95.

8. **Click Frame 95 of the Mouths layer, then Shift-click Frame 95 of the Background layer.**

9. **Press F5 to add new frames to all five selected layers.**

Because all of the layers now "exist" on Frame 95, all of the kiosk graphics are now visible on the Stage.

Note:

Content on the preceding frame automatically appears on a new keyframe. The Insert Blank Keyframe command adds a blank keyframe to the timeline that (as the name suggests) has no content. You can insert a blank keyframe to hide the layer content for a specific period of time.

Because all layers now extend to Frame 95, all graphics in the interface are visible on the Stage.

10. **Click Frame 1 of any layer to move the playhead to the beginning of the timeline.**

The playhead identifies the current point in time on the Flash timeline. If you don't move the playhead back to Frame 1, the background sound will not play.

11. **Press Return/Enter to test the movie on the Flash Stage.**

You should now hear two sounds: the character talking and the background music. The background music is an event sound (not related to the playhead), so it loops continuously.

Pressing Return/Enter causes the playhead to move, playing the movie directly on the Stage.

When a movie is playing on the Stage, pressing Return/Enter stops the playback but does not stop sounds that are playing.

12. Press the Escape key (ESC) to stop the background music.

13. Press Command-Return/Control-Enter to test the movie in a Player window.

The movie plays entirely through, and then starts over again (**loops**) — this is what would happen in the actual exported file.

To make the timeline play only once, you have to use code to intentionally stop the playhead from looping. This code will be implemented by your developer partner after you are finished creating the lip-syncing animation.

Note:

You can choose Control>Loop Playback to allow the playhead to loop on the Flash Stage.

14. Close the Flash Player window and return to Flash.

15. Save the file and continue to the next exercise.

PREPARE FOR LIP SYNCING

If you have ever watched cartoons, you have probably seen the results of the time-consuming and painstaking work involved in synchronizing a character's movements to sounds. Realistic lip syncing is an extremely complex art that requires precise attention to detail, as well as in-depth study of behavioral movement. Other projects, such as this one, do not call for the precision and detail required for lifelike animation; rather, they use representative movements to create the effect of a character talking.

1. Sit or stand in front of a mirror.

2. Say the following sentence slowly, paying careful attention to the shape of your mouth for each syllable:

Need help? Use the buttons to find exactly what you're looking for.

Note:

To better understand how to sync lip movements to sounds, you should study the different facial movements that are involved in spoken sound (called phonology).

3. With `atrium_kiosk.fla` open in Flash, expand the mouth graphics folder in the Library panel.

The illustrator for this project created eight different mouth shapes to represent the various "talking" sounds.

4. Click each mouth symbol in the Library panel and review the shapes.

Note that each symbol was created with the registration point at the center.

Symbol	Use for:	Symbol	Use for:
mouth1	Silent, M, B, P	mouth5	M, B, P
mouth2	C, D, G, J, K, N, R, S, Y, Z	mouth6	L, D, T, Th
mouth3	Short E, I, O, U Long A	mouth7	Short A, E Long I
mouth4	F, V	mouth8	Ch, Sh, Qu, W Long O, U

5. **In the timeline layers area, double-click the icon to the left of the Talking layer name to open the Layer Properties dialog box.**

6. **Choose 300% in the Layer Height menu and click OK.**

Double-click the layer icon to open the Layer Properties dialog box.

It's easier to sync movement to sound when you can see the variations in the sound file. By enlarging the layer height, you can see the peaks and valleys of the waveform directly on the timeline.

7. **Continue to the next exercise.**

 ## CREATE LIP SYNC ANIMATION

While lip syncing might seem complicated, it's actually quite simple — you show the graphic that supports the sound heard at a particular frame on the timeline. Because the different mouth shapes for this project have already been created, the most difficult part of the process is determining which shape to place at which point on the timeline.

1. **Click Frame 1 above the timeline to reset the playhead to the beginning of the movie.**

2. **Click the playhead and drag quickly to the right.**

   Dragging the playhead, a technique called **scrubbing the timeline**, allows you to manually preview portions of an animation. Because the sound on the Talking layer is a stream sound, you hear the sound as you drag the playhead. The background music — an event sound — is not related to the playhead, so scrubbing the playhead does not play the background music.

   As you drag the playhead from Frame 1, you hear the first sound in the spoken message beginning at Frame 4 (also indicated by the rise in the waveform).

Click the playhead and drag right to find the first spoken sound.

The active frame is identified here.

3. **Control/right-click Frame 3 of the Mouths layer and choose Insert Keyframe from the contextual menu.**

   Remember, a keyframe is the point at which something changes. In this case, you are going to change the mouth shape, so you need to add a keyframe at the appropriate point in time (when the mouth begins to move to make the spoken sound).

   Although the sound begins at Frame 4, people's mouths usually start moving before actual words are spoken. You are adding a keyframe one frame earlier than the sound to accommodate for this behavior.

4. **Click the mouth symbol on the Stage to show its properties in the Properties panel.**

   The object on the selected keyframe is selected on the Stage.

   The Properties panel shows the name of the symbol being used.

   The new keyframe is selected.

5. **With the mouth shape on the Frame 3 keyframe selected, click the Swap button in the Properties panel.**

   Lip syncing requires one primary task: swapping symbols to show the graphics that correlate to the sound at that particular moment.

6. **In the Swap Symbol dialog box, choose the mouth2 graphic symbol.**

   This is the mouth that correlates to the "N" sound at the beginning of the word "Need".

7. **Click OK to close the Swap Symbol dialog box.**

   The new mouth now appears on Frame 3. The mouth symbol (mouth1) on the previous keyframe will remain visible until the playhead reaches Frame 3.

   The new mouth shape appears, starting at Frame 3.

8. **Drag the playhead right to find the next significant change in sound.**

    The brief pause between the words "need" and "help" suggests a change in the speaker's mouth position at Frame 8.

9. **Insert a new keyframe at Frame 8 of the Mouths layer.**

10. **With the mouth on the Frame 8 keyframe selected, click the Swap button in the Properties panel. In the Swap Symbol dialog box, choose the mouth5 symbol and click OK.**

    This mouth shape is nearly closed, so it works well for the brief pause between words. It correlates to the short "I" sound, but it also works well as a good transition shape between a wide-open mouth and a closed mouth.

11. **Insert a new keyframe at Frame 10 of the Mouths layer. Open the Swap Symbol dialog box, and replace the mouth shape with the mouth3 symbol.**

    This shape correlates to the "short e" sound in "help". (The "h" sound typically blends into the vowel sound.)

12. **Return the playhead to Frame 1 and press Return/Enter to play the movie on the Stage.**

    So far you have only three changes in the character's mouth, but you should begin to see how the different symbols appear at the appropriate points in the playback. In general, lip syncing in Flash is a relatively simple process. The hardest parts are determining when to change the graphics in relation to the sound, and deciding which shape best suits the animation at any given point. Once you have determined these two elements, the actual syncing process is simply a matter of swapping symbols.

13. **Press the Escape key to stop the background music playback.**

14. **Applying the same process you used to create the first three mouth changes, continue scrubbing the playhead to identify points of change. Insert keyframes and swap symbols on the Mouths layer at the appropriate locations. In our example, we used the following locations and symbols:**

Frame	Symbol	Frame	Symbol	Frame	Symbol
15	mouth1	43	mouth4	64	mouth3
23	mouth8	46	mouth3	66	mouth2
27	mouth2	48	mouth2	68	mouth8
30	mouth6	50	mouth3	70	mouth2
31	mouth1	52	mouth2	72	mouth6
33	mouth3	55	mouth7	74	mouth2
36	mouth6	57	mouth2	79	mouth4
39	mouth2	60	mouth6	82	mouth8
41	mouth8	62	mouth2	84	mouth2

15. **Return the playhead to Frame 1, then press Return/Enter test the animation.**

    By swapping the mouth symbol at various points on the timeline in relation to the sounds on the Talking layer, you now have a character who appears to be talking.

16. **Save the file and continue to the next exercise.**

 ## DEFINE SOUND COMPRESSION SETTINGS

Before you export the final movie file, you should optimize the sounds to produce the smallest possible files while still maintaining the best possible quality. You can define default export settings for all stream sounds and all event sounds, but you can also experiment with different compression settings for individual sound files in the library.

1. **With atrium_kiosk.fla open, Control/right-click the atrium_jazz.mp3 file in the Audio folder of the Library panel. Choose Properties from the contextual menu.**

2. **In the resulting Sound Properties dialog box, leave MP3 selected in the Compresion menu, and uncheck the Use Imported MP3 Quality option.**

Flash supports five sound compression options:

- **Default.** This option uses the global compression settings (mp3, 16kbps, mono) defined in the Publish Settings dialog box when you export your SWF file. If you select Default, no additional export settings are available.

- **ADPCM.** This option converts sounds into binary data. ADPCM encoding is not as efficient as MP3 compression, but it is useful if you need to export a file to be compatible with older versions of Flash (version 3 or lower).

- **MP3.** Over the past few years, this format has become a *de facto* standard for audio on the Web. MP3 compression produces small files with very good quality, but it can cause problems for older computers with limited processing power.

- **Raw.** This option does not compress the audio data, which results in very large file sizes. This option should only be used for files that will be delivered on the desktop instead of over the Internet.

- **Speech.** This option uses a compression algorithm designed specifically for compressing spoken sounds. Sounds compressed with this option are converted to mono sounds (instead of stereo). Speech-compressed sounds require Flash Player 6 or higher.

Note:

The Preprocessing check box, enabled by default, converts stereo sounds to mono sounds.

3. **Choose 48 kbps in the Bit Rate menu.**

Depending on the selected compression option, you can also change the bit rate or the sample rate to affect the quality of the exported sound.

- The **Sample Rate** menu is available for ADPCM, Raw, and Speech compression; lower sample rates decrease file size, but can also decrease sound quality. The 22 kHz setting is recommended for reasonably good quality of most sounds.

- The **Bit Rate** menu is available for MP3 compression. This option determines the bits per second in the exported sound. Higher bit rates result in better sound quality. Most experts recommend at least 20 kbps for speech, and 48 kbps for reasonably good quality of complex sounds such as music.

Note:

Flash cannot increase the sample rate or bit rate of an imported sound above its original settings.

4. **Choose Best in the Quality menu.**

Three quality options — in order of file size (from small to large) and quality (from low to high) — are available for MP3 sounds: Fast, Medium, and Best.

The dialog box provides feedback regarding the size of the file using the selected settings.

5. **Click OK to change the export settings for the selected sound file.**

6. **Repeat Steps 1–5 for the remaining button sound files (dining, furnishings, music, and shoes).**

7. **Open the Sound Properties dialog box for the intro_talking sound file.**

8. **Choose Speech in the Compression menu.**

9. **Choose 11 kHz in the Sample Rate menu, and then click the Test button.**

   When the sound plays, you might notice some popping or hissing noises behind the spoken message.

   Click here to test sound quality using the defined settings.

10. **Choose 22 kHz in the Sample Rate menu, and then click the Test button.**

    This sample rate results in better quality, but a slight hissing is still audible behind the spoken message.

11. **Choose 44 kHz in the Sample Rate menu, and then click the Test button.**

    This sample rate results in much better quality. Because this kiosk will not be downloaded over the Internet, the larger file size is not a problem.

12. **Click OK to apply the new compression settings for this sound file.**

13. **Save the Flash file and close it.**

fill in the blank

1. In a Button symbol, the _____ defines the area where a user can click to trigger the button.

2. _____ to edit a symbol in place on the Stage.

3. The _____ marks the location of the defined X and Y values of a placed instance.

4. A(n) _____ defines the point in time when a change occurs.

5. _____ is the number of animation frames that occur in a second.

6. _____ sounds download completely before they play; they play from start to finish, and cannot be turned off midstream.

7. _____ sounds play as soon as enough of the data has downloaded to the user's computer; they can be switched off midstream.

8. The _____ sync method prevents more than one instance of the same sound from playing at the same time.

9. You can use the _____ dialog box to change the length of a specific sound file.

10. Use the _____ option to replace one symbol with another at a specific frame.

short answer

1. Briefly describe at least three uses of the Library panel.

2. Briefly explain the difference between event sounds and stream sounds.

3. Briefly explain the concept of lip syncing, as it relates to symbols and the Flash timeline.

Portfolio Builder Project

Use what you learned in this project to complete the following freeform exercise.
Carefully read the art director and client comments, then create your own design to meet the needs of the project.
Use the space below to sketch ideas; when finished, write a brief explanation of your reasoning behind your final design.

Your client is a company that provides technical support for children's online video games. The owner wants an introduction page for that site similar to the kiosk interface, with a talking character that identifies the options.

To complete this project, you should:

❏ Download the client's supplied files in the **FL5_PB_Project2.zip** archive on the Student Files Web page.

❏ Review the client-supplied sound and artwork files.

❏ Develop a site intro page with a talking robot and two different buttons.

❏ If you use the client's artwork, import the file into Flash and create movie clips as necessary from the different elements.

❏ If you don't use the supplied file, create or find artwork as appropriate.

We want to build a new introduction page to our video game site. We're using a robot avatar throughout the video game site, and want that character to be featured on the intro page — I even recorded the intro message with a "mechanical" sounding voice. (Feel free to re-record the audio if you want to, as long as the message stays the same.)

I found a robot illustration that I like, but I'm not an artist; I'd be happy to review other artwork if you have a better idea. I also want you to develop some kind of background artwork that makes the piece look like a cohesive user interface.

You need to include two buttons: one that links to online technical support and one that links to a telephone support page.

In the final file, I want the robot to look like it's talking, but I also want the robot to point to the related buttons when the appropriate part of the intro sound plays.

_____
_____
_____
_____
_____
_____
_____
_____
_____
_____
_____
_____
_____

Project Summary

This project introduced many of the basic concepts and techniques of animating objects in Flash. You learned about frames and keyframes, as well as two different types of symbols that will be used in many Flash projects, both throughout this book and in your professional career. You also learned how to import artwork that was created in Adobe Illustrator — a very common workflow in the graphic design/animation market.

You should understand how frames on the Flash timeline relate to the passage of actual time, and how keyframes are used to make changes at specific points in an animation. You should also understand the basic concept of symbols and instances, including the different ways to edit the conent of a specific symbol. You will build on these skills as you complete the rest of the projects in this book.

This project also showed you how to add audio content to a movie — placing a looped sound in the background of a file, triggering specific sounds with a button's Over state, and even synchronizing graphics to a spoken message.

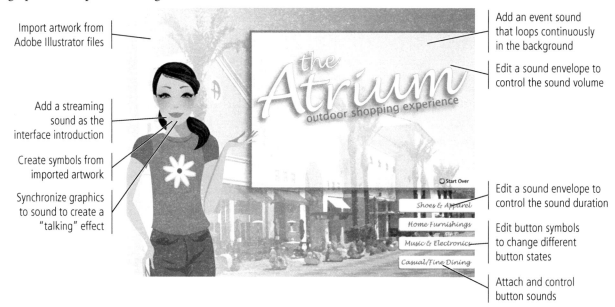

Import artwork from Adobe Illustrator files

Add a streaming sound as the interface introduction

Create symbols from imported artwork

Synchronize graphics to sound to create a "talking" effect

Add an event sound that loops continuously in the background

Edit a sound envelope to control the sound volume

Edit a sound envelope to control the sound duration

Edit button symbols to change different button states

Attach and control button sounds

Solar System Model

Your client, the City Children's Museum, is using a private grant to install a number of interactive video kiosks throughout the facility. The museum has a large, round room with the constellations painted across the "sky" (ceiling). They want to build a new planetary science exhibit to accompany the constellation map, which will include a video model showing how the planets revolve around the Sun.

This project incorporates the following skills:

❑ Creating a complex model based on scientific values

❑ Using masks to isolate specific elements of placed bitmap files

❑ Animating objects along a motion path

❑ Creating nested movie clips to animate multiple objects

❑ Placing static text in a Flash file

❑ Using behaviors to control movie clip playback

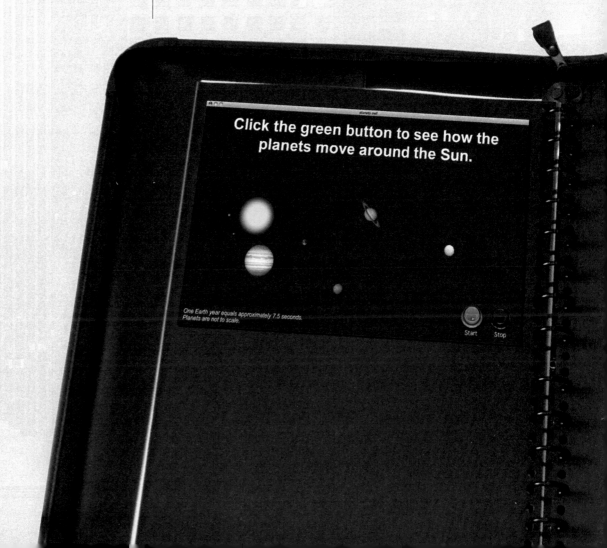

Project Meeting

client comments

We want the model to be an accurate representation — which is going to present a problem because the solar system is really a big place.

According to our calculations, the largest orbit will fit inside a 1:800 scale model screen space. Unfortunately, at 1:800 scale, the four inner planets would be too small to see and the Sun would fill the screen. If you use a smaller scale to fit the Sun, the orbits would be too small to see; if you use a bigger scale to see the inner planets, the orbits wouldn't fit in the window.

We've decided the best plan is to manipulate the scale as necessary so the orbits fit in the window. We'd like you to make the four inner planets two times the scale of the four outer planets, and create the Sun at 1:8000 scale. You can add text to the bottom of the screen explaining these anomalies.

Young children are familiar with the idea of the Moon moving around the Earth; if they see it rotating in the model, they might be able to associate that concept to the way the planets move around the Sun.

art director comments

According to the museum's technical director, the new kiosks have 1300 × 800-pixel screens. The final Flash movie has to fit in that space, so use those dimensions as the Stage size. This is a large file size, so keep file weight in mind. The final model is only going on kiosks for now, so download time isn't a consideration, but if the client decides to put the file on a Web site, it needs to download in a reasonable amount of time.

The client has sent all the scientific data we need to complete the model — planet sizes, orbit shapes, and the length of a year for each planet. I'll work out the frame lengths for each planet's orbit and send you that information as soon as it's ready.

Originally, the museum director asked us to create a very basic model with each planet represented by a circle, but I think we'll use photos instead. I found photos of the eight planets (and the Moon) that I'll send along, and then you can import them into Flash.

project objectives

To complete this project, you will:

❏ Use a semi-transparent gradient to blend objects into the background color

❏ Import and mask bitmap images of planets

❏ Create the solar system structure with movie clips

❏ Develop motion paths to animate planets' orbits around the Sun

❏ Use a nested movie clip to animate the Moon's orbit around the Earth

❏ Organize the Library panel for a complex movie file

❏ Create static text areas and control text properties

❏ Add buttons from built-in symbol libraries

❏ Name symbol instances so they can be affected by behaviors

❏ Assign built-in behaviors to button instances to control movie clip playback

Stage 1 Modeling Complex Animations

As always, the first step in starting a new project is creating a file and pulling together all of the required pieces. This project, however, also requires a good deal of planning to correctly and accurately place the various elements. For example, you have to use scientific information to create the planets' orbit paths, and then scale the planets appropriately based on what the client said during the planning meeting.

Although the client has decided to manipulate the relative scale of the inner planets, the overall time it takes for each planet to complete one orbit (a planetary "year") should be accurately represented in relation to the other planets. So regardless of how many frames represent a single orbit for the Earth, Mercury should still orbit about 6.5 times before the Earth has completed one year. This requires a careful calculation of the number of required frames relative to the movie's frame rate.

The following chart contains the scientific information provided by the client, as well as the art director's notes for applying the data in the Flash model. The times listed here will keep the orbits scientifically correct. At 12 frames per second — which is adequate for the computer kiosks that will display this animation — the longest orbit (Neptune) will be about 20 minutes; Earth will take about 7.5 seconds to complete its orbit.

Planet	Diameter (Miles)	Scale Diameter – Actual (in Pixels)	Scale Diameter – Applied (in Pixels)	Length of Year (in Days)	Length of Year (in Frames)
Sun	870,000	109	109		
Mercury	3,031	4	8	56.7	16
Venus	7,520	9	18	243.0	60
Earth	7,928	10	20	365.2	92
Mars	4,217	5	10	687.0	172
Jupiter	88,846	111	111	4,331.0	1,084
Saturn	74,898	94	94	10,760.0	2,692
Uranus	31,763	40	40	30,684.0	7,672
Neptune	30,775	38	38	60,188.3	15,048

 CREATE THE BASIC DOCUMENT

The kiosk window determines how much space is available to create the model, so you will use that as the basic Stage size. Keep in mind, however, that the Stage size contributes to the overall file weight (in addition to the size of embedded graphics, audio files, and other assets); larger Stage size allows more pixels, which means larger file size. Because this model might eventually be posted on the Internet, you're going to use a flat background color to help minimize the ultimate file size/weight — which will affect the file's download time.

1. **Download FL5_RF_Project3.zip from the Student Files Web page.**

2. **Expand the ZIP archive in your WIP folder (Macintosh) or copy the archive contents into your WIP folder (Windows).**

   This results in a folder named **Planets**, which contains the files you need for this project. You should also use this folder to save the files you create in this project.

3. **Create a new Flash document for ActionScript 3.**

4. **With the new file open, click the Edit button for the Size property (in the Properties panel).**

   When nothing is selected on the Stage, you can use the Properties panel to change document settings. Clicking the Edit button has the same effect as choosing Modify>Document.

   Click here to open the Document Settings dialog box.

5. **In the Document Settings dialog box, change the size of the document to 1300 pixels wide by 800 pixels high, change the Frame Rate to 12, and then click OK.**

6. **If you can't see the entire resized Stage in the document window, choose Fit in Window from the View Percentage menu.**

7. **With nothing selected in the Stage, click the Stage swatch in the Properties panel and change the background color to #003366 (a dark blue).**

Note:

The Properties panel Stage swatch is the same as the Background Color swatch in the Document Settings dialog box. If you only need to change the background color, you don't need to open the Document Settings dialog box.

8. **Save the file as a Flash document named planets.fla in your WIP>Planets folder, and then continue to the next exercise.**

USE TRANSPARENCY TO BLEND OBJECTS INTO THE BACKGROUND

Although gradients can increase file size, the flat-colored background saved a considerable amount of weight. In this exercise, you spend some of that "bandwidth capital" by blending a circle into the background to create the Sun.

1. **With planets.fla open, select the Oval tool and make sure you are working in object-drawing mode.**

2. **Set the stroke to None and set the fill to the black-white radial gradient.**

Apply None as the stroke color.

Choose the black-white radial gradient as the fill color.

Oval tool

Object-drawing mode should be active.

3. **Shift-click and drag to draw a circle on the Stage. With the circle selected, use the Properties panel to position the circle at X: 180, Y: 330, and set the circle diameter (W and H) to 140 pixels.**

   At 1:8000 scale, the Sun should be 109 pixels in diameter. However, you are going to use a radial gradient to create a glowing effect, so you are creating the shape larger than the necessary 109 pixels to accommodate the glow.

Use the X and Y fields to position the drawing object.

Use the W and H fields to resize the drawing object.

4. **Display the Color panel (Window>Color) if it isn't already visible.**

5. **Double-click the left gradient stop (the start color). In the pop-up Swatches palette, click the yellow swatch (#FFFF00) to change the color of the gradient stop.**

   Using a radial gradient, the start color will be at the center of the object, and the end color will be at the outside edge.

Double-click this gradient stop to change the start color.

6. **Double-click the right gradient stop (the end color). Change the stop color to the same yellow you used in Step 5, and then change the Alpha value of the selected stop to 0%.**

With this stop selected, change the Alpha field to 0%.

7. **Click below the gradient ramp to add a third gradient stop. Change the Alpha value of the new stop to 50%, and then drag it right to about three-quarters of the way across the gradient ramp.**

   When you add a gradient stop in the middle of the ramp, the new stop automatically adopts the color and Alpha value of the location where you click. Dragging the new stop right moves the 50% Alpha value farther along the gradient (and thus, farther out from the center of the selected circle).

Click below the gradient ramp to add a stop...

...change the Alpha value of the new stop to 50%...

...then drag the new stop right to extend the solid area of the gradient.

8. **Slide the left gradient stop (the start color) to about halfway along the ramp.**

Dragging this stop extends the fully opaque range of the gradient.

9. **Save the file and continue to the next exercise.**

IMPORT AND MASK PLANET IMAGES

In most graphics applications, a **mask** is used to isolate specific parts of an image or object, such as removing a photographed object from its background (often referred to as silhouetting). Anything outside the area of the mask will not be visible.

In Flash, masks are created by converting a specific layer to a mask. You can use a shape created with one of the Flash drawing tools (such as the Square or Oval tool), or you can use other objects (such as a bitmap image) in the mask layer. Objects on a mask layer are not visible in the final file; they are only used to define the visible area of underlying (masked) layers.

Note:

If more than one object exists on the mask layer, only the bottommost object on the layer will define the mask shape.

The photo was placed on Layer 1.   The oval was created on Layer 2.

After converting Layer 2 to a mask, only the area inside the oval shape is visible.

Note:

You can't create a mask layer inside a button, and you can't add another mask layer to an existing mask layer.

1. **With planets.fla open, choose File>Import>Import to Library.**

2. **Navigate to the WIP>Planets folder, select all JPEG files in the folder, and click Import to Library/Open.**

Note:

Press Command/Control to select multiple, non-contiguous files in the Import to Library dialog box.

3. **Drag the mercury.jpg bitmap from the Library panel onto the Stage.**

   The photo of Mercury includes a black background. To display only the planet, you will use a mask layer to remove the background.

4. **Control/right-click the mercury bitmap image and choose Convert to Symbol from the contextual menu.**

5. **Change the Name field to mercury_mc, choose Movie Clip in the Type menu, choose the center registration point, and then click OK.**

   The name "mercury" is already used by the bitmap image; you are simply adding the "_mc" to differentiate between the two library items.

Note:

Capitalization doesn't matter in this case. You can't have different symbols named "Mercury" and "mercury."

6. **Double-click the mercury_mc instance on the primary Stage to enter into the movie clip Stage.**

7. **Rename the default layer Mercury, and then add a new layer named Mask.**

   A mask in Flash requires a separate layer to hold the masking object.

The Edit bar shows you are editing the mercury_mc symbol.

8. **Choose the Oval tool and make sure object-drawing mode is active. Define any bright color with a 100% Alpha value as the fill and apply None as the stroke color.**

Using this mask shape, only the planet will appear in the final movie; the black background will be hidden. The masking shape will not be visible in the final movie, so the color of the oval is irrelevant.

9. **With the Mask layer active, Option/Alt-click the planet's center point and drag to create a circle from the center out.**

10. **Use the Free Transform tool to make the oval fit the planet.**

Using object-drawing mode, it is easier to manipulate the shape as necessary until it exactly matches the shape of the planet.

11. **Control/right-click the Mask layer in the timeline and choose Mask from the contextual menu.**

Note:

Object-drawing mode usually works better than standard-drawing mode for creating a mask shape.

Note:

It might be helpful to turn off snapping toggles (View>Snapping) when you resize these mask shapes.

Both layers are automatically locked. The layer immediately below is automatically masked by the Mask layer, and now you can see only the planet image; the fill attributes of the actual mask shape are hidden.

Note:

To reveal the mask shape for editing, simply unlock the Mask layer. When you are finished editing the shape, relock the Mask layer to reapply the mask.

12. Click Scene 1 in the Edit bar to return to the main Stage.

13. Select and delete the instance of the Mercury movie clip from the Stage.

14. Using the same process outlined in the previous steps, create a movie clip from each imported bitmap (the planets and the Moon) except Saturn:

- Place the bitmap on the Stage, and then convert the placed instance to a movie clip symbol using "_mc" in the symbol name and the center symbol registration point.

- Enter into the symbol and mask the bitmap image in the movie clip.

- Return to the main Stage and delete the movie clip instance from the main Stage.

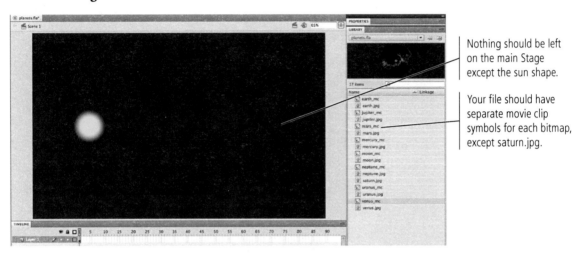

Nothing should be left on the main Stage except the sun shape.

Your file should have separate movie clip symbols for each bitmap, except saturn.jpg.

15. Save the file and continue to the next exercise.

CREATE A COMPLEX MASK SHAPE

The Saturn photo requires a slightly more complicated mask to reveal only the planet and its rings. In Project 1 you learned about the destructive editing characteristics of simple shapes. In this exercise you use that feature to create a compound shape that removes the inner shapes from the planet's rings.

1. With **planets.fla** open, drag saturn.jpg from the Library panel to the Stage.

2. Control/right-click the bitmap image on the Stage and choose Convert to Symbol from the contextual menu. Change the name of the new symbol to saturn_mc, choose Movie Clip in the Type menu, choose the center registration point, and then click OK.

3. Double-click the saturn_mc instance on the Stage to enter into the movie clip Stage. Rename the default layer Saturn, and then add a new layer named Mask.

4. Choose the Oval tool and make sure object-drawing mode is active. Define a red fill color and no stroke color.

   The actual fill color of the mask object doesn't matter; we're using red because it is easily visible against the blue background color.

5. **With the Mask layer selected, Option/Alt-click the symbol registration point and drag out to create an oval shape from the center point out.**

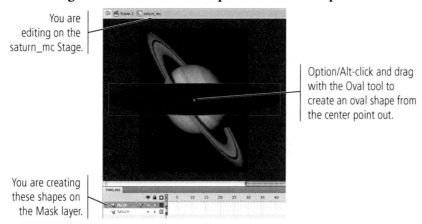

You are editing on the saturn_mc Stage.

Option/Alt-click and drag with the Oval tool to create an oval shape from the center point out.

You are creating these shapes on the Mask layer.

6. **Use the Free Transform tool to rotate the oval shape to match the angle of the rings in the image.**

Move the Free Transform tool cursor just outside a corner handle to rotate the shape to match the angle of the rings in the image.

7. **Drag the side handles of the shape until the rotated shape covers only the inner ring area.**

Drag the side handles to change the object's width and height to match the shape of the inner ring area.

8. **Copy the inner ring shape (Edit>Copy), then choose Edit>Paste in Place to duplicate the inner ring shape in the same position as the original.**

You are creating the inner-ring shape first so you can still see the planet image to create the outer-ring shape.

Note:

If you created the outer-ring shape first, you wouldn't be able to see the inner edge of the rings. That's why you need to create that shape first, and then rearrange the object stacking order.

9. **Use the Free Transform tool to drag the side handles of the second shape to match the outer ring edge.**

10. **Using the Oval tool, Option/Alt-click and drag to create the planet shape from the center out.**

11. **Using the Selection tool, choose the shape of the rings' outer edge and choose Modify>Arrange>Send to Back.**

12. **Change the fill color of the inner-ring shape to any color other than what you applied to the other two shapes (we used bright yellow).**

The inner-ring object must be a different color so the destructive editing capabilities recognize the inner-ring areas as different shapes after you break apart the drawing objects. The other two objects must be the same color so they will be recognized as a single shape.

13. **Using the Selection tool, Shift-click to select all three shapes and then choose Modify>Break Apart.**

After breaking apart the drawing objects, the crosshatch pattern indicates that you can select the areas of different colors.

14. **Click away from the selected objects to deselect them, then click to select the yellow areas and delete them.**

15. **Click inside the remaining shape to select it, then choose Modify>Shape> Expand Fill.**

When you use the destructive editing capability to remove the inner shapes, you might have very small gaps that — although not easily visible — can prevent the mask shape from working properly. By expanding the fill, you can remove these gaps and create a solid shape that works properly when you apply the mask.

16. **In the Expand Fill dialog box, change the Distance field to 1 px, choose the Expand option, and then click OK.**

17. **Control/right-click the Mask layer in the timeline and choose Mask from the contextual menu.**

18. **Click Scene 1 in the Edit bar to return to the main Stage, and delete the saturn_mc instance from the Stage.**

19. **Save the file and continue to the next stage of the project.**

Stage 2 Creating Animated Movie Clips

Animation — the true heart of Flash — can be created in a number of different ways. To create the animated solar system model, you will use a method called **classic tweening** to set each planet into orbit along a defined path.

If you completed Project 2 in this book, you already learned a bit about symbols in general, specifically button and graphic symbols. In this project, you work with movie clip symbols. Both graphic symbols and movie clip symbols can include animation, but movie clips offer a number of advantages over graphic symbols.

First, the animation contained in a movie clip requires only a single frame on the timeline where it is placed (called the **parent timeline**); a movie clip timeline might include 500 frames, but the entire animation will play on a single frame of the parent timeline. An animated graphic symbol, on the other hand, requires the same number of frames on the parent timeline that are present inside the symbol's timeline; in other words, a 500-frame animation inside the graphic symbol requires 500 corresponding frames on the timeline where the symbol is placed.

Because movie clip timelines function independently of the parent timeline, you can more easily incorporate animations of different duration onto the same parent timeline. In this project, the different planets' years vary significantly in length; you will create each planet's orbit in a separate movie clip so each can repeatedly revolve around the sun independently of the start and finish times of other planets.

At the end of this project, you will use basic programming techniques to add buttons that start and stop the planets' orbits, which requires some method for controlling the symbols that make up the digital solar system. Another advantage of movie clips is that placed instances can be named, which means they can be addressed — and controlled — using code. In other words, you need to create the motion in a movie clip symbol instead of on the main timeline or in a graphic symbol.

> *Note:*
>
> *Keep in mind that every symbol has its own timeline. Placed instances of a symbol might occupy only a single frame in the parent timeline, even if their internal timelines include hundreds or even thousands of frames.*

CREATE THE SOLAR SYSTEM STRUCTURE

Animating along a path is a two-step process — create the object that will be animated, and then create the path along which the object will move. In the first stage of this project, you created the masked planets that will orbit the Sun shape. You now need to define the orbits for each planet.

The Earth movie clip will also contain a secondary nested movie clip (i.e., the Moon movie clip, which will rotate around the Earth).

In this case, we completed the necessary research and calculations for creating the orbit shapes in the correct positions to ensure the solar system model appears realistic. In your professional career, you will likely have to complete this type of research on your own to create realistic, accurate animations.

1. With **planets.fla** open, rename the default layer **Sun**.

2. Create a new layer named **Planets** and make it the active layer.

3. Select the Oval tool, set the fill color to None, and set the stroke color to red.

   The line will not be visible after it has been converted to a motion guide, so the color of the stroke doesn't really matter. When you create a motion guide, use a stroke color that you can clearly see against surrounding objects.

4. Draw an oval in object-drawing mode. Use the Properties panel to set the oval's position and size as follows:

X: 160	Y: 420
W: 200	H: 70

Make sure the Constrain option is turned off (unlocked) so you can independently modify the height and width of the shape.

5. Using the Selection tool, Control/right-click the oval on the Stage and choose Convert to Symbol from the contextual menu.

6. Name the new symbol **Mercury_Orbit**, choose Movie Clip in the Type menu, choose the top-left registration point, and then click OK.

   Drawing-object parameters are based on the top-left corner of the object. By choosing the top-left symbol registration point, the symbol instance retains the same X,Y position as the original drawing object.

The selected oval is now an instance of the Mercury_Orbit movie clip symbol.

7. Using the Oval tool, create the orbit for Venus with the following parameters:

    X: 120   Y: 400
    W: 280   H: 108

8. Convert the second oval to a movie clip symbol named Venus_Orbit, using the top-left registration point.

9. Draw and position the remaining six orbit paths, and then convert each orbit path to a movie clip symbol using the top-left symbol registration point. Use the following data for the parameters of each orbit shape:

Planet	X	Y	W	H	Symbol Name
Earth	97	385	372	136	Earth_Orbit
Mars	87	375	478	164	Mars_Orbit
Jupiter	86	370	628	196	Jupiter_Orbit
Saturn	86	350	764	234	Saturn_Orbit
Uranus	77	350	934	280	Uranus_Orbit
Neptune	65	318	1176	328	Neptune_Orbit

Note:

You will create the orbit path for the Moon later in this project.

Because the Planets layer is above the Sun layer, the paths are in front of the Sun.

Controlling Frame and Tween Properties

With one or more frames selected in the timeline, you can use the Properties panel to control a number of options.

- **Name field.** Frames are sequentially numbered by default; you can also assign text-based labels to specific frames so you can more easily remember where in the timeline a specific action occurs. For example, "Arc_Tween" is more descriptive than "Frame 54."

- **Type menu.** If you assign a frame label, you can use this menu to treat the label as a regular name, as an anchor that can be targeted in a hyperlink, or as a comment.

- **Sound options.** The Properties panel includes several options for controlling sound files. You used these options in Project 2.

Motion and Shape Tween Properties

When a classic or shape tween is applied to selected frames, you can use the Properties panel to control a number of options related to the tween itself.

- **Ease.** This option is used to change the speed of movement as an object moves through a tween. You can set negative or positive values to increase or decrease speed at a consistent rate, or you can click the Edit button to define custom Ease values with different speeds at different points in the tween.

- **Rotate menu.** By default, an object simply moves from one place to another through the tween frames. You can choose Auto in the Rotate menu to rotate the object one time over the length of the tween; the object will turn in the direction that requires the least change. You can also exert greater control by choosing CW (clockwise) or CCW (counterclockwise), and then defining a specific number of times the object should rotate throughout the tween.

- **Snap option.** When this option is checked, the registration point of the tweened object attaches to the motion path.

- **Sync option.** This option synchronizes the number of frames in a tween within a graphic symbol to match the number of frames on the timeline where the graphic symbol is placed. With this option checked, replacing the animated symbol in the first frame of the tween replaces the symbol in all tweened frames.

- **Orient to Path.** If you are using a motion path, you can check this option to orient the baseline (bottom edge) of an object to the motion path.

With Orient to Path unchecked, the object remains horizontal throughout the tween.

With Orient to Path checked, the object's baseline rotates to match the shape of the curve.

- **Scale.** This option specifies custom ease settings for the scale of an animated object. If you modified the size of the object on the Stage, select Scale to tween the size of the selected item.

- **Blend menu.** When you apply a shape tween, you can use the Blend menu to control how shapes distort as they change from one shape to another. Distributive, the default option, creates smoother shapes throughout the transition. The Angular option can produce better results if the starting and ending shapes have sharp corners that you want to preserve throughout the transition.

10. Move the Sun layer above the Planets layer on the timeline.

If you don't put the Sun layer above the Planets layer, the Sun will remain behind the planets, even when the planets are supposed to appear to move behind the Sun.

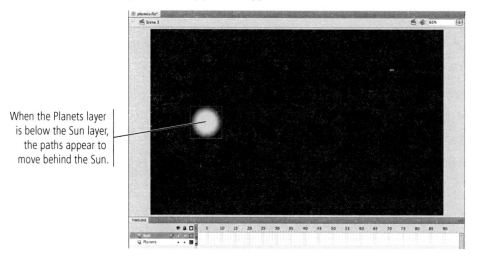

When the Planets layer is below the Sun layer, the paths appear to move behind the Sun.

11. Save the file and continue to the next exercise.

 CREATE MOTION PATHS TO ANIMATE THE PLANETS' ORBITS

A motion path is, by definition, a line with a start point and an end point; objects move from the beginning to the end of the line during the tween.

In the previous exercise, you used supplied data to create the shape for each planet's orbit path. For the planet movie clips to move along those paths, however, you must convert the oval shapes into lines with a start point and an end point.

1. With **planets.fla** open, double-click the Mercury_Orbit instance on the Stage.

You are now on the movie clip symbol Stage rather than the main Stage.

Note:

The Mercury orbit path is the smallest path, closest to the Sun.

2. Double-click the orbit path on the movie clip symbol Stage to enter into the drawing object.

You're going to use Flash's destructive editing capabilities to remove a small piece of the oval, which will convert the shape into a line with a start point and an end point. Because you created these shapes in object-drawing mode, you have to enter into the drawing object to use the Flash destructive editing capabilities.

You are editing the drawing object in the Mercury_Orbit movie clip, which is placed on the main Stage.

3. **Using the Selection tool, draw a small marquee to select a small area of the path where it falls behind the Sun, then press Delete/Backspace.**

By deleting the segment behind the Sun, the gap will be hidden when the movie plays.

Draw a small marquee with the Selection tool, then press Delete/Backspace to remove a small portion of the orbit — creating start and end points for the animation.

4. **Click Mercury_Orbit in the Edit bar to return to the movie clip Stage. Make sure you don't return to the main Stage (Scene 1) at this point.**

5. **Using the Selection tool, select the orbit path and choose Edit>Cut.**

6. **Control/right-click Layer 1 in the movie clip timeline and choose Add Classic Motion Guide from the contextual menu.**

A motion guide layer is a special layer designed to hold a path along which an object moves. Motion guide layers are automatically attached to the previously selected layer.

Note:

This is called a "classic" motion guide because this technique was available in previous versions of the application that did not include the Flash Motion Editor (which you will learn about in Project 4).

7. **With the new Guide layer selected, choose Edit>Paste in Place.**

This command pastes the orbit path in the exact position that it occupied on the main layer, but on the motion guide layer.

The orbit path has been cut from the regular layer and pasted in place on the motion guide layer.

8. **Select the main layer (Layer 1) in the timeline, and then drag the mercury_mc movie clip symbol from the Library panel onto the Stage.**

   To make the planet revolve around the Sun, you have to appropriately scale the movie clip instance and then align it to the motion guide.

9. **In the Properties panel, change the height and width values of the mercury_mc instance to 8 pixels.**

Note:

The appropriate size for each planet were provided by the client in the table on Page 119.

Note:

After resizing the planet, you might need to zoom out to find the placed instance on the Stage.

10. **Choose View>Snapping>Snap To Objects to make sure that option is toggled on.**

    If the menu option shows a checkmark, the option is already turned on.

This option should be checked.

11. **Using the Selection tool, drag the mercury_mc instance until the instance registration point snaps to the left end of the orbit path.**

The center point of the mercury_mc instance will snap to the end of the path as you drag it near the line.

This icon in the cursor indicates you can click and drag to move the movie clip instance.

Note:

Make sure the Guide layer is unlocked so the movie clip will snap into place on the path.

12. Control/right-click Frame 16 of Layer 1 (not the Guide layer) and choose Insert Keyframe.

In this case, the Mercury orbit animation needs to last 16 frames — representing one planetary year. Using a classic motion guide, you need to place a keyframe at the point where you want the tween to end.

Note:

You can also insert a keyframe by pressing F6, or by choosing Insert> Timeline>Keyframe.

The guide layer hasn't been extended, so the path is not visible at Frame 16.

The keyframe extends the layer, so the planet is visible at Frame 16.

Remember, keyframes are used when an object needs to change in some way. In this case, the mercury_mc instance needs to move to the end of the orbit path. When you create the motion tween, Flash will determine the position of the mercury_mc symbol for each intermediate frame (called **tween frames**).

13. Select Frame 16 of the Guide layer and press the F5 key to insert a regular frame.

The path on the guide layer also needs to exist on all 16 of those frames. Because the motion guide does not change over time, you use a regular frame instead of a keyframe.

Note:

You can also insert a regular frame by choosing Insert>Timeline>Frame.

The Guide layer needs a regular frame to keep the path in the movie for all 16 frames.

14. Click the Frame 16 keyframe on Layer 1 to select it, then drag the mercury_mc instance until the symbol's registration point snaps to the right end of the path.

15. **Control/right-click between Frames 1 and 16 of Layer 1, and then choose Create Classic Tween from the contextual menu.**

   Depending on your zoom percentage, you might not see the planet image after you create the motion tween. If you zoom out to see the entire orbit path, you'll find the planet at the correct position along the path for the current location of the playhead (wherever you clicked to create the motion tween).

Classic motion tween frames are identified in the Timeline by a blue arrow.

16. **Click Scene 1 in the Edit bar to return to the main Stage.**

   The Mercury orbit path is no longer visible; the planet instance is visible but currently hidden by the Sun.

Motion paths are not visible in the actual movie.

17. **Press Command-Return/Control-Enter to test the movie.**

   If you can't see the entire movie in the Player window, Control/right-click the Player window and choose Show All from the contextual menu.

You should be able to see the Mercury image moving along its motion path.

Note:

Remember, pressing Return/Enter plays the current timeline on the Stage. Because the main timeline has only one frame, this command would have no effect. Testing a movie on the Stage does not initiate the timeline of movie clips that are placed on the Stage.

18. **Close the Flash Player window. In Flash, save the file and continue to the next exercise.**

COMPLETE THE PLANETS' ORBITS

In this exercise, you use the method you learned in the previous exercise to set the remaining seven planets on their orbit paths, and extend each orbit across the correct number of frames. Each orbit must be timed correctly, relative to all other orbits.

Unfortunately, there is no way to automate these tasks, but by completing the same basic steps for eight different objects, you will be practicing a valuable skill.

1. **With planets.fla open, use the same process you learned in the previous exercise to animate each planet movie clip on the related orbit movie clip. Use the following information for sizing the planets and timing the orbits.**

Planet	Diameter (in Pixels)	Length of the Year (in Frames)
Venus	18	60
Earth	20	92
Mars	10	172
Jupiter	111	1,084
Saturn	75 wide, 94 high	2,692
Uranus	40	7,672
Neptune	38	15,048

Note:

For Saturn, you have to use non-proportional dimensions because the rings make the planet non-circular.

When you create the motion tweens for Saturn, Uranus, and Neptune, Flash has to add a significant amount of information to create thousands of frames. Give your computer ample time to complete the process.

Extending the Length of the Timeline

FLASH FOUNDATIONS

When you work on the outer planets, you will need to extend the timeline beyond what is available by default. To accomplish this, scroll the timeline all the way to the right, and then add a regular frame to the motion guide layer near the end of the visible timeline.

When you add a frame after the last visible frame, the timeline scroll bar moves to the middle of the panel, indicating that more frames are now available in the timeline. You can then scroll again to the new end of the timeline and add another frame, which again extends the length of the available timeline. Continue this process until you have the number of frames you need.

When you have added the final regular frame to the motion guide layer, you can easily add the necessary keyframe to the main layer below the guide layer.

The default timeline only goes up to a certain frame number.

After adding a regular frame near the end of the default timeline, the scroll bar indicates that more frames are available.

Continue adding regular frames and scrolling the timeline until you have the number of frames you need.

2. **Return to the main Stage of the Flash file and save the file.**

3. **Press Command-Return/Control-Enter to test the movie. (Fit the movie into the Player window if necessary.)**

   You should be able to see all of the planets moving along their orbits at one time.

4. **Close the Player window and return to Flash. Continue to the next exercise.**

 ## ORGANIZE THE LIBRARY

Because of the complexity in this movie, your Library panel is now crowded with more than 20 different symbols. To make the file easier to manage, you can organize library items into logical folders.

1. **With planets.fla open, select all three items related to the Earth (earth.jpg, earth_orbit, and earth_mc) in the Library panel.**

2. **Control/right-click any of the selected items and choose Move To from the contextual menu.**

3. **In the resulting dialog box, select the New Folder radio button. Type Earth Symbols in the field and click Select.**

4. **Collapse the Earth Symbols folder in the Library panel if it is expanded.**

5. **Repeat this process to group the related symbols into folders for better organization and easier navigation.**

6. **Save the file and continue to the next exercise.**

 ANIMATE A NESTED MOVIE CLIP

Although several planets have their own moons, your client asked you to include only the Earth's moon in this model so children will have a source of reference — something they are already familiar with. The Moon's orbit around the Earth takes approximately 27.3 days. Using the same time scale as the planets, the Moon's orbit should occupy 7 frames.

The process for animating the Moon around the Earth is basically the same as the process you used to animate the planets. The only difference is that you are creating the orbit motion guide inside the existing earth_mc movie clip.

Note:

You can't use fractions of frames, so we are rounding the orbit cycle to 7.

1. **With planets.fla open, expand the Earth Symbols folder in the Library panel. Double-click the earth_mc symbol icon to enter into that movie clip.**

2. **Select the Mask layer, and then add a new layer named Moon.**

   The new layer is automatically placed above the previously selected layer.

3. **Using the Oval tool with a red stroke and no fill, draw an oval shape for the orbit of the Moon. Use the following as the parameters of the shape:**

X: –465	Y: –50
W: 930	H: 280

   The planet object is centered on the symbol registration point. The negative X and Y values position the top-left corner of the orbit path relative to the center of the planet.

4. **Cut the oval object from the Moon layer.**

5. **Control/right-click the Moon layer in the timeline and choose Add Classic Motion Guide from the contextual menu. With the new Guide layer selected, paste the cut shape in place (Edit>Paste in Place).**

6. **Double-click the orbit shape to enter into the drawing object. Using the Selection tool, remove a small portion of the orbit (behind the Earth image).**

7. **Click earth_mc in the Edit bar to return to the symbol Stage.**

8. **Select the Moon layer in the timeline (not the Guide:Moon layer).**

9. **Drag an instance of the moon_mc symbol onto the Stage from the Moon Symbols folder in the Library panel. In the Properties panel, set the width and height of the placed Moon instance to 86 pixels.**

10. **Drag the Moon symbol until its registration point snaps to the beginning point of the motion guide.**

Note:

It isn't necessary to create a separate movie clip for the Moon orbit because you are creating the orbit inside the earth_mc symbol.

11. **Add regular frames to Frame 7 of the Earth, Mask, and Guide:Moon layers.**

If you don't add these frames, the masked Earth image will not be visible and the motion guide will not be available past the first frame.

12. **Add a keyframe at Frame 7 of the Moon layer.**

13. **With the Frame 7 keyframe of the Moon layer selected, drag the moon instance to snap to the end point of the motion path.**

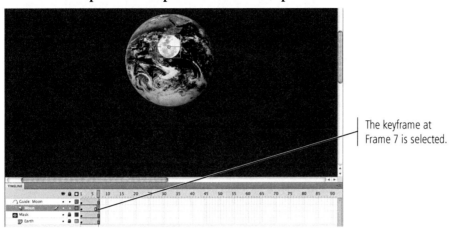

The keyframe at Frame 7 is selected.

14. **Create a classic tween between Frames 1 and 7 of the Moon layer.**

15. **In the Layers area of the timeline, select the Moon and Guide:Moon layers, and then drag them below the Earth layer.**

    As with placing the planets behind the Sun, the Moon needs to move behind the Earth as it orbits.

By rearranging the layers, the motion guide now moves behind the Earth image.

16. **Return to Scene 1 of the Flash file, and then press Command-Return/ Control-Enter to test your movie.**

There's the Moon, rotating around the Earth.

17. **Close the Player window and return to Flash.**

18. **Save the file and continue to the next stage of the project.**

Stage 3 Working with Text

One of the more frustrating aspects of Web design is working with text elements; this is because the appearance of type is dependent on the available fonts on a user's computer. Flash movies are not subject to this limitation because used fonts can be embedded in the exported SWF file; you can use any font in a Flash file, and it will appear exactly as expected in the movie as long as it is embedded.

If you're familiar with previous versions of Flash, you can use the Properties panel Text Engine menu to create a Classic Text object. In this case, you create one of three specific types of text object:

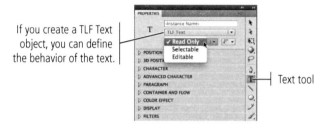

If you create a Classic Text object, you can also define the type of text.

Text tool

- **Static text** is placed, kerned, aligned, and manually edited with the Text tool. This type of text does not change.

- **Dynamic text** is basically an area into which information can be read; this type of text object can be named and addressed by code, which means the content can be changed as the result of a certain action.

- **Input text** is a field in which users can type to submit information (as in an online form).

Flash CS5 includes a new text engine — called Text Layout Framework (TLF) text — that makes it very easy to add text to a movie by clicking and dragging with the Text tool. You have a wide range of formatting options that define the behavior of the frame, as well as the appearance of text within the frame. Using TLF text, you don't need to specify whether the object is static or dynamic. Rather, you can determine whether text in the area is Read-Only, Selectable, or Editable.

If you create a TLF Text object, you can define the behavior of the text.

Text tool

 ## ADD TEXT TO THE MODEL

As your client mentioned, the planets in this model are not shown in a single, consistent scale. You have basically created a rough estimate of the solar system to show children how planets move around the Sun. Because your target audience is young children, the movie does not require a detailed or scientific explanation. You should, however, include a simple statement about the incorrect scale. You also need to add a large title at the top of the screen to describe what the model is showing.

1. **With planets.fla open in Flash, choose View>Magnification>Fit in Window.**

   You are going to create a heading across the top of the entire movie, so it will help to see the entire Stage.

2. **Add a new layer at the top of the layer stack named Text. Select the Text layer as the active layer.**

3. **Choose the Text tool in the Tools panel.**

4. **At the top of the Properties panel, make sure TLF Text is selected in the Text Engine menu and choose Read Only in the Text Type menu.**

Text Engine menu

Text Type menu

Text tool

5. **In the Character section of the Properties panel:**

   - **Change the Family menu to a sans-serif font such as Arial or Helvetica.**

   - **Choose a Bold, Black, or Heavy variation of the selected font in the Style menu.**

   - **Click the current Size link to access the field. Type 36 in the field and press Return/Enter.**

   - **Make sure the Leading menu is set to % and change the associated value to 110.**

   - **Click the Color swatch to open the Swatches panel. Choose white (#FFFFFF) as the text color, and make sure the Alpha value is 100%.**

   - **Choose Readability in the Anti-Alias menu.**

6. **In the Paragraph section of the Properties panel, click the Align Center option.**

   Any formatting you define before clicking with the Text tool will be applied in the new text area.

7. **Click near the top-left corner of the Stage and drag to create a rectangular text area about half the width of the movie.**

   To include text in a movie, you first have to create an area to hold the text characters. As you drag, notice that dragging affects only the width of the rectangle. The area's minimum height is determined by the currently defined text formatting options.

   When you release the mouse button, the text area appears as a white box. When the insertion point is flashing, you can type in the box to add text.

   Insertion point   Area handles

Note:

When the insertion point is flashing in a text area, you can't use the one-key shortcuts to choose other tools.

8. **Type** `Click the green button to see how the planets move around the Sun.`

   The text appears in the text area you just created, using the character and paragraph formatting options that you already defined. (Because you chose white as the text color, the text appears gray in the area so you can see it as you type.)

   Overset text icon

   Depending on the size of the area you created, the entire sentence might not fit into the area. The red plus sign icon (called the **overset text icon**) on the bottom-right corner of the area indicates that more text exists than will fit into the defined space. You can either change the size of the area to accommodate all of the text, or click the overset text icon to "load" the cursor with the rest of the text; once loaded with the overset text, clicking again on the Stage creates a second linked text area to contain the overset text.

9. **Choose the Selection tool, and then expand the Position and Size options in the Properties panel. Change the properties of the selected text area to:**

        X: 25   **Y: 25**
        W: 1250   **H: 50**

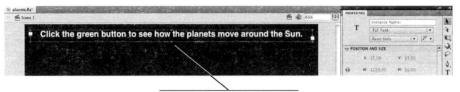

When the Selection tool is active, you can drag the area handles but you can't change the text content in the area.

Using the Position and Size properties, you can define specific numeric parameters for the area. You can also reposition a text area by clicking inside the area with the Selection tool and dragging to a new location, or resize the area by dragging any of the handles that appear on the outside edges of the object.

10. **In the Character section of the Properties panel, change the Size value to 60.**

When a text area is selected, changes to character and paragraph formatting apply to all text inside the area. You can change the formatting of only certain characters by highlighting the target characters with the Text tool before making changes in the Properties panel.

11. **Click the bottom-center handle of the text area and drag down until all of the text is visible.**

When you drag a text area handle with the Selection tool, text formatting is not affected.

Click the handle and drag down to change the area height.

Note:

If you use the Free Transform tool, dragging a text area handle will scale the contained text to match the transformed area.

12. **Click away from the text area to deselect it.**

13. **Choose the Text tool, then define the text properties as the italic/oblique, non-bold variant of whatever font you used for the heading, using 20-pt size and left paragraph alignment.**

14. **Create a new text area, and then type the following:**

> One Earth year equals approximately 7.5 seconds.
> Planets are not shown to scale.

15. **Using the Selection tool, resize the text area horizontally so each sentence fits on a single line (as shown below). Position the text area in the bottom-left corner of the Stage.**

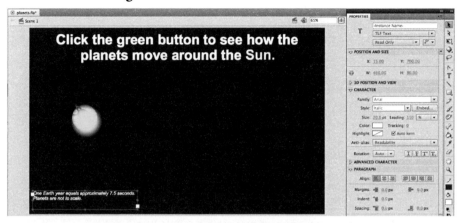

Controlling Text Properties

A number of text formatting options are available in the Properties panel when the Text tool is active.

Character Options

- **Family and Style menus.** As with any computer application, the font defines the appearance of the text. The entire list of fonts installed on your machine appears in the Family menu. The Style menu lists available variants of the selected font (Bold, Italic, etc.).

- **Embed button.** This button allows you to embed selected fonts or specific characters to ensure that text will appear on users' computers in the font you define.

- **Size.** The size of the text (in points) can be changed in the Font Size field or selected from the menu.

- **Leading.** This defines the distance between the bottom of one line of text and the bottom of the next line of text. You can define leading based on a percentage of the applied type size, or using a specific value.

- **Color.** This swatch changes the fill color of selected characters.

- **Letter Spacing (Tracking) field.** This option is used to increase or decrease the spacing between a selected range of characters.

- **Highlight.** This swatch defines the color immediately behind the selected text.

- **Auto Kern check box.** You can uncheck this option to prevent Flash from applying a font's default kerning values in static text.

- **Anti-aliasing menu.** This menu determines the level of anti-aliasing applied (if any).

- **Rotation menu.** This option changes the orientation of text within the area.

- **Type Style buttons.** These buttons change the style of text to (from left) underlined, ~~strikethrough~~, superscript (such as the TH in 4th), and subscript (the 2 in H_2O).

Paragraph Options

- **Paragraph Alignment buttons.** Text can be aligned to the left, right, or center of its containing area, or it can be justified so all lines fill the available horizontal space. If you use the Justify options on the right, you can also determine how the last line in the paragraph is formatted (left, centered, right, or forced).

- **Margins.** These options define how far text is placed from the left and right edges of the containing area.

- **Indent.** This option defines how far the first line of the paragraph is indented from the left edge of the remaining text in the same paragraph.

- **Spacing.** These options define how much space is added above or below each paragraph.

- **Text Justify.** When using justified paragraph alignment, this menu determines how extra space is distributed: between individual letters or only between words.

16. Expand the Container and Flow options in the Properties panel. Click the button to align the text to the bottom of the container.

One Earth year equals approximately 7.5 seconds
Planets are not shown to scale.

| Align Text to Top of Container | Align Text to Center of Container | Align Text to Bottom of Container | Justify Align Text within Container |

17. Save the file and continue to the next exercise.

Controlling Text Properties (continued)

When an existing text area is selected, other options become available for controlling the selected text.

Advanced Character Options

- **Link.** If you want selected text to act as a hyperlink, you can type the destination URL in this field.

- **Target.** This menu defines where the hyperlink target will open: in the same browser window (_self), in a new blank browser window (_blank), in the parent container of the SWF file (_parent), or in the main browser window that contains the frame with the link (_top).

- **Case.** This menu can be used to change text to all UPPER CASE, all lower case, or SMALL CAPS.

- **Digit Case.** This option can be used to apply Lining or Old Style character glyphs in place of regular numbers (if those options exist in the applied font).

- **Digit Width.** This option controls the horizontal spacing of number characters. Tabular forces all digits to occupy the same amount of space. Proportional allows each number to occupy only the space that is required for the digit shape.

- **Ligatures.** This option can be used to control the replacement of select character pairs (for example, fl or ff) with a single-character representation of those letters.

- **Break.** This menu can be used to force each selected character onto a new line (All), allow text to break naturally where necessary (Any), or prevent selected text from breaking across multiple lines (No Break).

- **Baseline Shift.** This option raises selected characters away from the invisible line on which the bottom of characters rest.

- **Locale.** This menu defines the language that is used for selected text.

Container and Flow Options

- **Behavior.** This menu can force text to only a Single Line of text, in which all text appears on one line regardless of return characters; display Multiline wrapped text in which text will reflow in the container if you change its width; or Multiline No Wrap text, in which new lines require pressing Return/Enter as you type.

- **Max Chars.** If you define the text type as Editable, you can use this value to limit how much text can be typed in an area.

- **Columns.** You can use this option to create multiple columns in a single text area. If you use multiple columns, you can also define the gutter width, or the space between columns.

- **Padding.** These fields define how far text is placed from the edge of containing area (sometimes called text inset, especially in applications such as Adobe InDesign).

- **Border Color** and **Background Color.** These swatches can be used to apply different colors to the text area.

- **1st Line Offset.** This menu can be used to adjust the position of the first line of text in the area, either by a specific distance or based on attributes of the applied font and formatting (Ascent and Line Height).

FLASH FOUNDATIONS

DEFINE FONT EMBEDDING

When you use text in a movie, the fonts you use must be available to other users who open your file. If not, the users' systems will substitute some font that is available — which can significantly impact the appearance of your movie. To solve this potential problem, you can embed fonts into your movies so the required fonts are always available. Flash stores all embedded font information in the SWF file to ensure the font displays properly, regardless of whether it's installed on the user's computer.

Note:

Embedding elements into a file — including font information — increases file size.

Keep in mind that embedding fonts adds to the resulting file size and increases the download time of Flash movies. The font outline (embedded character) is stored as part of the SWF file, so repeatedly using the same character of the same font in the movie does not increase the file size (the same theory as using instances of symbols). Keeping the number of fonts in a movie to a minimum ensures a faster-loading movie.

1. **With planets.fla open, select the Text tool.**

2. **Click inside the heading text area to place the insertion point and reveal the formatting for that area.**

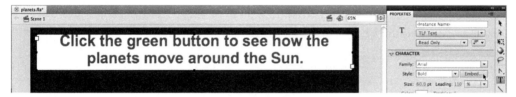

3. **In the Character section of the Properties panel, click the Embed button.**

   This button opens the Font Embedding dialog box. The currently applied font is automatically selected in the Family and Style menus.

4. **Change the Name field to Heading Font.**

5. **In the Character Ranges list, check the Uppercase, Lowercase, and Punctuation options.**

   Remember, embedding characters from fonts increases the resulting file size. You know only letters and punctuation were used in this document, so you can limit the embedded characters to only these ranges rather than embedding every possible character of the font.

Note:

Since you only used the period character, you could also type a period in the Also Include These Characters field rather than embedding the entire punctuation set.

6. **Above the list of fonts, click the Plus button to add another font to the list.**

   The new font defaults to the same as the previously selected font.

7. **Select Bold (Heading Font 1) in the Font list, then change the Name field to Footer Font.**

   The item on the left side of the dialog box won't reflect the new name until you click away from the Name field.

Note:

Some fonts can't be embedded; it depends on how the font was created and whether permission is intentionally enabled in that font. If a used font can't be embedded, it won't appear as you intended unless you convert the type to a drawing object.

8. **Choose Italic in the Style menu, and leave the same three Character Ranges options checked.**

   After you choose the new family, the item in the Font list (on the left side of the dialog box) reflects the new style.

9. **Click OK to close the dialog box.**

10. **Save the file and continue to the next stage of the project.**

Stage 4 Adding Movie Controls

The orbit animations exist within movie clips, which are placed on the first (and only) frame of the main timeline. By default, the timeline in a movie clip plays automatically as soon as the movie clip loads. Because the movie clips are all placed on Frame 1 of the main timeline, they begin playing as soon as the movie opens.

In this stage of the project, you add buttons and define behaviors to start and stop the orbit animation movie clips. This type of interactivity is one of the foundations of Flash — allowing users to click objects and cause something to happen somewhere in the movie.

 ### PREPARE INSTANCES FOR BUTTON CONTROL

Whether simply making an icon visible or starting and stopping the rotation of multiple planets around the Sun, you must name any placed instance you want to control with a script. It's a good idea to complete the naming process before you place the control buttons.

1. **With planets.fla open, hide the Sun layer on the main timeline.**

   Because the planets are behind the Sun, hiding that layer makes it easier to see and access the planets so you can name the placed instances.

2. **Using the Selection tool, click the first planet instance on the main Stage.**

3. **In the Properties panel, click the Instance Name field and type Neptune.**

Define the instance name in this field.

The Properties panel shows that the selected object is an instance of the Neptune_Orbit symbol.

4. **With the named instance selected, choose Modify>Arrange>Send to Back.**

   You selected this instance because it was at the top of the stacking order on the Planets layer. To be able to select the planets under the Neptune instance, you must rearrange the order of planets within the layer.

5. **Repeat Steps 2–4 to name the instances of the remaining planets. Use the Send to Back command as necessary until you have selected and named all placed instances of the planets.**

Use the proper (capitalized) name of each planet for the instance names. You will use these instance names in the next exercise when you define the actions that will start and stop the movie clips.

First, select a planet.   Second, determine which planet is selected.   Third, assign the appropriate instance name.

6. **Show the Sun layer in the timeline.**

7. **Save the file and continue to the next exercise.**

 ADD START AND STOP BUTTONS

Buttons can be used to perform many functions, such as navigating between pages in a Web site, loading external movies, or controlling the timeline of movie clips. In this exercise, you will define buttons that allow users to start and stop the planet orbit animations.

1. **With planets.fla open, add a new layer to the top of the layer stack and name it Buttons. Select this new layer as the active one.**

2. **Choose Window>Common Libraries>Buttons.**

The common libraries work exactly the same as any other external Flash library. Simply drag a symbol from the common library into your file; any symbol placed from an external library will be added to the Library panel in your file.

3. **Expand the classic buttons folder in the Library-Buttons.fla panel, and then expand the Arcade buttons subfolder.**

Note:

Flash includes a number of built-in libraries, which contain common objects such as the buttons you use in this model. Before you try to reinvent the wheel for common graphics such as buttons, look through the libraries included with the application.

4. **With the Buttons layer selected in the timeline, drag an instance of the arcade button – green symbol onto the Stage.**

5. **Drag an instance of the arcade button – red symbol from the Buttons library onto the Stage.**

   The two symbols are automatically added to your file's Library panel.

The Buttons layer is selected.

The green and red buttons have been dragged from the built-in Buttons library onto the Stage.

When you add a button to your movie Stage, it is automatically added to the file's Library panel.

6. **Close the Library-Buttons.fla panel.**

7. **Align the top edges of the two placed buttons, leaving approximately 20 pixels between the buttons.**

8. **Choose the Text tool. Use white as the color, 20 pt as the size, and apply the regular (non-bold, non-italic) style of the same font you used for the other text objects in the movie.**

9. **Add text areas below each button instance. Label the green button Start and label the red button Stop.**

   You could add these text fields inside the button symbols, but that isn't necessary.

10. **Select the Start text area and choose Modify>Break Apart.**

When you break apart a text area, each letter in the area becomes a separate object (as you can see by the individual bounding boxes around each character.

After breaking apart, each character is a separate object.

11. **With the individual letters still selected, choose Modify>Break Apart again.**

The second time you choose this command, the characters are converted to standard-drawing objects. These characters are no longer editable text, so you don't need to embed the font into the SWF file.

After breaking apart the second time, the text is converted to standard-drawing objects.

12. **With the drawing objects selected, choose Modify>Group.**

This enables you to select the entire word as a single object, even though it is made up of individual standard-drawing objects.

After grouping, you can select the entire "word" at once.

13. **Repeat Steps 10–12 for the Stop text area.**

14. **Using the Selection tool, draw a marquee around both buttons and their associated text areas. Drag the selected objects to the bottom-right corner of the Stage.**

Don't group the four elements. Simply select them all at once and drag them into position.

15. **Deselect the active selection, then click to select only the green button instance on the Stage. In the Properties panel, name the instance start_btn.**

16. **Select the red button instance on the Stage and name it stop_btn.**

17. **Save the file and continue to the next exercise.**

ASSIGN BEHAVIORS TO BUTTON INSTANCES

You could use a number of different methods to make the buttons start and stop the movie clip instances in this movie. To complete this project, you will use Flash's built-in behaviors to quickly and easily control what happens when users click these buttons.

1. **With planets.fla open, open the Behaviors panel (Window>Behaviors).**

2. **Select the red Stop button instance on the Stage and click the "+" button in the Behaviors panel.**

If you created the original Flash file for ActionScript 3, as instructed at the beginning of this project, you see a warning message. Built-in behaviors are not supported by ActionScript 3.0, so you have to target ActionScript 1.0-2.0 to use this functionality.

Note:

Click the "−" button in the Behaviors panel to remove a selected action from the object.

3. **Click the Publish Settings button in the warning dialog box to open the Publish Settings dialog box.**

4. **In the Flash tab of the Publish Settings dialog box, choose ActionScript 2.0 in the Script menu.**

Although ActionScript 3.0 is extremely versatile and powerful, non-programmers find it very confusing to assign the proper syntax for even the simplest actions (such as making a movie clip start or stop). By targeting ActionScript 2, you can use the more designer-friendly Behaviors panel to automatically assign basic behaviors.

Choose ActionScript 2.0 in this menu.

5. **Read the resulting warning message.**

There are trade-offs if you want to use the designer-friendly Behaviors panel. One of those trade-offs is that TLF text is not supported by ActionScript 2 or lower. Any TLF objects will be converted to static Classic Text objects.

6. **Click OK to dismiss the warning, then click OK in the Publish Settings dialog box to apply the change.**

7. **Review the two text areas in your movie.**

A number of TLF text formatting options are not available for classic text objects. If this change is ever necessary in your work, you should carefully review the results.

In the heading text, the space between the two lines is increased because leading is not an option for classic text objects. In the footer text, the text is attached to the top of the area because alignment within the container is not an option for classic text objects.

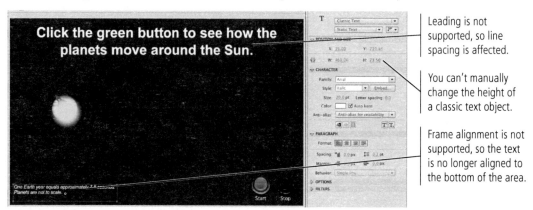

Leading is not supported, so line spacing is affected.

You can't manually change the height of a classic text object.

Frame alignment is not supported, so the text is no longer aligned to the bottom of the area.

8. **Click the footer text area to select it. Drag the area down so the bottom of the second line appears approximately 15 pixels from the bottom edge of the Stage.**

With a classic text object, you cannot adjust the height of a static text area. The height is always defined based on the applied formatting and the text contained in the area.

9. **Select the red button instance on the Stage again, then click the "+" button in the Behaviors panel and choose Moviecip>Goto and Stop at Frame or Label.**

10. **In the resulting dialog box, choose Earth as the movie clip instance you want to affect with this behavior.**

The Goto and Stop action requires two parameters: the instance you want to affect, and the frame at which you want to stop the movie clip's timeline.

By default, this behavior returns the movie clip playhead to Frame 1.

When a user clicks this button, the playhead in the Earth_Orbit movie clip (of which "Earth" is an instance) will return to Frame 1 and stop. In other words, the Earth_Orbit animation will stop playing.

11. Click OK to add the behavior to the selected instance.

In the Behaviors panel, the On Release event is added to the panel — and to the button instance.

The On Press event initiates an action as soon as a user clicks a button. On Release does not initiate the action until the user clicks the button and releases the mouse button within the button's hit area. This distinction allows a user to click, change his mind, and release the mouse button outside the button's hit area to cancel the action.

Note:

Double-clicking an action in the Behaviors panel reopens the target dialog box for that action; you can use this method to change the object affected by the selected action.

The behavior is now added to the selected instance.

12. Repeat this process to add seven more instances of the Goto and Stop behavior to the Stop button instance (one behavior for each planet).

With the instance selected, simply click the "+" button in the Behaviors panel and choose Movieclip>Goto and Stop at Frame or Label. In the resulting dialog box, select the next planet in the list and click OK.

Note:

Clicking an event in the Behaviors panel provides access to a menu, where you can choose a different trigger event.

The red button should have eight behaviors, one to stop each orbit.

13. Select the green button instance on the Stage. Repeat the same process from this exercise to add the Goto and Play at Frame or Label behavior, calling Frame 1, to the Start button (one behavior for each planet).

The green button should have eight behaviors, one to start each orbit.

14. Save the file.

15. Press Command-Return/Control-Enter to test the movie.

When the movie opens, the planets should immediately begin orbiting; by default, the orbit movie clips loop continuously until a user clicks the red button to stop them.

Click the buttons in the movie to test their behaviors. The red button should stop the orbits and move the planets to their original locations behind the Sun. The green button should set the planets back into orbit.

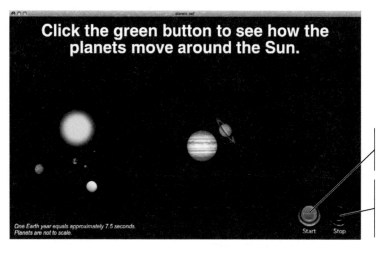

Clicking the green button should set the planets back into orbit.

Clicking the red button should stop the orbits and return the planets to their original positions behind the Sun.

16. Close the Player window and return to Flash.

17. Continue to the next exercise.

Export Movie File Types

FLASH FOUNDATIONS

When you choose File>Export>Export Movie, a number of formats are available in the Format/Save As Type menu. Each format has distinct uses, advantages, and disadvantages.

- **SWF Movie.** A Flash movie file can be placed into an HTML file, or it can be used in another Flash application.

- **QuickTime.** Selecting this option opens the Export QuickTime MOV dialog box, where you can set options such as dimensions, Stage color, last frame reached, time elapsed, and others.

- **Animated GIF.** Files exported in this format preserve all the animations in a single file. You can specify various options, such as dots per inch (dpi), image area, colors, and animation for the resulting GIF file. Setting the dpi is the same as setting the dimensions of the image; the number of times the animation needs to repeat can also be defined (0 creates an endless loop).

- **JPEG Sequence.** Selecting this option allows the file to be exported in the JPEG format. The Match Movie option matches the size of the exported file with that of the original document. When you use any of the sequence options, each frame of the movie is exported as a separate image.

- **GIF Sequence.** This format exports the files in GIF format, except the files are generated in a sequence for each frame animation. The animated GIF format exports a single file that contains all of the animations; this option generates a sequence of files.

- **PNG Sequence.** This option saves the files in the Portable Network Graphics (PNG) format, which supports transparency for objects that might need to be placed on various backgrounds. You can specify options such as dimension, resolution, colors, and filter options.

- **Windows AVI (Windows only).** This option exports the movie in the Windows format and results in huge file sizes. Choosing this option opens the Export Windows AVI dialog box, where you can set options such as dimensions and quality of the movie.

- **WAV Audio (Windows only).** This option exports only the sound file from the current document. You can specify the sound frequency and format of the sound file (stereo, mono, etc.), as well as ignore event sounds if you don't want them in the exported file.

PUBLISH THE FINAL MOVIE

Exporting a document refers to publishing it in a form that can be viewed in another application. The File>Export menu has two options: Export Image or Export Movie. If you choose **Export Image**, you can save your file as a static graphic (with no animation) in formats such as GIF or JPEG. **Export Movie** allows you to create a file (or sequence of files) that includes animation, which can be placed into an HTML document created in another application. You can export Flash movies in different formats, including SWF (the default format for Flash movies), QuickTime, or Animated GIF.

You can also use the Publish option (File>Publish) to generate the Flash SWF file, along with the necessary HTML document that inserts your Flash content into a browser window. (Publishing also creates JavaScript that lets your Flash file play automatically in browsers with that capability.)

1. **With planets.fla open, choose File>Publish Settings.**

2. **In the Formats tab of the Publish Settings dialog box, make sure the Flash and HTML options are selected.**

3. **Select the Windows Projector and Macintosh Projector options.**

   These two options create platform-specific executable applications, which can function without the Flash Player.

> **Note:**
>
> *By default, files are published in the same location as the FLA file. In this case, you are publishing the files in your WIP>Planets folder.*

4. **Click Publish to generate the necessary files.**

5. **When the publishing process is complete, click OK to close the Publish Settings dialog box.**

6. **Save the Flash file and close it.**

The Publish Settings dialog box (File>Publish Settings) contains all the necessary settings for publishing files from Flash. The Current Profile menu lists all available saved profiles. You can create a Publish profile that allows you to save your publish settings, which can then be imported by other users to publish documents with the same settings.

Remove Profile button
Rename Profile button
Duplicate Profile button
Create New Profile button
Import/Export Profile button

Formats Options. The Formats tab lists the options that are available for publishing files. The Flash (.swf) and the HTML (.html) formats are selected by default. For each file format, a field shows the default file names (with their respective extensions) that will be used. You can also specify custom names in these fields, and click the folder icon next to a file name to specify a different location to publish your files. (If you define different file names, you can click the Use Default Names button to restore the original default settings. If you select a location other than the default, the file name will show the entire path to that location.)

Flash Options. Options in the Flash tab determine how the animation is exported.

- The **Player** menu allows you to export the Flash movie to be compatible with an earlier version of the Flash Player, Adobe AIR 1.1, or various versions of Flash Lite.

- **Script** specifies which version of ActionScript (1, 2, or 3) is or will be used in the file. Clicking the Settings button opens a dialog box where you can specify the path of an external ActionScript file.

- **JPEG Quality** specifies the quality of JPEG images that are exported. If you choose a lower quality, the clarity of the image won't be particularly good, but the file size will be smaller. As the quality increases, so does the size of the file.

- **Enable JPEG Deblocking** helps smooth the appearance of JPEG files with very high levels of compression.

- **Audio Stream.** The Set button next to this field allows you to set the sample rate and compression of audio files used in the application. Clicking the Set button displays a dialog box where you can set the format, quality, and bit rate of sound. A streaming sound is played as soon as enough data is downloaded to play the file; the sound stops playing as soon as the movie stops.

- **Audio Event.** The Set button of this field performs the same function as the Set button in Audio Stream. The only difference is that an event sound does not play until it downloads completely, and it continues to play until explicitly stopped.

- **Override Sound Settings** allows Flash to override any setting that you define in the Audio Stream and Audio Event fields. If this option is deselected, Flash streams all the sound files using your settings.

- **Export Device Sounds** allows you to export sounds for different devices such as mobile phones, encoded in the native format of the device rather than a standard format such as AVI or WMV.

- **Compress Movie** is useful for reducing the size of the Flash file. If a file contains a large amount of ActionScript code, this option is useful for compressing the file and reducing its size, which also reduces the download time of the file. Compressed files can only be played in Flash Player 6 or later versions.

- **Include Hidden Layers** allows you to export hidden layer information in the exported file.

- **Include XMP Metadata** exports any metadata that has been entered in the File Info dialog box (File>File Info). The metadata is viewable when the SWF file is selected in Adobe Bridge.

- **Export SWC** can be checked to export a movie into a SWC file, which can be useful if you want to distribute the file as a component to be used in other Flash files.

- **Generate Size Report** creates a text file with information about the amount of data in the final Flash content.

- **Protect from Import** prevents others from importing your SWF file. This option also allows you to protect your SWF file with a password.

- **Omit Trace Options** allows Flash to ignore all the trace options, which are ActionScript functions that trace the results of a movie and display the output from the code in the output panel. (You'll use a Trace function in Project 6.)

- **Permit Debugging** allows you to debug your SWF file and allows other users to debug your SWF file remotely. Selecting this option also allows you to provide password protection for your SWF file; other users will have to enter the password in order to debug the file.

- **Password** is activated if you select the Protect from Import or the Permit Debugging option. You can specify a password that other users must enter in order to import the file or debug the movie.

- **Local Playback Security** options provide security for your application. If you select Access Local Files Only, then your SWF file can interact only on the local machine. If you choose Access Network Only, your SWF file can communicate with resources only on the network and not on the local machine.

- **Hardware Acceleration** options can be used to speed up the graphics performance of the exported movie.

- **Script Time Limit** can be used to define the maximum amount of time allowed for a script to run. If a script takes longer than the specified time, it is cancelled.

HTML Options. When you want to publish a Flash document on the Web, you need an HTML file that will embed your SWF file. The HTML tab (appropriately) includes options Flash uses to publish an HTML file.

- The **Templates** menu contains the various Flash templates in which an HTML file can be published. Selecting a template and then clicking the Info button shows a dialog box with information about the selected template.

- If you select **Detect Flash Version**, you can use the Version fields to define which is required. Flash Player detection code is embedded in the resulting file; when the user opens the HTML file, this code detects whether the particular version is available. If not, a link is provided to download the latest version of the Flash player. (Some templates do not support the Flash detection code.)

- You can specify the maximum dimensions for the published document. The **Match Movie** option uses the size of the SWF file when embedding the SWF file into the HTML file.

- Selecting the **Paused at Start** option keeps the SWF file from being played unless the user clicks a button or selects the Play option from the shortcut menu. By default this option is deselected, and Flash loads the SWF movie as soon as the movie is detected.

- The **Display Menu** option, selected by default, enables a shortcut when the user Control/right-clicks the SWF file in the browser. Deselecting this option shows only About Flash in the shortcut menu.

- The **Loop** option causes the Flash content to repeat after it reaches the final frame, so the movie plays in a continuous loop. This option is selected by default.

- Selecting the **Device Font** option displays users' system fonts instead of the fonts used in the SWF file, if those fonts are unavailable in the user's system.

- **Quality** specifies the quality of the SWF content embedded in the HTML file. Selecting Low loads your SWF file faster in the browser, but reduces the quality of the file. The Auto Low option gives preference to document loading rather than quality, but also tries to improve the quality of the SWF file. The Auto High feature treats loading and quality equally; when the loading speed is reduced, quality is compromised. The remaining three options are self-explanatory. In short — the lower quality you select, the faster the file will load (and vice-versa).

- **Window Mode** sets the value of the wmode attribute in the object and embed HTML tags. The default option (Window) does not embed window-related attributes in the HTML tags; the background of the Flash content is opaque. Opaque Windowless sets the background of the Flash content to opaque, which allows HTML content to appear on top of Flash content. Transparent Windowless sets the background of the Flash content to transparent.

- **HTML Alignment** allows you to realign the Flash content in the browser window. The Default option displays the SWF file in the center of the browser; you can also choose Left, Right, Top, or Bottom.

- **Scale** controls the display of Flash content when you change the dimension of the Flash content in the HTML file. Default (Show All) displays the entire document in the specified area. No Border fits the document in the specified area and maintains the quality of the SWF file by avoiding distortion. Exact Fit fits the entire SWF file in the specified area, but this option compromises the quality of the SWF file. No Scale prevents the Flash content from being scaled in the HTML file.

- **Flash Alignment** allows you to set the horizontal and vertical alignment of Flash content in the HTML file.

- The **Show Warning Messages** option displays all warning and error messages whenever a setting for publishing the content is incorrect.

Project Review

fill in the blank

1. Objects on a _____ layer are not visible in the final file; they are only used to define the visible area of underlying layers.

2. A _____ timeline functions independently of other symbols in the same file.

3. You can check the _____ option to align the bottom edge of an object to a motion path.

4. A(n) _____ is a special layer designed to hold a path along which an object moves.

5. _____ are required when an object needs to change in some way at a given point in time.

6. _____ is simple text that does not change.

7. _____ is essentially a text area that can be populated with the contents of an external file.

8. _____ solves the potential problem of used fonts not being available on a user's computer.

9. You must create the file for _____ to use built-in Flash behaviors.

10. _____ is the default extension for exported file movies.

short answer

1. Briefly explain how a movie clip symbol relates to the primary timeline of a file.

2. Briefly explain the purpose and creation process of a mask.

3. Briefly explain the purpose of the Behaviors panel.

Use what you learned in this project to complete the following freeform exercise.
Carefully read the art director and client comments, then create your own design to meet the needs of the project.
Use the space below to sketch ideas; when finished, write a brief explanation of your reasoning behind your final design.

art director comments

The museum director is very pleased with your work on the solar system animation. He has hired you to create additional video models for other areas of the museum.

To complete this project, you should:

❏ Research the topic you are going to model and determine what (if any) data will be required to create a scientifically accurate illustration.

❏ Create or locate images or graphics that will result in a "kid-friendly" learning experience.

❏ Develop a video model that can be deployed as HTML or as a stand-alone module on both Windows or Macintosh computers.

client comments

We would like you to create a series of videos over the next year (as the grant funds become available). The first one we want is an illustration of gravity. We're not entirely sure how it should look or function. We kind of like the legend of Isaac Newton sitting under an apple tree, when an apple fell on his head. If you could figure out how to make that work, great. If not, we're happy to consider other solutions.

As more funds become available, we're also going to want movies to illustrate other scientific principles. Our current list includes tectonic plate movement, tidal patterns, volcanic eruptions, and friction.

It will be easier to secure the secondary grants for later projects if we can include a specific plan for the different programs. Once you finish the gravity illustration (which we already have the money for), can you sketch out plans for at least two others?

project justification

_____

_____

_____

_____

_____

_____

_____

_____

_____

_____

_____

_____

_____

The ability to control object movement is one of the most important functions in designing complex animations. In this project, you used motion guides to create the solar system orbits. You now know how to move objects in any direction — whether the path is defined artistically or scientifically.

Your solar system model also required two new skills — object masking and creating static text — that will be important in many Flash projects. Object masking allows you to isolate specific areas of an object; areas outside the mask shape will not be visible in the final file. Most pieces will involve some text, even if that text is eventually converted into drawing objects; you now know how to create and format text to communicate the client's message directly within a Flash file.

Managing the 20+ symbols in this solar system model clearly illustrated the importance of organizing complex animation files. When you create a project with more than a few library items, it's best to organize your work in a logical manner, using descriptive names for all assets. Using folders and a logical hierarchy can also be very helpful when you or someone else needs to open and modify a file in the future.

Finally, you learned how to apply built-in behaviors to control objects in a Flash file. If you target ActionScript 2.0, you can use these behaviors to accomplish many common tasks without manually writing a single line of code. This is a tremendous benefit to designers who are more visually oriented and have no programming background.

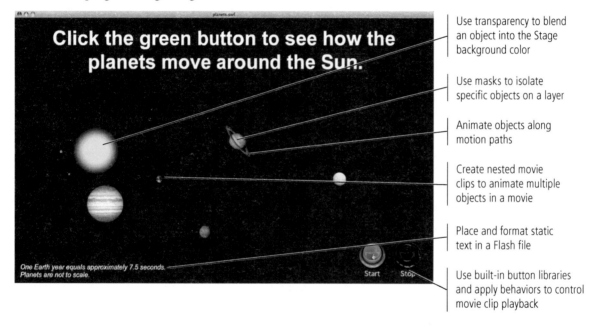

Use transparency to blend an object into the Stage background color

Use masks to isolate specific objects on a layer

Animate objects along motion paths

Create nested movie clips to animate multiple objects in a movie

Place and format static text in a Flash file

Use built-in button libraries and apply behaviors to control movie clip playback

Ocean Animation

Your client, Bay Ocean Preserve, wants to add an interactive animation to the kids' side of its Web site. As part of the Flash development team, your job is to build the required animations, and then add the necessary controls to make the buttons function as expected.

This project incorporates the following skills:

❏ Importing and managing artwork from Adobe Photoshop

❏ Importing symbols from external Flash file libraries

❏ Understanding the different types of Flash symbols

❏ Building frame-by-frame animations

❏ Creating motion tweens to animate various object properties

❏ Creating an animated armature

❏ Animating in three dimensions

❏ Preparing symbol instances for scripting

❏ Adding basic button controls to instances on the Stage

client comments

Our organization focuses on natural resource conservation and habitat preservation on the central California coast. This area is home to a number of endangered species, and we work to educate people about observing those creatures without interacting and interfering with them.

We've been told that some kind of interactivity will be an important part of capturing a younger audience. Although we think cartoon fish dancing across the screen would minimize the seriousness of our message, we understand that we have to do something to make the site more interesting for children.

We were thinking about an "aquarium" screen saver we used to have, and we thought that kind of thing would be a good balance between user interactivity and pointless arcade games.

art director comments

Since the client clearly wants to avoid a cartoon look, I had the staff artist create some fish and other illustrations that are fairly realistic. I also found a good photo of a turtle that will work well with the other elements.

One of the animations — the swaying kelp forest — should play constantly, and will not be controlled by buttons.

Three animations will be controlled by the buttons. First, a fish hiding in a cave will appear and blow bubbles. Second, a turtle will swim across the scene and get bigger, to create the effect of the turtle swimming toward you. Finally, a school of different fish will swim in the other direction, in a "train" across the scene.

One other animation — the organization's logo — will play as soon as the file opens, and then not again until the entire file is reset.

The programming for this isn't very complicated, so you should be able to create it with Flash's built-in Code Snippets.

project objectives

To complete this project, you will:

- ❑ Create symbols from imported Photoshop artwork
- ❑ Import symbols from other Flash files
- ❑ Place and manage instances of symbols on the Stage, and control the visual properties of those symbols
- ❑ Control timing using keyframes
- ❑ Create animated movie clip symbols
- ❑ Generate motion tweens to animate changes in object properties
- ❑ Use the Motion Editor to numerically control properties at specific points in time
- ❑ Animate a bone armature
- ❑ Animate an object in three-dimensional space
- ❑ Add interactivity to button symbols

Stage 1 Importing Bitmaps and Symbols

In this project, much of the artwork was created in Adobe Photoshop — a common workflow for Flash animation projects. It's important to understand that artwork from a Photoshop file is imported into Flash as bitmap objects, which (as you learned in Project 1) are raster images that can result in large file sizes. Fortunately, the Flash symbol infrastructure means that objects in a file's library are downloaded only once; you can use multiple instances of a symbol without increasing overall file size.

You should also keep in mind that the quality of a bitmap object is defined by its resolution. Bitmap objects can typically be reduced in size, but enlarging them much beyond 100% could significantly reduce the image quality.

Finally, it's important to realize that Flash is designed to create files that will be viewed on a digital screen. Flash recognizes the actual number of pixels in a bitmap image rather than the defined pixels per inch (ppi). If you import a 3″ × 3″ bitmap image that is saved at 300 ppi (typical of print-quality images), that image is 900 pixels × 900 pixels high. In Flash, the image is still 900 pixels × 900 pixels, but those pixels occupy 12.5″ at 72 ppi (typical screen resolution).

 ## IMPORT ADOBE PHOTOSHOP ARTWORK

Importing a Photoshop file to the Flash Stage is very similar to importing an Illustrator file. Because of the different nature of the two applications, however, you have fewer options when you work with Photoshop files.

1. **Download FL5_RF_Project4.zip from the Student Files Web page.**

2. **Expand the ZIP archive in your WIP folder (Macintosh) or copy the archive contents into your WIP folder (Windows).**

    This results in a folder named **Aquarium**, which contains the files you need for this project. You should also use this folder to save the files you create in this project.

3. **In Flash, create a new Flash document for ActionScript 3.0.**

4. **Choose File>Save. Save the file in your WIP>Aquarium folder as a Flash file named ocean.fla.**

5. **Open the Flash Preferences dialog box and click PSD File Importer in the list of categories.**

6. **Choose Lossless in the Compression menu and click OK.**

    When you import a Photoshop file, you can define the compression settings for each resulting bitmap object. By default, Flash applies lossy compression, which can create smaller file sizes but can also degrade the quality of resulting images. By changing the setting in the Preferences dialog box, you are changing the default setting that will be applied to all bitmap objects that are created when you import a Photoshop file to the Flash Stage. This means you won't have to change the option for individual objects.

Choose Lossless in this menu.

> *Note:*
>
> *Learn more about Adobe Photoshop in the companion book of this series, **Adobe Photoshop CS5: The Professional Portfolio**.*

> *Note:*
>
> *Preferences are accessed in the Flash menu on Macintosh or the Edit menu on Windows.*

7. **Choose File>Import>Import to Stage. Navigate to the file `ocean.psd` in your WIP>Aquarium folder and click Open/Import.**

8. **In the resulting dialog box, click the first item in the list of Photoshop layers, and then review the options on the right.**

    Flash recognizes individual layers in the native Photoshop file; objects on each individual layer will be imported as separate bitmap objects. For each layer/bitmap object, you can choose to automatically create a movie clip instance from the imported artwork.

Each layer in the Photoshop file will be imported as a separate bitmap object.

Layer groups are recognized, and can be maintained in the imported artwork.

If you select multiple layers in the list, you can merge those layers into a single bitmap object.

Note:

When artwork is created in Photoshop, each object that needs to be managed separately in Flash should be created on a separate Photoshop layer.

Photoshop File Import Preferences

FLASH FOUNDATIONS

You can define the default options for importing native Photoshop files in the PSD File Importer pane of the Preferences dialog box. (Remember, preferences are accessed in the Flash menu on Macintosh and in the Edit menu on Windows.) Most of these options will become clearer as you work through this project and learn more about the different types of symbols. In some cases, the options refer to specific features in the native application.

-   The **Import Image Layers As** options determine whether applied layer styles are editable (if possible) in the Flash file. Photoshop layer styles include drop shadows, beveling, and others.

-   The **Import Text Layers As** options determine how Photoshop text layers are managed. These options are the same as the Import Text As options for importing Illustrator files. The default here, however, is to import Photoshop text layers as flattened bitmap images, which means you can't edit the text or the vector letter shapes.

-   The **Import Shape Layers As** options determine how vector-based shape layers in the Photoshop file import into Flash. If you choose Editable Paths and Layer Styles, vector shapes in the Photoshop file are imported as vector paths; styles applied to the shape layer in Photoshop are imported as styles in the Flash file (if those styles are supported by Flash). If you choose Flattened Bitmap Images, Photoshop shape layers are flattened in Flash, which means you cannot access or edit the vector information within the Flash file.

-   **Layer Groups** and **Merged Bitmaps** in the native Photoshop file can be automatically converted to a single movie clip if these options are checked.

-   **Movie Clip Registration** defines the default registration options for any objects you import as movie clip symbols.

-   **Publish Settings** defines the type of compression applied and the quality of the resulting files.

9. **Click the Cave item in the list of layers and review the options.**

   If a Photoshop file includes a layer group, the group is recognized in the Import dialog box. You can choose to create a single movie clip from the entire layer group, and name the instance that is placed on the stage.

10. **Check the Create Movie Clip for this Layer option. In the Instance Name field, type caue_mc, and choose the bottom-right registration option.**

    If you don't choose this option, the layer group is maintained in the imported artwork as a layer group in the Flash timeline.

The icon shows that this layer group will now be imported as a movie clip instance.

11. **Make sure Flash Layers is selected in the Convert Layers To menu. Check the options to place layers at their original position, and to set the stage size to match the Photoshop canvas.**

    These options have the same general purpose as the similar options when you import a native Illustrator file. (The Photoshop document area is called the canvas; the Illustrator document area is an artboard.)

12. **Click OK to complete the import process, and review the results.**

    If you had not chosen to make a movie clip instance from the layer group, those layers would have been imported as a layer group in the Flash timeline. The default Layer 1 from the original file is maintained at the bottom of the layer stack.

The symbol registration point indicates that this object is an instance of a movie clip symbol.

Because you created a movie clip instance from the layer group, only one layer is created to contain the instance.

Each resulting bitmap exists inside a folder that is named based on the imported Photoshop file.

Objects from the Cave layer group are nested in a folder that is named based on the layer group name.

13. **Delete Layer 1, then save the file and continue to the next exercise.**

When objects already exist in a Flash file, it is a fairly simple process to copy them from one file to another. If both files are open, you can simply copy a symbol instance from the Stage of one file and paste it into the Stage of the other file; the necessary assets are automatically pasted into the library of the second file. You can also simply open the Library panel of an external file, which enables you to access the assets in that library without opening the second file's Stage.

1. **With ocean.fla open, choose File>Open. Navigate to creatures.fla (in the WIP>Aquarium folder) and click Open.**

   When more than one file is open, each file is represented by a tab at the top of the document window. You can click any document tab to make that file active.

2. **In the Library panel, Shift-click to select the Fish1, Fish2, and Turtle items in the library. Control/right-click one of the selected items and choose Copy from the contextual menu.**

The document tabs show there are two open files.

The Library panel shows the library for the currently active file.

3. **Click the Library menu at the top of the Library panel and choose ocean.fla to display that file's library.**

Use this menu to switch between the libraries of all open files.

4. **Control/right-click the empty area at the bottom of the Library panel (below the existing assets) and choose Paste from the contextual menu.**

   The Air bitmap item is also pasted because it is used in the Fish2 movie clip.

Although creatures.fla is active, the Library panel now shows the library of the ocean.fla file.

5. Click the Close button on the creatures.fla document tab to close that file.

None of the pasted symbols is added to the Stage; they are only placed in the ocean.fla file's library.

The three selected items from the creatures file are pasted into the ocean.fla library.

The Air bitmap, which is used in the Fish2 movie clip symbol, is also pasted into the ocean.fla library.

6. With `ocean.fla` still open, choose File>Import>Open External Library.

7. Select `buttons.fla` (in the WIP>Aquarium folder) and click Open.

You can use this option to open the library of another file without opening the external FLA file. The external library opens as a separate panel; the file name is included in the panel tab.

Note:

The keyboard command for opening an external library is Command/ Control-Shift-O.

8. Shift-click the Reset, Showcave, Showfish, and Showturtle button symbols.

9. Click any of the selected items and drag to the ocean.fla Library panel.

The files don't disappear from the external library; they're simply duplicated in the ocean.fla Library panel. The Starfish bitmap object is also copied because it is used in the four button symbols.

The external library opens in a separate panel.

The cursor icon shows that you're dragging to copy assets from one library into another.

10. Click the Close button of the buttons.fla Library panel to close the external file's library.

Only one instance of the starfish bitmap is copied into the ocean.fla library, even though all four buttons use the same image.

11. Save the ocean.fla file and continue to the next exercise.

ALIGN OBJECTS ON THE STAGE

The four buttons for this project need to be placed across the bottom of the Stage, aligned to appear equally distributed across the Stage area. The Align panel makes it very easy to position multiple selected objects relative to one another.

1. **With `ocean.fla` open, select the Buttons layer to make it active.**

2. **Drag instances of the four button symbols to the middle of the Stage, arranged so they do not overlap.**

3. **Select the placed Showfish button instance. Using the Properties panel, position the instance at X: 20, Y: 510.**

Place the symbols (from left to right) Showfish, Showturtle, Showcave, and Reset across the Stage.

Use the Properties panel to position the Showfish button instance.

4. **Using the Selection tool, Shift-click to select all four button instances on the Stage.**

5. **In the Align panel, turn off the Align To Stage check option and then click the Align Bottom Edge button.**

   The Align options position objects based on the selected edge. Because you used the Align Bottom Edge button, the selected objects are all moved to the bottom edge of the bottommost object in the selection.

Align Bottom Edge button

Align To Stage should not be checked.

The selected objects move to align with the bottom edge of the bottommost selected object.

6. **Select only the Reset button and set the X position to 605.**

7. **Select the four placed button instances.**

8. **In the Align panel, click the Space Evenly Horizontally button.**

   This option calculates the overall space across the selection, then shifts the objects so the same amount of space appears between each object in the selection. Because the buttons are different widths, this option creates a better result than the distribution options.

   Space Evenly Horizontally button

   The middle objects are moved to create equal space between all objects in the selection.

9. **Save the file and continue to the next exercise.**

 ## TRANSFORM SYMBOLS AND INSTANCES

Placed instances of a symbol are unique objects, which means they can be manipulated separately without affecting other instances of the symbol. Each instance remains linked to the primary symbol, however, so transforming the actual symbol affects all placed instances of that symbol.

1. **With ocean.fla open, Control/right-click the Kelp object on the Stage and choose Convert to Symbol from the contextual menu.**

   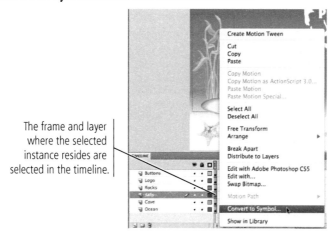

   The frame and layer where the selected instance resides are selected in the timeline.

2. **In the resulting dialog box, type Seaweed in the Name field and choose Movie Clip in the Type menu. Choose the bottom-center registration point and click OK.**

The Properties panel now shows that the selected object is an instance of the Seaweed symbol, which has been added to the Library panel.

Because you defined bottom-center registration, measurements are based on the bottom-center handle of the instance (hidden by the rock bitmap).

There's the new symbol.

3. **Using the Selection tool, Option/Alt-click the existing instance and drag right to clone a second instance of the Seaweed symbol.**

4. **Repeat Step 3 to clone one more instance.**

5. **Deselect everything on the Stage. Choose the Free Transform tool in the Tools panel and click the middle Seaweed instance to select it.**

   The Free Transform tool is used to change the size or shape of an object. Remember, all transformations are applied around the transformation registration point.

Note:

If the Free Transform tool is active when you click and drag to move an object, make sure you don't click the object's transformation registration point before you drag the object.

Free Transform tool

Transformation registration point

6. **Drag the transformation registration point until it snaps to the bottom-center bounding box handle.**

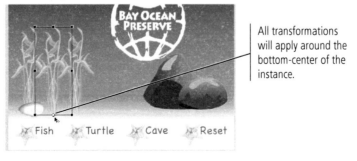

All transformations will apply around the bottom-center of the instance.

7. **Click the top-center bounding box handle and drag down to make the selected instance shorter.**

Transformations applied to individual instances have no effect on the original symbol or on other placed instances.

Because the bottom-center is the transformation registration point, dragging the top-center handle makes the instance shorter, but does not move the bottom of the instance.

Understanding Transformation Options

FLASH FOUNDATIONS

The Transform Panel

At times, you might need to apply very specific numeric transformations, such as scaling an object by a specific percentage. Rather than manually calculating new dimensions and defining the new dimensions in the Properties panel, you can use the Transform panel (Window>Transform) to make this type of change.

Reset

Constrain

Duplicate Selection and Transform

Remove Transform

When you change a value in the Transform panel, press Return/Enter to apply the change, or click the Duplicate Selection and Transform button to make a copy of the object and apply the change to the copy instead of the original.

When you transform objects in Flash (either numerically or in Free Transform mode), Flash remembers the original properties of the object. You can restore the original settings by clicking the Remove Transform button at the bottom.

The Modify>Transform Submenu

The Modify>Transform submenu hosts a number of valuable options for transforming objects.

Free Transform displays a set of eight bounding box handles, which you can drag horizontally or vertically to scale, stretch, skew, and rotate an object. During a free transform, an object's overall shape is maintained (an oval remains an oval, a square remains a square, and so on).

Distort displays a set of eight bounding box handles. If you drag one of the corner handles, you can "stretch" the object out of its original shape. For example, you can drag one corner of a rectangle to create a polygon with odd angles.

Scale and Rotate opens a dialog box where you can define specific, numeric scale percentages or rotation. You can also use the **Rotate 90°** (Clockwise and Counterclockwise) options for a selected object.

Envelope adds control handles to the object's anchor points, which you can use to warp the shape. You can drag the handles to reshape the connecting curves, and/or drag the anchor points to new positions to create an entirely different shape than the original.

Anchor point

Handle

Scale is a subset of Free Transform. You can see the eight bounding box handles, but you can only scale or stretch the object; you can't rotate or skew it.

Rotate and Skew are also subsets of Free Transform. You can see the eight bounding box handles, but you can only skew or rotate the object; you can't scale or stretch it.

Flip Horizontal or **Flip Vertical** options allow you to flip objects on either axis.

Even though you can transform objects, Flash remembers the object's original size and shape. You can remove any transformation — except envelope distortion — using the **Remove Transform** option. To remove an envelope distortion, you have to choose Modify>Combine Objects>Delete Envelope.

Project 4: Ocean Animation   175

8. **In the Library panel, double-click the Seaweed symbol icon to enter into the symbol Stage.**

The crosshairs identify the **symbol registration point**, or the location of X:0, Y:0 for placed instances; all measurements for placed instances begin at this location.

Even though you changed the transformation registration point of the placed instance on the main Stage, the registration point is in the center on the symbol Stage. The transformation registration point is specific to each placed object or instance.

The Edit bar shows you are now working on the Seaweed symbol Stage.

The transformation registration point is particular to each instance of an object or symbol.

The symbol registration point appears on the symbol Stage.

9. **With the Free Transform tool still selected, drag the transformation registration point until it snaps to the bottom-center bounding box handle of the object on the Stage.**

10. **Show the Transform panel (Window>Transform).**

The Transform panel can be used to make precise numerical changes, or simply to monitor the changes you make with the Free Transform tool.

11. **In the Transform panel, make sure the Link icon is not active and then change the Scale Height value to 80%.**

If the Link icon shows two solid chain links, changing the height of an object would proportionally affect the width of the object (and vice versa). Because you only want to change the height, you need to break the Link icon.

Scale Width

Scale Height

When this icon shows a broken link, you can change the width and height independently.

The transformation applies around the transformation registration point.

12. In the Edit bar, click Scene 1 to return to the main Stage.

When you modify the original symbol, the changes ripple through all placed instances.

Editing the actual symbol affects all three placed instances on the Stage.

The instance you resized on the main Stage is still proportionally sized.

13. Save the file and continue to the next exercise.

 ## WORK WITH LAYERS IN AN IMPORTED MOVIE CLIP SYMBOL

When you imported the project artwork, the two pieces of the cave were created on separate layers — in a layer group — because you need to place a fish inside the cave, stacked between the two boulders. If the two boulders had existed on a single layer, the result would have been a single bitmap object, which could not be broken apart in Flash to accomplish the desired effect.

1. With `ocean.fla` open, use the Selection tool to click the Cave movie clip instance on the Stage.

2. In the Properties panel, change the X position of the instance to 850.

If the cave objects had been placed in the correct position in the Photoshop file, the imported bitmap objects would have been clipped at the Stage edge. If you create artwork in Photoshop, make sure pieces are entirely inside the Canvas edge if you don't want them clipped when they are imported into Flash.

Note:

Remember, the symbol registration point marks the location of the defined X and Y values on the main Stage.

Because you defined the bottom-right corner as the symbol's registration point, that point is positioned at X: 850.

3. Double-click the Cave movie clip instance on the Stage to edit the symbol in place on the Stage.

Because this movie clip (and instance) was created based on a layer group in the imported artwork, the layers that made up the group are maintained in the symbol timeline.

These are the two layers that made up the layer group in the original Photoshop file.

4. **Change the name of Layer 1 to Fish.**

5. **Drag an instance of the Fish2 movie clip symbol onto the Stage, near the existing cave pieces.**

   Because the Fish layer is below the two Boulder layers, the Fish2 instance should be at least partially hidden by the two pieces of the cave.

6. **In the Timeline panel, drag the Fish layer above the Boulder 1 layer.**

   The Fish2 instance is now between the two pieces of the cave.

7. **Drag the Fish2 instance so only the head appears to the left of the front rock.**

   In the second stage of this project, you will learn a number of techniques for creating animations — including making this fish blow bubbles that rise up and off the Stage.

8. **Click Scene 1 in the Edit bar to return to the main Stage.**

9. **Save the file and continue to the next exercise.**

 ## USE THE SPRAY BRUSH

Although you could simply place multiple instances of the Rock bitmap without converting it to a formal symbol, you can use the Spray Brush tool to quickly and easily add numerous instances of the object.

1. **With ocean.fla open, click the Rock bitmap on the Stage to select it.**

2. **In the Transform panel, make sure the Link icon at the top of the panel is solid.**

   When this icon appears as two connected chain links, the object's width and height are constrained to maintain equal proportions. If this icon is a broken chain, you can change one value without affecting the other.

3. **Place the mouse cursor over the Scale Width value and drag left until the W value is 35%.**

   This technique is called **scrubbing**; you can use it to change any hot-text value in the application interface.

Click over hot text and drag left or right to dynamically change the value.

4. **Control/right-click the rock (on the Stage) and choose Convert to Symbol.**

5. **In the resulting dialog box, type Gravel in the Name field. Choose Graphic in the Type menu, select the center registration point, and click OK.**

   You are going to create many instances of this symbol as decoration on the Stage. Because you don't need to address the instances with script, you don't need to name the instances. You also don't need to animate anything inside the Gravel symbol, so the Graphic type is appropriate.

6. **Choose the Spray Brush tool (nested under the Brush tool) in the Tools panel.**

Use the Properties panel to define what will be sprayed and how it will spray.

Spray Brush tool

Spray Brush tool cursor

7. **In the Properties panel, click the Edit button in the Symbol area. Choose Gravel in the resulting dialog box, and then click OK.**

8. **Check the Random Scaling, Rotate Symbol, and Random Rotation options. Change the Brush Width and Height values to 75 pixels.**

9. **In the timeline, make sure the Rocks layer is active. Zoom out so you can see the entire Stage, and some of the surrounding area on the left and right.**

10. **Click the left edge of the Stage over the brown area of the gradient. Hold down the mouse button and drag slowly to the right across the entire Stage.**

   The dozens (or even hundreds, depending on how you dragged) of instances do not increase the file size because the symbol needs to download only once.

Note:

When you spray with the Spray Brush tool, one mouse click creates a single group.

As you learned in Project 1, you have to enter into the group (double-click) to access the individual instances.

Using the Random Scaling, Rotate Symbol, and Random Rotation options, you used a single symbol to create a field of ocean rocks.

Because the Buttons layer is higher than the Rocks layer, the bottom edges of the sprayed instances are hidden.

Each time you click and drag with the Spray Brush tool, the resulting instances are grouped. If you click again to add more rocks, you will have more than one group of rock instances.

11. **Save the file and continue to the next exercise.**

ORGANIZE YOUR LIBRARY WITH FOLDERS

As you saw in Project 3, folders make it easy to organize the assets that make up a movie, and easy to find the assets you need.

1. **With ocean.fla open, click the Library panel to activate it.**

2. **In the Library panel, change the name of the ocean.psd Assets folder to Bitmaps.**

   Changing a library folder name has no effect on placed instances of the symbols inside that folder.

3. **Select the two bitmap objects in the nested Cave folder and move them into the first-level Bitmaps folder.**

   Moving symbols to a new location in the Library panel has no effect on placed instances of the moved symbols.

4. **Select the three bitmap objects in the first level of the library and drag them into the Bitmaps folder.**

5. **Drag the nested Cave folder from the Bitmaps folder to the main level of the Library panel.**

6. **Change the Cave folder name to Movie Clips, then drag the three movie clip symbols from the main level of the Library into the Movie Clips folder.**

Drag the nested folder to the empty area at the bottom of the panel to move it to the first level of the library.

Note:

In this case, we're using simple names for the symbol folders. The names you assign to symbol (or layer) folders aren't functional; they just need to make sense to you (or other people working with your files).

7. **Create a new folder named Buttons at the first level of the library. Drag the four button symbols into the new folder.**

   New folders are created at the same nesting level as the current selection. To create a new folder at the first level of the library, click the empty area at the bottom of the panel to deselect any files before clicking the New Folder button.

8. Create another new folder named Graphics at the main level of the Library folder. Drag the one remaining graphic symbol into the folder.

9. Save the file and continue to the next stage of the project.

Stage 2 Animating Symbols

In Project 2, you created simple animation by swapping symbols at specific points in time; although nothing technically changed position, replacing one object with another is still considered "animation." In Project 3, you used classic tweening to move objects along a path; this technique creates smooth motion by defining the start point keyframe, end point keyframe, and path shape. In this project, you learn several different techniques for creating various types of animation, including animating specific properties of an object.

 ## CREATE A BASIC FRAME ANIMATION IN A MOVIE CLIP SYMBOL

Movie clips are animated symbols that reside on a single frame of the timeline. In its simplest form, a movie clip can include a solitary fish swimming across the ocean; at its most complex, a movie clip can include fully interactive elements in a video game. In this exercise, you create the most basic type of animation — a frame animation.

1. With **ocean.fla** open, make sure nothing is selected on the Stage.

2. In the Properties panel, change the FPS hot text to 15 frames per second.

    Using 15 fps for a movie — especially one that's going to run on the Web — provides decent quality. The default 24 fps is not necessary for standard computer viewing, and could create large files that take too long for many users to download.

Set this value to 15 FPS.

3. On the Stage, double-click the Cave symbol instance to enter into the symbol Stage (edit in place).

4. **Double-click the placed Fish2 instance to enter into the nested symbol. Click away from the selected objects, and then select only the air bubbles.**

When you first enter into a symbol, all objects in the symbol are automatically selected. You are going to move only the bubbles, which are an instance of the Air bitmap object that is placed inside the Fish2 symbol. You are editing in place on the main Stage so you can see when the bubbles are entirely outside the Stage area.

5. **In the timeline, Control/right-click Frame 7 of the default Layer 1. Choose Insert Keyframe from the contextual menu.**

As you already know, **keyframes** are special frames where something happens to an object: it appears or disappears, changes size, moves to another position, changes color, and so on. When you add a new keyframe, a regular frame is automatically added immediately before the previous keyframe; objects on the preceding keyframe will remain in place until the playhead reaches the new keyframe.

6. **With Frame 7 selected in the timeline, deselect the fish graphic, and then reposition the air bubbles graphic directly above the original position.**

When you select a keyframe, all objects on that keyframe are automatically selected (just as when you first enter into the symbol). You can Shift-click the fish instance to deselect that object, leaving only the air bubbles object selected.

Note:

If you change an object on a regular frame in the middle of a movie, all frames between the two surrounding keyframes (or the nearest preceding keyframe and the final frame) reflect that change.

You are working on the Fish2 symbol, which is nested inside the Cave symbol.

With the Frame 7 keyframe active, move the bubbles up from their previous position.

When you add a keyframe, a regular frame is automatically added directly before it.

7. **Repeat Steps 5–6 six more times, adding a new keyframe every seven frames and moving the air bubbles up until they are outside the top edge of the Stage.**

Because you're editing the symbol in place, you can see how far you need to move the bubbles until they are outside the Stage area. If you edited this symbol on its own Stage, you would have to guess about positioning, return to the main Stage to test your guess, return to the symbol to add more frames, return to the main Stage to test again, and so on.

At Frame 49, the bubbles are entirely off the Stage.

8. **Select Frame 56 on the timeline and press F5 to add a regular frame.**

   This regular frame at Frame 56 extends the timeline by half a second, which prevents the bubbles from reappearing in the fish's mouth (Frame 1) immediately after they move past the top of the Stage (Frame 49).

9. **Click the playhead above the timeline and drag left and right.**

   Scrubbing the playhead allows you to look at specific sections of a movie over time so you can see if they work the way you expect.

10. **Click Scene 1 in the Edit bar to return to the main Stage.**

11. **Press Return/Enter to play the current timeline on the Stage.**

    When you test the movie, nothing seems to happen because there is only one frame on the main timeline.

You are now on the main Stage.

The main timeline has only one frame, so the playhead has nowhere to go.

12. **Press Command-Return/Control-Enter to test the movie.**

    You can see the air bubbles moving up in a continuous loop. Even though the primary Stage has only one frame, the movie clip's timeline continues to play as long as the movie remains open.

The animation plays in the Flash Player window.

13. **Close the Flash Player window and return to Flash.**

14. **Save the file and continue to the next exercise.**

CREATE AN OBJECT-BASED ANIMATION

You might have noticed that the frame-by-frame animation you just created is rather choppy. Although this can be the effect you want, there are also times when you want smooth, continuous movement. Rather than defining each individual frame manually — which could take days, depending on the length of your animation — you can let Flash define the frames that are in between two keyframes (called tween frames).

Flash CS5 incorporates technology that makes it very easy to define smooth animations by simply moving a symbol object around on the Stage.

1. **With ocean.fla open, create a new layer named Turtle immediately above the Logo layer. Select the Turtle layer as the active layer.**

2. **Drag an instance of the turtle bitmap image from the Library panel onto the Stage. Use the Transform panel to scale the instance to 50%, and then position it beyond the right edge of the Stage, higher than the Cave instance.**

3. **Control/right-click the turtle instance and choose Convert to Symbol from the contextual menu.**

4. **In the resulting dialog box, type Swimmer in the Name field, choose Movie Clip in the Type menu, and choose the center registration point.**

5. **Click the Folder link. Select the Existing Folder radio button and choose movie clips in the list. Click Select to return to the Convert to Symbol dialog box, and then click OK to create the new symbol.**

6. **Click Frame 90 on the Turtle layer and press F5 to add a new regular frame.**

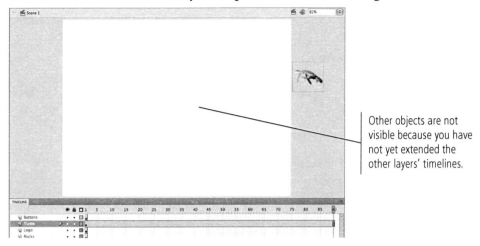

Other objects are not visible because you have not yet extended the other layers' timelines.

7. **Control/right-click any frame on the Turtle layer and choose Create Motion Tween.**

Control/right-click anywhere on the timeline between keyframes to add a motion tween between keyframes (or between a keyframe and the final frame on that layer).

Note:

We enlarged our workspace by collapsing docked panels to icons so we could see the entire Stage and all 90 frames in the timeline.

8. **Click Frame 90 to select that frame.**

   Flash creates a motion tween in the frames between keyframes. Because Frame 1 is the only keyframe on this layer, the motion tween is created between Frame 1 and the last frame on the layer.

9. **Select the Turtle image located at the right of the Stage, and drag it off the left edge of the Stage.**

   Because Frame 90 is within the range of the motion path, a new keyframe is automatically added on Frame 90 to mark the new position of the Swimmer symbol. A line — the motion path — shows the path of movement from the symbol's position on Frame 1 to its position on Frame 90. The small dots along the motion path correspond to the frames within the tween.

Note:

The motion path line corresponds to the color of the layer containing the path.

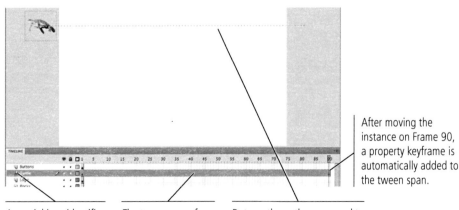

After moving the instance on Frame 90, a property keyframe is automatically added to the tween span.

A special icon identifies motion path layers.   The tween spans from Frame 1 to Frame 90.   Dots on the path correspond to individual frames in the tween.

10. **Click Frame 1 to move the playhead back to the beginning of the timeline, and then press Return/Enter to play the timeline on the Stage.**

The turtle moves across the Stage as the playhead progresses.

11. **Select Frame 90, then click the turtle instance to select it. Scale the selected instance to 200% of its current size. If necessary, reposition the resized turtle so it is entirely outside the edge of the Stage.**

The term "motion path" is deceptive because you can animate much more than just motion when you apply a motion tween. By scaling the object on Frame 90, you told Flash to change both the symbol size and position as the timeline progresses.

Note:

Because you scaled the object to 50% before you created the Swimmer symbol, resizing this instance to 200% restores the bitmap to its original size.

12. **Return the playhead to Frame 1, and then press Return/Enter to play the timeline on the Stage.**

Now the turtle gets larger as it moves across the stage, creating the effect of the turtle swimming closer. Flash automatically calculates the appropriate position and size of the symbol for all frames between the Frame 1 and Frame 90 keyframes.

Using a motion tween, only two keyframes are required to smoothly move and resize the symbol instance.

13. **Save the file and continue to the next exercise.**

Using Onion Skins

Onion skinning, accessed through a set of buttons at the bottom of the timeline, is a technique that allows you to view more than one frame of an animation at a time.

- Clicking the **Onion Skin** button toggles the feature on or off.

- Clicking the **Onion Skin Outlines** button turns all visible skins to outlines (or wire frames). Combining outlines and onion skins allows you to clearly see the components of your animations without fills or (true-weight) strokes.

- Clicking the **Edit Multiple Frames** button allows you to edit multiple frames at the same time: moving an entire animation, for example, or simply changing single frames within a tween. Without this feature, you would have to move objects one frame at a time. With the feature, you can see previous or subsequent frames, which often helps when you're fine-tuning an animation and you need to move an object in one frame relative to its position in other frames.

- Clicking the **Modify Onion Markers** button allows you to select from a range of predefined skins, or turn onion skinning off. You can choose to have onion skins span two frames, five frames, or ten frames. You can also manually adjust the onion skin markers and bypass these presets.

The following illustrations show a simple motion tween that moves the circle symbol across the Stage, from left to right.

Onion Skin   Onion Skin Outlines   Edit Multiple Frames   Modify Onion Markers

When the Onion Skin feature is active, you can see multiple frames at once (around the playhead).

These markers show the range of frames that is visible on the Stage.

Click the Modify Onion Markers button to show predefined skinning options.

When Onion Skin Outlines is active, frames within the visible onion skin display as wireframes.

Click an onion skin marker and drag to manually change the number of visible frames.

EDIT THE SHAPE OF THE MOTION PATH

As you learned in the previous exercise, moving an object and changing its size (or other properties) can be as simple as creating a motion tween and adjusting the symbol at specific frames on the timeline. You don't need to manually create keyframes because Flash adds them for you whenever you change the symbol at a particular point in the timeline. In this exercise, you work with the motion path line, which can be edited like any other line in Flash — giving you precise control over the course of a tween.

1. **With ocean.fla open, click the Swimmer symbol on the Stage to select it and reveal the related motion path.**

2. **Move the Selection tool cursor near the center of the motion path until you see a curved line in the cursor icon. Click near the path and drag up to bend the motion path.**

Bending the path shape with the Selection tool has no effect on the timeline.

3. **Return the playhead to Frame 1 on the timeline, and then press Return/Enter to play the timeline.**

   The turtle now follows the new shape of the motion path.

4. **Click Frame 45 of the Turtle layer to select that frame. Using the Selection tool, click the Swimmer symbol instance and drag down.**

   Flash automatically adds another keyframe to the motion tween, and the motion path bends again to reflect the defined position for the turtle at the selected frame. Flash adds an anchor point to the path at the new keyframe.

Moving the object affects the shape of the path by adding a new position keyframe to the timeline.

5. **Choose the Subselection tool in the Tools panel, and then click the new anchor point in the middle of the path.**

   Remember from Project 1 that the Selection tool selects entire paths. The Subselection tool selects the anchor points and handles that make up a shape.

Controlling Animation Speed with Easing

Physical objects are subject to physical laws; in the real world, friction, momentum, and mass (among other things) affect how an object moves. A bouncing ball is a good example of these laws. If you throw a ball at the ground, how hard you throw the ball determines its beginning speed. When the ball hits the ground, it transfers energy to the ground and then rebounds, causing the ball to move away from the ground (its first bounce), at which point it is moving slightly faster than when you threw it. As the ball arcs through the bounce it slows down, then starts to drop and hits the ground again, repeating the process in ever-decreasing arcs until it finally gives up its energy and then stops. The speed of the ball changes when the energy behind the ball changes.

In animation terms, these changes in speed are called **easing**. In Flash, you can control easing in the Properties panel when a tween is selected in the timeline.

- Positive Ease values decrease the distance of movement on subsequent frames, causing the object to slow down as it moves through the tween.

- Negative Ease values increase the distance of movement on subsequent frames, causing a moving object to speed up through the tween.

- Ease values closer to 100 or −100 result in greater apparent changes in speed.

The accompanying illustrations show a simple 50-frame motion tween that moves a circle symbol across the Stage.

We turned on onion skins for all frames to show the posiiton of the symbol at each frame in the tween.

We clicked inside the tween span to select the motion tween.

The Properties panel shows options related to the selected tween.

By increasing the Ease value, the object moves farther on early frames than on later frames.

This creates the effect of the object slowing down over the course of the animation.

The Properties panel shows the positive Ease value as "out" — it slows down.

By decreasing the Ease value, the object moves farther on later frames than on early frames.

This creates the effect of the object speeding up over the course of the animation.

The Properties panel shows the negative Ease value as "in" — it speeds up.

6. Click the selected anchor point and drag left.

Moving the anchor point changes the shape of the motion path, just as it does when you edit a regular Bézier curve. You can also adjust the handles of the point to change the shape of the motion path between the two connecting anchor points (the selected point and the point at the left end of the path).

When you change the position of the anchor point, notice that the number of dots (representing frames in the tween) on either side of the point remains unchanged. Because you effectively shortened the left half of the path, the same number of frames display over a shorter distance than the same number of frames to the right of the selected point. In effect, you made the turtle swim faster in the first half of the animation (moving a longer distance) and slower in the second half (moving a shorter distance).

Note:

You can use the Convert Anchor Point tool to convert a smooth anchor point on a motion path to a corner anchor point, allowing you to change directions in the tween.

Note:

By default, motion paths are created with a non-roving keyframe property, which means the anchor points along the path are attached to specific keyframes in the timeline.

Frames to the left of the repositioned keyframe are closely spaced. | The keyframe still exists on Frame 45. | Frames to the right of the repositioned keyframe are more widely spaced.

7. Control/right-click anywhere within the motion tween (in the timeline), and choose Motion Path>Switch Keyframes to Roving in the contextual menu.

When you choose this option, the dots along the path redistribute to equal spacing across the entire length of the tween, and the keyframe from Frame 45 is removed from the layer timeline. The shape of the path is not affected.

Note:

If you convert keyframes to roving, frames are redistributed along the entire span of the tween. If you then convert the frames back to non-roving, the location of keyframes added to the tween is determined by the location of anchor points on the path.

A roving-property keyframe is not attached to any particular frame in the tween. This type of keyframe allows you to create a custom-shaped motion path with consistent speed throughout the tween.

After choosing the Roving option, the frames along the path are redistributed to be equally spaced across the entire path.

The property keyframe is removed from the timeline.

8. Save the file and continue to the next exercise.

Motion Tween Properties and Presets

In Flash CS5, the motion path includes all information for the animation, including the length of the animation and specific object properties at various points along the path. A motion path is actually a specific type of object rather than simply a guide; the Properties panel shows a number of options that relate to the selected motion path.

Because a motion path is an actual object, you can attach any symbol to the path by simply dragging a new symbol onto the Stage when the motion path layer is selected.

Use this field to define a name for the motion path instance.

Use Ease values to speed up or slow down an animation over time.

Use this option to rotate a symbol X number of times as it moves along the motion path.

Check this option to rotate the object so its bottom edge follows the contour of the path.

Use these options to change the position and size of the overall path.

Check this option to synchronize the number of frames in a tween within a graphic symbol to match the number of frames on the timeline where the graphic symbol is placed.

We dragged the Fish 3 symbol onto the Stage while the motion path layer was active.

A warning asks if you want to replace the current symbol on the selected motion path.

After clicking OK in the warning, the Fish 3 symbol follows the same motion path.

A special icon identifies a motion path layer.

Flash includes a number of predefined motion presets (Window>Motion Presets), which you can use to add common animations to your files. You can also save your own motion presets by Control/right-clicking an existing motion path and choosing Save as Motion Preset from the contextual menu. (User-defined presets are stored and accessed in a Custom folder in the Motion Presets panel. Custom presets do not include previews.)

COPY AND PASTE FRAMES

Your turtle currently swims from right to left across the Stage. When the animation loops, however, it would seem to miraculously jump back to the right and swim across again. For a more realistic effect, you are going to make a copy of the motion path animation and reverse it so the turtle swims back across the Stage before the animation loops.

1. **With ocean.fla open, Control/right-click anywhere in the Turtle layer motion tween and choose Copy Frames from the contextual menu.**

   You could also use the options in the Edit>Timeline submenu, but the standard Edit menu commands (and the related keyboard shortcuts) do not work when you want to copy or paste frames in the timeline.

2. **Control/right-click Frame 95 of the Turtle layer and choose Paste Frames.**

   Note:

   You are allowing five extra frames between the time the turtle leaves and then re-enters the Stage area (ostensibly enough time for it to turn around before it swims back).

   You pasted an exact copy of the selected frames (the motion tween) — including the position of the symbol at various keyframes. In other words, the turtle is on the right at Frame 95 and on the left at Frame 184 (the end of the pasted animation).

Creating and Controlling Shape Tweens

In addition to changing object properties in a motion tween, you can also create a **shape tween** to change one shape into another over time. Unlike motion tweens, which do not require a second bounding keyframe, a shape tween requires two existing keyframes — one with the starting shape and one with the ending shape.

If you Control/right-click between two keyframes, choosing Create Shape Tween generates the shape tween; the tween frames automatically change the shape of the object as necessary to convert Shape A into Shape B. The following illustrations show a simple shape tween that changes a blue square into a green circle.

The blue square exists on the Frame 1 keyframe.

The green circle exists on the Frame 50 keyframe.

Control/right-click between the two keyframes and choose Create Shape Tween.

Because the two keyframe objects are different colors, the tween also calculates the required change in color for each frame.

Playing the animation shows the object twisting from a square to a circle.

The shape tween frames (between keyframes) are highlighted in green.

In many cases, shape tweens don't work exactly as expected. In the previous examples, the shape tween animation twists the square shape over time into the circle shape. If you want the square corners to simply move without twisting (for example), you can use **shape hinting** to control the change that occurs in a shape tween.

Choosing Modify>Shape>Add Shape Hint places a shape hint in the center of the selected object.

We added three more shape hints and dragged one to each corner.

When you select the next keyframe in the tween, the shape hints from the previous keyframe are already in place in the middle of the object.

We dragged the four shape hints to the outside edges of the circle on Frame 50.

Letters on each shape hint correspond to the letters of shape hints on the first keyframe object.

Flash adjusts the shape tween to move the same-lettered shape hints from their positions on the first keyframe object to their positions on the second keyframe object.

3. **Control/right-click anywhere between Frame 95 and Frame 184 and choose Reverse Keyframes.**

Reversing the keyframes moves the turtle to the left at Frame 95 and the right at Frame 184.

4. **Select the Frame 95 keyframe in the timeline. Click the turtle instance with the Selection tool, then choose Modify>Transform>Flip Horizontal.**

For the turtle to realistically swim back across the Stage, you have to flip the symbol instance to face in the correct direction.

5. **Click Frame 184 to make that the active frame. With the turtle on the Frame 184 keyframe selected, choose Modify>Transform>Flip Horizontal again.**

The turtle now faces to the right throughout the entire second half of the animation.

6. **Add new regular frames to Frame 184 of the remaining layers on the timeline.**

Remember, you have to manually extend each layer so they will exist throughout the length of the entire animation.

7. Click Frame 1 to reposition the playhead, then press Return/Enter to play the movie on the Stage.

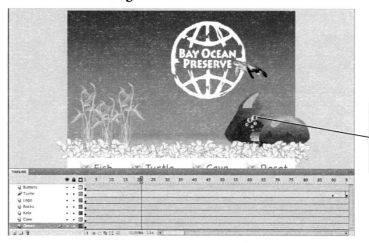

The air bubbles in the Cave movie clip instance do not move because that animation exists only inside the movie clip timeline.

8. Press Command-Return/Control-Enter to test the movie in Flash Player.

Both animations — the swimming turtle and the moving air bubbles — now play.

9. Close the Flash Player window and return to Flash.

10. Save the file and continue to the next exercise.

USE THE MOTION EDITOR

In addition to making changes on the Stage, you can also use the Motion Editor panel to define specific changes to specific properties at specific points in time. In this exercise, you use the Motion Editor to animate the seaweed with a tween that creates the effect of a smooth, swaying motion.

1. With **ocean.fla** open, double-click the Seaweed symbol icon in the Library panel to enter into the symbol Stage.

2. In the timeline, select Frame 40 and press F5 to insert a new regular frame.

You can also Control/right-click the frame and choose Insert Frame from the contextual menu.

3. **Control/right-click anywhere between Frame 1 and Frame 40 and choose Create Motion Tween.**

4. **Read the resulting message.**

   Motion tweens only work with symbol instances. As you see in the warning dialog box, Flash can automatically convert the placed bitmap instance to a movie clip symbol.

5. **Click OK in the message to create a symbol from the selected object.**

   You are not creating this tween on the main Stage because you want the animation to loop continuously regardless of the position of the playhead on the main timeline. Even though you are already inside of a symbol, you need to create a nested symbol structure for the motion tween to work properly.

6. **In the Library panel, change the name of Symbol 1 to Seaweed Sway, and then move the symbol into the Movie Clips folder.**

The selection is now an instance of the new Seaweed Sway movie clip.

There's the new (renamed) symbol.

7. **Choose the Free Transform tool in the Tools panel. Select the object on the Stage, and drag the transformation registration point to the bottom-center handle.**

8. **Open the Motion Editor panel (Window>Motion Editor). If it is grouped with the Timeline panel, click the Motion Editor tab and drag it away from the group so you can see both panels at once.**

The Motion Editor Panel in Depth

The Motion Editor panel can control any property that can be animated on a motion path. All available properties are listed in the left side of the panel. The right side shows a graph with the number of frames defined in the bottom-left corner; the active frame, and the value of each property at that frame, appears at the left edge of the graph. (You can change the number of viewable frames in the bottom-left corner of the dialog box to see an overview of the entire path animation.)

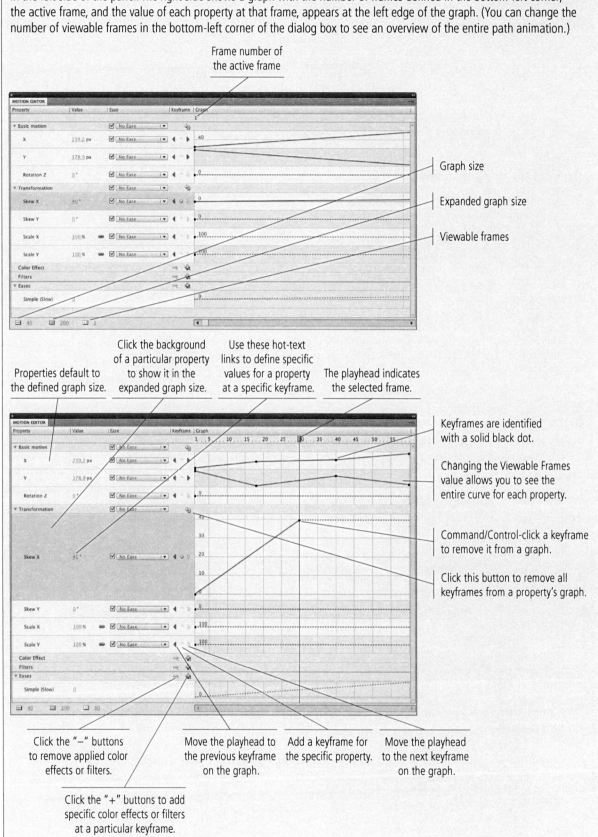

Frame number of the active frame

Graph size

Expanded graph size

Viewable frames

Properties default to the defined graph size.

Click the background of a particular property to show it in the expanded graph size.

Use these hot-text links to define specific values for a property at a specific keyframe.

The playhead indicates the selected frame.

Keyframes are identified with a solid black dot.

Changing the Viewable Frames value allows you to see the entire curve for each property.

Command/Control-click a keyframe to remove it from a graph.

Click this button to remove all keyframes from a property's graph.

Click the "−" buttons to remove applied color effects or filters.

Move the playhead to the previous keyframe on the graph.

Add a keyframe for the specific property.

Move the playhead to the next keyframe on the graph.

Click the "+" buttons to add specific color effects or filters at a particular keyframe.

FLASH FOUNDATIONS

9. **Click Frame 10 in the timeline to select it. In the Motion Editor panel, scroll until you find the Skew X option. Click the hot text for that option and change the value to 5°.**

   The concept here is the same as in the previous exercise: select the frame, and then change the object properties to what you want at that particular point in time. The difference is that you're using the Motion Editor panel to easily define numeric values for specific properties at specific points in time.

Note:

We docked the Motion Editor panel above the timeline panel so we could see both panels and the symbol Stage.

The transformation registration point is at the bottom-center.

The Motion Editor graph shows that the skew transition will be a gradual change — a tween.

Frame 10 is selected.

10. **Click Frame 30 in the timeline to select it. In the Motion Editor panel, change the Skew X value to –5°.**

    You don't need to manually move the skew back to 0°; the tween frames do that for you.

Note:

Selecting a different frame in either panel changes the selected frame in the other panel.

The dotted lines show the projected value of the property at specific frames.

As you can see by the dotted line after the Frame 30 keyframe, the Skew X transition would stay at –5° until the animation looped, when it would jump back to 0°. To avoid this jump, you need to manually set the skew back to 0° at the last keyframe.

Note:

The object must be selected to change its properties. Selecting the frame in the timeline also selects the object on that frame.

11. **Click Frame 40 in the timeline to select it. In the Motion Editor panel, change the Skew X value to 0°.**

The animation will now flow smoothly from –5° to 0° before it loops back to Frame 1.

Graphics vs. Movie Clips

Both graphics and movie clips can include animation. However, there are two fundamental differences in the capabilities of the two symbol types.

First, movie clip symbol instances can be named, which means they can be addressed by code. You can write scripts to control the timeline within a movie clip symbol independently of other objects in the file. Graphic symbol instances can't be named, which means you can't affect them with code.

Second, if you create animation inside of a graphic symbol, the timeline where you place the instance determines how much of the graphic symbol's animation plays. In other words, frames in the graphic symbol must correspond to frames on the parent timeline.

In this example, the seaweed animation was created in a graphic symbol instead of a movie clip.

On the main Stage, playing the animation requires the same number of frames that are contained in the graphic symbol timeline.

In the example here, the 40-frame seaweed animation was created in a graphic symbol (as you can see in the Edit bar above the symbol Stage). For the instances on the main Stage to play properly, you need to extend all of the layers to 40 frames (above right).

If the parent timeline includes more frames than the graphic symbol (as in the example on the right, where the main timeline has 94 frames) the graphic symbol's timeline will play slightly less than 2.5 times before looping back to the beginning — causing a visible jump in the animation.

If you have a number of animations of different length, you should use movie clip symbols, which function independently of the timeline where they are placed and can loop continuously regardless of the length of other animations on the same parent timeline.

If you extend the timeline to create other animations, the graphic symbol animation repeats as long as the timeline allows.

The 40-frame seaweed animation would play 2 full times plus 14 frames before the main timeline looped back to Frame 1.

12. **Click Scene 1 in the Edit bar to return to the main Stage.**

13. **Press Command-Return/Control-Enter to test the movie in a Player window.**

    Because you created the animation inside of the Seaweed movie clip symbol, all three instances of the symbol sway continuously as long as the animation is open.

14. **Close the Player window and return to Flash. Save the file and continue to the next exercise.**

 ## ANIMATE EFFECTS AND FILTERS

In addition to changing the common symbol properties — position, size, etc. — a motion tween can be used to animate a number of other options. Effects and filters, which can add visual interest to most objects on the Stage, can also be animated to change over time. In this exercise, you are going to cause the client's logo to fade into view over time, changing from blurry to clear by the time it is fully visible.

1. **With `ocean.fla` open, Control/right-click the logo instance on the Stage and choose Convert to Symbol.**

2. **Name the new symbol BOP, choose Movie Clip as the type, and choose the center registration point. Use the Folder link to place the new symbol inside the Movie Clips folder. Click OK to create the symbol.**

3. **Using the Selection tool, double-click the Logo instance on the Stage to edit the symbol in place. Select Frame 60 on the Layer 1 timeline and press F5 to add a new regular frame.**

    Because movie clips are self-contained animations, every movie clip in the file can last a different amount of time. You also need to be able to control this animation separately from other animations, which is why you are creating the tween inside of the symbol.

4. **Control/right-click between Frame 1 and Frame 60 and choose Create Motion Tween from the contextual menu.**

5. **Click OK in the resulting warning. Rename the new Symbol 1 as BOP Animated, and then move the symbol into the Movie Clips folder.**

6. **Click to select Frame 1 in the Layer 1 timeline, and then click the symbol instance on the Stage to select it.**

7. **In the Properties panel, open the Style menu in the Color Effect section and choose Alpha. Drag the resulting slider all the way to the left to change the Alpha value to 0.**

   The Alpha value controls an object's opacity; a value of 0 means the object is not visible.

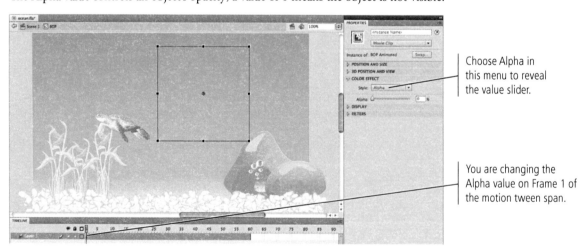

Choose Alpha in this menu to reveal the value slider.

You are changing the Alpha value on Frame 1 of the motion tween span.

8. **Click Frame 30 on the Layer 1 timeline to select it, and then click the symbol registration point on the Stage to select the symbol instance.**

   Because the current Alpha value is 0, you can't see the actual object to select it; you have to rely on the registration point to select the instance on the Stage.

9. **In the Properties panel, change the Alpha value back to 100.**

10. **Click Frame 1 to select it, and then press Return/Enter to play the animation.**

    By animating the Alpha property, the logo becomes entirely visible after 30 frames.

11. **With the BOP Animated instance selected on the Stage, open the Motion Editor panel (if necessary) and move the playhead to Frame 1.**

The object is again invisible because the Alpha value at the selected frame is set to 0.

Click above the graph to move the playhead in the Motion Editor panel.

Click the "+" button to add a filter to the selected tween.

12. **Scroll through the Motion Editor properties until you find the Filters option. Click the "+" button for Filters and choose Blur from the resulting menu.**

13. **Make sure the Blur X and Blur Y values are linked, and then change the Blur X value to 30 px.**

This icon should be a solid chain.

The Blur X and Blur Y values are 30 px at Frame 1.

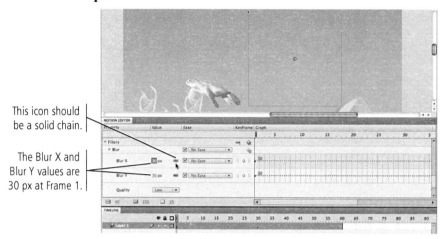

14. **Click Frame 30 to select it. In the Motion Editor panel, click the Add Keyframe button for the Blur X property, and then change the Blur X value to 0 px.**

The object is now visible because the Alpha value at Frame 30 is 100%.

Click here to select Frame 30.

Click this button to add a keyframe at the selected frame.

This slope marks a transition from a 30-px blur to a 0-px blur.

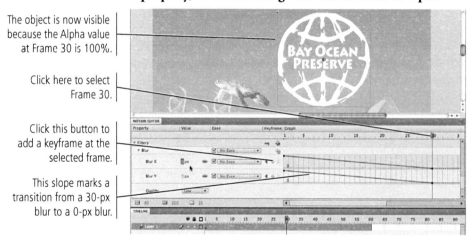

15. **Return the playhead to Frame 1, and then press Return/Enter to preview the animation.**

The BOP Animated movie clip gradually becomes clearer and more visible between Frame 1 and Frame 30.

16. **Save the file and continue to the next exercise.**

ANIMATE IN 3D

As you know, you can change the X (left/right) and Y (up/down) properties to move an object around the Stage. Flash CS5 adds the third dimension — the Z dimension (near/far or front/back) — so you can animate movie clips in three dimensions.

1. **With `ocean.fla` open, make sure you are editing the BOP movie clip in place on the Stage.**

2. **Click Frame 45 in the Layer 1 timeline to select it, and then choose the 3D Rotation tool in the Tools panel.**

   When a movie clip is selected with the 3D Rotation tool, a visual indicator overlays the selected instance. Each axis (X, Y, or Z) is controlled by a different aspect of the overlay.

   If you look carefully, you can see the related axis in the cursor icon when you move over a specific element in the overlay graphic.

3. **Click the Y Axis overlay and drag right to rotate the movie clip around the Y axis.**

The shaded area of the overlay shows how far you have rotated the object.

4. **In the Motion Editor panel, make sure the graph view shows at least 60 frames.**

Depending on how you dragged, your slope might go up to a positive number instead of down to a negative number.

Change this option to 60 to show the entire graph.

5. Review your Rotation X, Rotation Y and Rotation Z properties.

Simply dragging the overlay allows you to rotate the object, but it is not guaranteed to produce the results you want. Before you finalize the animation, you should use the Motion Editor graph to verify that what you get is what you want (a single, full revolution).

6. Make sure the Rotation Y property is –180 (one half of an entire revolution), and the other two rotation properties are 0.

The negative value causes the rotation to occur from left to right. Positive values cause the rotation to occur from right to left.

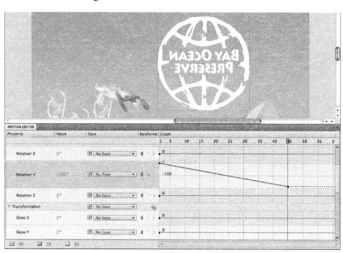

Note:

If you use a mouse with a scroll wheel, be very careful scrolling through the Motion Editor panel. The menus and hot-text values in the panel are also scrollable. If your cursor moves over one of these values or menus as you try to scroll, you will inadvertently change the values or menu where you scroll.

7. Click Frame 60 to select it. In the Motion Editor panel, click the Add Keyframe button for the Rotation Y property and change the value for that keyframe to –360.

Using the negative number, you are causing the object to make one full revolution; the constant downslope in the Motion Editor panel confirms this. If you had simply used 0, the object would revolve halfway, then go back in the opposite direction for the second half of the revolution. Because the slope is steeper from Frames 45–60, the second half of the rotation will occur more rapidly than the first half of the rotation.

8. **Select Frame 30 in the Motion Editor, and then click the Rotation Y Add Keyframe button. Change the value of the new keyframe to 0.**

The two halves of the revolution will now occur at the same speed; none of the revolution will take place until the logo is entirely visible and unblurred.

The constant downslope shows that the object will make one complete revolution in the same direction.

The flat line shows that the Rotation Y value will not change until the playhead reaches Frame 30.

9. **Click Scene 1 in the Edit bar to return to the main Stage.**

10. **Press Command-Return/Control-Enter to test the animation.**

Because the Rotation Y value is a continuous slope, the logo completes one entire revolution in the same direction between Frame 30 and Frame 60.

11. **Save the file and continue to the next exercise.**

 ## WORK WITH THE BONE TOOL

The Bone tool can be used to link symbols to one another in a "chain" effect, or to define complex motion for simple objects. As the name implies, you use the Bone tool to create "bones" and "joints" where the bones connect. In this exercise, you use the Bone tool to create a school of fish that swims in a line across the Stage.

Note:

*The process underlying the Bone tool is called **inverse kinematics**.*

1. **With ocean.fla open, create a new layer named Fish above the Turtle layer in the main timeline.**

2. **Choose Insert>New Symbol. Name the new symbol School and choose Movie Clip as the symbol type. Use the Folder link to place the new symbol inside the Movie Clips folder. Click OK to create the new symbol.**

3. **Using the Selection tool, drag a copy of the Fish1 movie clip onto the Symbol Stage. Align the top-right corner of the instance to the symbol registration point.**

When you use the Insert>New Symbol command, the Stage automatically switches to a new blank symbol Stage.

4. **Press Option/Alt, click the Fish1 instance, and then drag left to clone a second instance of the Fish1. Repeat this process to add two more Fish1 instances.**

5. **Click Scene 1 in the Edit bar to return to the main Stage.**

6. **With Frame 1 of the Fish layer selected, drag an instance of the School movie clip symbol onto the Stage. Position the School instance in the top half of the Stage, but entirely outside the left edge of the Stage.**

7. **Double-click the placed School instance to edit the symbol in place on the Stage.**

   You're going to make this school of fish swim across the top of the movie. Editing the symbol in place allows you to see how far you need to move the fish to ensure they go all the way across the ocean.

8. **Choose the Bone tool in the Tools panel.**

9. **Click the first Fish symbol instance, hold down the mouse button, and drag to the middle of the second Fish instance.**

   When you use the Bone tool, a new Armature layer is added to the timeline. The objects connected to the armature joints — called IK nodes — are moved from their original layer to the Armature layer.

Solid lines of the armature represent bones.

Circles on the armature represent joints.

Bone tool

10. **Click the second Fish instance, hold down the mouse button, and drag to the middle of the third Fish instance.**

11. **Click the third Fish instance, hold down the mouse button, and drag to the middle of the fourth Fish instance.**

The empty keyframe on Layer 1 shows that all four symbol instances are now part of the armature.

12. **Save the file and continue to the next exercise.**

 ## ANIMATE THE BONE ARMATURE

Now that you have the armature structure in place, you can use it to animate the instances' movement in both time and space.

1. **With ocean.fla open, make sure you are editing the School symbol instance in place on the Stage.**

2. **In the timeline, click Frame 45 of the Armature layer to select it, and then press F5 to insert a new regular frame.**

3. **Choose the Selection tool in the Tools panel, and then choose Edit>Select All to select all four instances on the armature.**

4. **Hold down the Option/Alt key, click any of the selected instances, and then drag the selection until the front fish is about halfway across the Stage and approximately one inch down.**

   You can Option/Alt-drag instances to move them to a new position without rotating the object or bending the armature.

Option/Alt-drag to move the selected objects (and the armature) without bending the armature or rotating the objects.

The registration point shows the symbol's original starting point.

Changing an object on the armature automatically adds a keyframe.

5. **Deselect all instances, click only the back Fish instance on the armature, and then drag up to the top of the Stage.**

As you drag the Fish instance without pressing Option/Alt, notice how other instances on the armature are affected, and how the different objects (including the one you drag) are rotated around the joints.

Click and drag to move the object and bend the armature.

All instances move according to the new armature shape, and they rotate around the joints.

6. **Press Option/Alt, click the second Fish instance, and drag down and right until this instance is partially on top of the first Fish instance.**

Option/Alt-drag to move one instance on the armature without affecting the position of other instances.

7. **Repeat Step 6 for the other two instances on the armature.**

8. **In the timeline, insert a new regular frame at Frame 90 to extend the timeline of the armature tween. Select all four Fish instances on the armature, press Option/Alt, and move all four objects past the right edge of the Stage and up near the top of the Stage.**

9. **Deselect the four objects, select only the fourth Fish instance, and then Option/Alt-drag down to change the direction of the armature.**

10. **Using the Transform panel, change the rotation of the selected fish as necessary so it appears to point up and away from the Stage.**

Change the Rotate value to adjust the orientation of the selected symbol instance.

Note:

You can use the Transform panel to precisely control the position and rotation of a specific instance on an armature.

11. **Repeat the process from Steps 9–10 to change the relative position of the fish in the school.**

We spread out the fish so they no longer overlap, and rotated each to point in the same general direction.

12. **Click Scene 1 on the Edit bar to return to the main Stage.**

13. **Press Command-Return/Control-Enter to test the movie, including the armature animation.**

14. **Close the Player window and return to Flash. Save the file and continue to the next stage of the project.**

Stage 3 **Programming Basic Timeline Control**

You now have all of the pieces in place for the ocean scene, including a number of animations that play automatically when the movie opens. According to the project specs, however, most of these animations should not play until a user clicks the appropriate button at the bottom of the screen. For everything to work properly, you need to complete several additional steps to accomplish the following goals:

- Play the logo animation only once when the movie first loads.

- Play the school of swimming fish when the Fish button is clicked.

- Play the swimming turtle when the Turtle button is clicked.

- Show the cave with the bubbly fish when the Cave button is clicked.

- Hide the cave, stop the turtle and school of fish, and replay the logo animation when the Reset button is clicked.

 CONVERT A MOTION TWEEN TO A MOVIE CLIP

At this point, all but the swimming turtle animations are contained inside of various movie clip symbols. In order to add code that controls the turtle animation independently of the main timeline, you need to move the symbol instance and motion tween into a symbol, and then place a symbol of that instance on the Stage.

1. **With ocean.fla open, click anywhere in the Frame 1–94 tween on the Turtle layer.**

Clicking within the tween selects the entire tween.

The regular keyframe starts a second tween, which is not selected.

2. **Press Shift, then click in the Frame 95–184 tween to add it to the selection.**

Because Frame 95 is a regular keyframe and not a property keyframe within the tween, the two tweens are technically treated as separate. You have to manually select both tweens to copy them into a symbol.

3. **Control/right-click inside the selected frames and choose Copy Frames in the contextual menu.**

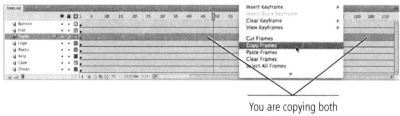

You are copying both selected tweens.

4. **Choose Insert>New Symbol. In the resulting dialog box, type** Swimming Turtle **in the Name field and choose Movie Clip in the Type menu. Use the Folder link to place the new symbol in the Movie Clips folder, then click OK.**

5. **Control/right-click Frame 1 of the new symbol's timeline and choose Paste Frames from the contextual menu.**

This pastes the full set of contents of the selected frames — including the turtle instance and the motion tweens — inside the symbol.

The motion path and attached symbol instance are added to the symbol's Stage.

Symbol registration point

Both tweens are pasted onto the timeline.

6. **Click anywhere within the Frame 1–94 tween, then choose Edit>Select All to select the motion path and the turtle symbol instance.**

This command selects both the motion path and the attached instance, so you can drag the entire piece as a single group.

7. **Drag the selection until the right end of the motion path aligns to the symbol registration point.**

The existing Swimmer symbol uses the center registration point. You're going to swap symbols, and the registration point in this symbol will align to the position of the previous one. For the tween to work as it does on the main timeline, you need to place the right end of the motion path at the registration point. (This will make more sense shortly).

The right end of the motion path should align with the symbol registration point.

8. **Repeat Step 7 for the Frame 95–184 tween.**

When you select the second tween, you see that the motion path remains where it was first pasted.

The right end of the second tween motion path must also align to the symbol registration point.

9. **Click Scene 1 in the Edit bar to return to the main Stage.**

10. **Control/right-click the Frame 1–94 tween on the Turtle layer and choose Remove Tween from the Contextual menu.**

The tweens now exist in the new Swimming Turtle movie clip symbol, so they are no longer needed on the main timeline.

After removing the tween, the frames remain but all property keyframes are removed.

The second tween is still in place after the Frame 95 keyframe.

11. **Repeat Step 10 for the Frame 95–184 tween on the same layer.**

12. **Click Frame 2 of the topmost layer to select it.**

13. **Scroll the Timeline panel as necessary until you see Frame 184. Press Shift, then click the last frame on the bottommost layer to select all frames from 2–184 on all layers.**

Click Frame 2 of the top layer...

...then Shift-click Frame 184 of the bottom layer to select all contiguous frames between the two you click.

14. **Control/right-click anywhere within the selected frames and choose Remove Frames from the contextual menu.**

Because all animation in this movie occurs within the timelines of various movie clip symbols, you don't need 90 frames on each layer of the main timeline.

You can't simply press the Delete key to remove frames. You must use the contextual menu (or the related commands in the Edit>Timeline submenu).

Because all of the animations are now contained within movie clip symbols, the main timeline now has only a single frame for each layer.

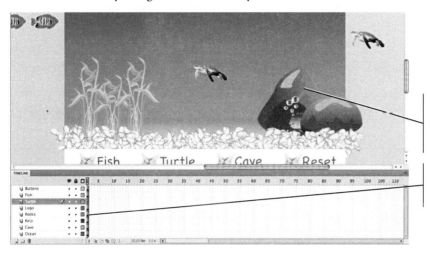

All objects are still in place because they exist on the Frame 1 keyframes of their respective layers.

Each layer on the main timeline now has only a single frame.

15. **Click the existing turtle instance on the Stage to select it.**

As you can see in the Properties panel, this is currently an instance of the Swimmer movie clip. You need to replace it with the Swimming Turtle movie clip.

Symbol registration point

16. **In the Properties panel, click the Swap button. Choose the Swimming Turtle movie clip in the resulting dialog box and click OK.**

When you swap symbols, the registration point of the new symbol is put in exactly the same spot as the registration point of the replacement symbol — which is why you moved the right end of the motion path to align with the symbol's registration point.

Although you can't see the motion path, you know the center of the turtle was aligned to the right end of the path at Frame 1.

17. **Save the file and continue to the next exercise.**

PREPARE SYMBOL INSTANCES FOR ACTIONSCRIPT

As you know, when you drag a symbol from the Library panel to the Stage, you create an instance of the symbol. Named instances are instances that have been assigned a unique identifier or name, which allows them to be targeted with ActionScript code.

1. **With ocean.fla open, make sure you are working on the main Stage.**

2. **Using the Selection tool, click the School instance to the left of the Stage. In the top field of the Properties panel, type school_mc.**

Use the Properties panel to assign instance names.

3. **Define names for the rest of the placed instances as follows:**

Remember, the Cave instance was named cave_mc when you created it during the import process.

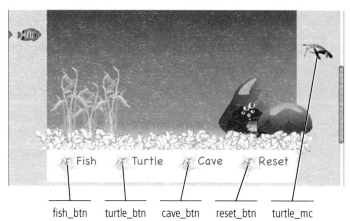

fish_btn   turtle_btn   cave_btn   reset_btn   turtle_mc

Note:

You don't need to name the seaweed instances because those will not be targeted with scripts.

Note:

The "_mc" and "_btn" naming convention is common in the world of Flash development. This convention allows programmers to easily recognize the type of a particular instance when they add scripts to the file.

4. **In the Timeline panel, click the Logo layer name to select the layer.**

   Remember, selecting a layer reveals the bounding boxes for all objects on the layer.

5. **Click the symbol registration point to select the logo.**

   Because the logo object has an Alpha value of 0, this is the easiest way to select the instance so you can name it.

6. **In the Properties panel, type bop_mc as the instance name.**

Click the layer name to reveal the instance...

...then click the symbol registration point to select the instance...

...then type the instance name in the Properties panel.

7. **Save the file and continue to the next exercise.**

 ADD MOVIE CLIP CONTROLS

The Code Snippets panel is a new feature of Flash CS5 that is intended to make it easier for non-programmers to add a certain level of interactivity to a Flash movie. Items in the panel, written in plain English, automatically add whatever code is necessary to perform the listed function. In this exercise, you will add four commands to dictate what is visible when you first open the movie.

1. **With ocean.fla open, open the Code Snippets panel from the Window menu.**

   Different types of common commands are available, grouped into logical sets or folders.

2. **Expand the Actions folder in the Code Snippets panel, and then roll your mouse over the Stop a Movie Clip item.**

   Each item includes a plain-English name, and a more detailed explanation in a tool tip.

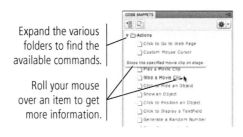

Expand the various folders to find the available commands.

Roll your mouse over an item to get more information.

Note:

Beginning in Project 5, you will work in depth with ActionScript code. Although the Code Snippets panel is supposed to make coding more user friendly for non-programmers, the various options in the panel will make more sense after you have at least a basic understanding of how ActionScript works. You should explore the different Code Snippets on your own, especially after completing the next project.

3. Select the Swimming Turtle instance on the stage and then double-click the Stop a Movie Clip item.

Adding the snippet automatically opens the Actions panel, showing the new code.

Code snippets include instructions in the form of comments, which are enclosed by /* and */.

The actual command uses dot syntax, defining what instance is being affected and what will happen to that instance.

The code is added to the selected frame on a new layer named Actions.

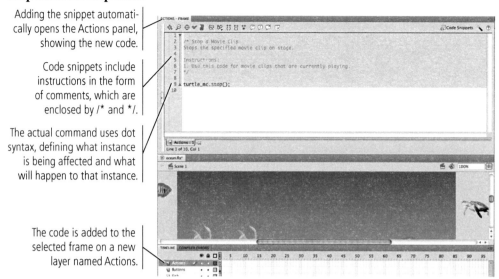

It might seem that by first selecting the object, you are attaching script to that object. Instead, you are telling Flash which object you want the command to address. In ActionScript 3, all scripts are placed on the timeline frames rather than attached to specific objects on the Stage. In the Timeline panel, a new layer named Actions is added to the top of the layer stack. (Although not required, this separate layer for the code is a common convention among developers.)

In the Actions panel, which opens automatically when you add the snippet, you can see that the stop command has been added to Frame 1 of the Actions layer. The command references turtle_mc, which is the instance name you defined. In other words, this command stops the turtle_mc instance from playing. The instance is stopped as soon as the main timeline reaches the command; because the command is on Frame 1 of the main timeline, the instance is stopped as soon as the movie opens.

Note:

The format or syntax of the added code is called **dot syntax**: *it first defines the object you are addressing, then adds a dot, then defines what you want to do to that object.*

4. Select the School instance and then double-click the Stop a Movie Clip item.

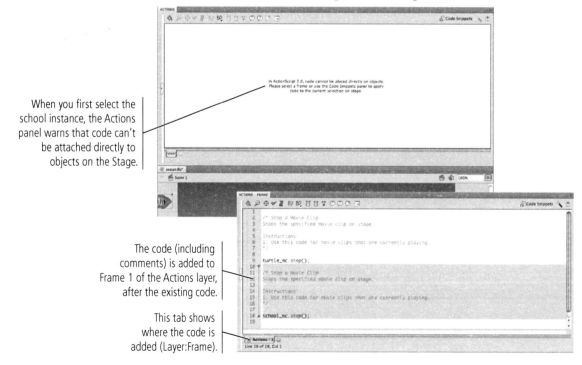

When you first select the school instance, the Actions panel warns that code can't be attached directly to objects on the Stage.

The code (including comments) is added to Frame 1 of the Actions layer, after the existing code.

This tab shows where the code is added (Layer:Frame).

5. **Select the Cave instance and then double-click the Stop a Movie Clip item.**

6. **Select the Cave instance again and double-click the Show an Object item.**

Unfortunately, there is no snippet to simply hide an item without requiring the user to click something. (The Click to Hide an Object item is not appropriate because you want to hide the instance as soon as the movie opens, and not as a reaction to the user's click.)

However, the added Show an Object statement shows that the value "true" is attached to the visible property of the instance. To make the instance *not* visible, you simply have to change the property's value in the code.

7. **In the Actions panel, change the word true to false on Line 36.**

8. **Press Command-Return/Control-Enter to test the movie.**

The three movie clips are stopped, and the cave is hidden. However, the logo animation still plays continuously and you want it to play only once when the movie opens.

9. **Close the Player window and return to Flash.**

10. **In the Library panel, double-click the BOP movie clip symbol icon to enter into the symbol's Stage.**

   You can't stop the BOP instance on the main Stage because you want the animation to play one time when the movie first opens. To accomplish this goal, you need to add a stop command to the end of the movie clip timeline.

11. **Click the last frame in the Layer 1 timeline, then click the logo instance on the Stage to select it.**

12. **Expand the Timeline Navigation folder in the Code Snippets panel, then double-click the Stop at this Frame item to add the necessary code.**

   Timeline Navigation snippets can be used to control the timeline (and thus, the playback) of specific symbols. The Stop at this Frame command affects the active timeline at the selected frame, so a specific instance is not referenced in the resulting code.

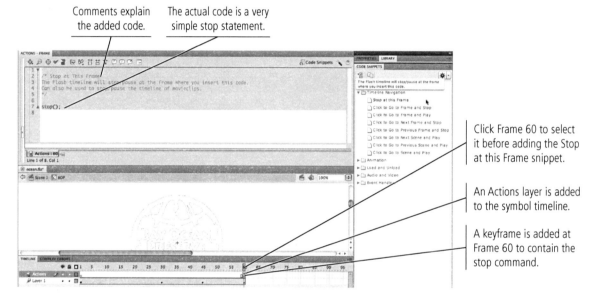

Comments explain the added code.

The actual code is a very simple stop statement.

Click Frame 60 to select it before adding the Stop at this Frame snippet.

An Actions layer is added to the symbol timeline.

A keyframe is added at Frame 60 to contain the stop command.

13. **Click Scene 1 in the Edit bar to return to the main Stage, then press Command-Return/Control-Enter to test the movie.**

   The logo animation now plays only once and then stops.

14. **Close the Player window and return to Flash, then save the file and continue to the next exercise.**

ADD EVENT HANDLERS TO BUTTONS

As you saw in the previous exercise, ActionScript 3 requires code to be attached to a frame on the timeline. To affect a specific object on the Stage, you have to use the defined instance names as reference in the code. Programming a button requires more complex code called an **event handler**, with (at least) two referenced objects — the instance that triggers the action, and the instance that is affected by the action.

The Code Snippets panel includes options for creating event handlers with the proper syntax, although defining what occurs as a result of the event might require a few workaround steps. Even using code snippets, it is helpful if you are familiar with the basics of ActionScript code.

1. **With ocean.fla open, expand the Timeline Navigation folder in the Code Snippets panel.**

2. **Select the Fish button instance on the Stage, then double-click the Click to Go to Frame and Play item in the Code Snippets panel.**

   The added code is not attached to the selected instance; it is added to Frame 1 of the existing Actions layer, after all code that you already added.

The selected instance becomes the object that can trigger the function.

The specific trigger (CLICK) is defined inside the event listener.

This is the event listener statement.

This is the function that is called when the defined event occurs.

The function name is the same in the event listener and the defined function.

Although you do not need to know every detail of ActionScript code to use Code Snippets, there are a few important points that you should understand:

- The first line of added code defines what will happen to trigger the function (the **event listener**). Inside the parentheses, the MouseEvent.CLICK statement says that the following function will be called when the fish_btn instance is *clicked*.

- The first line of code includes a **function name** immediately before the closing parenthesis. That same name is defined at the beginning of the following function so the file knows what function to play when the defined button is clicked.

- The **function body** — between the two braces — defines what occurs when the event is triggered.

3. **Place the insertion point before the gotoAndPlay command inside the function body and click the Insert Target Path button at the top of the Actions panel.**

The statement inside this function currently says "go to Frame 5 and play the timeline". Because the statement does not address a specific instance, the code will be interpreted to mean the timeline on which the code is placed (in this case, the main Stage timeline). You want the function to play the School movie clip instance, so you have to add the appropriate reference.

Insert Target Path button

Click here to place the insertion point.

4. **Choose school_mc in the Insert Target Path dialog box and click OK.**

This dialog box lists every nameable instance on the Stage, so you can choose from the list instead of trying to remember the exact name you defined for a specific object.

The insertion point flashes immediately after the added instance name.

Note:

If an item in the Insert Target Path dialog box appears in parentheses, the instance is not yet named; selecting it will prompt you to define an instance name.

The word "this" in the instance name refers to the timeline where the instance is placed. It is automatically included when you use the Insert Target Path dialog box. It is not strictly necessary in this case because the instances are all on the main timeline of the file you are building, but you do not need to remove it from the code.

5. **Type a period (dot) immediately after the instance name to separate it from the gotoAndPlay command.**

Remember, dot syntax requires a period separating the different parts of code — in this case, the instance that will be affected by the gotoAndPlay command.

6. **Change the number inside the parentheses to 1.**

This number defines the frame number of the instance that will be called when a user clicks the button. You want the instance to start at the beginning, so you are changing the frame reference to 1.

Add this dot...   ...and change this number to 1.

7. Repeat Steps 2–6 to create an event handler for the Turtle button that plays the turtle_mc movie clip instance from Frame 1.

Notice that a sequential number is added to the function name, both in the event listener statement and in the first line of the function. Every function in a file must have a unique name so it can be called when necessary.

8. Repeat Steps 2–6 to create an event handler for the Cave button that plays the cave_mc movie clip instance from Frame 1.

```
60
61    turtle_btn.addEventListener(MouseEvent.CLICK, fl_ClickToGoToAndPlayFromFrame_3);
62
63    function fl_ClickToGoToAndPlayFromFrame_3(event:MouseEvent):void
64    {
65        this.turtle_mc.gotoAndPlay(1);
66    }
67
68    /* Click to Go to Frame and Play
69    Clicking on the specified symbol instance moves the playhead to the specified frame in the timeline and cont
70    Can be used on the main timeline or on movie clip timelines.
71
72    Instructions:
73    1. Replace the number 5 in the code below with the frame number you would like the playhead to move to when
74    */
75
76    cave_btn.addEventListener(MouseEvent.CLICK, fl_ClickToGoToAndPlayFromFrame_4);
77
78    function fl_ClickToGoToAndPlayFromFrame_4(event:MouseEvent):void
79    {
80        this.cave_mc.gotoAndPlay(1);
81    }
82
```

9. Select the cave_mc instance on the Stage (not the Cave button) and double-click the Show an Object item in the Actions folder of the Code Snippets panel.

The Cave button needs to show the instance before it plays, so this button function needs two lines of code. Unfortunately, the Code Snippets panel was not designed to add code inside of an existing function. The Show an Object snippet is added at the end of the existing code, *after* the function that is called when a user clicks the cave_btn instance. As a workaround, you have to add the necessary command and then paste it into the function body.

The "show" command is added outside of the existing function.

10. Select the line of code that makes the cave_mc instance visible (Line 90 in the above example) and press Command/Control-X to cut the selected code.

You have to use the keyboard shortcuts to copy (Command/Control-C), cut (Command/Control-X), or paste (Command/Control-V) code in the Actions panel. The menu commands do not work while you are active in the Actions panel.

11. Place the insertion point immediately after the opening brace in the function (Line 79 in our example) and press Return/Enter to add a new line in the function body. Press Command/Control-V to paste the code that you cut in Step 10 to the function body.

12. Delete the extra lines of comments at the end of the code.

13. Press Command-Return/Control-Enter to test the movie.

Test the buttons that you just programmed. Each should play the relevant movie clip.

14. Close the Player window and return to Flash, then save the file and continue to the next exercise.

COMBINE MULTIPLE EVENT HANDLERS IN A BUTTON

The final element of this project is the Reset button, which needs to accomplish a number of things. As the name suggests, clicking this button should restore the movie to exactly what happens when it first opens. Because the symbols in this movie are controlled with code, you need to add more code that defines what happens when this button is clicked.

1. With ocean.fla open, select the Reset button on the Stage.

2. Double-click the Click to Go To Frame and Stop item in the Timeline Navigation folder of the Code Snippets panel.

3. Add a reference to the school_mc instance, and change the referenced frame to 1.

4. **Select the line inside the function body (Line 96 in our example) and copy it.**

5. **Place the insertion point at the beginning of the existing function body (Line 96) and paste it three times.**

6. **Change the second and third lines to reference the turtle_mc and cave_mc instances, respectively.**

7. **Change the fourth line to reference the bop_mc instance, and change the command to gotoAndPlay.**

   When a user clicks the Reset button, the logo animation should replay from the first frame. It will replay only once because you already added the stop command inside the movie clip's timeline.

These lines will stop the first three animations and effectively hide the first two on the Stage.

This command will cause the logo animation to play once.

8. **Select the Reset button on the Stage again, and double-click the Click to Hide an Object item in the Actions folder of the Code Snippets panel.**

9. **In the resulting function, change the referenced instance to cave_mc.**

   By default, this snippet hides the object that triggers the function. Because you want to hide the cave and not the Reset button, you need to change the instance name inside of the function body.

10. **Cut the function body (Line 113 in our example) from the code and then paste it inside the body of the previous function.**

    In this case, it is not necessary to have two separate event handlers for the same button.

Note:

You don't need to hide the turtle and school instances because Frame 1 of those movie clips exists entirely out of the Stage area so they won't be visible when their timelines are reset.

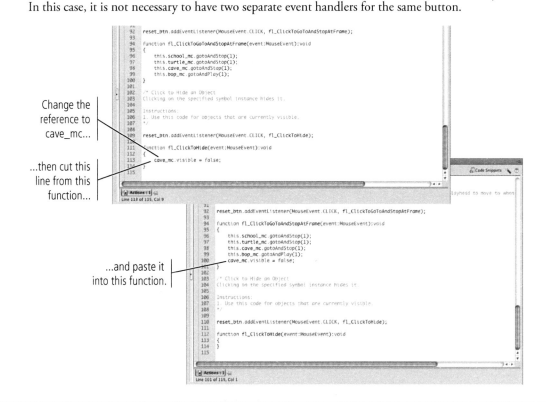

Change the reference to cave_mc...

...then cut this line from this function...

...and paste it into this function.

11. Delete all code related to the second reset_btn event handler (Lines 103–115 in our example above).

Because you combined this function body with the other event handler for the same button, this code is no longer necessary.

```
87
88    Instructions:
89    1. Replace the number 5 in the code below with the frame number you would like the playhead to move to when
90    */
91
92    reset_btn.addEventListener(MouseEvent.CLICK, fl_ClickToGoToAndStopAtFrame);
93
94    function fl_ClickToGoToAndStopAtFrame(event:MouseEvent):void
95    {
96        this.school_mc.gotoAndStop(1);
97        this.turtle_mc.gotoAndStop(1);
98        this.cave_mc.gotoAndStop(1);
99        this.bop_mc.gotoAndPlay(1);
100       cave_mc.visible = false;
101    }
102
```

12. Press Command-Return/Control-Enter to test the movie.

Test the buttons that you just programmed. The Reset button should stop and hide all animations except for the swaying seaweed.

13. Close the Player window and return to Flash, then save the file and close it.

Project Review

fill in the blank

1. Objects from a Photoshop file should be created on _____ if they need to be managed separately when imported into Flash.

2. The _____ tool places multiple instances of a selected symbol; you can use the Properties panel to randomize the instances that are placed.

3. The _____ defines the point around which object transformations are made.

4. The X and Y position of a symbol instance is based on the _____.

5. You can use the _____ panel to define numeric scale, skew, and rotation values for the selected object.

6. Animation in a _____ requires the same number of frames on the timeline where the instance is placed.

7. Animation in a _____ plays regardless of the number of frames in the timeline where instances are placed.

8. _____ is the format required by ActionScript 3 code.

9. Using ActionScript 3, code is attached to a specific _____, and uses instance names to address specific objects.

10. In ActionScript, a(n) _____ includes a statement defining the instance that triggers an event and the function that is called when the defined event occurs.

short answer

1. Briefly explain the concept of "tweening."

2. Briefly explain the difference between a graphic symbol and a movie clip symbol.

3. Briefly define an event handler.

Portfolio Builder Project

Use what you learned in this project to complete the following freeform exercise.
Carefully read the art director and client comments, then create your own design to meet the needs of the project.
Use the space below to sketch ideas; when finished, write a brief explanation of your reasoning behind your final design.

The media director for the Chicago Wild Animal Park is re-branding the facility from the "City Zoo" image it has had for the past twenty years. He has hired you to create a series of animated icons for the park's new interactive Web site.

To complete this project, you should:

❑ Use the drawing tools to develop icons for the main areas of the facility. Create each of the icons in the same shape and size, and use the same general style for each.

❑ Add some kind of animation to each icon. Use any combination of frame animations, shape tweens, and/or motion tweens.

We've gotten rid of the cages and created realistic natural habitats for the animals. Our main goal now is rehabilitation, preservation, and education. We're going to have educational programs and exhibits throughout the facility, but we don't want people to be scared off by the idea of learning!

We have many international visitors, so most of our collateral — including our new Web site — is based on images that can be understood in any language. Although there will be text as well, the icons should very clearly indicate what users will find when they click on any specific one (even if they can't read the words).

We need a series of six animated icons that will label the different areas of the facility. The six main sections are: the tropics, the desert, the Arctic, the forest, the ocean, and the sky. There will also be a special children's section that needs its own icon.

_____
_____
_____
_____
_____
_____
_____
_____
_____
_____
_____
_____
_____
_____

This project incorporated artwork that was created in Adobe Photoshop, which is a common development workflow. You also worked with symbols that were created in another Flash file, which is also a common collaborative process.

The second stage of this project focused on different methods of creating animation — frame-by-frame to move something in jumps, motion tweening to move objects smoothly, tweening to change only certain properties over time, and even tweening to rotate an object in three-dimensional space. To create these animations, you have also learned a number of techniques for transforming objects on the Stage; the Transform panel, the Free Transform tool, and the Properties panel all play valuable roles in Flash development.

Finally, you were introduced to the object-oriented model of ActionScript 3 when you added button controls using the Code Snippets panel. With very little (if any) knowledge of coding or programming, you were able to use the built-in functionality to meet the project's interactive requirements.

Import artwork from an Adobe Photoshop file

Import symbols from an external Flash library

Create frame animations to move objects over time

Animate Alpha properties, graphic filters, and 3D attributes

Animate multiple symbols on an armature

Define movie clip symbols to create tween animations

Define a graphic symbol and spray multiple instances

Add code to control the playback of various movie clip instances.

Gator Race Game

Your client publishes children's books. The marketing manager has found that the more time kids spend on the company's Web site, the more sales the company makes. To entice children to visit the site more often and for longer periods, the client hired your agency to build an interactive children's game featuring Baggy Gator, one of the publisher's most well-known characters.

This project incorporates the following skills:

❑ Preparing objects on the Stage for ActionScript

❑ Getting help in the Actions panel

❑ Using functions to control movie clip timelines and object properties

❑ Creating event handlers and custom functions

❑ Working with variables and arrays

❑ Scripting loops and conditional statements

❑ Adding sound with ActionScript

Project Meeting

client comments

We're adding a number of kid-friendly tools to our Web site, including a talking introduction screen and interactive games. The more time kids spend on our site, the more they see (and learn to recognize) different characters from our books — and the more they want to read the books where those characters are involved.

We want the first game to feature Baggy Gator and his friends. We thought a foot race would be familiar enough for young children to understand and non-violent enough for parents to allow.

There are a few technical requirements that we think are important:

- The game should be no longer than 10 seconds to accommodate children's short attention spans.

- There should be constant action to keep the kids interested and engaged.

- There should be sound effects while the race is running.

art director comments

The client mentioned three specific requirements, so make sure you keep those in mind while you develop this piece.

- The entire movie needs to be 10 seconds long. Translate that to frames when you combine all the pieces.

- The movie needs to have constant action. Different characters need to "take the lead" at different points in the race. If you move one character every second, that should meet this requirement.

- Add sound effects. Races have audiences, and audiences cheer. I think a cheering crowd sound will help kids to get into the spirit of the race. Let's also add some "running feet" sounds to make the running animation seem more realistic.

I asked our illustrator to build the necessary graphics for the project. As our resident coding expert, I need you to put all the pieces together and make the movie work.

project objectives

To complete this project, you will:

- ❏ Define instance names
- ❏ Add motion to the background
- ❏ Use functions to control movie clip timelines
- ❏ Create scripts to control object properties
- ❏ Write event handlers and functions
- ❏ Create an event listener
- ❏ Define a custom function
- ❏ Script with variables and random numbers
- ❏ Create an array to store racer positions
- ❏ Define a loop to evaluate array elements
- ❏ Use an if condition to call movie clip frames
- ❏ Program the Restart button functionality
- ❏ Test the movie and change cursor styles
- ❏ Create access for sound files in the library
- ❏ Develop scripts to call sounds

Stage 1 Preparing for ActionScript

The best way to start a complicated project such as this one is to develop a clear plan of what needs to take place. Consider the sketch from the original project-planning meeting (shown at right). You need to complete a number of different tasks to create the final game. Some of these tasks, such as the various actions for each character, can be accomplished with frame animations and tweens. The rest of the tasks, however, require more complicated interaction between the elements of the movie. Fortunately, ActionScript provides the mechanism for creating and controlling this type of interaction.

This project was designed to give you an idea of what you can do with ActionScript. To enhance your marketability as a professional Flash programmer, we encourage you to continue your ActionScript education beyond this book.

REVIEW THE FILE STRUCTURE

When you work as part of a development team, it's always best to review the various elements in a file before you begin any programming activities.

1. **Download FL5_RF_Project5.zip from the Student Files Web page.**

2. **Expand the ZIP archive in your WIP folder (Macintosh) or copy the archive contents into your WIP folder (Windows).**

   This results in a folder named **Gators**, which contains the files you need for this project. You should also use this folder to save the files you create in this project.

3. **In Flash, choose File>Open and navigate to the WIP>Gators folder. Select gator_race.fla and click Open.**

   The basic file for this movie has already been created, with most of the pieces in place. Each element (character, buttons, and the racetrack background) is a different movie clip on a separate layer. Your task is to turn the various symbols into an interactive game.

4. **Choose View>Magnification>Show All to see all contents of the movie.**

The Racetrack movie clip instance extends far beyond the boundaries of the Stage.

The Stage area is marked in the file by page guides.

Each element is placed on a separate layer.

5. **Choose View>Magnification>Fit in Window to enlarge the movie so the Stage area (but not the entire movie) is visible.**

6. **In the timeline, hide the Background layer.**

   The Racetrack movie clip (which occupies the Background layer) is larger than the actual Stage, so the actual Stage area is visible when the Background layer is hidden. The original designer placed guides to mark the edges of the Stage, which will be helpful as you create the interactive elements of the game.

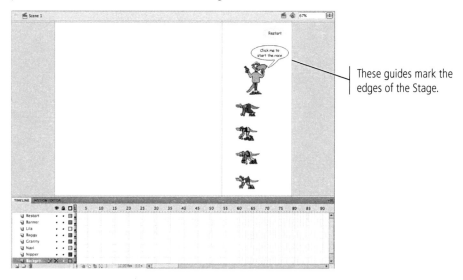

   These guides mark the edges of the Stage.

7. **Show the Background layer again.**

8. **Open the Library panel and expand the Gators folder.**

9. **Select the Baggy movie clip in the Library panel and click the Play button in the preview area.**

   Each racer movie clip was created with frame animations to simulate the effect of getting set for the race (Frame 5), running (Frames 10–17), crying (Frames 20–23), and cheering (Frames 26–29).

   Click the Play button to preview the animation in the Baggy movie clip.

   Each character is created as a separate movie clip symbol.

   The crying frame animation will be called if the character loses the race. The cheering animation will be called if the character wins the race.

10. **Select the Lila movie clip in the library and click the Play button.**

    Lila is the race starter. This movie clip includes a frame animation with Lila tapping her foot while waiting for a user to start the race (Frames 1–20). Beginning at Frame 21, Lila looks up from her watch, and then raises the starting pistol and fires (Frame 24).

11. **Save the file and continue to the next exercise.**

DEFINE INSTANCE NAMES

Instance names are required if you want to target individual objects using ActionScript. You need to provide an instance name for a symbol instance before you can refer to that object in your code.

1. **With gator_race.fla open, use the Selection tool to click the Lila movie clip instance on the Stage.**

2. **In the Properties panel, type lila_mc in the Instance Name field.**

Use this field to name the selected instance.

3. **Using the same technique, assign unique instance names to the remaining elements, using the instance names listed in the following table.**

Object to Select	Instance Name
Baggy movie clip instance	char1_mc
Granny movie clip instance	char2_mc
Navi movie clip instance	char3_mc
Nipper movie clip instance	char4_mc
Racetrack movie clip instance	racetrack_mc
Banner movie clip instance	banner_mc
Restart button instance	restart_btn

Note:

Although it might seem as though you should use the character names as the instance names, using the numerals 1–4 to name the instances will be important later when you write the ActionScript to make the game work properly.

The characters "_mc" and "_btn" in the instance names help differentiate movie clip instances from button instances. Although not strictly necessary, many Flash programmers use this naming convention.

restart_btn
banner_mc
lila_mc
char1_mc
char2_mc
char3_mc
char4_mc
racetrack_mc

4. **Save the file and continue to the next exercise.**

ADD MOTION TO THE BACKGROUND

The Background movie clip is currently a static movie clip (although there are animated movie clips nested within the Background movie clip). The individual racer movie clips and the race starter movie clip already contain frame animations. After you add the necessary looping, the frame animations will make it appear as though the racers are running along the track. The overall effect is not complete, however, because the background does not yet move in time with what appears to be running gators. You correct that problem in this exercise.

1. **With `gator_race.fla` open, double-click the racetrack_mc instance on the Stage to edit the movie clip symbol in place.**

2. **Select Frame 6 of the Track layer and insert a new keyframe.**

    To add a new keyframe, choose Insert>Timeline>Keyframe, press F6, or Control/right-click the frame and choose Insert Keyframe from the contextual menu.

    When the race starts, the running gators take five frames to "get set" before they begin running. Adding this keyframe keeps the track in place until the gator animations actually start "running."

You are working on the Racetrack movie clip Stage.

3. **Select Frame 100 of the Track layer and add a new regular frame.**

    To add a new regular frame, choose Insert>Timeline>Frame, press F5, or Control/right-click the frame and choose Insert Frame from the contextual menu.

    Later in this project, you will add ActionScript to change the racers' positions eight times (i.e., every second); the final movement occurs at Frame 96. Shortly after the final change of position, the race "ends" at Frame 100.

4. **Control/right-click anywhere between the keyframe at Frame 6 and the regular frame at Frame 100 and choose Create Motion Tween from the contextual menu.**

5. **Read the resulting warning and click OK to convert the objects on the Stage to a single movie clip symbol.**

6. **In the Library panel, rename the new Symbol 1 Racetrack_Group.**

7. **Select Frame 100 on the Track layer. Using the Selection tool, click the Racetrack_Group movie clip on the Stage to select it. Press Shift and drag right until the finish line graphic is on top of the guide where the starting line was located (as shown in the following image).**

If you switch between the two keyframes, the background jumps from its original location to the ending position. To fix this problem, you need to use tweening to create a continuous-motion effect.

The finish line graphic should be centered on the guide in the Stage area.

Frame 100 is selected.

8. **Select Frame 120 on the Track layer and add a new regular frame.**

If the entire movie lasts 10 seconds, at 12 fps, 120 frames are required. You want the race to end before the actual movie file, which is why you placed the finish line at Frame 100 instead of Frame 120.

Adding the new frame extends the tween after the last keyframe; the symbol on the tween remains in the same position as it was on the last keyframe in the tween.

The blue frames identify the length of the tween, even when nothing is moving (i.e., after Frame 100).

Between Frame 6 and Frame 100, the graphics move from left to right (from the starting line section to the finish line section).

Between Frame 100 and Frame 120, the racetrack remains fixed, showing the "finish line" section of the graphics.

9. **Click Scene 1 on the Edit bar to return to the main Stage.**

10. **Press Command-Return/Control-Enter to test the movie.**

As the movie plays, the background moves smoothly to the right. When the playhead reaches the final frame of the background timeline, the timeline returns to Frame 1 and automatically plays again.

If you watch the individual characters, you see the different animations included in each movie clip. At this point, each character simply plays from start to finish, and then starts over again. Later in the project, you will add ActionScript to control which frames play at specific points throughout the movie.

The racetrack moves…

…but the characters remain fixed in place.

11. **Close the Player window and return to Flash.**

12. **Save the file and continue to the next exercise.**

MOVE THE STARTER OFF THE STAGE

In the Lila movie clip, the race starter looks up from her watch at Frame 21, and then fires the gun at Frame 24. After Lila starts the race, she needs to move off the Stage to complete the illusion of the racers running away from the starting line. To create the desired effect, you need to add a motion tween within the Lila movie clip.

1. **With `gator_race.fla` open, double-click the lila_mc instance on the Stage to edit the movie clip in place.**

2. **Insert a new regular frame at Frame 35, and then create a motion tween between Frames 24 and 35.**

You are working in the Lila symbol Stage.

3. **Read the resulting warning, and then click OK to convert the objects on the Stage to a single movie clip symbol.**

4. **In the Library panel, rename the new Symbol 1 Lila_Move and drag it into the Gators library folder.**

5. **Select Frame 35. Click the lila_mc instance on the Stage, and then Shift-drag the movie clip right until the instance is outside the Stage boundary.**

   You might need to scroll or zoom out to show the gray area to the right of the Stage (where you want to place the Lila instance).

Lila should be entirely off the Stage.

The tween causes Lila to move smoothly out of the scene.

Frame 35 is selected.

Note:

You are not moving the banner because it should simply disappear when the race starts (instead of moving to the right). Later, you will add ActionScript to control the visibility of this element.

6. **Click Scene 1 on the Edit bar to return to the main Stage.**

7. **Press Command-Return/Control-Enter to test the movie.**

   Lila now moves out of the scene after she fires the starting pistol. The timelines still loop, however, so Lila reappears in the scene after Frame 35.

Lila moves out of the scene after firing, but her timeline automatically loops after Frame 35, so she reappears.

8. **Close the Player window and return to Flash.**

9. **Save the file and continue to the next stage of the project.**

Stage 2 Working with ActionScript 3

ActionScript moves basic animation to a higher level, allowing the end user to interact with a movie. As you add more complex scripts, users can move objects around, change their colors, toggle soundtracks on and off, and even play games. Experienced developers use ActionScript to enable Flash to communicate with other programming languages (including XML) to create complex, data-driven Flash sites for electronic commerce, news feeds, and various forms of entertainment.

In Project 3, you used built-in behaviors for ActionScript 2 to define object-based event handlers and their resulting actions. In other words, you defined what happened (the action) when the user did something (the event handler) to an object (the trigger). ActionScript 2 is perfectly usable, and can be more friendly to designers and graphics-oriented users — particularly since a number of common programming tasks are made available in the built-in behaviors, and require very little manual programming.

ActionScript 3, the current version, is a complex language that adds incredible programming power to Flash. In Project 4, you got a brief introduction to ActionScript 3 when you used built-in code snippets to add user controls in the ocean animation. Although it can be intimidating at first — especially for graphic designers with no programming experience — it is well worth the effort to understand the basics of ActionScript 3, if for no other reason than to enhance your understanding of what you can create with this powerful tool.

Using ActionScript 2, you attach scripts directly to symbol instances. With ActionScript 3, you write code on different frames of the timeline and attach specific bits of code to certain objects. Although a bit more complicated, the logic behind ActionScript 3 allows far more complexity in a Flash animation than can be accomplished with ActionScript 2.

To complete the gator race game, you need to create a number of different actions that control the various elements of the game (the race characters and the Background movie clip, as well as the button that allows the user to start the game). You will use ActionScript 3 to attach the necessary scripts to specific frames in the timeline — both in the main Stage and in the individual movie clip Stages.

Planning Your Script

FLASH FOUNDATIONS

It is better to prepare your ActionScript in a logical way before you add a single line of code into the Actions panel. You might use an entire notebook to plan your movie before you begin coding, but doing so will save hours of troubleshooting time later. There are five questions you can use as a guide for applying ActionScript:

What are you trying to do with the script? You should know what you are trying to achieve before you begin. Something as basic as the difference between tinting a solid color and tinting a gradient could change what script you use, so be specific about what you want the script to do.

What are you trying to affect? ActionScript can modify or reference the entire movie, external movies, external scripts, movie clips, buttons, frames, keyframes, and even shapes. Before you start scripting, knowing what you want to reference changes what script is available.

What script is most appropriate to create the desired result? Once you know what you are trying to do and what will be affected, you can begin to determine what actions might achieve your desired result. Programming languages often use terms that you won't find in conversational language, but ActionScript is easier

than most in this regard. At times you might have to think in synonymous terms to find the script you need. For example, you could research how to *start* a movie clip for quite some time to no avail, but if you researched how to *play* a movie clip, you would quickly find it.

What makes this script occur in the movie? After you know what script you want to use, the next step is to determine what will trigger the action. Does the action happen when a button is clicked? Does it occur when the playhead crosses the fourth frame of a movie clip? Many actions are designed to execute when the movie first starts.

Where should the script be attached? Even though you know what script to use, what it should do, what it references, and what triggers the action, if you put the script in the wrong place, it could either fail to work, or at the very least, require different syntax.

Understanding ActionScript Terminology

The terminology of ActionScript — and the vocabulary used to refer to scripting elements — can be unfamiliar and even intimidating to people whose backgrounds are more design oriented, rather than grounded in computer programming. Keep in mind the following definitions as you work through the rest of this project:

- When working with ActionScript, everything in Flash is treated as an **object**; this includes not only actual objects, but also frames, timelines, scenes, etc.

- Objects in Flash are divided into **classes** (they are "classified"). Different classes of objects (Bitmap, Movie Clip, etc.) have different available properties, methods, and events because, for example, a movie clip can do different things than a bitmap image.

- In the Flash Actions panel, classes are grouped into **packages**, which simply provide a convenient way to manage large groups of related elements.

- **Properties** are the characteristics of an object, such as position, color, and visibility.

- **Methods** are the things an object can do, such as sending the playhead to a specific frame.

- **Events** are the triggers that an object can react to, such as a button being clicked or the playhead crossing a certain frame on the timeline.

- An **event listener** (also called an **event handler**) tells Flash when to react, and what to do when Flash "hears" the triggering event. Essentially, the code says, "When A happens, do B." In this plain-English example, the entire statement is the event listener; A is the event and B is the function that will occur.

- **Function** is simply a generic term for an overall chunk of code. A function can include the object that will be affected, the event that causes the action, and the method that will be applied as a result of the event.

Understanding Dot Syntax

Syntax refers to the structure of the language, including placing all characters in the proper order. Leaving out a single character (such as a semicolon) can render the code unreadable (known as a **syntax error**). Scripting in ActionScript 3 uses **dot syntax** to apply script commands to different objects. For example:

> **char4.y = 350;**

Because you aren't attaching a script to a specific object, you first have to tell the script which object you want to affect with a specific action. The first part of the script, then, identifies the object you are targeting. In this example, the script affects an object with the instance name **char4**.

The second part of the script (**y = 350**) is the property you want to affect with the action. In this case, the line of code moves the **char4** object vertically (the y axis) on the Stage. The dot that separates the object from the action is where the term "dot syntax" originates.

Before you can begin programming the functionality of the game, you need to add some basic controls to the movie clips in the file. Specifically, you need to:

- Stop the Racetrack movie clip from moving until the race starts

- Prevent the Racetrack movie clip from looping when it reaches the final frame

- Loop the Lila animation so she continues to tap her foot until a user clicks to start the race (in other words, prevent Lila from firing the starting pistol before a user starts the race)

- Prevent the individual racers from running before a user starts the race

- Loop the three animations in each racer's movie clip so each character can run continuously, cry continuously, or cheer continuously, depending on the current context of the game

By adding simple functions to control the timelines of the movie clips, you can easily address of all these issues. Functions, as stated above, are bits of programming that perform certain sets of actions. The structure (syntax) of a function is shown below:

Function name (Argument 1, Argument 2, …) : return type {}

Functions should start with the name of the function, followed by the arguments that the function accepts. The function name can be predefined in ActionScript (such as "stop") or user-defined. You will create your own functions later in this project.

Arguments (also known as **parameters**) are the values the function needs as input (for example, the specific frame to go to for the gotoAndPlay function). The number of arguments can vary, depending on the function you're using. Some functions, such as the stop function, do not accept or require any arguments. The arguments of a function are placed inside parentheses. The parentheses are required for all functions, even if a specific function does not accept any arguments.

The third section is the **return type** of a particular function (for example, a certain function might return a bit of text from a specific text field). The **void** value means the function does not return any value. (If this section is left blank, it is assumed the function returns no value.)

The braces (curly brackets) represent the opening and closing of the **function body**. All code that needs to execute when the function is called is written between this pair of braces. This will be important later when you define your own function to perform a number of different actions at once. For basic functions such as stop, the braces are unnecessary.

1. **With gator_race.fla open, double-click the racetrack_mc instance to edit the movie clip in place on the Stage.**

2. **Create a new layer named Actions at the top of the layer stack in the Timeline panel for the movie clip symbol.**

    It is common practice among developers to use a dedicated Actions layer in a complex project, making the scripts easier to find and manage. You cannot add actions to frames on a motion tween layer, so in this case you *must* add a separate layer to attach the actions.

3. **Select the keyframe at Frame 1 of the Actions layer, and then open the Actions panel (Window>Actions).**

Note:

Press Option-F9/F9 to open the Actions panel.

FLASH FOUNDATIONS

In the Actions panel, the **Actions toolbox** contains all of the functions of the ActionScript language, sorted into **classes** (or categories that share the same basic methods and properties). A menu at the top of the Actions toolbox allows you to switch between versions of the ActionScript language.

Clicking a class in the toolbox expands that class to show the options contained within the class, which might include a number of sub-classes. Double-clicking an item in one of the Actions toolbox packages adds that item to the script in the Script pane; this is designed to help you construct scripts with correct syntax.

Script pane

Actions toolbox

Click this button to collapse or expand the Actions toolbox.

Script navigator

This tab shows the selected layer and frame.

The **Script navigator** allows you to navigate through the various elements (movie clips, frames, etc.) in the document.

Above the Script pane, a series of useful tools can help make it easier to write your own scripts.

A The **Add a New Item to the Script** button opens a menu with the same elements that are available in the Actions toolbox.

B Clicking the **Find** button opens the Find and Replace dialog box, which you can use to find specific text in the document, and then replace that text with other text.

C The **Insert Target Path** button lets you choose which object you want to affect with a function or event, with either an absolute or relative path.

D **Check Syntax** helps you check the syntax of your code so errors will not display when the movie runs. If the code you write is correct, a dialog box tells you the script contains no errors. If the script has errors, a dialog box shows you the error location and description.

E **Auto Format** allows you to format and indent the code as you enter it, which helps you manage the code. This is also useful in spacing the code appropriately. This option is available only if the code does not contain any syntax errors.

F When you type a period in the Script pane, the **Show Code Hint** feature opens a pop-up window that shows relevant options to the code you are typing.

G The **Debug Options** help you debug your code, allowing you to set breakpoints into the code for finding errors. When the program reaches a particular frame where the code contains an error, it stops immediately. You can insert breakpoints in the appropriate locations if the program returns errors.

H The **Collapse Between Braces** option shrinks the code between braces (for example, curly braces or brackets), which helps you navigate through the code.

I For easier navigation, you can select a particular block of code and then click the **Collapse Selection** option. The whole block of code collapses.

J The **Expand All** option expands all pieces of collapsed code.

K Clicking the **Apply Block Comment** button places /**/ into the code. Anything you type between the two asterisks is considered a comment. If you select an existing piece of code in the Script pane before clicking this button, the selected text will be surrounded by the comment characters (e.g., /*selected text*/). Comments are used to add explanations or other non-script elements to the code; they are ignored when the script is compiled.

L Clicking the **Apply Line Comment** button adds two forward slashes to the script. Text on the line following this notation will be ignored when the script is compiled.

M Clicking the **Remove Comment** button removes the selected comment from the code.

N Clicking **Show/Hide Toolbox** expands and collapses the Actions toolbox on the left side of the panel.

O Clicking the **Code Snippets** button opens the Code Snippets panel (refer to Project 4 for more on working with code snippets).

P **Build Scripts mode** prompts you for the various elements needed to create a script, using various fields and other notes above the Script pane.

Q The **Help** feature allows you to get assistance on certain topics, which is especially useful in discovering the use of functions, events, etc. Whenever you require details about how a particular function works, use the Help feature as your primary resource.

4. **Place the insertion point in the first line of the Script pane in the Actions panel. Click the Insert Target Path button above the Script pane.**

Most functions need to begin with a statement that determines which object should be affected by the function. The Insert Target Path dialog box presents a list of available objects, which can be useful if you are working with a complex project — or if you simply forget the exact name of an instance.

5. **Make sure the Relative option is selected at the bottom of the Insert Target Path dialog box.**

A **relative path** refers to the position of an object in relation to the currently selected object. Relative paths use the syntax **Object(this).racetrack_mc**, where "this" refers to the timeline containing the script.

An **absolute path** refers to the position of an object in relation to the main file. Absolute paths are written as **Object(root).racetrack_mc**, where "root" refers to the main timeline (Scene 1) of the active file.

Note:

As long as you are maintaining scripts in the same file as the objects you are manipulating, relative references are fine; absolute references will be important if you work with scripts that are external to the Flash file.

You are working inside the Racetrack symbol Stage.

Insert Target Path button

This tab shows where you are adding script (in this case, Frame 1 of the Actions layer).

Frame 1 is selected on the Actions layer in the Racetrack symbol Stage.

6. **With root selected at the top of the list, click OK to add the target path reference to the script.**

7. **In the Actions toolbox, expand the flash.display>MovieClip class, and then expand the Methods folder.**

The flash.display package provides controls for classes of objects you see on the Stage (including movie clips), so the events, methods, and properties of movie clips are accessed in the flash.display>MovieClip class.

8. **Double-click "stop" in the Actions toolbox to insert the command for the respective movie clip.**

When you add this function after the existing "**this**" reference, Flash automatically adds the dot that is required for proper dot syntax.

Double-click the command to insert it into the script, including the necessary punctuation.

Function

Affected object

Location of function

The stop function stops the timeline at a particular frame. In plain English, the code says:

At Frame 1	the background timeline will	stop playing
[where the action was created]	**this**	**stop()**

9. **Place the insertion point at the end of Line 1 in the Script pane, and type a semicolon.**

A semicolon is required at the end of each line of code. If you forget to add this character at the end of a line, your code will result in an error.

10. **Add a new keyframe at Frame 120 of the Actions layer, and then click inside the Actions panel Script pane to place the insertion point on Line 1.**

When the Actions panel is open, selecting a new keyframe in the timeline shows the script associated with the selected keyframe. Simply click in the Script pane to edit the script for the currently selected keyframe.

11. **Type this.stop(); on Line 1 of the Script pane.**

Although you can always use the Actions toolbox to add elements of ActionScript code, in the case of basic functions such as this one, it is usually easier to simply type the command directly in the Script pane.

Type the stop( ) function, including the required path in the Script pane.

Frame 120 of the Actions layer is selected.

If you don't add the stop function at the final keyframe, the Racetrack movie clip would still play only once, but the timeline would automatically return to Frame 1 — which shows the starting line — before stopping. To prevent this, you have to add the stop function at both the beginning and ending frames.

Note:

A small "a" appears in the frame where an action is attached, allowing you to more easily locate the actions in non-dedicated layers.

12. **Click Scene 1 in the Edit bar to return to the main timeline.**

13. **Press Command-Return/Control-Enter to test the movie.**

    Now when you test the movie clip, the racetrack remains stationary. Later in the project, you will add code that causes the racetrack to start moving when Lila fires the starting pistol (which happens only after a user clicks the lila_mc instance).

14. **Close the Player window and return to Flash.**

15. **Save the file and continue to the next exercise.**

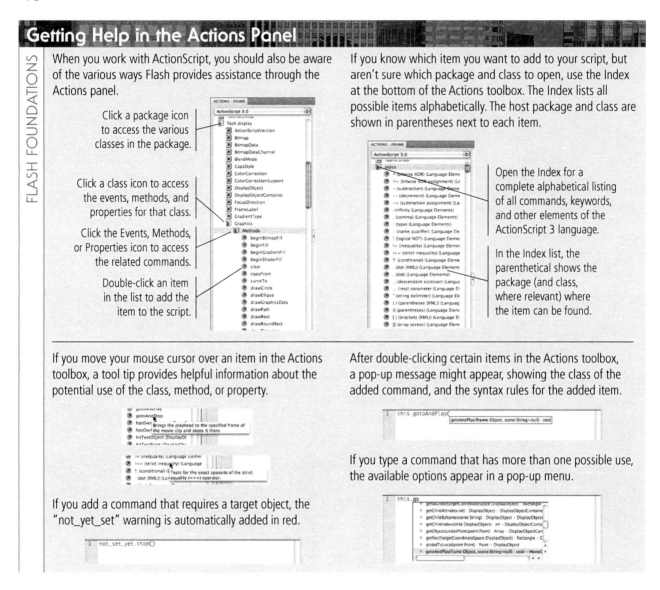

Getting Help in the Actions Panel

When you work with ActionScript, you should also be aware of the various ways Flash provides assistance through the Actions panel.

Click a package icon to access the various classes in the package.

Click a class icon to access the events, methods, and properties for that class.

Click the Events, Methods, or Properties icon to access the related commands.

Double-click an item in the list to add the item to the script.

If you know which item you want to add to your script, but aren't sure which package and class to open, use the Index at the bottom of the Actions toolbox. The Index lists all possible items alphabetically. The host package and class are shown in parentheses next to each item.

Open the Index for a complete alphabetical listing of all commands, keywords, and other elements of the ActionScript 3 language.

In the Index list, the parenthetical shows the package (and class, where relevant) where the item can be found.

If you move your mouse cursor over an item in the Actions toolbox, a tool tip provides helpful information about the potential use of the class, method, or property.

If you add a command that requires a target object, the "not_yet_set" warning is automatically added in red.

After double-clicking certain items in the Actions toolbox, a pop-up message might appear, showing the class of the added command, and the syntax rules for the added item.

If you type a command that has more than one possible use, the available options appear in a pop-up menu.

USE FUNCTIONS TO LOOP FRAME ANIMATIONS

When you tested the movie at the end of the previous exercise, the Background movie clip did not move, but the different characters' timelines were moving. You have to use the same stop function to prevent the characters from running until you want them to run.

You also need to use basic functions to create the loops for the different animations contained in each character's movie clip — running, crying, cheering, and (in Lila's case) foot tapping.

1. **With `gator_race.fla` open, double-click the Baggy movie clip icon in the Library panel (Gators folder) to enter into the movie clip Stage.**

2. **Click the first keyframe on the timeline (Frame 1) to select it.**

    Although it is common to use a separate Actions layer in the timeline — and is required if the layer has a motion tween — the separate Actions layer is not strictly necessary.

3. **In the Actions panel (Window>Actions), click in the Script pane to place the insertion point.**

    From this point forward, we will assume the panel is open. Remember, you can access all panels in the Window menu.

4. **Type `this.stop();` in the Script pane.**

    As in the previous exercise, you are controlling the timeline of the current movie clip, so the "**this**" reference is sufficient.

You are adding the stop function to Frame 1 of the Baggy Anim layer.

5. **Click the Frame 17 keyframe.**

    The "running" animation exists from Frame 10 to Frame 17. For the character to run as long as necessary without creating extra frames, you have to create a loop that sends the playhead from Frame 17 back to Frame 10. The gotoAndPlay function is used for this purpose — moving the playhead from one frame to another in the timeline.

6. **Type `this` on Line 1 in the Script pane.**

    Again, the reference "**this**" refers to the current timeline — in this case, the Baggy movie clip timeline.

7. **In the Actions toolbox, expand flash.display>MovieClip>Methods.**

8. Double-click gotoAndPlay in the Actions toolbox.

Double-clicking inserts the gotoAndPlay function into the Script pane. Because you used the Actions toolbox, Flash adds the required dot between the path and the function.

Double-clicking an item in the Actions toolbox adds the necessary code, including punctuation (except the terminal semicolon).

The gotoAndPlay function is accessed in the flash.display>MovieClip> Methods package.

9. Type 1 0 inside the parentheses of the gotoAndPlay function, and type a semicolon at the end of the line of code.

This code creates a loop so, when the Baggy movie clip reaches Frame 17, the playhead moves back to Frame 10 — resulting in a continuous running effect using only eight frames.

The entire function includes the object path, the command, the function arguments (the frame where you are sending the playhead), and the semicolon.

10. Click Frame 23 in the timeline. On Line 1 in the Script pane, type

> **this.go**

When you type in the Script pane, a code hint menu shows all available options for the current context. As you type, the menu automatically scrolls to the first command that matches what you type.

Note:

Each racer's movie clip includes frame animations for crying when the character loses (Frames 20–23) and cheering when the character wins (Frames 26–29). The gotoAndPlay function is necessary to loop both of these animation sequences.

11. Press Return/Enter to apply the gotoAndPlay function from the pop-up menu.

The opening parenthesis of the gotoAndPlay statement is automatically added to the code; a tool tip hint shows you the syntax rules for the added item. Bold elements in the tool tip — frame, in this case — are required.

12. With the insertion point after the opening parenthesis, type 20);.

Like the stop command, you can simply type the gotoAndPlay command rather than using the Actions toolbox. As you type, the Actions panel provides assistance in the form of pop-up code hint menus and tool tips.

When you write ActionScript, remember that capitalization counts. Make sure you capitalize words in the functions exactly as we show them here. "GoToAndPlay" is not the same as "gotoAndPlay."

Note:

As you become more comfortable working with ActionScript, you'll also become more comfortable typing your own code.

```
1   this.gotoAndPlay(20);
```

13. Click Frame 29 in the timeline. On Line 1 in the Script pane, type

```
this.gotoAndPlay(26);
```

You can use the code hint menu to add the gotoAndPlay command, or simply type the entire statement.

Note:

Because the last frame includes a function to loop the playhead, you don't need to add the stop function to the last frame of the racers' movie clips.

It is not necessary to return to the main Stage before entering into a different symbol's Stage (which you do in the next step).

14. Double-click the Granny movie clip icon in the Library panel to enter into the movie clip Stage. Add the same functions to the Granny movie clip that you added to the Baggy movie clip:

Add the stop() function at Frame 1.

Add the gotoAndPlay() function at Frame 17, referencing Frame 10.

Add the gotoAndPlay() function at Frame 23, referencing Frame 20.

Add the gotoAndPlay() function at Frame 29, referencing Frame 26.

15. **Repeat Step 14 for the Navi and Nipper movie clips.**

16. **Double-click the Lila movie clip in the Library panel to enter into it.**

    - **Add an Actions layer at the top of the timeline, and place new keyframes at Frame 20 and Frame 35.**

      The main layer of the Lila movie clip contains a motion tween, so the extra Actions layer is required to contain the scripts to control this movie clip.

    - **Add the gotoAndPlay() function to Frame 20 of the Lila movie clip, sending the playhead back to Frame 1.**

    - **Add the stop() function to the final frame of the Lila movie clip.**

Note:

The Lila movie clip does not need a stop function in Frame 1 because she should start tapping her foot as soon as the movie opens. Because the final frames of the Lila movie clip are not looped, you need to stop the Lila movie clip when it reaches the final frame.

17. **Click Scene 1 in the Edit bar to return to the main Stage.**

18. **Press Command-Return/Control-Enter to test the movie.**

    When the movie opens, the background and racers remain fixed in position, and Lila taps her foot while waiting to be clicked. You can see the Restart button, which should not appear until the race is finished. Before programming the actual race functionality, you should add the necessary code to hide the Restart button until the race is over.

Lila continuously taps her foot because the movie clip timeline returns to Frame 1 when it reaches Frame 20.

The background and all the characters are fixed in place by the stop functions on Frame 1 in each movie clip.

19. **Close the Player window and return to Flash.**

20. **Save the file and continue to the next exercise.**

USE SCRIPTING TO CONTROL OBJECT PROPERTIES

In addition to controlling the playhead, you can use ActionScript to change the properties of specific objects — including visibility — at different times in a movie. In this case, the Restart button should be hidden when the race starts, and then become visible when the race is over. To accomplish this goal, you use the main movie timeline to add scripts at different points in the race.

1. **With `gator_race.fla` open, add a new layer named Actions at the top of the layer stack on the main timeline.**

   Just as using a different layer for each graphic element makes it easier to manage complex graphics, so can using a dedicated layer (or layers) for actions make it far easier to manage the scripts in a complex movie.

2. **Select Frame 1 of the Actions layer, and then place the insertion point in the first line of the Actions panel Script pane.**

3. **Click the Insert Target Path button above the Script pane.**

4. **Make sure the Relative option is selected at the bottom of the dialog box, and then click restart_btn in the list.**

   Because you are targeting a specific object, the target path is more complex than the simple "this" statement that refers to the current timeline. **Object(this).restart_btn** means the target is an *object* on *this* timeline with the instance name of *restart_btn*.

Targeting a specific object requires the instance name in the path.

Frame 1 of the Actions layer in the main timeline is selected.

5. **Click OK to add the path to the Script pane.**

6. **In the Actions toolbox, expand flash.display>DisplayObject>Properties and double-click visible in the list.**

   The button is visible on the Stage, so it falls into the DisplayObject class. Visibility is an object property, so you can access that option in the Properties set of commands.

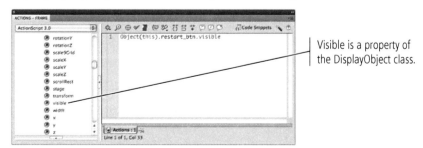

Visible is a property of the DisplayObject class.

7. Type `=false;` at the end of the function line.

An option such as visibility has only two possible options — true (visible) or false (not visible). You could also use the Language Elements>Statements, Keywords & Directives class in the Actions toolbox to add the property value to the code, but it is easier to simply type "true" or "false" to change the visibility property.

Note:

*The true-or-false value of the visible property is called a **Boolean value**.*

The command in the Script pane does not affect the object's appearance on the development Stage.

8. Select Frame 120 of all layers on the main timeline. Press the F5 key to insert new frames to all layers at once.

As stated earlier in the project, the entire movie needs to last 10 seconds — or 120 frames. Before you can use the main timeline to program different actions at various points in the movie, you first have to create the necessary frames in the main timeline.

Because the Actions layer has no content on the Stage, the frames are white instead of gray.

All nine layers should extend to Frame 120.

9. Add a keyframe to Frame 105 of the Actions layer.

10. With Frame 105 of the Actions layer selected in the timeline, place the insertion point in the first line of the Script pane.

11. Repeat the same basic process from Steps 3–7 to add a function that sets the visibility property of the Restart button to true.

The Restart button will only be visible when the Background timeline reaches Frame 105 (i.e., after the race is over).

Note:

Even though the Background movie clip contains 120 frames (enough to create the animation for that movie clip), it is not a good idea to control objects on the main timeline entirely from within a nested movie clip.

12. Press Command-Return/Control-Enter to test the movie.

If you watch for ten seconds, you will see the Restart button reappear shortly before it disappears again. This is because the main timeline loops in the same way any other timeline loops — playing from start to finish and then returning to the beginning.

When the movie first opens, the Restart button is not visible.

The Restart button appears after approximately nine seconds because you haven't yet stopped the main movie timeline.

13. Close the Player window and return to Flash.

14. Select Frame 1 of the Actions layer. Click in the Actions panel Script pane to place the insertion point at the end of the existing script (on Line 1).

15. Press Return/Enter to add a new line, and then press Return/Enter again to move to Line 3.

This extra line is called **white space**, which visually separates different pieces of code within the Script pane.

16. Type this.stop(); on Line 3 of the Script pane.

This statement prevents the movie from playing automatically when it is loaded. You're referring to the current timeline rather than a specific object, so the **this** reference is sufficient in this case.

You can use lines of white space to visually separate sections of code.

17. Add a keyframe to Frame 120 of the Actions layer.

New scripts require keyframes, which means you have to add a keyframe at Frame 120 before you can add the stop function.

18. With Frame 120 of the Actions layer selected, click in the Script pane and add the stop function.

This prevents the timeline from looping back to Frame 1, which means the Restart button remains visible.

19. Save the file and continue to the next stage of the project.

Stage 3 Creating Custom Functions

If you play the movie now, nothing will happen — which is exactly what you want. The action in this movie is entirely dependent on a user clicking the Lila movie clip instance. When a user clicks the Lila movie clip instance, several things need to happen:

- The main timeline needs to start moving. You stopped the main timeline at Frame 1 in an earlier exercise; when a user clicks the Lila instance, the main timeline needs to move past the stop function and start moving (in other words, go to Frame 2).

- The Lila movie clip needs to stop looking at her watch and fire the pistol, and then move to the right and off the Stage area. This animation is already prepared within the movie clip (beginning on Frame 21), and you already created the tween to move the character off the Stage area after firing the pistol.

- Each racer needs to "get set" (Frame 5) and start "running" (Frame 10). You already created the loops, so the characters can run continuously until something stops them.

- The background needs to start moving to simulate the effect of the runners moving across the track. You already created the tween that moves the background to the right, but you also added a stop function that prevents the background from moving when the file opens.

- The "Click me" banner needs to disappear.

Because all these things need to happen when a user clicks Lila, the most logical solution is to define a custom function that triggers when the user clicks the character.

CREATE AN EVENT LISTENER

Creating an event is essentially a two-stage process:

- Add an event listener to a specific object (for example, a button users can click to make something happen), and define the event handler that names the function that will be called and run when the event listener is triggered.

- Define the actual function that is called by the event handler (i.e., exactly what to do when the triggering event occurs).

1. **With gator_race.fla open, add a new layer named Event Handlers to the top of the layer stack on the main timeline.**

2. **Select Frame 1 in the Event Handlers layer. Click in the Actions panel Script pane to place the insertion point.**

   As mentioned earlier, most programmers insert a specific layer for coding events. You can even use separate layers for different types of scripts — as we are doing here by using a separate layer to contain the event handlers in this movie.

3. **On Line 1 of the Script pane, add a relative reference to the lila_mc instance.**

You are attaching an event handler to a specific instance rather than the main timeline, so the path must contain the instance name.

You are using a separate layer to manage the event handler code.

4. **In the Actions toolbox, expand flash.events>EventDispatcher>Methods.**

The flash.events package consists of all the classes that are necessary for performing the specific actions when an event occurs. For example, you can load a movie clip or move images and graphics from one location to another when a particular event occurs.

5. **Double-click addEventListener in the list to add it to the script.**

To perform a set of actions when a particular object is clicked, you must first add an event listener to that object. If you want to perform an action when the user clicks an object, for example, define MouseEvent as the first argument. If you want to trigger an action based on pressing a certain key, specify KeyEvent as the first argument.

The addEventListener function accepts two arguments between the parentheses. The first argument specifies the event that will trigger the action (in other words, the event to listen for). The second argument is the (user-defined) name of the function that will be called when the defined event occurs.

Double-click to add the necessary code.

Note:

When you use the Actions toolbox to place the addEventListener code, the code hints menu automatically appears. You can simply ignore it and type inside the parentheses.

6. **Place the insertion point between the function parentheses.**

7. **Expand flash.events>MouseEvent>Properties, and then double-click CLICK to insert the required code.**

Because you want to initiate an event on the click of the mouse, you are using the CLICK event of the MouseEvent class.

Double-clicking the property adds the appropriate event type (MouseEvent) and specific event (CLICK).

8. **After CLICK and before the closing parenthesis, type , raceStart and add a semicolon after the closing parenthesis.**

The word **raceStart** is the name of the function that you will define in the next exercise.

A user-defined function can have any name. Keep in mind, however, that capitalization counts in ActionScript. RaceStart is not the same function as raceStart or racestart.

Instance name (triggering object)   Event listener   Event listener type   Function name

9. **Save the file and continue to the next exercise.**

DEFINE A CUSTOM FUNCTION

Because stop, gotoAndPlay, and similar functions are so common, they are built into the ActionScript 3 dictionary. Remember, however, that a function is simply a block of code that you want to execute at a certain time — whether at a certain frame or as the result of a button being clicked. Functions can be as basic or complex as necessary — they can execute a single action (such as stopping a timeline) or multiple actions at once.

To complete this project, you need to control nine different elements when a user clicks the Lila instance. Rather than defining nine separate functions for a single event listener, you can combine all nine actions into the single custom function that you named raceStart in the previous exercise.

1. With `gator_race.fla` open, select Frame 1 of the Event Handlers layer. Click to place the insertion point at the end of Line 1 in the Script pane.

2. Press Return/Enter twice to move the insertion point to Line 3.

3. Expand Language Elements>Statements, Keywords & Directives>Definition Keyword in the Actions toolbox.

The Language Elements package contains all syntax and code of the ActionScript language; it contains all keywords and other expressions used to write ActionScript code.

4. Double-click function in the list to add it to the script.

Clicking this option in the Actions toolbox adds the function keyword, as well as the required punctuation (parentheses and braces).

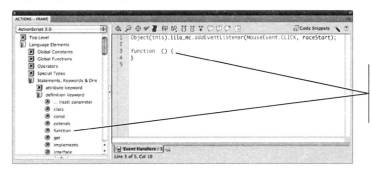

Double-clicking the function keyword adds the required punctuation to the script.

5. Type `raceStart` before the opening parenthesis of the function.

This code links the function to the event handler you defined in the previous exercise. In other words, you're writing the function that will execute when the event handler triggers.

6. Type `event:` between the opening and closing parentheses.

When possible, Flash presents a list of available options in the form of code hints. These menus show a list of options relevant to the code you are currently typing. For example, when you type **event:**, Flash recognizes that the next step is to define the type of event, so it displays code hints for the available types of events.

Note:

Code hints show different options depending on the context of the code you are typing.

7. **Type Mou, then scroll through the code hint menu to find MouseEvent. With MouseEvent highlighted, press Return/Enter to add it to the script.**

This function needs to be called on the click of the mouse, so you use MouseEvent as the argument.

Typing scrolls the code hint menu to the first item that matches what you type.

Pressing Return/Enter adds the highlighted item to the script.

Note:

You can also double-click a code hint to add the item to the script.

A new Line 1 is added to the top of your script; basically, the line tells the file to import a predefined package that defines all of the methods and properties that can be applied to a MouseEvent.

When you write ActionScript inside of Flash, these import statements are not typically necessary because Flash manages this issue for you in most cases (of course, there are exceptions). However, if you write ActionScript code outside of Flash (or export the code to be used in some other application), the import statements must be included at the beginning of the code so the code can accurately process and compile the types of objects (called **classes**) that are used in the code.

Note:

If you accidentally click the Mouse event instead of the MouseEvent event in the code hint list, the wrong import statement will be added to Line 1. You would have to delete the incorrect code and then redo Steps 6–7 to add the correct import statement.

Although this statement is not strictly necessary in the case of this project, Flash automatically adds it for you based on the code you have added through the Actions toolbox; it doesn't hurt anything to leave it there.

```
1   import flash.events.MouseEvent;
2
3   Object(this).lila_mc.addEventListener(MouseEvent.CLICK, raceStart);
4
5   function raceStart (event:MouseEvent) {
6   }
7
```

8. **Type a colon outside the closing parenthesis, and then choose void from the code hint menu.**

The last part of this function (void) specifies the return type for the function. You have to provide the void value if your function returns no value.

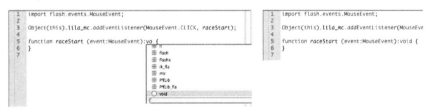

Note:

Every function has a return type that specifies the type of data (integer, string, etc.) that returns to the function. Void is used if the function returns no data.

9. **Click after the opening brace and press Return/Enter to add a line between the function braces.**

Although not required, coding convention typically places each action of a function on a separate line in the script.

10. **Type this.gotoAndPlay(2);.**

Because you are adding the function on the main timeline, **this** refers to the main movie timeline.

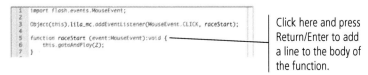

Click here and press Return/Enter to add a line to the body of the function.

11. **Press Return/Enter to move to the next line in the script.**

12. **On the new line, add a relative reference to the lila_mc instance.**

    This line of code commands a specific object on the timeline, so the target path needs to include the specific instance name.

Note:

When you use the Actions toolbox to add a function, the code automatically includes the opening and closing braces. If you simply type the function keyword, make sure you add the closing brace at the end of the lines that make up the function body.

13. **With the insertion point after the relative reference, type .gotoAndPlay(21);.**

    ```
    1  import flash.events.MouseEvent;
    2
    3  Object(this).lila_mc.addEventListener(MouseEvent.CLICK, raceStart);
    4
    5  function raceStart (event:MouseEvent):void {
    6      this.gotoAndPlay(2);
    7      Object(this).lila_mc.gotoAndPlay(21);
    8  }
    9
    ```

    When a user clicks the Lila instance, the Lila movie clip timeline moves to Frame 21, where Lila stops looking at her watch and fires the starting pistol.

14. **Press Return/Enter to move to the next line.**

15. **Add additional commands to the function to set the remaining movie clips in motion. Use the Actions toolbox or simply type the necessary code:**

    ```
    Object(this).racetrack_mc.gotoAndPlay(2);
    Object(this).char1_mc.gotoAndPlay(5);
    Object(this).char2_mc.gotoAndPlay(5);
    Object(this).char3_mc.gotoAndPlay(5);
    Object(this).char4_mc.gotoAndPlay(5);
    ```

    ```
    1  import flash.events.MouseEvent;
    2
    3  Object(this).lila_mc.addEventListener(MouseEvent.CLICK, raceStart);
    4
    5  function raceStart (event:MouseEvent):void {
    6      this.gotoAndPlay(2);
    7      Object(this).lila_mc.gotoAndPlay(21);
    8      Object(this).racetrack_mc.gotoAndPlay(2);
    9      Object(this).char1_mc.gotoAndPlay(5);
    10     Object(this).char2_mc.gotoAndPlay(5);
    11     Object(this).char3_mc.gotoAndPlay(5);
    12     Object(this).char4_mc.gotoAndPlay(5);
    13 }
    ```

    Moving the playhead to Frame 2 of the Racetrack symbol bypasses the stop function, which allows the movie clip's timeline to play. Frame 5 in each racer's movie clip represents the "get set" position before the characters start running.

Note:

*The code between the braces represents the **function body** — the actions that will be performed when the function is called.*

16. **Press Command-Return/Control-Enter to test the movie. In the Player window, click the Lila movie clip.**

    When you click the starter, the racetrack and characters all move as they should:

    • Lila raises the gun and fires.

    • The four racers get into the set position, and then start running.

    • The racetrack moves to the right.

    • After the main timeline reaches Frame 105 (approximately 9 seconds), the Restart button appears.

The banner_mc instance still remains visible throughout the race.

17. **Close the Player window and return to Flash.**

18. **With Frame 1 of the Event Handlers layer selected, click in the Script pane to place the insertion point after the last command in the raceStart function.**

Note:

You still need to program the Restart button, but the necessary functions won't make sense until you program the rest of the game's functionality. You will create the second event handler and function later in this project.

19. **Press Return/Enter to add a new line to the function. Type the following code to hide the banner_mc instance after a user clicks the Lila instance:**

```
Object(this).banner_mc.visible=false;
```

```
1   import flash.events.MouseEvent;
2
3   Object(this).lila_mc.addEventListener(MouseEvent.CLICK, raceStart);
4
5   function raceStart (event:MouseEvent):void {
6       this.gotoAndPlay(2);
7       Object(this).lila_mc.gotoAndPlay(21);
8       Object(this).racetrack_mc.gotoAndPlay(2);
9       Object(this).char1_mc.gotoAndPlay(5);
10      Object(this).char2_mc.gotoAndPlay(5);
11      Object(this).char3_mc.gotoAndPlay(5);
12      Object(this).char4_mc.gotoAndPlay(5);
13      Object(this).banner_mc.visible=false;
14  }
```

Add this line of code to the function to hide the banner when a user clicks Lila.

20. **Save the file and continue to the next stage of the project.**

Stage 4 Working with Variables and Arrays

When you last tested your movie, you saw that clicking the Lila instance correctly sets all the pieces of the movie into motion. You might have noticed, however, that the racers keep running after the race is over, and all four runners are in an even tie throughout the race.

Programming the remaining game functionality requires two additional blocks of code: one to move a different character at specific intervals throughout the race, and another to determine which character wins the race. To create the first half of this functionality, you will use variables and randomly generated numbers.

Variables are named spaces in the memory that hold values. A variable exists as soon as you declare it; in other words, a variable exists because you say so.

Data types define the type of information a particular variable can hold. ActionScript 3 defines several primitive data types:

Note:

A variable is simply a container that holds information needed in other parts of the code.

- The **number** data type can hold any number.

- The **integer** (int) data type can hold any whole number (a number with no decimal point).

- The **unsigned integer** (uint) data type can hold any whole, non-negative number.

- The **string** data type holds the actual characters within a set of quotation marks.

- The **boolean** data type can have only one of two values: true or false.

- The **null** data type contains only one value: null

- The **void** data type contains only one value: undefined.

To declare a variable, you need to use the var statement.

> **var myAge : uint;**

In this statement, you have declared a variable named *myAge*. The second part of the statement determines that the variable value must be a non-negative whole number (as ages typically are, unless you refer to yourself as "something and a half").

When you declare a variable, you can also define an initial value at the same time by using the equal sign (called an **assignment operator**):

> **var myAge : uint = 40;**

Note:

You can declare a variable without declaring its type, but the best practice is to declare a variable with its data type.

SCRIPT WITH VARIABLES AND RANDOM NUMBERS

At several times throughout the race, one of the racers will move to the left, basically "taking the lead." To accomplish this movement, you need a mechanism to randomly move one character instance to the left. ActionScript 3 includes the tools you need to accomplish this task.

Here's a plain-English explanation of the script you will write in this exercise:

- The first part of the script will generate a random number between 0 and 1.

- That number will be multiplied by 4 so it can be associated with one of the characters' numbers (1–4). Since the characters are numbered 1, 2, 3, and 4 — whole numbers — you also have to round up the randomly generated number to match one of the character numbers.

- The second part of the script will add strings of text to the generated number to create the instance name of the character that will move when the script runs.

This script will repeat a number of times throughout the race. Every time the code runs, a different character moves or "takes the lead" in the race. (Because the process is random, the same racer might move more than once.)

1. **With gator_race.fla open, add a keyframe at Frame 24 of the Actions layer on the main timeline.**

2. **With Frame 24 selected, click in the Script pane of the Actions panel and type var temp.**

   The word *temp* is the name of the variable you are defining. As with instances of symbols, you have to name variables if you want to use them in ActionScript.

Note:

You can declare a variable using the Language Elements> Statements, Keywords & Directives>Definition Keyword class in the Actions toolbox.

3. **Type a colon after the variable name in the script, and then choose Number from the code hint menu.**

   This command declares one variable (*temp*) of a Number data type. You defined this variable to hold a number that will be generated through the use of random numbers.

Note:

A variable exists as soon as you declare it — in other words, simply because you say so.

4. **Type a semicolon at the end of the line and press Return/Enter twice to move to Line 3 in the Script pane.**

5. **Type `temp=` in Line 3 of the Script pane.**

   Remember, *temp* is the name of the variable you just declared. The next step is to assign a value to this variable.

6. **In the Actions toolbox, expand Top Level>Math>Methods. Double-click random in the list to insert it into the script.**

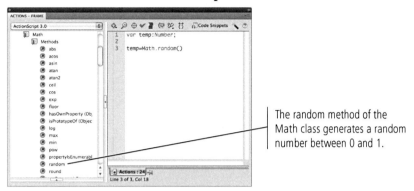

The random method of the Math class generates a random number between 0 and 1.

7. **Type `*4;` after the Math.random function.**

   Because there are four participants in this race, you also have to multiply the random number by 4. Every time the value is generated, it is converted into a value ranging from 0 to 4. (Don't worry if this sounds a bit confusing; it will make more sense shortly.)

8. **On the next line in the Script pane, type `temp=`.**

9. **In the Actions toolbox, double-click ceil (in Top Level>Math>Methods).**

10. **Type `temp` in the parentheses of the Math.ceil function, and then add a semicolon at the end of the line.**

    The ceil method converts a number — in this case, the value in the *temp* variable — to the nearest integer that is either greater than or equal to that number; in other words, it rounds up to the next whole number.

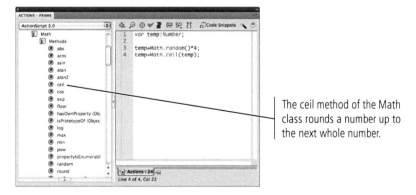

The ceil method of the Math class rounds a number up to the next whole number.

Together, these two lines of code generate a random number (between 0 and 1), multiply that number by 4, and round the number up to the nearest whole number. The result is stored as the value of the temp variable.

11. Press Return/Enter twice to move to Line 6 of the Script pane, and then type

```
this["char"+temp+"_mc"]
```

This statement calls the particular racer whose value is generated by the *temp* variable. (Remember, you previously assigned instance names char1, char2, char3, and char4 to the different character instances.)

The brackets after the word "**this**" contain a single piece of code that defines the instance name. Within the brackets:

- **"char"** and **"_mc"** (including the quotation marks) are strings; the actual characters inside the quotation marks will be used.

- **+** is the addition operator; although commonly used for actual mathematical operations, the **+** operator can also be used to combine different data types.

- *temp* is the variable you defined earlier; it contains a whole number between 1 and 4.

Note that the variable name is not surrounded by quotation marks because you want to use the value of the variable. If you surrounded the variable name with quotes, the function would treat the variable name as a text string.

12. Outside the closing bracket, type .x=.

As we stated earlier, you are writing this code to move one character to the left. By adding the x property (including the required dot) to the statement, this statement now refers to the horizontal (x) position of the instance, which is determined by the randomly generated variable.

The x property determines an object's horizontal position (across) on the Stage. The y property determines the object's vertical position (up or down) on the Stage. To move something left on the Stage, you have to subtract from the object's x position.

13. After the "=" in the Script pane, type

```
this["char"+temp+"_mc"].x-50;
```

Remember, the right side of the statement is assigned to the left side of the statement. This line of code moves the selected character 50 pixels left from its previous position.

14. Select Lines 3–6 in the Script pane, and then press Command/Control-C to copy the selected code.

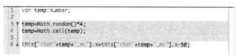

15. In the timeline, add keyframes at Frames 36, 48, 60, 72, 84, and 96 of the Actions layer.

Note:

In this case, you do not need to add the dot between the word "this" and the statement that defines the appropriate character name.

Note:

The different operators in ActionScript 3 can be accessed in the Language Elements>Operators class in the Actions toolbox.

Note:

*The equal sign (**assignment operator**) assigns values from right to left and not vice-versa.*

Note:

Add to the x property to move an object right.

Subtract from the x property to move an object left.

Add to the y property to move an object down.

Subtract from the y property to move an object up.

16. **Select Frame 36 and paste (Command/Control-V) the copied code into the Script pane.**

You don't need to declare the variable every time you want to use it, so you didn't need to copy Line 1 of the script in Frame 24.

When the main timeline reaches Frame 36, the temp variable gets a new value, which maps to a (possibly) different character. The character identified by the new variable value will then move 50 pixels to the left.

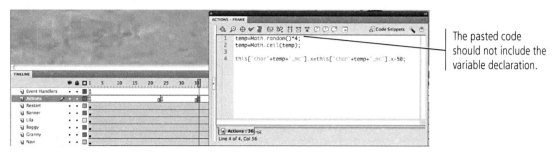

The pasted code should not include the variable declaration.

17. **Repeat Step 16 to paste the copied code into Frames 48, 60, 72, 84, and 96 of the Actions layer.**

One character will move left every second of the race.

This code is pasted into the keyframes at Frame 36, 48, 60, 72, 84, and 96 to move one character every second.

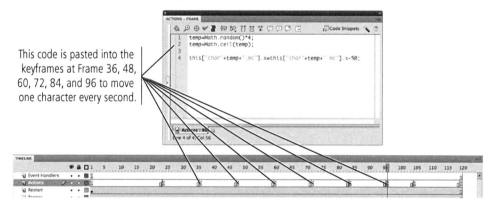

18. **Save the file and continue to the next exercise.**

Translating ActionScript to Plain English

Have you ever heard the terms "left-brain thinker" and "right-brain thinker"? Right-brain thinkers are typically more visually oriented, while left-brain thinkers are typically more logically oriented.

This delineation is why ActionScript sometimes causes problems for graphic designers, who are frequently right-brain thinkers. To put it simply, ActionScript is computer programming. Being successful at computer programming requires a good understanding of logic and quantitative reasoning — which can be a challenge for many right-brain thinkers.

Using examples is the best way to explain the code you are creating in this project. The table to the right shows what is happening with the *temp* variable.

Random number	*4	Ceiled	Calls character
0.1	0.4	1	char1_mc
0.2	0.8	1	char1_mc
0.3	1.2	2	char2_mc
0.4	1.6	2	char2_mc
0.5	2.0	2	char2_mc
0.6	2.4	3	char3_mc
0.7	2.8	3	char3_mc
0.8	3.2	4	char4_mc
0.9	3.6	4	char4_mc

CREATE AN ARRAY TO STORE OBJECT POSITIONS

To determine which character wins the race, you need to write a script that captures the positions of each racer instance after the race is over. An **array** is essentially a type of variable that stores a group of values instead of a single value. A simple array declaration uses the following syntax:

> **var classmates:Array = new Array();**

This statement declares an array variable named *classmates* of unlimited size, so you can enter any number of elements into this particular array. You can limit the number of values in an array by typing a number between the array object parentheses:

> **var classmates:Array = new Array(3);**

You can also directly define elements of the array by typing the values inside the array object parentheses:

> **var classmates:Array = new Array("Linus", "Sally", "Charlie");**

If you don't directly define the array elements, you can define them in a list based on the array **index value**, which is simply the numbered position of specific elements in the array, beginning with 0. Array indexes always begin with 0, not 1.

> **classmates[0]="Linus"**
>
> **classmates[1]="Sally"**
>
> **classmates[2]="Charlie"**

Note:

Array indexes always begin with 0, not 1.

1. **With gator_race.fla open, insert a keyframe at Frame 100 of the Actions layer on the main timeline.**

   The final change of character position occurs at Frame 96, and the racetrack tween stops moving at Frame 100. You define the race winner as soon as the race ends — at Frame 100 on the main timeline.

2. **With Frame 100 selected, click in the Actions panel Script pane and type**

   var arrPosition:

3. **Choose Array from the code hint menu and press Return/Enter.**

Frame 100 of the Actions layer is selected.

4. Type =new Array(4); at the end of the line.

There are only four participants in this race, so you are creating an array object that can have only four elements. The next step is to store the positions of each racer in the different elements of the array.

```
1  var arrPosition:Array=new Array(4);
```

5. On the next line of the Script pane, type:

```
arrPosition[0]=this.char1_mc.x;
```

Each array element is identified by an index value in brackets; the first element of the array always has an index value of 0, the second element has an index value of 1, and so on.

The left half of this statement says that you are defining the first element (**arrPosition [0]**) in the array. The right half of the statement (after the equal sign) assigns a value to that array element.

In plain English, this line says that the first value in the array (**arrPosition[0]**) equals the current x position of char1.

```
1  var arrPosition:Array=new Array(4);
2  arrPosition[0]=this.char1_mc.x;
```

6. Beginning on Line 3, add the following three lines of code to store the x positions of the other race participants in the different array positions:

```
arrPosition[1]=this.char2_mc.x;
arrPosition[2]=this.char3_mc.x;
arrPosition[3]=this.char4_mc.x;
```

Make sure each line of code has a different index number in the array position brackets (e.g., **arrPosition[0]**, **arrPosition[1]**, etc.), as well as a different character number in the instance names.

```
1  var arrPosition:Array=new Array(4);
2  arrPosition[0]=this.char1_mc.x;
3  arrPosition[1]=this.char2_mc.x;
4  arrPosition[2]=this.char3_mc.x;
5  arrPosition[3]=this.char4_mc.x;
```

7. Save the file and continue to the next stage of the project.

Note:

This array stores the positions of each racer at Frame 100 (after the position changes that occur throughout the race). The current x position of char1 is stored in the first array element, the position of char2 is stored in the second element, and so on.

Stage 5 Scripting Loops

In the previous exercise, you defined an array to store the position of each racer. The next step is to write code that compares the different values stored in the array to determine which value is lowest. Whichever character is farthest to the left (the lowest x value) "wins" the race.

To successfully evaluate each value in the array, you need to run the comparison script for each element in the array; in the case of the *arrPosition* array, you run the script four times. ActionScript loops are useful whenever you need something to happen more than once. There are five basic types of loops in ActionScript 3.

A **for loop** takes three arguments between the parentheses on the first line: the initialization value for a variable that has already been declared (**a=0**), the condition that determines how long the loop lasts (**a<5**), and the increment statement that increases the value of the variable each time the loop is run (**a++**). All actions you want to execute are contained in the braces.

```
for (a=0; a<5; a++) {
        char1.x = char1.x–50;
}
```

In plain English, this code says:

> Start with the variable *a* equal to zero. Perform the actions within the braces (i.e., move the instance named char1 left 50 pixels), and then add one to variable *a*. As long as variable *a* is less than five, repeat these actions.

A **while loop** has only one argument — the condition in which the loop runs. The variable is incremented at the end of the loop action. The while loop assumes the variable is declared and initialized outside the loop.

```
while (a<5) {
        char1.x = char1.x–30;
        a++;
}
```

A **do while loop** is basically the same as a while loop, except the condition is placed at the end of the loop, which allows the loop to run at least once even if the condition is false. For example:

```
do {
        char1.x = char1.x–30;
} while (a<5)
```

If the variable *a* has a value greater than 5 before the program reaches this loop, the char1 instance will still move one time before the loop condition is determined to be false and the loop is exited.

The **for...in loop** evaluates the elements of an array. The for...in loop uses the following syntax:

```
for (var i in array) {
        Perform some action;
}
```

The first part of the condition (*variable* in *array*) declares a variable that represents the current index value in the array. The second part of the condition identifies the specific array being evaluated.

A for…in loop automatically executes the braced code for each element stored in the array. If an array stores four elements, for example, the loop will execute four times. The first time the loop runs, the variable value is 0 (the first index value). The second time the loop runs, the variable value is 1 (the second index value). This continues until the loop has evaluated all elements in the array, at which point the loop is exited.

The **for each…in loop** is similar to the for…in loop, except the variable in the array condition is the actual value in the array elements. For example:

var array=new array ("Patty", "Lucy", "Schroeder");

for each (var i in array) {

　　Perform some action;

}

Using a for…in loop, the value of *i* increments to the next array position every time the loop iterates, so:

First pass	**i=0**
Second pass	**i=1**
Third pass	**i=2**

Using the for each…in loop, the variable in the loop condition equals the actual value of the array element, so:

First pass	**i="Patty"**
Second pass	**i="Lucy"**
Third pass	**i="Schroeder"**

DEFINE A FOR…IN LOOP TO EVALUATE ARRAY ELEMENTS

At this point in the race movie, you have stored each racer's position in an array named *arrPosition*. The next task is to add a mechanism to evaluate the different values stored in the array to determine which character's movie clip instance is farthest left on the Stage, effectively "winning" the race. As we explained, a for…in loop is specifically designed to cycle through all of the values in an array.

Several variables are required to compare the different array values:

lowest This variable will be initialized as the x position of the first character, creating a basis of comparison. The loop will then compare this value to the next value in the array to determine which is lower.

pos This variable will hold the index value of the lowest array value (0, 1, 2, or 3) as determined by the comparison.

i This variable will represent the current index position in the array evaluated in the for…in loop.

1. With `gator_race.fla` open, select Frame 100 of the Actions layer in the main timeline.

2. Place the insertion point at the end of the existing script (in the Actions panel Script pane) and press Return/Enter twice to move to Line 7.

3. At the current insertion point, type the following code to declare a variable named "lowest" of the integer data type.

    `var lowest:int`

4. After the variable declaration, add the following code to initialize the lowest variable to equal the first value stored in the arrPosition array.

    `=arrPosition[0];`

   By initializing the variable as the first value in the array, you establish a basis for comparing the other values in the array.

Add an equal sign and the specific array position to initialize the variable.

Frame 100 of the Actions layer is selected.

5. Press Return/Enter to move to the next line in the Script pane.

6. On Line 8 of the Script pane, type:

    `var pos:int=0;`

   This declares a variable named *pos* of the integer data type with an initial value of 0. This variable will store the array position associated with the lowest value in the array. (If you do not initialize the variable to 0, running the game multiple times in the Flash Player can cause problems in determining the true winner of the race.)

7. Press Return/Enter twice after the second variable declaration to move to Line 10 in the Script pane.

8. In the Actions toolbox, expand Language Elements>Statements, Keywords & Directives>Statement and double-click for..in.

   As with other pieces of code, using the Actions toolbox adds the necessary syntax for a specific command. We recommend using the Actions toolbox for loops and conditions until you are familiar and comfortable with the syntax rules.

Add the for...in statement to the script.

9. **Between the parentheses of the for statement, type:**

> **var i in arrPosition**

In plain English, this line means, "while the value of i is within the length of the array named arrPosition." In other words, this loop will execute while the value of *i* is less than or equal to the number of values stored in the *arrPosition* array.

The first time the loop runs, *i* is 0 (the first index value in the array). Each time the loop **iterates** (repeats), the value of *i* becomes the next index value in the array; so the second time the loop runs, *i* is 1 (the second index value in the array), and so on. The number of elements in the array is four, so this loop will continue until the value of *i* reaches 4.

Note:

When you create a for…in loop, you can declare the variable inside the loop condition. It is not necessary to declare the variable before entering the loop.

```
1   var arrPosition:Array=new Array(4);
2   arrPosition[0]=this.char1_mc.x;
3   arrPosition[1]=this.char2_mc.x;
4   arrPosition[2]=this.char3_mc.x;
5   arrPosition[3]=this.char4_mc.x;
6
7   var lowest:int=arrPosition[0];
8   var pos:int=0;
9
10  for (var i in arrPosition) {
11  }
12
```

10. **Place the cursor after the opening brace and press Return/Enter.**

Like the custom function you defined earlier, any code you want to execute during the loop must be placed within the braces.

11. **In the Actions toolbox, double-click if (in Language Elements>Statements, Keywords & Directives>Statements) to add the condition to the script.**

The if statement is a called a **conditional statement**. In other words, you are now writing code to determine what happens *if a certain condition is true*.

The if statement has its own parentheses (where you define the condition to check) and braces (where you define the action to perform if the condition is true).

This closing brace closes the entire for statement.

12. **Between the parentheses of the if statement, type:**

> **arrPosition[i]<lowest**

Remember that in Step 4, you initialized the variable lowest to equal the first value stored in the array. In this conditional statement, you compare the value of the current array position to the value of the variable *lowest*.

```
1   var arrPosition:Array=new Array(4);
2   arrPosition[0]=this.char1_mc.x;
3   arrPosition[1]=this.char2_mc.x;
4   arrPosition[2]=this.char3_mc.x;
5   arrPosition[3]=this.char4_mc.x;
6
7   var lowest:int=arrPosition[0];
8   var pos:int=0;
9
10  for (var i in arrPosition) {
11      if (arrPosition[i]<lowest) {
12  }
13
14  }
```

The variable *i* represents the current array position based on the for…in loop.

- The first time the loop runs, *i* = 0. The conditional if statement compares the value in arrPosition[0] to the value of the variable *lowest*.

- The second time the loop runs, *i* = 1. The conditional if statement compares the value in arrPosition[1] to the value of the variable *lowest*.

- The third time the loop runs, *i* = 2. The conditional if statement compares the value in arrPosition[2] to the value of the variable *lowest*.

- The fourth time the loop runs, *i* = 3. The conditional if statement compares the value in arrPosition[3] to the value of the variable *lowest*.

13. **After the opening brace of the if statement, press Return/Enter. On Lines 12 and 13 of the script, type:**

```
lowest=arrPosition[i];

pos=i;
```

The statements between the conditional if braces determine what happens if the condition is true. In other words:

```
5   arrPosition[3]=this.char4_mc.x;
6
7   var lowest:int=arrPosition[0];
8   var pos:int=0;
9
10  for (var i in arrPosition) {
11      if (arrPosition[i]<lowest) {
12          lowest=arrPosition[i];
13          pos=i;
14      }
15
16  }
17
```

If the value of arrPosition[i] is less than the value of the *lowest* variable,

then the value of arrPosition[i] becomes the new value of the *lowest* variable

and the value of *i* becomes the new value of the *pos* variable.

Since the x-axis origin ("0") is the left edge of the screen, smaller numbers are closer to the left edge and thus "in the lead" — ultimately, the character with the lowest x value will win the race.

This loop compares each value in the array to find the smallest number — the winner. When the comparison finds a value that is less than the current value of the *lowest* variable, that value becomes the new value of the *lowest* variable. The associated array position (i) is then stored in the *pos* variable to identify the location of the winning character.

> *Note:*
>
> *The two closing braces (}) — one for the if conditional statement and one for the for...in loop — were added by clicking the commands in the Actions toolbox. If you type your own code, you need to remember to close the braces manually.*

14. **Save the file and continue to the next exercise.**

Translating ActionScript to Plain English, Part 2

Suppose the racers' x positions at the end of the race are:

char1_mc (Baggy)	25	so	arrPosition[0] = 25
char2_mc (Granny)	23	so	arrPosition[1] = 23
char3_mc (Navi)	20	so	arrPosition[2] = 20
char4_mc (Nipper)	21	so	arrPosition[3] = 21

Before the program enters the for...in loop, the variable *lowest* contains the value of arrPosition[0], or 25. When the program reaches the for...in loop:

First run of the loop:	i = 0	arrPosition[0] < 25 ?	(Is 25 less than 25?)	False
Second run of the loop:	i = 1	arrPosition[1] < 25 ?	(Is 23 less than 25?)	True, so
				lowest = arrPosition[1] = 23
				pos = 1
Third run of the loop:	i = 2	arrPosition[2] < 23 ?	(Is 20 less than 23?)	True, so
				lowest = arrPosition[2] = 20
				pos = 2
Fourth run of the loop:	i = 3	arrPosition[3] < 20 ?	(Is 21 less than 20?)	False
Fifth run of the loop:	i = 4, which is not a position in the arrPosition array			

The loop is exited.

When the loop is finished, the *lowest* variable is the leftmost x position of the four characters — the winning character (in this example, Navi). The *pos* variable equals the index value of the array position in the *lowest* variable.

In this example, arrPosition[2] holds the lowest value, so the *pos* variable equals 2.

USE AN IF ELSE CONDITION TO CALL MOVIE CLIP FRAMES

In the previous exercise, you defined a script that identifies the lowest value in the arrPosition array. Next, you need to write a script that maps the index value of the lowest array value (which you stored in the *pos* variable) to the appropriate character instance on the Stage — effectively identifying the "winner" of the race.

You also need write a script to tell each character what to do, based on the results of evaluation. Because you have four characters, you need to execute the script four times; a for loop is ideally suited for running a set of actions a specific number of times.

For each character (each iteration of the loop), you will write a conditional if else statement that tells the character what to do. If the character wins, the script should call Frame 26 of the movie clip's timeline. If the character does not win, the script should call Frame 20 of the movie clip's timeline.

Note:

Remember, each character's movie clip contains a "winning" (cheering) frame animation beginning on Frame 26 and a "losing" (crying) frame animation beginning on Frame 20.

1. **With `gator_race.fla` open, select Frame 100 of the Actions layer on the main timeline. Place the insertion point at the end of the code in the Actions panel Script pane. Press Return/Enter twice to add white space.**

2. **Declare a variable named "chk" that will hold an integer value; initialize the value of this variable as "pos+1" by typing:**

   ```
   var chk:int=pos+1;
   ```

   Remember, the *pos* variable holds the array position of the lowest value in the array. Because the array positions are numbered from 0–3 and the characters are numbered from 1–4, you have to add 1 to the array position of the lowest value to determine which character wins the race.

   ```
   1   var arrPosition:Array=new Array(4);
   2   arrPosition[0]=this.char1_mc.x;
   3   arrPosition[1]=this.char2_mc.x;
   4   arrPosition[2]=this.char3_mc.x;
   5   arrPosition[3]=this.char4_mc.x;
   6
   7   var lowest:int=arrPosition[0];
   8   var pos:int=0;
   9
   10  for (var i in arrPosition) {
   11      if (arrPosition[i]<lowest) {
   12          lowest=arrPosition[i];
   13          pos=i;
   14      }
   15
   16  }
   17
   18  var chk:int=pos+1
   19
   ```

   You're still working on Frame 100 of the Actions layer on the main Timeline.

3. **On the next line of the script, declare a variable named "a" that will hold an integer value by typing:**

   ```
   var a:int;
   ```

   This variable will be incremented in a loop and compared to the variable *chk* to define the action of each character instance.

4. **Press Return/Enter twice to move to Line 21. In the Actions toolbox, expand Language Elements>Statements, Keywords & Directives>Statement and double-click for in the list.**

5. Between the parentheses of the for statement, type:

    `a=1; a<=4; a++`

```
18  var chk:int=pos+1;
19  var a:int;
20
21  for (a=1; a<=4; a++) {
22  }
23
```

The first argument (**a=1**) initializes variable *a* to 1.

The second argument (**a<=4**) adds a condition so the loop executes only while the value of *a* is less than or equal to 4.

The third argument (**a++**) increments the value of *a* by 1.

6. Place the cursor after the opening brace and press Return/Enter.

7. In the Actions toolbox, expand Language Elements>Statements, Keywords & Directives>Statement and double-click if in the list.

8. Between the parentheses in the if condition, type:

    `a==chk`

The **equality operator** (**==**) determines whether the two variable values are equal. In plain English, this line of code checks to see if the value of variable *a* is equal to variable *chk*.

```
18  var chk:int=pos+1;
19  var a:int;
20
21  for (a=1; a<=4; a++) {
22      if (a==chk) {
23      }
24
25  }
26
```
— This brace closes the if statement.
— This brace closes the for statement.

Note:

*Remember, **chk = pos+1**, or the number of the character instance with the lowest x position.*

This loop runs until *a* is less than or equal to 4; *a* is incremented each time the loop runs.

First run:	a = 1	The program enters the if condition, compares the value of *a* to the value of *chk*.
Second run:	a = 2	The program enters the if condition, compares the value of *a* to the value of *chk*.
Third run:	a = 3	The program enters the if condition, compares the value of *a* to the value of *chk*.
Fourth run:	a = 4	The program enters the if condition, compares the value of *a* to the value of *chk*.
Fifth run:	a = 5	The variable *a* is not less than or equal to 4, so the program exits the loop.

You now need to tell the program what to do when *a* equals *chk* (the character wins the race), and what to do if *a* does not equal *chk* (the character does not win the race).

9. After the opening brace of the if condition, press Return/Enter.

10. On Line 23 of the Script pane, type:

    `this["char"+a+"_mc"].gotoAndPlay(26);`

This statement applies the same technique you used earlier to move a character based on a randomly generated number. In other words, you are appending strings to the value of variable *a* to result in a character instance name (char1_mc, char2_mc, and so on).

```
18  var chk:int=pos+1;
19  var a:int;
20
21  for (a=1; a<=4; a++) {
22      if (a==chk) {
23          this["char"+a+"_mc"].gotoAndPlay(26);
24      }
25
26  }
27
```

So if the value of *a* equals the value of *chk*, the character wins the race. The gotoAndPlay command calls Frame 26 of that movie clip's timeline.

Note:

In the Script pane, text strings (including the enclosing quotation marks) appear in green. If you forget to include a quotation mark in your code, the script will not work properly. Use the colors in the Script pane as an indication of potential errors:

Text strings appear in green.

Code elements (functions, methods, etc.) appear in blue.

Variable names, parameters, and values appear in black.

11. **Press Return/Enter to move to the next line in the Script pane.**

12. **In the Actions toolbox, double-click else (Language Elements>Statements, Keywords & Directives>Statement).**

The previous line defines what happens if *a* is equal to *chk*. Using the else command, you define what happens if *a* is not equal to *chk*.

```
18   var chk:int=pos+1;
19   var a:int;
20
21   for (a=1; a<=4; a++) {
22       if (a==chk) {
23           this["char"+a+"_mc"].gotoAndPlay(26);
24           } else {
25
26   }
27
28   }
29
```

Double-clicking else in the Actions toolbox adds a closing brace for the if statement and an opening brace for the else statement.

This is now the closing brace for the else statement.

This is still the closing brace for the for statement.

13. **In the empty line after the opening brace of the else statement (Line 25 in our example), type:**

```
this["char"+a+"_mc"].gotoAndPlay(20);
```

If *a* is not equal to *chk*, this line of code calls Frame 20 of the character's movie clip (the beginning of the "losing" animation).

```
18   var chk:int=pos+1;
19   var a:int;
20
21   for (a=1; a<=4; a++) {
22       if (a==chk) {
23           this["char"+a+"_mc"].gotoAndPlay(26);
24           } else {
25   this["char"+a+"_mc"].gotoAndPlay(20);
26   }
27
28   }
29
```

14. **Click the Auto Format button in the Actions panel to clean up the code.**

You have the correct code after the previous step, but it might be difficult to decipher visually. Although double-clicking an item in the Actions toolbox adds the necessary code (including punctuation), the code is not always formatted to be readable by humans. Clicking the Auto Format button makes the code easier to read.

If your script contains syntax errors, clicking the Auto Format button warns you of the errors; code with syntax errors is not reformatted.

```
19
20   var chk:int = pos + 1;
21   var a:int;
22
23   for (a=1; a<=4; a++)
24   {
25       if (a == chk)
26       {
27           this["char" + a + "_mc"].gotoAndPlay(26);
28       }
29       else
30       {
31           this["char" + a + "_mc"].gotoAndPlay(20);
32       }
33
34   }
```

Auto Format button

Using the Auto Format button indents the pieces of the else statement to show their positions within the main for statement.

15. **Save the file and continue to the next exercise.**

PROGRAM THE RESTART BUTTON FUNCTIONALITY

Now that you understand what is happening throughout the race, you can determine what needs to happen when a user clicks the Restart button and the game is reset:

- The "Click Me" banner needs to become visible.

- The main movie timeline needs to return to Frame 1.

- The Restart button instance needs to be hidden.

- The lila_mc instance needs to return to her original position and start tapping her foot.

- The racetrack_mc instance needs to return to its original position.

- The baggy_mc, granny_mc, navi_mc, and nipper_mc instances need to stop moving, and then return to their original positions.

Because all of these actions need to occur simultaneously when a user clicks the Restart button, the best way to accomplish these tasks is to use an event listener and custom function.

1. **With gator_race.fla open, select Frame 1 of the Event Handlers layer on the main Stage.**

2. **Place the insertion point at the end of the existing script and press Return/ Enter twice.**

3. **On Line 16 of the Script pane, add a relative reference to the restart_btn instance.**

4. **In the Actions toolbox, expand flash.events>EventDispatcher>Methods, and double-click addEventListener.**

Add the second event handler immediately after the existing code.

You're working on Frame 1 of the Event Handlers layer on the main timeline.

5. **Inside the parentheses of the addEventListener function, type MouseEvent. and then choose CLICK from the code hint menu.**

6. **After the word CLICK, type `, raceReset` as the name of the function that will be called when the event is triggered.**

7. **Add a semicolon outside the closing parenthesis.**

raceReset is the name of the function that will be called when the restart_btn instance is clicked. Next, you need to define the raceReset function.

8. **Press Return/Enter twice to move the insertion point to Line 18 of the Script pane.**

9. **On Line 18 of the Script pane, type:**

   `function raceReset () {}`

```
15
16   Object(this).restart_btn.addEventListener(MouseEvent.CLICK, raceReset);
17
18   function raceReset() {}
```

10. **Place the insertion point inside the function parentheses and type `event:` and then choose MouseEvent from the resulting code hint menu.**

11. **Type a colon outside the function parameter parentheses, and then choose void from the code hint menu.**

Because this function returns no value, you have to use the void return type.

```
16   Object(this).restart_btn.addEventListener(MouseEvent.CLICK, raceReset);
17
18   function raceReset(event:MouseEvent):void {}
```

The function name goes before the parentheses.

Add the void return type here.

12. **Place the insertion point between the function braces, and then press Return/Enter twice to add an empty line between the opening and closing braces.**

13. **On Line 19 (within the function braces), add the following code:**

   `Object(this).banner_mc.visible=true;`

The banner_mc instance is hidden by the function called when a user clicks the lila_mc instance. This command shows the banner_mc instance again.

14. Beginning on Line 20 of the Script pane (still within the function braces), add lines of code to reset the main movie timeline, the Racetrack movie clip, and the lila movie clip:

```
this.gotoAndStop(1);
Object(this).racetrack_mc.gotoAndStop(1);
Object(this).lila_mc.gotoAndPlay(1);
```

Frame 1 of the Actions layer on the main timeline includes a function to hide the Restart button instance, so you don't need to add a separate command to hide the Restart button here.

Although the main timeline and the racetrack timeline include stop functions at Frame 1, the commands in this function override the stop commands. To prevent the main timeline and Racetrack movie clip timeline from automatically playing when the race resets, you have to use the gotoAndStop command instead of gotoAndPlay.

```
16  Object(this).restart_btn.addEventListener(MouseEvent.CLICK, raceReset);
17
18  function raceReset(event:MouseEvent):void {
19      Object(this).banner_mc.visible=true;
20      this.gotoAndStop(1);
21      Object(this).racetrack_mc.gotoAndStop(1);
22      Object(this).lila_mc.gotoAndPlay(1);
23  }
```

15. Add four more lines to the raceReset function to reset the timelines of each racer's movie clip:

```
Object(this).char1_mc.gotoAndStop(1);
Object(this).char2_mc.gotoAndStop(1);
Object(this).char3_mc.gotoAndStop(1);
Object(this).char4_mc.gotoAndStop(1);
```

These lines of code move each racer's movie clip timeline to its original position, where the racers wait for a user to click the Lila movie clip.

```
16  Object(this).restart_btn.addEventListener(MouseEvent.CLICK, raceReset);
17
18  function raceReset(event:MouseEvent):void {
19      Object(this).banner_mc.visible=true;
20      this.gotoAndStop(1);
21      Object(this).racetrack_mc.gotoAndStop(1);
22      Object(this).lila_mc.gotoAndPlay(1);
23      Object(this).char1_mc.gotoAndStop(1);
24      Object(this).char2_mc.gotoAndStop(1);
25      Object(this).char3_mc.gotoAndStop(1);
26      Object(this).char4_mc.gotoAndStop(1);
27  }
```

16. Using the Selection tool, click the Baggy instance on the Stage. Note the x position in the Properties panel.

Because the characters move only as a result of code throughout the race, their positions on the development Stage never change. All four racers have the same horizontal (x) starting position.

Note:

You have already used most of the commands that are needed in this function. You can simply type the necessary code or use the Actions toolbox to add the various elements.

Note:

The gotoAndStop command is similar to the gotoAndPlay command, except the playhead does not automatically move from the referenced frame.

Note:

You can access the gotoAndStop command in the Actions toolbox by expanding flash.display> MovieClip>Methods.

17. Add four more lines to the raceReset function, changing the x property of each racer movie clip instance to the same x position you noted in Step 16:

```
Object(this).char1_mc.x=780;

Object(this).char2_mc.x=780;

Object(this).char3_mc.x=780;

Object(this).char4_mc.x=780;
```

Note:

Access the x property in the Actions toolbox by expanding flash.display> DisplayObject> Properties.

```
15
16   Object(this).restart_btn.addEventListener(MouseEvent.CLICK, raceReset);
17
18   function raceReset(event:MouseEvent):void {
19       Object(this).banner_mc.visible=true;
20       this.gotoAndStop(1);
21       Object(this).racetrack_mc.gotoAndStop(1);
22       Object(this).lila_mc.gotoAndPlay(1);
23       Object(this).char1_mc.gotoAndStop(1);
24       Object(this).char2_mc.gotoAndStop(1);
25       Object(this).char3_mc.gotoAndStop(1);
26       Object(this).char4_mc.gotoAndStop(1);
27       Object(this).char1_mc.x=780;
28       Object(this).char2_mc.x=780;
29       Object(this).char3_mc.x=780;
30       Object(this).char4_mc.x=780;
31   }
```

18. Save the file and continue to the next exercise.

 ## TEST THE MOVIE AND CHANGE CURSOR STYLES

Most programmers have a motto that says code once, test often (or something to that effect). When you are writing code — regardless of how basic or complex — it's a good idea to test your scripts as often as possible. Even the best planner can overlook a critical design element during initial development. Problems or issues only become obvious when you watch the actual movie as it will appear when exported.

Note:

Because the motion in the Background and Lila movie clips is based on tweens, moving the playhead for those movie clips restores them to their original positions.

The racers' movement, however, is based on random numbers generated in ActionScript code; to return the racers to their original positions, you have to use ActionScript to change the x properties of those movie clip instances.

1. With gator_race.fla open, press Command-Return/Control-Enter to test the movie.

2. In the Player window, click Lila to play the race.

3. After the race is over, click the Restart button to verify that everything resets properly. The race should play again.

There is one remaining issue that you should address. Users typically expect to see a pointing-hand cursor when the mouse hovers over a button. The Restart button is an instance of a button symbol, so the cursor changes to a pointing hand when the mouse is over the button instance. The Lila instance, which starts the race, functions as a button, but it was created as a movie clip because it contains a number of frame animations. To meet users' expectations, you should change the cursor style for the lila_mc instance.

4. **Close the Player window and return to Flash.**

5. **Select Frame 1 of the Event Handlers layer on the main timeline.**

6. **Place the insertion point at the beginning of Line 3 in the Script pane. Press Return/Enter to move the existing script to Line 4.**

7. **On Line 3 of the Script pane, type:**

   Object(this).lila_mc.buttonMode=true;

   This code allows the movie clip instance to appear to behave as a button without being created as a formal button symbol. When a user moves the mouse over the movie clip in the movie, the cursor will change to a pointing-hand icon that indicates a clickable object.

Note:

The buttonMode command can be accessed in the Actions toolbox by expanding flash.display> MovieClip>Properties.

```
1   import flash.events.MouseEvent;
2
3   Object(this).lila_mc.buttonMode=true;
4   Object(this).lila_mc.addEventListener(MouseEvent.CLICK, raceStart);
5
6   function raceStart (event:MouseEvent):void {
```

8. **Press Command-Return/Control-Enter to test the movie. Move your mouse cursor over the Lila instance.**

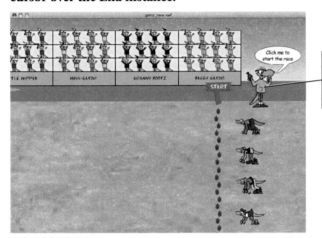

You set the buttonMode property of the movie clip instance to true, so the cursor changes to a pointing hand.

9. **Close the Player window and return to Flash.**

10. **Save the file and continue to the final stage of the project.**

Stage 6 Adding Sound with ActionScript

When you last tested the movie, all elements moved correctly. The overall file, however, is perfectly silent — which doesn't create the effect you are trying to achieve. To bring life into the race game, you need to add sounds to the graphic elements, including a gun shot when Lila starts the race, the sounds of clattering feet as the gators run, and the cheers from the crowd as they watch the race.

In Project 2, you learned how to import sound files into Flash, and to control sound files on the timeline. The sound files for this project have already been imported into the Library panel; your job is to use ActionScript to add the different sounds at appropriate points in the movie.

 ## CREATE ACCESS FOR SOUND FILES IN THE LIBRARY

ActionScript 3 contains a built-in Sound class in the flash.media package that contains the events, methods, and properties related to controlling sound files. To access sound files from the Library panel, however, you have to create a linkage for each sound file — defining a new custom class that is essentially a sub-grouping of the main sound class.

If this seems confusing, don't worry; it will make more sense as you complete the following exercises.

1. **With gator_race.fla open, expand the Sounds folder in the Library panel.**

2. **Control/right-click the baggy_running.wav file and choose Properties from the contextual menu.**

3. **If the resulting Sound Properties dialog box opens in basic mode, click the Advanced button to show additional options.**

If this button shows "Advanced" click to show the Linkage options.

4. In the Linkage area, check the Export for ActionScript option.

The first step in adding sound through ActionScript requires making those sounds available without placing them on a timeline. This is called **linkage**. You must create a new class for each sound file, and the new class must be linked to the primary sound class.

By default, the Export in Frame 1 option is also selected. The Base Class field shows that the file is recognized as part of the flash.media.Sound class.

5. Change the Class field to baggyFeet.

This is the name of the new class you are creating to make this file accessible in ActionScript.

Check this option to make the file available for ActionScript.

This is the custom class you will use to access the sound file in ActionScript.

6. Click OK.

Flash displays a warning that a definition for the class does not exist, so the class will be defined for you when the file is exported.

The class name appears in the Linkage column of the Library panel.

7. Click OK to close the warning dialog box.

8. Repeat Steps 2–7 for the five remaining sound files, using the following custom class names:

crowd_cheers.wav	cheer
granny_running.wav	grannyFeet
gun_shot.wav	shot
navi_running.wav	naviFeet
nipper_running.wav	nipperFeet

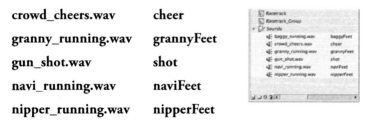

9. Save the file and continue to the next exercise.

Now that the library sounds are accessible to ActionScript, you have to write the code to play the different files at the appropriate points in the movie.

- The gun shot sound should play when Lila fires the starting pistol.

- The crowd cheering sound should play when the crowd is visible on the Stage, based on the motion tween in the Racetrack movie clip.

- The running feet sounds should play for each racer, based on the running animation in each character's movie clip.

1. **With gator_race.fla open, select Frame 1 of the Event Handler layer on the main timeline.**

2. **In the Actions panel, click at the end of the last line in the raceStart function body and press Return/Enter twice.**

   The gun shot sound should play when the race starts, so you are adding a command as part of the raceStart custom function.

3. **On Line 16 of the script, type:**

   ```
   var audioGun:shot=new shot();
   ```

   You created the audioGun variable as an object of the shot class. The custom shot class has only one possible value — gun_shot.wav — so the variable audioGun of the shot class is the gun_shot.wav file.

   ```
   3   Object(this).lila_mc.buttonMode=true;
   4   Object(this).lila_mc.addEventListener(MouseEvent.CLICK, raceStart);
   5
   6   function raceStart (event:MouseEvent):void {
   7       this.gotoAndPlay(2);
   8       Object(this).lila_mc.gotoAndPlay(21);
   9       Object(this).racetrack_mc.gotoAndPlay(2);
   10      Object(this).char1_mc.gotoAndPlay(5);
   11      Object(this).char2_mc.gotoAndPlay(5);
   12      Object(this).char3_mc.gotoAndPlay(5);
   13      Object(this).char4_mc.gotoAndPlay(5);
   14      Object(this).banner_mc.visible=false;
   15
   16      var audioGun:shot=new shot();
   17  }
   18
   19  Object(this).restart_btn.addEventListener(MouseEvent.CLICK, raceReset);
   20
   21  function raceReset(event:MouseEvent):void {
   ```

   You are adding the sound to the raceStart function body.

   Frame 1 of the Event Handlers layer is selected.

   Event Handlers : 1

4. **Press Return/Enter to movie to Line 17 of the Script pane, and then type:**

   ```
   audioGun.play();
   ```

   ```
   13      Object(this).char4_mc.gotoAndPlay(5);
   14      Object(this).banner_mc.visible=false;
   15
   16      var audioGun:shot=new shot();
   17      audioGun.play();
   18  }
   ```

5. **Double-click the Baggy movie clip icon in the Library panel to enter into the movie clip Stage.**

   Because the feet sounds need to loop along with the running animation for each gator, you are going to script the running feet sounds directly on the timeline for each racer.

6. **Select Frame 10 on the timeline and click in the Script pane of the Actions panel.**

7. **Declare a new variable named "audioBaggy" of the "baggyFeet" class by typing:**

   ```
   var audioBaggy:baggyFeet=new baggyFeet();
   ```

Note:

You can access the play function in the Actions toolbox by expanding flash.media> Sound>Methods.

8. **On the next line of the Script pane, add the play command for the audioBaggy variable by typing:**

   ```
   audioBaggy.play();
   ```

   Sounds added using ActionScript are **stream sounds** — they play one time from start to finish. The running feet sounds will loop because the timelines for those movie clips loop. The sound files play once each time the movie clip timelines hit Frame 10.

The sound will play when the movie clip timeline reaches Frame 10.

9. **Repeat Steps 5–8 for the three remaining racer movie clips. Use an appropriate variable name for each character, and use the appropriate class for each sound file.**

10. **Click Scene 1 in the Edit bar to return to the main Stage.**

11. **Choose View>Magnification>Fit In Window to make the entire Stage area visible.**

12. **Double-click the racetrack_mc instance on the Stage to edit the symbol in place.**

13. **Click the playhead and drag right until the second crowd (near the finish line) moves into the Stage area (past the guide that marks the left edge of the Stage).**

    Our timeline shows the crowd appearing at Frame 74.

This guide marks the left edge of the Stage.

At Frame 74 the crowd moves into the Stage.

14. **Add a new layer named Sound at the top of the main timeline. Insert keyframes at Frames 2 and 74 of the Sound layer.**

    The existing layer contains a tween, so you are using a separate layer to contain the sound actions. Layers are not only useful for organizing visual elements, they also help in systematic development of a project that contains sounds. By inserting the sound file in a separate layer, you can more easily modify or delete that particular file (if necessary).

15. **Select Frame 2 of the Sound layer and click in the Actions panel Script pane.**

16. **Declare a variable named "audioCrowd" of the "cheer" class by typing:**

    ```
    var audioCrowd:cheer=new cheer();
    ```

17. **On the next line of the Script pane, add the play command for the audioCheer variable by typing:**

    ```
    audioCrowd.play();
    ```

18. **Select Frame 74 of the Sound layer. In the Script pane of the Actions panel, add the play command for the audioCheer variable by typing:**

    ```
    audioCrowd.play();
    ```

    Note:

    You don't need to declare the variable every time you want to use it.

19. **Press Command-Return/Control-Enter to test the completed game.**

     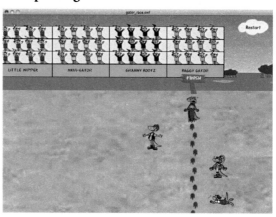

20. **Close the Player window and return to Flash.**

21. **Save and close the completed Flash file.**

Project Review

fill in the blank

1. _____ are required to target specific symbol instances using ActionScript.

2. A(n) _____ relates a trigger object and event to a defined function.

3. Scripting in ActionScript 3 uses _____ to apply script commands to specific objects.

4. The _____ contains all of the functions of the ActionScript language, sorted into classes.

5. In the Actions panel, the _____ button lets you choose which object you want to affect with a function or event.

6. In the Actions panel, _____ show different options depending on the context of the code you are typing.

7. The code between braces represents the _____, or the actions that will be performed when the function is called.

8. _____ is also known as the assignment operator.

9. A(n) _____ is used to define actual characters (inside of quotation marks) in a script.

10. _____ is the numbered position of specific elements in an array.

short answer

1. Briefly define "variable." Provide two examples of how variables can be useful.

2. Briefly define "array." Provide two examples of how arrays can be useful.

3. Briefly define "loop." Include a short explanation of at least three different types of loops.

Portfolio Builder Project

Use what you learned in this project to complete the following freeform exercise.
Carefully read the art director and client comments, then create your own design to meet the needs of the project.
Use the space below to sketch ideas; when finished, write a brief explanation of your reasoning behind your final design.

art director comments

To help promote the new adventure book, *Up and Away*, your client has asked you to create a game similar to the gator race.

To complete this project, you should:

❑ Download the client's supplied files in the **FL5_PB_Project5.zip** archive on the Student Files Web page.

❑ Review the client's supplied artwork. If you use this artwork, import the file into Flash and create the necessary movie clips from the different elements.

❑ If you prefer, find or create other artwork as appropriate for a hot air balloon race.

❑ Add animations to the different elements of the race.

❑ Program the game functionality using ActionScript.

client comments

When we thought of this game, we were thinking about the carnival games where kids shoot water guns at a lever, and the balloons rise up a pipe based on how much water hits the trigger mechanism. We don't need something that complicated; we only need a Start button so kids can set the balloons flying. (And don't forget to add a Restart button so the kids can play the game more than once.)

We've supplied you with an Illustrator file that's being kicked around as the back-cover artwork, but you can use a different background or balloon artwork if you have something else.

We do want you to add some kind of frame animation to the balloons so they do more than just rise when the game is started. You also need to come up with some way to differentiate between the winner and the losers. We thought about the losers deflating and falling, but again, we're open to suggestions.

project justification

_____

_____

_____

_____

_____

_____

_____

_____

_____

_____

_____

_____

_____

_____

Project Summary

This project was designed as an introduction to ActionScript. By completing these exercises, you learned how to use many foundational programming techniques — event handlers, variables, operators, loops, and conditional statements — to control the elements in a Flash movie. You also learned about the terms related to writing code, and you discovered how functions relate to a Flash movie.

Many designers devote their entire careers to building applications with ActionScript. To enhance your marketability as a professional Flash developer, we encourage you to continue your ActionScript education beyond this project.

Use ActionScript to add sound files at appropriate points in the movie playback

Create an event handler and custom function to set all elements in motion when a user clicks the race starter

Use basic functions to stop and loop frame animations

Use ActionScript to control object position and visibility

Create an event handler and custom function to reset all elements to their original positions

Use a random-number variable to change the position of one character several times

Create a loop to determine which character won the race

Define a conditional statement to call the appropriate animation for each character at the end of the game

Gopher Golf Game

Your client operates a family entertainment complex in suburban Pittsburgh. The facility includes a nationally recognized professional golf course, as well as a miniature golf course to lure families looking for inexpensive entertainment. You have been hired to develop an interactive game for the client's Web site that appeals to both children and adults.

This project incorporates the following skills:

❏ Importing and analyzing artwork from an Adobe Illustrator file

❏ Creating various types of symbols based on imported artwork

❏ Editing symbol artwork to meet the unique needs of the job

❏ Using a mask to hide parts of a tween animation

❏ Writing scripts to animate different symbols in a random sequence

❏ Defining a variable to control game duration

❏ Programming a symbol instance to function as the cursor throughout the game

❏ Using dynamic text areas to track user actions

❏ Adding script to show specific symbols based on the user's performance

I was at the amusement park with my niece last weekend and she played Whack-A-Mole for nearly an hour! I swear, it was contagious, because I played right along with her the whole time! That would be just the thing for our site.

To appeal to both adults and children, we also thought it would be fun to use gophers instead of moles — call it Gopher Golf. The kids will like the silly cartoon animals, and we think most adults will understand the gopher-on-the-golf-course reference.

I had our staff illustrator build all of the necessary artwork components in Adobe Illustrator, so you should be able to import the file and get straight to work on the animation and programming. The artist is very good, but some organization will be part of your job simply because you have a better idea of the game structure than the illustrator does.

This game is going to require some random-number generation to make different gophers pop up around the golf course. You also need to use variables to control the game's duration and keep track of the user's hits and misses.

Rather than just clicking on the gophers, I thought it would be fun to use a golf club as the cursor so users "whack" the gophers with a driver. You need to add script to hide the regular pointer, and then force the club symbol to follow the path of the mouse as it is dragged.

Finally, make sure the game can be played more than once. The Replay button should reset the counting variables and make gophers randomly pop up again.

To complete this project, you will:

❏ Import provided artwork

❏ Define symbols and instances

❏ Organize layers and library folders

❏ Map timeline frames and keyframes

❏ Change button states

❏ Add dynamic text areas

❏ Animate the pop-up gopher movie clip

❏ Mask a motion tween

❏ Add timeline controls

❏ Program basic game functionality

❏ Use the trace function and code comments

❏ Change the mouse cursor to a movie clip

❏ Animate the golf club cursor

❏ Track user actions

❏ Pass values to the parent timeline

❏ Program the game results

Stage 1 **Preparing Game Artwork**

The best way to start a complicated project such as this one is to develop a clear plan of what needs to take place. Consider the sketches from the original project-planning meeting; as you can see, you need to complete a number of tasks to create the final game.

IMPORT PROVIDED ARTWORK

The first step in most Flash projects is creating a new file. Then you can import the provided artwork and review the content.

1. **Download FL5_RF_Project6.zip from the Student Files Web page.**

2. **Expand the ZIP archive in your WIP folder (Macintosh) or copy the archive contents into your WIP folder (Windows).**

    This results in a folder named **Gophers**, which contains the files you need for this project. You should also use this folder to save the files you create in this project.

3. **In Flash, create a new Flash file for ActionScript 3.**

4. **Using the Properties panel, change the file frame rate to 15 fps.**

    Don't worry about the Stage size. You're going to change that shortly, based on the size of imported artwork.

5. **Choose File>Import>Import to Stage. Navigate to the file gophers.ai in the WIP>Gophers folder and click Open.**

6. **In the Import to Stage dialog box, review the primary level of items that will be imported.**

7. **At the bottom of the dialog box, make sure the Flash Layers option is selected in the Convert Layers To menu.**

8. **Check the Place Objects at Original Position and Set Stage Size options.**

Layers in the Illustrator file are highlighted.

Check this option to keep imported artwork in the same position as it was on the Illustrator artboard.

Check this option to change the Stage size to match the size of the Illustrator artboard.

9. **Click OK to import the file.**

10. **Click away from the Stage area to deselect all imported objects. If necessary, use the Fit In Window magnification option to show the entire Stage in the document window.**

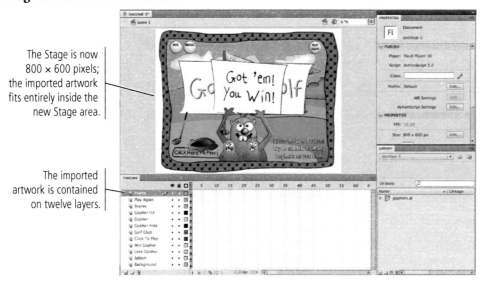

The Stage is now 800 × 600 pixels; the imported artwork fits entirely inside the new Stage area.

The imported artwork is contained on twelve layers.

11. **Save the file as gophers.fla in your WIP>Gophers folder and continue to the next exercise.**

DEFINE SYMBOLS AND INSTANCES

When you work with provided artwork, you never know what you are going to get. Some designers simply illustrate with no concern for how the file will be used. Others understand the requirements of artwork that will be used in a Flash movie, and organize files as much as possible to ensure an almost seamless transition from an Illustrator artboard to the Flash Stage. The artwork for this project — like the majority of artwork you'll receive from external sources — falls somewhere in between these two extremes.

Note:

Many Flash projects involve artwork created in Adobe Illustrator. The amount of required setup work depends on the complexity of the project, but also on the quality of the artwork.

1. **With gophers.fla open, hide all but the top layer (Frame).**

   The Frame layer has no functional purpose other than (as the name suggests) framing the overall artwork. You don't need to address this object in any way, so you don't need to convert it to a symbol.

2. **Hide the Frame layer and show the next layer in the stack (Play Again).**

   This layer contains the artwork for a button that users can click to replay the game.

3. **Control/right-click inside the selected object on the Play Again layer and choose Convert to Symbol from the contextual menu.**

4. **In the resulting dialog box, name the new symbol Replay, choose Button from the Type menu, and choose the center registration point. Click OK to create the new symbol.**

You are using the Button type for this symbol because you are going to use the special button frames to change the text color when a user clicks the button.

Note:

If the Convert to Symbol dialog box appears in Advanced mode, click the button to collapse it to Basic mode.

5. **With the symbol instance selected on the Stage, type replay_btn in the Instance Name field of the Properties panel.**

Name the instance on the Stage "replay_btn".

6. **Hide the Play Again layer and show the next layer in the stack (Scores).**

This layer contains two groups, which will track the users' "hits" and "misses" as they play the game. These don't need to be clickable, but you do need to address them with ActionScript — and that means you must convert each group to a movie clip symbol.

7. **Using the Selection tool, click the Hits group to select it.**

If you clicked the Scores layer name in the timeline after showing the layer, both objects on the layer will be automatically selected. If this is the case, click away from the two groups to deselect them so you can select only the Hits group.

8. **Control/right-click the Hits group and choose Convert to Symbol from the contextual menu. Name the new symbol Hits, choose Movie Clip in the Type menu, and choose the center registration point. Click OK to return to the Stage.**

The original artist grouped related objects in the Illustrator file, so the entire "Hits" golf ball artwork is a single group.

9. **With the Hits instance selected on the Stage, type hits_mc in the Instance Name field.**

Keep in mind that ActionScript is case sensitive. When you write script to address this instance, you must use the lowercase instance name that you defined in this step.

The instance on the Stage is named "hits_mc".

The Hits symbol is a movie clip.

10. Repeat Steps 8–9 for the Misses golf ball, naming the instance `misses_mc`.

11. Hide the Scores layer and show the next layer in the stack (Gopher Hit).

This layer contains artwork that will be part of the pop-up gopher animation, which you will create later. You are going to create the animation on a motion tween, which means you need to convert this artwork to a movie clip symbol.

12. Click the visible object on the Stage to select the group. Using the same method from Step 8, create a new movie clip symbol named `Gopher_Hit`, using the bottom-center registration point.

13. After you create the symbol, delete the selected instance from the Stage.

This symbol will be used inside another movie clip; it does not appear by itself in the game, so you can delete the instance from the Stage.

The hollow circle identifies a blank keyframe.

14. **Using the same process outlined in the previous steps, review the contents of each layer and create the necessary symbols. Use the following information to create each movie clip and instance:**

Layer	Symbol Name	Symbol Type	Registration Point	Action to Take on the Stage
Gopher	Gopher	Movie clip	bottom-center	Delete the instance from the Stage
Gopher Hole	Gopher_Hole	Movie clip	bottom-center	Delete the instance from the Stage
Golf Club	Golf_Club	Movie clip	bottom-left	Name the instance **club_mc**
Click To Play	Play	Button	center	Name the instance **play_btn**
Win Gopher	Win_Gopher	Movie clip	bottom-center	Name the instance **win_mc**
Lose Gopher	Lose_Gopher	Movie clip	bottom-center	Name the instance **lose_mc**
Splash	Splash_Gopher	Movie clip	bottom-center	Name the instance **splash_mc**
Background		None		

When you get to the Splash layer, the artist did not group all the objects that make up the layer. You must be certain to select all of the pieces before creating the movie clip for this layer's contents.

Although this process can be time consuming, reviewing the provided artwork and creating the necessary components is a vital part of any Flash project. (To minimize the amount of required set-up work for this project, we optimized the original artwork significantly. When you work on your own projects, you never know what you will get until you start clicking in the imported artwork.)

Note:

Symbol and instance names should reflect the content and purpose. Descriptive names will help significantly when you create the required ActionScripts.

15. **Save the file and continue to the next exercise.**

 ## ORGANIZE FILE LAYERS

Before you build the animations and scripts that are required for this game, you need to complete one more organizational step. To more easily manage the large number of components throughout the project, you should remove unnecessary layers and add any new layers that you know you will need.

Of course, you can add layers at any time in a project, but taking the time to properly set up a project at the beginning of the process can make your work easier and more efficient. This process also helps you to get into the habit of analyzing a project's needs before you create a single animation or script — a vital step in successful Flash development.

1. **With gophers.fla open, show all layers on the timeline.**

   To help you more easily manage the various components at different points in time, the final game will include seven basic layers:

   - The Background and Frame layers, which already contain the necessary artwork
   - A Splash layer to manage the objects that appear when the movie first opens
   - A Content layer that manages the pop-up gopher animations and the counters
   - Two results layers to contain the "Win" and "Lose" movie clips, respectively
   - An Actions layer to manage the various scripts

2. **Lock the Background and Frame layers.**

Note:

You will use ActionScript to control the visibility of the "Win" and "Lose" movie clips, so you could use a single layer for the two results movie clips. However, using separate layers makes it easier to manage the separate objects during development.

3. **Select the three layers with no content and delete them.**

   You can identify empty layers by the blank keyframe icon (the open circle).

The blank keyframes identify the empty layers.

4. **Click the Click To Play layer name to select the objects on that layer. Choose Edit>Cut.**

5. **Click the Splash layer name to select that layer, and then choose Edit> Paste in Place.**

   The Paste in Place command makes it easy to move objects from one layer to another.

Paste in Place puts the cut object in the same spot on the Splash layer.

Note:

Press Command/Control-Shift-V to paste the copied object in place.

6. **Delete the now-empty Click To Play layer.**

7. **Double-click the Scores layer name and change it to Content.**

   It's always a good idea to use descriptive names for assets, including layers.

8. **Repeat Steps 4–6 to move the club_mc instance from the Golf Club layer to the Content layer.**

9. **Repeat Steps 4–6 to move the replay_btn instance from the Play Again layer to the Win Gopher layer.**

10. **Select the Frame layer, and then click the New Layer button. Name the new layer Actions.**

By selecting the top layer before adding the layer, the new layer automatically appears at the top of the stack in the timeline.

11. **In the timeline, drag the Splash layer above the Content layer.**

Although not strictly necessary, it can be easier to understand complex processes if you arrange layers in a linear (top-to-bottom) manner, in the order their content appears when the movie plays.

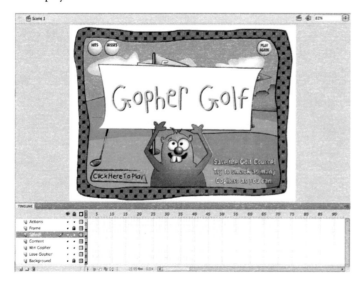

12. **Save the file and continue to the next exercise.**

MAP TIMELINE FRAMES AND KEYFRAMES

In this exercise, you add keyframes and manipulate regular frames to define the basic timeline structure for the three stages of the final game:

- The splash screen and Play button appear when the movie first opens.

- The pop-up gophers and score clips appear when a user clicks the Play button.

- The results and "Play Again" button appear after the game is finished. The score clips should remain visible in the third stage.

1. **With gophers.fla open, click the keyframe on the Content layer to select it. Click the selected frame again, and then drag it to Frame 2.**

   You can't simply click and immediately drag a frame. You have to first select the frame(s), release the mouse button, and then click again to drag the selected frame(s).

   When the movie opens, only the splash objects and Play button should be visible. By moving the Content layer keyframe from Frame 1 to Frame 2, you effectively hide the Content layer objects until a user clicks the Play button. (Later in this project, you will add a script to prevent the timeline from automatically playing when the game first opens.)

Click the frame to select it...

...then click the selected frame again and drag it to Frame 2.

2. **Click the keyframe on the Win Gopher layer, then Shift-click to select the keyframe on the Lose Gopher layer. Click either selected frame and drag them both to Frame 3.**

   The third phase of the game shows the user's results. The Play Again button and the "Win" or "Lose" movie clip should not be visible until the third phase — which you accomplish by moving these layers to Frame 3.

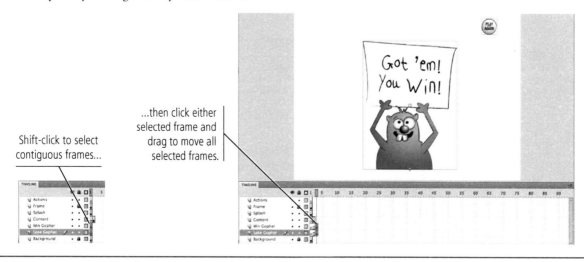

Shift-click to select contiguous frames...

...then click either selected frame and drag to move all selected frames.

3. **Click Frame 3 of the Actions layer to select it. Press Command/Control and then click Frame 3 of the Frame, Splash, Content, and Background layers to add them to the selection.**

   Command/Control-clicking selects individual noncontiguous frames. Shift-clicking selects all contiguous frames between your first and second selections.

   Command/Control-click to select non-contiguous frames.

4. **Press the F5 key to add new regular frames to all selected frames.**

   All layers now extend to Frame 3, and the background and frame graphics are visible on all frames of the movie.

   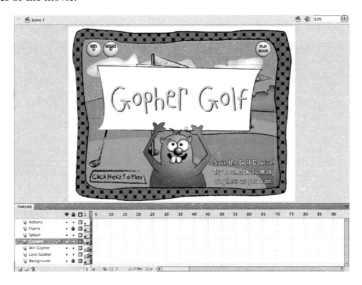

5. **Click Frame 3 of the Actions layer, and then Shift-click Frame 3 of the Background layer to select Frame 3 on all layers.**

6. **Click any of the selected frames and drag to Frame 22.**

   The pop-up gopher animation requires 20 frames. Although the animation will occur within the timeline of its own movie clip, you have to allow enough time for the movie clip timeline to finish before the main timeline reaches the next process.

   Because the content layer begins on Frame 2, allowing 20 frames for the animation means the main content should end on Frame 21. The third phase (the results) must then begin on Frame 22.

   When you drag frames, keyframes are automatically added to those frames. You can remove any of these that are not necessary.

Note:

Be patient; it might take a few seconds for Flash to add the necessary frames to all the layers.

7. **On the Splash layer, select Frame 2, and then Shift-click Frame 22 to select all but Frame 1 on that layer. Control/right-click any of the selected frames and choose Remove Frames from the contextual menu.**

Shift-click to select all but Frame 1 on the Splash layer...

...then use the Remove Frames command to delete the selected frames.

Note:

You can't simply press Delete to remove frames; you have to choose the Remove Frames command.

The objects on this layer should only be visible when the game first opens, so it is not necessary to extend the layer to the end of the movie. Rather than simply deleting the unnecessary keyframe, you are deleting all unnecessary frames from the layer.

8. **Control/right-click Frame 22 of the Frame layer and choose Clear Keyframe from the contextual menu.**

If you choose Remove Frame, the keyframe is deleted but so is the regular frame — which would cause the layer to have only 21 frames instead of the necessary 22.

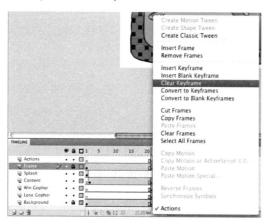

9. **Repeat Step 8 for the Background layer.**

Clearing the keyframe does not remove the regular frame.

10. **Save the file and continue to the next exercise.**

CHANGE BUTTON STATES

The game requires two buttons (Play and Replay), which should change in appearance when the user's mouse rolls over them. In Project 2, you learned about the special frames that are created in a button symbol. In this exercise, you change the Over frame of the two button symbols.

1. **With gophers.fla open, double-click the Play button symbol icon in the Library panel to enter into the symbol Stage.**

2. **Control/right-click the Over frame in the timeline and choose Insert Keyframe from the contextual menu.**

3. **With the Over frame selected, double-click the artwork on the Stage to enter into the group.**

4. **Double-click the blue area in the background to enter into the nested group.**

5. **Double-click the blue area again to access the blue drawing object.**

   Depending on how the imported artwork was created, you might have to drill down several grouping levels to access the individual drawing objects.

The Edit bar shows when you have reached the actual drawing object.

6. **Click the drawing object to select it, and then use the Color or Properties panel to change the fill color to a bright green.**

7. **In the Library panel, double-click the Replay button symbol icon to enter into the symbol Stage.**

   It is not necessary to return to the main Stage before you enter a different symbol Stage.

8. **Control/right-click the Over frame and choose Insert Keyframe from the contextual menu.**

9. **With the Over frame selected, double-click the artwork on the Stage to enter into the group, and then double-click any of the letters to enter the group containing just the words.**

10. **With the individual letter objects selected, use the Color or Properties panel to change the fill color to the same green you used in the Play button symbol.**

You should be in the nested group that contains only the letters.

11. **Click Scene 1 in the Edit bar to return to the main Stage.**

12. **Save the file and continue to the next exercise.**

ADD CLASSIC DYNAMIC TEXT AREAS

Throughout a game, the "Hit" and "Miss" golf balls in the top-left corner should reflect the user's score. To accomplish this, you need to add dynamic text fields, which can contain variable text. (You will write the scripts for these fields later.)

TLF Text areas, which you used in Project 3, allow a large number of formatting options that are not available for Classic Text areas. The text areas you need for this project, however, will contain nothing more than basic numbers with no special formatting; Classic Text is suitable for this type of application.

1. **With gophers.fla open, double-click the Hits movie clip icon in the Library panel to enter into the symbol Stage.**

2. **Choose the Text tool in the Tools panel.**

3. **In the Properties panel, choose Classic Text in the Type menu and choose Dynamic Text in the secondary menu.**

4. **In the Character options, choose a sans-serif font such as Arial or Helvetica. Set the size to 12 pt, and choose a bright green color.**

5. **In the Paragraph options area, click the Align Center button.**

   By defining character and paragraph properties before creating a text area, the properties will be applied to new text areas you create. Although the dynamic text area has no content of its own, the formatting will be applied to text that is scripted into the area.

Choose Classic Text in the Type menu.

Choose Dynamic Text in the secondary menu.

Before you create the text area, set the character and paragraph options.

6. **Click and drag over the ball shape to create a new text area. Use the handles to resize the text area to fit within the ball shape, below the word "HITS."**

7. **With the text area active on the Stage, type hit_count in the Instance Name field of the Properties panel.**

   Later in the project, you will use ActionScript to dynamically change the value in this text area — hence, the name "dynamic text area." Like symbol instances, text areas must be named before they can be addressed in ActionScript.

As with symbols, dynamic text areas must be named to be addressed in ActionScript.

8. **In the Properties panel, click the Embed button in the Character area.**

9. **In the Options area, check the Numerals box. Leave all other options at their defaults, and click OK.**

   Because these areas can only display numbers, you only need to embed the font's numeral characters.

10. **Repeat this process to add a dynamic text area named** `miss_count` **in the Misses movie clip symbol. Use red as the text color for this area.**

Make sure you add this text area inside the symbol Stage, and not on top of the placed instance on the main Stage.

You can skip Steps 8–9, because the font is already embedded (assuming you use the same font for both text areas).

11. **Click Scene 1 in the Edit bar to return to the main Stage.**

12. **Save the file and continue to the next exercise.**

 ANIMATE THE POP-UP GOPHER MOVIE CLIP

The final step in preparing this file for scripting is animating the pop-up gophers. When you imported the artwork, you created three separate movie clip symbols, which you need to combine into an animated movie clip. The animation is a simple up-and-down motion tween, with a few extra steps required to create the desired effect.

1. **With** `gophers.fla` **open, choose Insert>New Symbol. Name the new symbol** `Gopher_Popup`, **choose Movie Clip in the Type menu, and click OK.**

2. **On the new symbol Stage, change the name of Layer 1 to** `Hole`.

3. **Drag an instance of the Gopher_Hole movie clip onto the Stage. Using the Align panel, align the bottom center of the symbol instance to the symbol Stage's registration point.**

When the Align To Stage option is active, the Align buttons position the object relative to the symbol Stage's registration point.

4. **Add a new layer named** Gopher **to the top of the layer stack in the timeline.**

5. **Drag an instance of the Gopher movie clip symbol onto the Stage. Using the Properties panel, define the position of the symbol instance as X: 0, Y: 50.**

   Remember, the symbol's X/Y position is based on the symbol's registration point.

6. **With the Gopher instance selected on the Stage, type** gopher_tracked **in the Instance Name field of the Properties panel.**

   You are going to write a script that tracks the number of times the user clicks this symbol. To be addressed by ActionScript, the instance must be named.

7. **Select Frame 20 of both layers and press the F5 key to insert a new frame and extend the timeline on both layers.**

8. **Control/right-click anywhere between Frame 1 and Frame 20 on the Gopher layer and choose Create Motion Tween.**

9. **Select Frame 10 of the Gopher layer. Click the Gopher instance on the Stage to select it, and then change the Y position of the instance to –15.**

10. **Select Frame 20 of the Gopher layer. Click the Gopher instance, and then change the Y position back to 50.**

By changing only the Y position, the motion tween moves the gopher straight up and then straight down over the 20 frames in the tween.

11. **Control/right-click Frame 21 of the Gopher layer and choose Insert Blank Keyframe.**

If the user clicks ("hits") the gopher in Frames 1–20, a different gopher will move back down into the hole. Frames 21–30 will include the "pop-down" animation for the Gopher_Hit movie clip.

Because the keyframe is blank, there is no content on the Stage at Frame 21.

12. **Drag an instance of the Gopher_Hit movie clip onto the Stage, and position it at X: 0, Y: –15.**

This is the same position as the regular gopher at the height of the up-and-down tween (on Frames 1–20).

Later you will add ActionScript to determine whether a user clicks the pop-up gopher instance (named "gopher_tracked" from Step 4) in the tween on Frames 1–20. The instance on Frame 21 will only appear if the user clicks the gopher_tracked instance, based on th code you will later create. You don't need to name the Gopher_Hit instance on Frame 21 because you are not going to directly address that instance.

13. **Add a new frame at Frame 30 of both layers to extend the timeline of both layers.**

Because you inserted a blank keyframe at Frame 21, Frames 21-30 are not part of the motion tween.

Note:

Press F5 to insert new frames at the selected frames on the timeline.

14. **Create a motion tween between Frame 21 and Frame 30 on the Gopher layer.**

You are adding a second, separate tween to the layer.

15. **Select the Gopher_Hit instance on Frame 30 and change its position to Y: 50.**

16. **Press Return/Enter to play the timeline on the Stage.**

The first tween moves the Gopher movie clip up and down.

Beginning on Frame 21, the "hit" gopher appears and then sinks down into the hole.

17. **Save the file and continue to the next exercise.**

 MASK A MOTION TWEEN

Your current animation has two problems. First, the gopher pops up and sinks down, then jumps to show the "hit" gopher, which also goes back down into the hole. You will use ActionScript to solve this problem later.

Second, the gopher animation appears entirely in front of the hole artwork because the Gopher layer is on top of the Hole layer. If you move the Gopher layer down in the stacking order, however, the entire tween will fall behind the hole graphic. To achieve the desired effect of the gopher rising up from inside the hole, you need to create a mask to show only a specific part of the gopher animation.

1. **With gophers.fla open, make sure you are editing the Gopher_Popup symbol, and make the rulers visible (View>Rulers).**

2. **Click Frame 10 to select it.**

This frame shows the gopher at the highest point in the animation. You need to know this position so you can define the area for the mask.

3. **Click the horizontal ruler at the top of the document window and drag down to create a guide that marks the top edge of the Gopher instance.**

Drag a guide from the ruler to the top edge of the Gopher instance.

Frame 10 marks the highest point of the animated symbol.

4. **Click the vertical ruler on the left edge of the document window and drag right to create a guide that marks the left edge of the Gopher instance.**

5. **Drag a second guide from the vertical ruler to mark the right edge of the Gopher instance.**

6. **Create a new layer named Mask above the Gopher layer, and then hide the Gopher layer.**

7. **Select Frame 1 of the Mask layer. Using any method you prefer, draw a shape with a bright-colored fill that covers the entire area of the gopher. Use the guides as references for the top, left, and right sides of the shape. Adjust the bottom edge of the shape to match the front of the hole (as shown here).**

If you remember from Project 3, a mask object is not visible; it simply defines the area that will be visible on the masked layer; it doesn't matter what colors you use.

Use the guides as references to position the top, left, and right edges of the mask shape.

Because the Gopher layer is hidden, you can see the line that marks the "front" of the hole.

8. **Show the Gopher layer, then Control/right-click the Mask layer name and choose Mask from the contextual menu.**

After creating the mask, only the area of the Gopher layer that is inside the mask shape is visible.

9. **Click Frame 1 of any layer to select it, and then press Return/Enter to test the animation.**

When the timeline reaches Frame 21, you can see that the "hit" gopher artwork is higher than the regular gopher. This tells you that some of the artwork falls outside the mask area.

10. **In the timeline, unlock the Mask layer.**

By default, a mask layer is locked as soon as it is created.

11. **Click Frame 21 to show the "hit" gopher at its highest point.**

12. **Use any method you prefer to move the top edge of the mask shape up so it extends beyond the top edge of the "hit" gopher artwork.**

We used the Subselection tool to move up the anchor points on the top corners of the mask shape.

Because Frame 21 is selected, you can see where you should place the top edge of the mask shape.

13. Lock the Mask layer.

When a mask layer is locked, you can't see (or edit) the mask object.

14. Click Scene 1 on the Edit bar to return to the main Stage.

15. Select Frame 2 of the Content layer. Drag eight instances of the Gopher_Popup movie clip onto the Stage, and arrange the instances around the golf course.

Space the instances around the Stage to leave enough room above each instance so the gophers do not pop up on top of other instances. (Use the image after Step 16 as a rough guide for placing the instances.)

16. Select each Gopher_Popup instance and assign instance names using the gopher1_mc naming convention.

Each instance name should contain the word "gopher", a sequential number (1–8), then "_mc". For the ActionScript that you will write later to work properly, you must follow this naming convention exactly.

Name each instance "gopherX_mc", using a sequential number for X in each instance.

Place eight instances of the Gopher_Popup movie clip on the Stage.

17. Save the file and continue to the next stage of the project.

Stage 2 Programming Interactivity

After considerable setup, all the pieces of your game are now in place. Now you are ready to begin scripting. The skills you learned in Project 5 (the Gator Race) are foundational building blocks for programming in ActionScript; some of those same methods are useful in developing this game — as they will be in many Flash projects. Others — specifically the interactive elements — require different methods.

To complete this project, you will script the following functionality:

- Program button functionality for the Play and Replay buttons.

- Pop up only one gopher at a time, repeating 10 times.

- Change the mouse cursor to the golf club graphic throughout the game, which animates when the user clicks.

- Based on hits and misses, show the correct gopher during the "down" half of the animation.

- Track a user's hits and misses throughout the game.

- Calculate a win or loss based on the number of hits, and then show the appropriate movie clip after the game is complete.

ADD TIMELINE CONTROLS

Rather than beginning as soon as the file opens, you need to stop the timeline until a user clicks the Play button. In this exercise, you add basic functions to control the playback of the main and gopher animation timelines.

1. **With gophers.fla open, press Command-Return/Control-Enter to test the movie.**

    By default, the timeline plays from beginning to end and then loops (starts over). All eight gophers pop up at the same time when the main timeline reaches Frame 2. The first task, then, is to stop the animations from playing as soon as the file opens.

2. **Close the Flash Player window and return to Flash.**

3. **Select Frame 1 of the Actions layer on the main timeline and open the Actions panel (Window>Actions).**

4. **Click in the Actions panel Script pane to place the insertion point, and type stop();.**

This statement stops the active timeline. It is basically the same thing as the statement **this.stop();** that you used in Project 5; the only difference is the omitted object path, which is unnecessary when referring to the current timeline. (This type of shortening is common in code.)

5. **Select the keyframe on Frame 22 of the Actions layer. In the Actions panel Script pane, type stop();.**

If you don't add the stop function to the final frame, the timeline automatically returns to Frame 1 after it plays the whole way through. This would show the splash screen graphics again (which is incorrect).

6. **Double-click the Gopher_Popup symbol icon in the Library panel to enter into the symbol Stage.**

7. **Add a new layer named Actions at the top of the timeline.**

8. **Select Frame 1 of the Actions layer. In the Script pane, type stop();.**

You can tell by the existing layers that you are inside the Gopher_Popup movie clip symbol.

9. **Insert a new keyframe on Frame 20 of the Actions layer. In the Script pane, type stop();.**

In this movie clip, two sections of the Gopher layer represent the "down" half of the animation. This stop function prevents the movie clip timeline from showing both "down" tweens.

10. **Click Scene 1 on the Edit bar to return to the main Stage.**

11. **Press Command-Return/Control-Enter to test the movie.**

Because you added the stop functions to the main timeline and the gopher animation timeline, nothing happens in the movie.

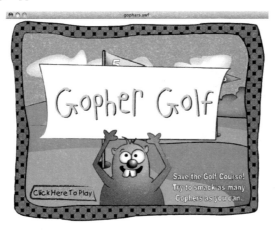

12. **Close the Flash Player window and return to Flash. Save the file and continue to the next exercise.**

 PROGRAM BASIC GAME FUNCTIONALITY

When a user clicks the Play button, the game should begin. The Gopher_Popup instances should randomly animate ten times, and the user's mouse action should be tracked to determine "hits" and "misses." This functionality requires a number of variables, loops, and conditional statements, which you learned about in Project 5.

1. **With gophers.fla open, select the Frame 1 keyframe on the Actions layer of the main timeline.**

2. **Type the following code beginning on Line 3 of the Actions panel Script pane:**

```
play_btn.addEventListener(MouseEvent.CLICK, playgame);

function playgame (event:MouseEvent):void {
    play();
```

When you type the opening brace of the function and press Return/Enter, Flash automatically adds the required closing brace for you.

> *Note:*
>
> *Remember, the actions of a function must be contained within the braces of the function.*

This is the same basic technique you used in Project 5 to make the gators start running when a user clicked the race starter. The first line attaches an event listener to the play_btn instance on the Stage. When a user clicks the button (**MouseEvent.CLICK**), the function **playgame** is called. The second half of the script is a custom function named "playgame", which simply plays the current timeline.

> *Note:*
>
> *The import statement is added on Line 1 as soon as you define the argument of the function (event:MouseEvent); this moves the code you are typing so it begins on Line 5.*

The next step is to create code that makes something happen when the main timeline reaches Frame 2.

3. **Insert a new keyframe on Frame 2 of the Actions layer. On Line 1 of the Script pane, insert code to declare a random-number variable, multiplied by 8, and then rounded to the next highest whole number (ceiled):**

```
var randomGopher = Math.ceil(Math.random()*8);
```

In Project 5, you did the same basic thing in two lines: one line to generate the random number (and multiply it by the required whole number), and one line to ceil that number. In this case you are combining the two lines, generating the random number as the argument of the ceil function. The two methods accomplish the same goal.

Note:

All code in this exercise was explained in Project 5. Refer to that chapter for detailed discussion.

4. **On Line 2 of the Script pane, add the gotoAndPlay function, using the random-number variable to call one of the eight Gopher instances:**

```
this["gopher"+randomGopher+"_mc"].gotoAndPlay(2);
```

5. **Press Command-Return/Control-Enter to test the movie. Click the Play button to test the animation.**

Because you used the random-number generator, a single gopher pops up when the main timeline reaches Frame 2. You haven't yet defined a loop to show more than one gopher. When the timeline reaches Frame 22, the movie stops.

6. **Close the Flash Player window and return to Flash.**

The final game requires ten random gophers to pop up. To accomplish this task, you will increment a variable and use a conditional statement to make the timeline loop ten times.

7. **Select Frame 1 of the Actions layer. On Line 11 of the Script pane, define a number-type variable named counter, initialized to 0:**

```
var counter:Number = 0;
```

This variable will be used in a conditional statement to determine how many times the timeline loops.

This statement declares a variable that will loop the animation.

8. **Select Frame 2 of the Actions layer. Place the insertion point at the beginning of the existing script and press Return/Enter twice to add space above the script.**

9. **On Line 1 of the Script pane, add code to increment the counter variable:**

    `counter++;`

Each time the main timeline hits Frame 2, the counter variable is incremented.

You are adding this script to Frame 2, where the Content layer begins.

10. **Insert a new keyframe at Frame 21 of the Actions layer. With the Frame 21 keyframe selected, add a conditional statement that evaluates the value of the counter variable, and then directs the timeline to the correct frame (based on that value):**

    ```
    if (counter<10) {
        gotoAndPlay(2);
    } else {
        nextFrame();
    }
    ```

    The variable is evaluated at Frame 21, after at least one animation has played.

    The nextFrame and prevFrame commands control the timeline of the defined movie clip, moving the playhead forward or backward one frame from the current position. (Because these commands control movie clip timelines, they are part of the flash.display>MovieClip>Methods package.)

11. **Press Command-Return/Control-Enter to test the movie.**

12. **Click the Play button in the Flash Player window to test the randomness of the animated gophers. Watch the pop-up gophers to see if any overlap with other instances.**

    After 10 gophers appear, the main timeline moves to Frame 22 (accomplished by the nextFrame statement that appears on Frame 21).

13. Close the Flash Player window and return to Flash.

14. If any pop-up gophers overlapped with other instances when the movie played, rearrange the instances on the Stage as necesary.

15. Save the file and continue to the next exercise.

 USE THE TRACE FUNCTION AND CODE COMMENTS

When you work with variables that control internal functionality, it can be difficult to understand exactly what is happening behind the scenes. The trace function can be very useful — especially during development — in understanding how variables work in relation to your scripts.

1. With **gophers.fla** open, select the Frame 2 keyframe on the Actions layer of the main timeline.

2. Place the insertion point at the end of the existing script and press Return/ Enter twice.

3. Type `trace(counter);` at the current location in the script.

   This line tells the script to show (trace) the value of the counter variable in the Flash Output panel.

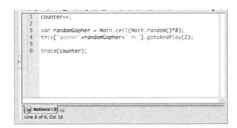

4. Press Command-Return/Control-Enter to test the movie.

5. Move the Flash Player window on your screen so you can see both the Player window and the timeline.

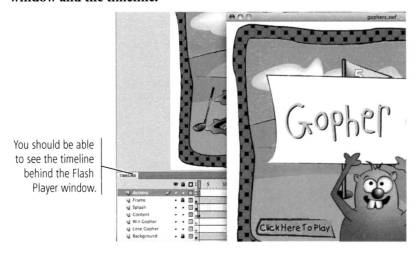

You should be able to see the timeline behind the Flash Player window.

6. Click the Play button in the test movie.

7. While the movie plays, watch the timeline in the Flash application.

When the trace function occurs in a script, the Flash Output panel automatically appears in the same position as it was last used. If you have never used the Output panel, it is docked with the timeline by default.

Because you added the trace function to show the value of the counter variable, you can better understand how the conditional loop makes the correct number of gophers pop up throughout the game:

- Clicking the Play button plays the current timeline, so the timeline moves to Frame 2.
- The counter variable is incremented when the timeline reaches Frame 2.
- Each time the timeline reaches Frame 21, the if condition evaluates the value of the counter variable.
- If the value of the counter variable is less than 10, the timeline loops back to Frame 2, where the counter variable is incremented again.
- When the timeline has looped enough times to increment the counter variable to 10, the timeline continues and shows one more instance of the pop-up animation (the tenth gopher).
- When the timeline reaches Frame 21 after the counter has been incremented to 10, the if condition determines that 10 (the value of the counter variable) is not less than 10 (the defined condition) and sends the timeline to the next frame (the else condition).

Each time the Timeline reaches Frame 2, the counter variable is incremented.

The Output panel shows each time the counter variable changes.

8. Close the Player window and return to Flash.

9. Place the insertion point before the trace function in the Script pane and type //.

Two forward slashes identify a **comment**, which is simply a non-functioning line in the Script pane; comments are ignored when the movie plays. Using comments is an easy way to temporarily show or hide specific lines of code during development.

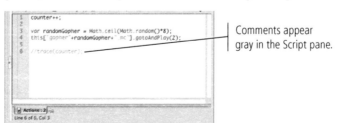

Comments appear gray in the Script pane.

Note:

You can also convert multiple lines of code to a comment by typing / at the beginning of the first line and */ at the end of the last line you want to comment. This is called a **block comment**.*

10. **Place the insertion point at the beginning of Line 3 in the Script pane (where you declare the randomGopher variable).**

11. **Press Return/Enter twice, and then move the insertion point back to Line 3 in the script. Type:**

    ```
    //Generate a random number that calls one of the gopher
    animation instances.
    ```

    Comments are also useful for creating text-based notes to yourself or other programmers.

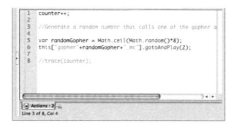

Note:

Clicking the Remove Comment button removes all comment notations and converts commented lines to regular code. The commented lines remain in the script.

12. **If the entire comment does not fit into the Script pane, open the panel Options menu and choose Word Wrap.**

13. **Save the file and continue to the next exercise.**

 ## CHANGE THE MOUSE CURSOR TO A MOVIE CLIP

At this point, the ten gophers randomly pop-up, but nothing happens when you click them. In this exercise, you write script that programs the actual game functionality — including changing the user's cursor to the golf club.

1. **With gophers.fla open, select the Frame 2 keyframe on the Actions layer of the main timeline.**

    You're adding this script to Frame 2 because that is where the game functionality begins.

2. **Place the insertion point at the beginning of the existing script and press Return/Enter twice to add space above the script.**

3. **With the insertion point on Line 1 of the Script pane, expand flash.display> Sprite>Methods. Double-click startDrag to add it to the script.**

Sprite is simply a term for a type of object that can appear in a Flash Player window; sprites are simple objects that do not have a timeline. A movie clip, which *does* have a timeline, is actually a subclass of sprite, which means that sprite methods — including startDrag and stopDrag — are also available to movie clips.

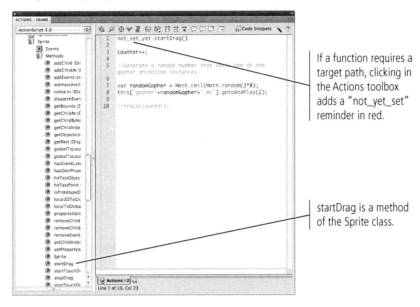

If a function requires a target path, clicking in the Actions toolbox adds a "not_yet_set" reminder in red.

startDrag is a method of the Sprite class.

4. **Highlight the existing path ("not_yet_set") and type `club_mc`.**

This command causes the specified instance to follow the path of the user's mouse cursor.

5. **Inside the parentheses of the startDrag function, type `true`. Type a semicolon at the end of the statement.**

The Boolean value is a parameter of the startDrag function, which defines where the object appears relative to the mouse cursor. If the value is true, the registration point of the symbol follows the mouse cursor. If the value is false, the movie clip is attached to the mouse cursor relative to the first place you click.

Note:

You can always use the Insert Target Path button if you forget the exact names you defined for specific symbol instances.

6. **Press Command-Return/Control-Enter to test the movie. Click the Play button, and then drag around the Player window and track movement of the golf club.**

As you drag the mouse around the Player window, the bottom-left corner of the golf club (the symbol's registration point) follows the mouse cursor.

7. **Close the Flash Player window and return to Flash.**

8. **Place the insertion point at the beginning of the existing script and press Return/Enter twice to add space above the script.**

9. **With the insertion point on Line 1 of the Script pane, type Mouse.hide();.**

   This command hides the basic mouse pointer.

Note:

You can also access Mouse.hide from the flash.ui>Mouse>Methods package in the Actions toolbox.

10. **Press Command-Return/Control-Enter to test the movie. Click the Play button, and then drag around the Player window and track the movement of the golf club.**

Because you used the Mouse.hide command, the regular mouse cursor is no longer visible.

11. **Close the Flash Player window and return to Flash.**

12. **Select the Frame 22 keyframe on the main Actions layer.**

13. **On Line 2 of the Script pane, type stopDrag();.**

   An object remains draggable until you tell it otherwise, or until you make a different object draggable (only one object can be dragged at a time).

14. **On Line 3 of the Script pane, type Mouse.show();.**

   This command shows the regular mouse cursor again, which is important because the golf club no longer shows the location of the cursor.

When the game reaches the "results" phase, the user can no longer drag the golf club and the regular cursor reappears.

15. **Save the file and continue to the next exercise.**

ANIMATE THE GOLF CLUB CURSOR

Although the golf club movie clip is draggable, it still follows the same structure and rules as any other movie clip; it can have its own timeline animation, which can be targeted and controlled using events and other scripts. To make the cursor/movie clip change position when a user clicks anywhere on the Stage, you must attach an event listener to the Stage rather than to a specific object.

1. **With gophers.fla open, double-click the Golf_Club movie clip icon in the Library panel.**

2. **Add a keyframe at Frame 2 of Layer 1 (the only layer in the movie clip).**

3. **With the Frame 2 keyframe selected, choose the Free Transform tool and select the artwork on the Stage.**

4. **Move the transformation registration point to the symbol registration point (at the bottom-left corner of the artwork).**

5. **Click outside the top-right handle and drag slightly down and right to rotate the golf club artwork.**

Move the transformation registration point to the bottom-left corner…

…and then rotate the artwork slightly clockwise.

6. **Select the Frame 1 keyframe. In the Actions panel Script pane, type stop();.**

   As with any other animation, the timeline of this movie clip would automatically loop if you didn't intentionally stop it.

7. **Click Scene 1 on the Edit bar to return to the main Stage.**

8. **Select the Frame 2 keyframe on the Actions layer. Place the insertion point at the end of the existing code and press Return/Enter twice.**

9. **Define event listeners and custom functions to call the appropriate frame of the golf club movie when a user clicks and when a user releases the mouse button:**

```
stage.addEventListener(MouseEvent.MOUSE_DOWN, playClubDown);
stage.addEventListener(MouseEvent.MOUSE_UP, playClubUp);

function playClubDown(event:MouseEvent):void{
    this.club_mc.gotoAndStop(2);
}

function playClubUp(event:MouseEvent):void{
    this.club_mc.gotoAndStop(1);
}
```

If you don't define the playClubUp function, the club will remain in the rotated position from Frame 2.

The Stage reference at the beginning of the event listener declarations attaches these listeners directly to the Stage, and not to a specific symbol instance. Clicking anywhere in the Player window initiates these functions.

10. **Press Command-Return/Control-Enter to test the movie. Click the Play button, drag around the Player window, and click to test the playClubDown and playClubUp functions.**

If you drag over any of the gophers, you will notice that the golf club moves behind the gopher holes — which is incorrect. This occurs because you placed the hole instances on the same layer where the golf club already existed. Objects exist by default in the order they are placed; so for the game to work properly, you need to move the golf club to the front of the stacking order.

Because the golf club is lower in the stacking order on the layer, it appears behind the gopher hole graphics.

11. **Close the Flash Player window and return to Flash.**

12. **Select the golf club instance on the Stage and choose Modify>Arrange> Bring to Front.**

13. **Press Command-Return/Control-Enter to test the movie. Click the Play button and drag around the Player window.**

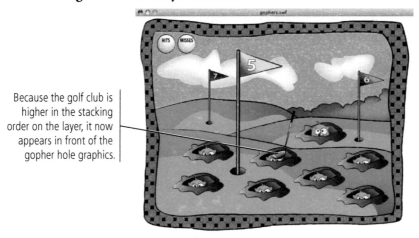

Because the golf club is higher in the stacking order on the layer, it now appears in front of the gopher hole graphics.

14. **Close the Flash Player window and return to Flash.**

15. **Select the Frame 22 keyframe on the Actions layer. Move the insertion point two lines after the existing code.**

16. **In the Actions toolbox, expand flash.events>EventDispatcher>Methods and double-click removeEventListener.**

If you remember from the first half of this project, the club_mc instance exists on the Content layer, but not on Frame 22.

If a user clicks when the timeline is stopped at Frame 22, an error occurs because the playMouseDown and playMouseUp functions reference an object that doesn't exist at that point in time.

To avoid this problem, you are removing the event listeners at the "results" frame.

17. **Highlight the target path ("not_yet_set") and type stage. Add a semicolon at the end of the statement.**

The stage reference is required because that is where you added the event listeners.

18. **Place the insertion point inside the parenthesis of the statement and type**

   MouseEvent.MOUSE_DOWN, playClubDown

19. **Add a second removeEventListener statement for the playClubUp function:**

   stage.removeEventListener(MouseEvent.MOUSE_UP, playClubUp);

20. **Save the file and continue to the next exercise.**

TRACK USER ACTIONS

The third element of this game's interactivity requires some method of tracking a user's mouse clicks. You first need to determine whether a user clicked the pop-up Gopher instance; then you can call the correct animation based on the user's action; and finally, you can use variables to count of the number of hits and misses in a single game.

1. **With gophers.fla open, double-click the Gopher_Popup symbol icon in the Library panel to enter the symbol Stage.**

2. **Add a new keyframe at Frame 2 of the Actions layer.**

3. **With the Frame 2 keyframe selected, define an event listener and custom function so that, if a user clicks the gopher, the timeline moves to Frame 21 (the "hit" gopher going back into the hole):**

    ```
    gopher_tracked.addEventListener(MouseEvent.CLICK, clicked);

    function clicked(event:MouseEvent):void{
        gotoAndPlay(21);
    }
    ```

    Remember, gopher_tracked is the instance name you defined for the Gopher symbol instance when you created the pop-up gopher animation. This is a movie clip symbol, so you don't have to define a specific hit-frame area; any click within the movie clip area will trigger the function (score a "hit").

4. **Click Scene 1 on the Edit bar to return to the main Stage.**

5. **Select the Frame 1 keyframe on the Actions layer.**

6. **At the end of the existing script, define two new number-type variables to store the number of hits and misses, and initialize both values to 0:**

    ```
    var hitcount:Number = 0;
    var misscount:Number = 0;
    ```

7. **Select the Frame 2 keyframe on the Actions layer. Place the insertion point immediately after the counter increment (Line 7) and press Return/Enter twice.**

Note:

The import statement is added on Line 1 as soon as you define the argument of the function (event:MouseEvent).

8. **With the insertion point on the new empty Line 9, click the Insert Target Path button.**

   As we mentioned earlier, this dialog box can be useful if you forgot the names you used for specific symbol instances. It is also useful for creating the correct path to objects nested in other objects, such as the dynamic text areas in the Hits and Misses movie clips.

9. **Click the arrow/plus sign to the left of hits_mc to show the nested object. Select the nested hit_count object in the dialog box and click OK.**

10. **At the end of the path, type .text=hitcount;.**

    This statement changes the text property (**.text**) of the hit_count dynamic text area (**Object(this).hits_mc.hit_count**) to the value of the hitcount variable (**=hitcount**).

11. **Add another statement that maps the misscount variable to the miss_count dynamic text area:**

    ```
    Object(this).misses_mc.miss_count.text=misscount;
    ```

12. **Save the file and continue to the next exercise.**

PASS VALUES TO THE PARENT TIMELINE

You still need some way to increment the hitcount and misscount variables. Because different frames in the animation represent "hits" and "misses," the easiest way to accomplish this is to create simple statements that are triggered when the playhead reaches specific frames.

1. **With gophers.fla open, double-click the Gopher_Popup symbol icon (in the Library panel) to enter the symbol Stage.**

2. **Select the Frame 20 keyframe on the Actions layer.**

3. **After the existing script, type the following code:**

   MovieClip(parent).misscount++;

   The **MovieClip(parent)** statement refers to the object that contains the current movie clip (its parent). In this case, the gopher instances are placed on the main Stage, so the **MovieClip(parent)** statement refers to the main timeline. The **misscount++** statement increments the value of the misscount variable, which you declared on Frame 1 of the main timeline.

4. **Add a new keyframe on Frame 21 of the Actions layer.**

5. **Add a statement to Frame 21 that increments the hitcount variable on the main timeline:**

   MovieClip(parent).hitcount++;

The timeline reaches Frame 21 only if the "clicked" function is called by the gopher_tracked instance being clicked (a "hit").

6. **Click Scene 1 on the Edit bar to return to the main Stage.**

7. **On Frame 2 of the Actions layer, select and copy the code on Lines 9–10.**

8. **Select the Frame 22 keyframe. Place the insertion point at the beginning of the existing script and press Return/Enter two times.**

9. **Move the insertion point to Line 1 and paste the code you copied in Step 7.**

When the timeline reaches Frame 21 and **counter=10**, the main timeline moves to Frame 22; the timeline on the gopher movie clip might not have triggered the final hitcount or misscount increment, so the final score only reflects the first nine user results.

If a user clicks the gopher at Frame 15 of the pop-up animation, that action triggers the 10-frame pop-down animation of the "hit" gopher. The entire revolution takes 25 frames to complete, which means the main timeline will have reached Frame 22 before the final hit or miss was mapped to the dynamic text areas.

If you don't include these statements on Frame 22, the final "hit" or "miss" (from the tenth run) might not reflect in the counters.

10. **Press Command-Return/Control-Enter to test the movie. Play the game and review the tracking functionality in the dynamic text objects.**

11. **Close the Flash Player window and return to Flash.**

12. **Save the file and continue to the next exercise.**

PROGRAM THE RESULT

The final tasks are to show the correct "results" movie clip when the game is finished, and to program the Replay button. Like the first exercise in Stage 2 of this project, both of these tasks require code that you learned about in Project 5.

1. **With `gophers.fla` open, select the Frame 22 keyframe on the Actions layer of the main timeline.**

2. **After the existing script, define a conditional "if…else" statement that shows the lose_mc instance if the hitcount value is less than 10, and the win_mc instance if the hitcount value is 10:**

```
if (hitcount<10) {
    lose_mc.visible=true;
    win_mc.visible=false;
} else {
    win_mc.visible=true;
    lose_mc.visible=false;
}
```

Notice that each condition defines the visibility property of both movie clips. Also notice that the else statement does not define a specific condition; the code assumes only two possibilities: *if* the condition is true, or *else* it is not.

The condition in the if statement (hitcount<10) requires a user to hit all 10 gophers in order to win the game. You could set a lesser threshold for victory by reducing the number in the condition, or even use both variables in the condition to define a victory as any game with more hits than misses (misscount<hitcount).

3. **Define a new event listener and function to reset the game when a user clicks the Replay button:**

```
replay_btn.addEventListener(MouseEvent.CLICK, replay);

function replay (event:MouseEvent):void {
    counter=0;
    hitcount=0;
    misscount=0;
    gotoAndPlay(2);
}
```

The variables that control the timeline loop and increment the counters are initialized to 0 in Frame 1. However, this function resets the game to Frame 2, so the variables need to be reset to 0 within the function body.

4. **Press Command/Control-Enter to test the movie. Play the game at least twice to test the Replay functionality.**

5. **Close the Player window and return to Flash.**

6. **Save the Flash file, then export the movie (File>Export Movie) as a SWF file named** `gophers.swf` **in your WIP>Gophers folder.**

7. **Close the file.**

Using the Compiler Errors Panel

When you test a file that includes ActionScript, your code must be processed or compiled before you can preview the file in the Flash Player window. If your script contains errors when you try to test the movie, Flash shows a list of the problems in the Compiler Errors panel (grouped with the Timeline panel by default).

In addition to simply reviewing the list of problems, you can use the Compiler Errors panel to navigate to the specific problem. If you select an item in the list and click the Go To Source button (or simply double-click the problem in the list), the Actions panel displays the relevant line code.

In the example shown here, Flash could not find a property named "Hitcount". The source of the problem shows that the programmer was trying to reference the variable named "hitcount", but accidentally typed a capital H instead of lowercase — a very common error, especially for new programmers.

ActionScript is case-sensitive; if you define a variable with a lowercase name, you must always use the lowercase name when referring to that variable. Although certainly not the only potential error in a script, capitalization is a good place to begin searching for the root cause of compiler errors.

Go To Previous

Go To Source   Go To Next   Clear

1. The _____ command makes it easy to move objects from one layer to another without changing the objects' X,Y position.

2. _____ to delete selected frames from the timeline.

3. Press _____ to select noncontiguous frames in the timeline.

4. When named, a _____ can be addressed by ActionScript to display variable values in the exported movie.

5. The _____ operator is used to increase the value of a variable by 1.

6. The _____ function can be used during development to show specific results in the Output panel.

7. Type _____ at the beginning of a line of code to convert that line to a comment.

8. A _____ appears between /* and */ in the Script pane.

9. The _____ command hides the basic mouse pointer in the Flash Player window.

10. The _____ code is used to send values from a movie clip's timeline to the timeline on which the symbol instance is located.

1. Briefly explain how dragging frames on the timeline affects objects on the Stage.

2. Briefly explain two examples of how the Output panel can aid in development.

3. Briefly explain two advantages of dynamic text.

Portfolio Builder Project

Use what you learned in this project to complete the following freeform exercise.
Carefully read the art director and client comments, then create your own design to meet the needs of the project.
Use the space below to sketch ideas; when finished, write a brief explanation of your reasoning behind your final design.

The assistant program director for the Field Museum in Chicago has hired you to create an interactive map that can be accessed on kiosks placed throughout the facility, as well as using hand-held digital devices.

❑ Download the museum's floor plans (www.fieldmuseum.org/plan_visit/floor_plans.htm).

❑ Create symbols and buttons to identify the different facilities and services (stairs, restrooms, elevators, etc.) throughout the museum.

❑ Add artwork, images, and color however you prefer to identify the different exhibit halls and other areas of the museum.

We currently have PDF maps that people can download and print from the Internet, but we are in the process of building an interactive electronic self-guided tour that can be rented from the information services office. We're planning on something a bit larger than a hand-held MP3 player; it will be able to play audio files about different exhibits or even video files about related topics. We think the interactive map will be an excellent added service for this program.

Can you use the PDF maps we have now to create new interactive versions? We hunted through our archives — we don't have the original art files of the floor plans, so we're hoping you can create new line art for the floor plans as well.

The devices we're using are fairly advanced, so you can add color or illustrations however you like to make the map more attractive. Just make sure the map is easily readable; don't let the artwork or imagery clutter the basic floor plan too much.

Project Summary

To complete this project, you worked with artwork imported from an Adobe Illustrator file. In this case, the artwork was prepared with a high degree of concern for integration into Flash. You saw, however, that even "good" supplied artwork will almost always require some additional setup once you import it into Flash. You also used Flash to create basic up-and-down tweens that, although very simple, still provide the underlying basis of the entire game. Different frames of the animation are called based on where the user clicks.

As you learned in this project, interactivity is far more than simply clicking a button. Using ActionScript 3, you can build complex games and other interactive tools that allow the user to control the behavior of every element on the screen.

Track user actions with dynamic text areas

Force a symbol instance to track the mouse movement

Hide the regular mouse pointer

Randomly animate symbol instances throughout the game

Pass values from a movie clip timeline to the main timeline

Show different symbol instances based on user results

Travel Video Module

Your client is a travel company that offers a variety of customized and personalized tourism packages. As part of their promotional efforts, the client wants to include a series of video clips on their Web site to show examples of the tours they offer. They hired you to build a video-viewing module in Flash, including a series of thumbnail images that a user can click to watch the related videos.

This project incorporates the following skills:

❏ Using the Adobe Media Encoder application to encode video files for Flash

❏ Importing video files into Flash

❏ Defining video playback parameters

❏ Creating dynamic video captions

❏ Building thumbnail navigation

❏ Linking thumbnails to movies and captions

❏ Editing component skins and dynamic text styles

Project Meeting

client comments

Our primary focus is building custom trips to meet any need or interest. We've taken people all over the world, and we can build packages for groups of any size — from two to two hundred.

We think the best way to promote our services to potential clients is to show them what we have done for other clients. Our Web site already includes testimonials from satisfied clients, but we also want to add actual trip videos on our home page.

We've taken hundreds of videos over the years, but we've narrowed down the field to eight movies that we want to show on the home page. Because the videos will be on our home page, we want each one to last only about 10 seconds. We might decide to expand the library later; if we do, we might add longer videos on other pages.

The module needs to include some way for users to select which video they want to see, and for each video, please include a caption that explains what the video is all about.

art director comments

Flash includes many built-in tools for working with video, but you have to start by encoding the client's files into a format that Flash can read. You can then import the video into Flash, build the rest of the module components, and tie everything together.

You could manually program the module functionality, but using the TileList component is the easiest way to create a thumbnail navigation system. This tool condenses several hours or days of work in ActionScript into a very simple, panel-based set of parameters.

Because there is only a single caption for each video, you can use a script to change the content in a dynamic text area based on which thumbnail is clicked. You'll use the same scripting methodology to change the specific video that displays in the playback component.

project objectives

To complete this project, you will:

❑ Use the Adobe Media Encoder to encode video files to a format appropriate for Flash

❑ Import video into Flash

❑ Define FLVPlayback component parameters

❑ Use the TextArea component for captions

❑ Add content to the TileList component

❑ Adjust TileList parameters

❑ Define a change event to link thumbnails to movies and captions

❑ Edit an interface component skin

❑ Format component text styles using ActionScript

❑ Export the video module for upload to a Web server

Stage 1 **Encoding Video for Flash**

Before you build the video viewer module, you should understand the common file formats used for publishing video files on the Web:

- **AVI** is the abbreviation of Audio Video Interleave. Video files in this format can be played on most computers, as long as the computers have the required plugins.

- **MOV** is the extension for the QuickTime multimedia format. Using the required plugins and applications, video files in this format can be viewed on most computers.

- **MPEG** is the abbreviation for Moving Pictures Experts Group, a group that specializes in video and audio encoding. Video files compressed using the .mpeg algorithms are most commonly used on the Web.

- **WMV** is the abbreviation for Windows Media Video. Video files of this type are used in Windows Media Players.

- **RM** is the file extension for RealVideo files. These files are popular for their streaming capabilities; they are played in Real Media Players.

Compression is the process of reducing video file size relative to the original file size. There are two general types of compression:

- **Spatial compression** removes redundant data from a file. Instead of defining each pixel, an area is specified using coordinates. Spatial compression is often called **intraframe** compression.

- **Temporal compression** identifies differences between frames and stores only the differences. By doing so, a large portion of the file is deleted, and each frame is described based on the difference from the preceding frame. Temporal compression is often called **interframe** compression.

> *Note:*
>
> *A device used to compress data is known as an **encoder** or **coder**, and a device that decompresses data is known as a **decoder**. A device that can both compress and decompress a file is known as a **codec**.*

Both spatial and temporal compression are considered **lossy** methods, which means that redundant data is discarded during the compression process. The discarded data is not available when the file is decompressed for playback. (**Lossless compression** results in an exact copy of all original data when the file is decompressed.)

CREATE A QUEUE IN THE ADOBE MEDIA ENCODER

To work correctly in Flash, video files must be converted to the FLV/F4V (Flash Video) format. You can use the Adobe Media Encoder, a standalone application included with Flash Professional, to create F4V files from other video file formats.

1. **Download FL5_RF_Project7.zip from the Student Files Web page.**

2. **Expand the ZIP archive in your WIP folder (Macintosh) or copy the archive contents into your WIP folder (Windows).**

   This results in a folder named **Tourism**, which contains the files you need for this project. You should also use this folder to save the files you create in this project.

3. **Launch the Adobe Media Encoder application.**

   On Macintosh, you will probably find this application in the Applications>Adobe Media Encoder CS5 folder on your hard drive.

   On Windows, click the Start menu and choose All Programs. Look for the Adobe Media Encoder application in the main Start menu.

4. **Open the Preferences dialog box for the Adobe Media Encoder.**

As with any other application, preferences are accessed in the Application menu on Macintosh and the Edit menu on Windows.

5. **In the Preferences dialog box, check the Remove Completed Files option.**

If you do not check this option, the application maintains the queue from the last time it was used.

6. **Uncheck the Start Queue Automatically option.**

If you leave this option checked, the encoding process automatically begins 2 minutes after adding files to the queue. Unchecking this option allows you to control the entire process, including when it begins.

7. **Check the Place Output Files In option.**

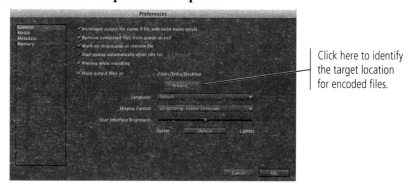

Click here to identify the target location for encoded files.

8. **Click Browse, and then navigate to the F4U folder that is in your WIP>Tourism folder. Click Choose/OK.**

The original, unencoded movie files exist here.

The encoded movie files will be saved here.

Note:

If you don't define a target folder, the encoded files will be placed in the same folder as the source files.

You will save the primary Flash file for this project in the WIP>Tourism folder. The individual movie files will be exported to the F4V folder. References from the main Flash file to the various movie files will use the path from the main file to the individual movies in the F4V folder.

9. **Click OK to close the Preferences dialog box.**

10. **In the Adobe Media Encoder application, click the Add button.**

11. **Navigate to the WIP>Tourism>Movies folder. Shift-click to select all eight files in the Movies folder.**

Note:

You can also add files to the queue by dragging them onto the Adobe Media Encoder window.

Note:

Click and drag to reorder files in the queue.

12. **Click Open to add the selected files to the Media Encoder queue.**

Click here to add files that need to be encoded.

The main screen of the Adobe Media Encoder displays the Source Name, Format, Preset settings, Output File location, and Status of the selected video files.

The status of each video displays in the queue. Files recently added are marked as "Waiting" until you encode them.

13. **Continue to the next exercise.**

 DEFINE ENCODER SETTINGS

When you encode video files, you can control numerous export options in the various tabs of the Export Settings dialog box.

1. **In the Adobe Media Encoder application, click away from the added movie files to deselect them.**

2. **Click the F4V-Match Source Attributes link (to the right of the Preset menu) for the video1.mov file.**

    The profiles in the Preset menu determine the Flash Player version and level of compression that will be applied to the video clip. The F4V-Same as Source (Flash 9.0.r115 and Higher) profile is selected by default.

    Click the hot text link to open the Export Settings dialog box so you can define custom export settings.

    Clicking this link opens the Export Settings dialog box, where you can define custom output settings for the selected file.

The available video export options depend on the file format you are exporting — F4V or FLV (controlled in the Format tab). The following is a brief explanation of the various export options.

- **Codec.** The word "codec" is the shortened form of enCOder/DECoder. This option refers to the software method used to compress video data on video frames, to reduce the size of the file and improve file transfer time.
  - Using the F4V format, video is compressed using the MainConcept H.264 codec.
  - Using the FLV format, video is compressed using the On2 V6P codec.
- **Encode Alpha Channel.** Color information in a video is contained in three channels: red, green, and blue. Video can also include an additional fourth channel, called an **alpha channel**, which contains transparency information. If your video includes alpha channel information, check this option so you can place transparent video content over other Flash content.
- **Resize Video.** Check this option to change the physical height and width (in pixels) of frames in the video.
- **Frame Rate.** This option specifies the number of frames per second in the exported video file. Increasing the frame rate might produce smoother motion (depending on the frame rate of the source clip, project, or sequence), but also results in larger file size.

- **Field Order.** Interlaced video consists of two fields for each video frame. Each field contains half the number of horizontal lines in the frame; the upper field contains the odd-numbered lines and the lower field contains the even-numbered lines.

  An interlaced display (such as a television) displays each frame by first drawing all lines in one field, and then drawing all lines in the other field. You can use the Field Order menu to determine which fields load first.

  A progressive display (such as a computer monitor) draws all horizontal lines from top to bottom in a single pass. Choosing None (Progressive) in the Field Order menu exports the video without fields, as necessary for noninterlaced displays.
- **Bitrate Encoding.** This option defines whether the encoding produces a constant or variable bitrate.
  - CBR (**constant bitrate**) results in the same bitrate for every frame in the video, regardless of the complexity of each frame.
  - VBR (**variable bitrate**) results in different bitrates for different frames, allowing greater compression for less-complex frames to reduce overall file size.

	FLV	F4V
Basic Video Settings		
Codec	On2 V6P	MainConcept H.264
Encode Alpha Channel	On/Off	NA
Resize Video (Frame Width and Height)	On/Off	On/Off
Frame Rate	Same As Source, 1, 5, 8, 10, 12, 12.5, 15, 24, 25, 29.97, 30	Same As Source, 10, 12, 12.5, 15, 24, 25, 29.97, 30
Field Order	NA	None (Progressive), Upper, Lower
Profile	NA	Baseline, Main, High
Level	NA	1.0–5.1
Bitrate Settings		
Bitrate Encoding	CBR, VBR	CBR; VBR 1 Pass; VBR 2 Pass
Encoding Passes	One, Two	NA (Managed in Encoding Type)
Bitrate	5–10 kbps	NA
Target Bitrate	NA	0.19–50 Mbps
Maximum Bitrate	NA	0.19–50 Mbps
Advanced Settings		
Set Key Frame Distance	On/Off	On/Off
Simple Profile	On/Off	NA
Undershoot [% Target]	0–100%	NA
Quality	Speed, Good, Best	NA

3. Click the Format tab and make sure the F4V option is selected.

A file with the extension ".F4V" is an MP4 video file utilized by Adobe Flash Player version 9 and higher. The FLV (Flash Live Video) format is designed for Web playback, offering high compression rates to deliver video over the Internet using Adobe Flash Player version 6 and higher.

Note:

If you ever need to stretch or shrink a video in only one direction, click the chain icon to unconstrain the dimensions.

Preview of the selected movie

Use these tabs to review and change options in different categories.

Use these options to change the in point (start) and out point (end) of the movie that will be exported.

Understanding Video Export Settings (continued)

FLASH FOUNDATIONS

- **Encoding Passes.** For variable-bitrate encoding, this option determines how many times video frames are analyzed to determine the appropriate compression for individual frames. Using two passes takes more time than a single pass, but results in higher output quality.
  - Using the F4V format, you can choose VBR 1 Pass or VBR 2 Pass directly in the Bitrate Encoding menu.
  - Using the FLV format, you can choose One or Two in the separate Encoding Passes setting when you use the On2 V6P codec.

- **Bitrate.** This option defines the number of megabits per second of playback in the encoded file.
  - Using the FLV format, you can define the average bitrate that you want to allow in the exported file.
  - Using the F4V format, you can define both the target bitrate and maximum bitrate that you want the encoder to allow in the exported video.

- **Set Key Frame Distance.** By default, the Adobe Media Encoder places a keyframe every 30 frames in the encoded video file. Only data different from the preceding keyframe is stored in frames between the keyframes. If you check the Set Keyframe Distance option, you can define a specific number of frames between keyframes in an encoded video.

- **Simple Profile.** Selecting this option optimizes high-resolution video content that will be played back on older output devices.

- **Undershoot.** This option defines the target data rate percentage so additional data is available in the buffer.

- **Quality.** Use this option to determine whether speed or quality is more important in the encoding process (for example, speed might be more important when encoding for testing purposes, while quality is more important in the final application deployment). The Good setting balances image quality and the amount of time it takes to encode video. The Best setting favors the best possible image quality, but takes substantially longer to encode video. The Speed setting favors the fastest possible encoding, resulting in lower quality video.

- **Render at Maximum Depth** and **Use Maximum Render Quality.** These options can be used to render video higher than 8 bits per pixel.

- **Use Frame Blending.** This option can be used to create smoother motion when you are exporting to a different frame than the original source video file.

4. In the top-left corner of the dialog box, click the Crop button.

5. Set the Top field value to 10. Click away from the field to apply the value; do not press Return/Enter.

Cropping a video means changing the physical area of the video that will be included in the output. Areas outside the crop area are not included in the exported video. When the Crop button is active, you can use the Left, Top, Right, and Bottom fields (above the preview image) to crop a specific number of pixels from each edge of the image. You can also use the handles in the preview to crop the file to a specific point.

Crop button

Change these values to define how many pixels to crop from each edge.

You can also click and drag these handles to change the crop area.

6. Click the Crop button again to exit Crop mode.

7. Click the Video tab and review the options.

8. In the bottom-right section of the dialog box, check the Resize Video option. With the Constrain option turned on, change the Frame Width to 330 pixels. Click away from the field to apply the value; do not press Return/Enter.

When the Constrain Width/Height option is checked, changing the frame width to 330 automatically applies a proportional change in the frame height.

If you don't see the chain icon, click here to constrain proportions.

Click here, then type the new width.

Note:

If you press Return/ Enter after changing a value in this dialog box, you return to the Adobe Media Encoder queue. You can always return to the Export Settings dialog box by clicking the Preset hot-text link.

9. Click the Out Point handle below the preview area and drag left until the time stamp below the preview shows approximately 8 seconds.

These handles allow you to shorten the duration of a video clip. When you change the in point or out point of a video file, the new duration displays below the preview image.

Out Point handle

Note:

The files for this project do not include audio information. If a video file includes audio information, you can use the options in the Audio tab to control the quality of audio included in the movie.

10. **Click OK to return to the main window of the Adobe Media Encoder.**

11. **In the main Adobe Media Encoder dialog box, click the Start Queue button.**

    You can click the Stop Queue button to stop the encoding process midstream; you will see a warning dialog box asking if you want to finish encoding the current file. If you click No in the warning, the current file shows Skip in the Status column. You can select a skipped file and choose Edit>Reset Status to place the file into the Waiting queue.

Note:

For the sake of this project, you are using the default settings for the remaining seven files.

12. **When all eight files have been encoded, quit the Media Encoder application.**

13. **Continue to the next exercise.**

 ## PREPARE THE CONTAINER FLASH FILE

The basic Flash file for this project will contain three primary elements: a video player, a caption area, and a scrolling area for numerous thumbnail images that will function as links. Now that the necessary video files have been converted to the F4V format, your next task is to create the Flash file itself.

1. **In Flash, create a new Flash file for ActionScript 3.0.**

2. **Choose File>Save As. Save the file as** `travel_videos.fla` **in your WIP>Tourism folder.**

3. **Click the Edit button in the Properties section of the Properties panel to open the Document Settings dialog box.**

4. **Change the document to 330 pixels wide and 425 pixels high. Click the Background Color swatch and choose #006666 from the Swatches panel. Set the Frame Rate to 24 fps.**

5. **Click OK to apply the changes.**

6. **Rename Layer 1 as Background.**

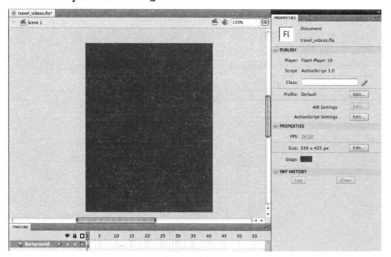

7. **Save the file and continue to the next exercise.**

 ## IMPORT VIDEO INTO FLASH

There are three different ways to deliver video using the Flash Player.

Embedded Video. Using this method, video content is placed on the Flash timeline and stored in the SWF file with other content. This method is popular because it is easier to visualize the interaction of the video with other elements on the timeline. There are, however, several disadvantages to embedding video on a timeline:

- Each frame in a video file will map to a single frame in the Flash timeline. This method can significantly reduce the video playback quality because the video will play back at the frame rate defined for the Flash file. (Video is typically captured at 24 fps or higher.)

- You might have problems synchronizing audio and video because the frame rates of the video and the Flash movie do not always match.

- Embedding video into a Flash file can significantly increase the file size and download time of the final SWF movie file.

Progressive Download. Using this method, the video file remains separate from the primary Flash file. When the video file is called by the SWF file, the video downloads from its source location on the Web server. As soon as enough information has downloaded, the video begins playing (although you can prevent automatic playback if you prefer). Because the video file remains external to the SWF file, this method offers the following benefits:

- You do not need to republish the SWF file to change content in the video file.

- The SWF file is considerably smaller than an embedded video file, so it takes less time to download the SWF file.

- Because the video file and the SWF file are separate, the video can maintain a higher frame rate; this also prevents problems with synchronization between the audio and video components of the video file.

Streaming Video. Using this method, each user (client) opens a connection to the streaming server; the streaming server streams the video bits to each individual client. These bits are used by the client, and then immediately discarded. (As with progressive download files, streaming video files remain external to other Flash content. Unlike progressive download video, which can be deployed with any Web server, streaming video requires streaming server software.) Streaming video offers the following advantages:

- With streaming video, the server can precisely control and deliver any portion of the stream to individual clients. Users can go to any point in the video and play it immediately.

- Streaming allows real-time broadcasting of live events, as well as the ability to control the playback of the content. Live video can be delivered from any connected video camera or Web cam.

- Streaming immediately serves the requested video; users do not need to wait until the entire video has downloaded.

The disadvantage to streaming video is that slow connection speed or bandwidth congestion might result in decreased quality.

In this exercise, you import the first client video into the Flash file. This video will be the default playback when a user opens the module. Later in the project, you will use ActionScript to change the video that appears in the module, based on a series of thumbnail images.

1. With **travel_videos.fla** open, create a new layer named **Video** at the top of the layer stack.

2. Choose **File>Import>Import Video.**

The Import Video command works like a wizard, walking you through the necessary steps of the video import process. In the first screen, you define the location of the video file you want to import (whether on your local drive or already deployed on a Web server).

The Import Video dialog box provides three import options:

- **Load External Video with Playback Component.** If this option is selected, the video imports into an instance of the FLVPlayback component to control video playback. When you publish the Flash document as a SWF and upload it to your Web server, you must also upload the video file and configure the FLVPlayback component with the location of the uploaded video file.

- **Embed FLV in SWF and Play in Timeline.** You can use this option to embed an FLV/F4V into the Flash document. When you import video this way, the video is placed in the timeline; individual frames in the video correspond to individual frames on the Flash timeline.

- **Import as Mobile Device Video Bundled in SWF.** Similar to embedding a video in a Flash document, this option allows you to bundle a video into a Flash Lite document for deployment on a mobile device.

Note:

The F4V format is a later variant of the FLV format. The Import Video dialog box only mentions FLV files, but the options also apply to F4V as well.

3. **Make sure the Load External Video with Playback Component is selected, then click the Browse button.**

4. **Navigate to video1.f4v in your WIP>Tourism>F4V folder and click Open to return to the Import Video dialog box.**

   Because the F4V folder is located in the same place as the Flash file, the Flash file can create an accurate relative path from the main file to the video file. If you change the relative location of either file — either on your local computer or when you upload files to the Web server — you will have to correct the video's link path.

5. **Click Continue/Next to show the Skinning screen of the Import Video dialog box.**

   A **skin** is simply the superficial appearance of a component. The selected skin determines which controls are included in the video playback component created by the Import Video process.

6. **In the Skin menu, choose SkinUnderPlaySeekStop.swf.**

   The video files for this project do not include audio information, so you do not need to include volume and mute controls in the skin.

This is a preview of the selected skin, showing the controls that are included.

7. **Click Continue/Next to show the Finish Video Import screen of the Import Video dialog box.**

8. **Read the information in the Finish Video Import screen.**

As we mentioned earlier, the relative path from the exported SWF file (and the working Flash file) must be maintained. This screen also tells you that the skin you selected is actually a separate SWF file, which must also be available on the Web server for the video to work properly.

9. **Click Finish to add the video playback component to the Stage.**

When you import the video with the FLVPlayback component, the component is automatically centered on the Stage. (The skin is not considered in the object size for centering.) The playback component defaults to the same physical size as the video file you imported.

10. **Make sure the component is selected on the Stage. In the Properties panel, unlink the width and height properties, then change the component's size to W: 320, H: 220.**

This defines the size of the component, which is the actual object on the Stage. Changing the size of the FLVPlayback component has no effect on the size of the video that plays inside the component.

11. Change the position of the component to X: 5, Y: 5.

This position provides 5 pixels of "breathing space" around the left, top, and right sides of the component.

12. Type player in the Instance Name field.

Later in this project, you will use ActionScript to change the content in the playback component, based on which thumbnail is clicked. Like other elements on the Stage, the playback component instance must be named so it can be addressed in ActionScript.

The source parameter shows the file that will play in the component.

13. Save the file, and then press Command-Return/Control-Enter to test the movie.

By default, the video is proportionally scaled to fit into the defined component size, and then the component is resized to fit the scaled video. You will change the playback component settings later to keep the playback component at the size you defined.

Note:

You might need to click away from the selected component before you can test the file.

14. Close the Player window.

15. On your desktop, open your WIP>Tourism folder and review the contents.

A SWF file for the selected skin has been added to the folder with the test movie. This file is required to display the selected FLVPlayback component skin.

This is the SWF file generated by the Test Movie command.

16. Return to Flash, and then continue to the next stage of the project.

Stage 2 Working with Components

Flash CS5 includes a set of useful tools for building a variety of common interface elements — from scrolling panes to form fields to working video players with all of the necessary playback controls. These tools are very appealing to visually oriented designers because, in most cases, the tools can be used instead of writing complicated ActionScript — even when developing fairly complex interactive elements. (Many components still require some coding, but not as much as creating the components from scratch would require.)

User Interface Components

FLASH FOUNDATIONS

Two sets of components are available in the Components panel: User Interface and Video. User Interface components, described here, help you create common interactive elements.

Button. This component creates a rounded-corner button with a text label. You can change the text label on the button by changing the Label parameter for the component. One unique feature of the Button component (compared to regular button symbols) is the Toggle parameter; if you set this parameter to True, the button maintains the clicked state until a user clicks it a second time.

CheckBox. This component creates a standard toggle control with the label to the right of the check box shape.

ColorPicker. This component creates a color swatch that, when clicked, opens the Color Picker palette in the SWF file. You can use ActionScript to define the specific colors available in the palette.

ComboBox. This component creates a pop-up menu list. Double-clicking the dataProvider parameter for this component opens the Value dialog box, where you can define the labels and data for individual menu items.

DataGrid. This component creates a table to contain data in columnar format; the resulting grid is scrollable and sortable, based on column headings. The contents of the DataGrid component must be defined through ActionScript.

Label. This component creates a text area that is basically a dynamic text field. (There is no real reason to use this component; a standard dynamic text area serves the same purpose.)

List. This component creates a scrollable selection list. As with the ComboBox component, double-clicking the dataProvider parameter opens the Value dialog box, where you can define the necessary list items.

NumericStepper. This component creates a specialized field that contains only numbers. You can define the initial value in the field, minimum and maximum values, and the increments used by the Up Arrow and Down Arrow buttons attached to the field.

ProgressBar. This component creates a small animated bar that indicates a process is not yet finished.

RadioButton. This component creates a toggle control similar to a check box. The primary difference is that radio buttons are typically part of a group, from which a user can select only one option. You have to use ActionScript to define each radio button as part of the same group.

ScrollPane. This component creates an area intended to contain large images. You can define the size of the pane in the Properties panel, and then control the pane's content and scrolling behavior in the Properties panel.

Slider. This component creates a number-based slider bar. Like the NumericStepper component, you can define the initial, minimum, and maximum possible values, as well as the intervals at which the slider handle can stop.

TextArea. This component creates a stylized dynamic text area that can scroll both horizontally and vertically (if necessary). For smaller blocks of text that don't require scrolling, a regular dynamic text area might be easier to manage because you don't have to use ActionScript to control the appearance of text.

TextInput. This component creates a field in which users can input text.

TileList. This component creates a scrollable grid of images. You can double-click the dataProvider parameter to add items to the component, or you can use ActionScript to manually define the component contents. (If you use the dataProvider option, each item will include a label, which will be added to the selected thumbnail. If you don't want to include labels for the items, you should use ActionScript to manually define the items.)

UILoader. This component creates an invisible area you can use to easily load other files into a movie. You can use the Properties panel to define the file to load.

UIScrollBar. This component can be dragged onto a scrollable dynamic text field to easily add scrollbars to the text area. (To make a dynamic text area scrollable, Control/right-click a dynamic text area and choose Scrollable from the contextual menu.) The scrollbar component snaps to the closest edge of the text area, depending on where you drag the component.

DEFINE FLVPLAYBACK COMPONENT PARAMETERS

When you use the Import Video command and dialog box, the selected video is placed onto the Stage within an instance of the built-in FLVPlayback component. Although you can create custom players, this component includes skins with controls that are already designed to control the video inside the player. By selecting different skins and modifying the component parameters, you can customize the component to meet most video player needs without having to learn complex ActionScript.

1. **With travel_videos.fla open, select the FLVPlayback component on the Stage.**

   Components are controlled using built-in sets of parameters, which you can define in the Component Parameters section of the Properties panel.

2. **In the Component Parameters section of the Properties panel, uncheck the autoPlay option.**

3. **Open the scaleMode menu and choose exactFit.**

Uncheck this option to prevent the movie from playing when the file first opens.

Choose exactFit to force the video file into the defined component size.

4. **Click the skinBackgroundColor swatch and choose the light gray swatch (#CCCCCC) from the pop-up color palette.**

5. **Change the skinBackgroundAlpha value to 0.5 to increase the transparency of the skin.**

   By default, the FLVPlayback skin is partially transparent. The skinBackgroundAlpha parameter controls the transparency from 0 (fully transparent) to 1 (fully opaque).

Note:

Because you added the video using the Import Video command, the source path is already defined. You can also drag the FLVPlayback component from the Components panel, and then use the Source parameter to define which video to play.

Note:

The skinAutoHide value is set to false by default. If you change this parameter to true, the skin will only appear when a user rolls the mouse over the FLVPlayback component.

6. **Press Command-Return/Control-Enter to test the movie.**

   When the player module opens, the movie does not play until you click the Play button in the component skin. This follows the rule you defined using the autoPlay parameter.

7. **Close the Player window and return to Flash.**

8. **Save the file and continue to the next exercise.**

FLVPlayback Component Parameters

You can customize the FLVPlayback component by changing many parameters in the Properties panel.

- **align.** This determines where the video is placed inside the FLVPlayback component if the video is physically smaller than the space available in the playback component. (When you place a video using the Import Video dialog box, the playback component automatically scales to match the physical size of the imported video.)

- **autoPlay.** This parameter has two options: true or false. Your choice determines whether the defined video plays as soon as the module opens.

- **cuePoints.** This parameter describes cue points for the selected video file. Cue points synchronize certain points in the video file with animation, text, or graphics.

- **isLive.** This parameter allows you to set a Boolean value that, if true, specifies that the video is streaming live from Flash Media Server (FMS). The default value is false.

- **preview.** This parameter has no function in Flash CS5; it is a remnant of CS4 (and earlier) technology, when the application could not display the actual video content on the Flash Stage.

- **scaleMode.** This determines whether the video will scale to fit the space available in the FLVPlayback component. You can choose maintainAspectRatio to scale the video proportionally (horizontal and vertical dimensions keep the same aspect ratio as the original), noScale (the video displays at its original size), and exactFit (the video scales to fit the available space, distorting the original aspect ratio if necessary).

- **skin.** This parameter enables you to customize the location of controls, as well as the specific options included in the component skin. Double-clicking this parameter opens the Select Skin dialog box, which includes the same options you saw in the Skinning screen of the Import Video dialog box.

- **skinAutoHide.** This parameter has two possible options: true or false. If you select true, the skin controls will only be visible when a user moves the mouse over the FLVPlayback component.

- **skinBackgroundAlpha.** This parameter controls the transparency of the component skin. Alpha can be set from 0 (fully transparent) to 1 (fully opaque).

- **skinBackgroundColor.** This parameter controls the color of the component skin.

- **source.** This parameter specifies the path to the video to be played. If a video file has already been uploaded to a Web server, you can specify the HTTP or RTMP (Real-Time Messaging Protocol) path in this parameter.

- **volume.** This parameter controls the default volume for the video in the component. Volume can be set from 0 (silent) to 1 (full volume).

USE THE TEXTAREA COMPONENT FOR CAPTIONS

The TextArea component is basically an enhanced dynamic text area that defaults to show a white background and a slightly beveled edge. (You can edit this appearance by editing the component skins.)

1. **With travel_videos.fla open, create a new layer named Caption at the top of the layer stack.**

2. **Open the Components panel (Window>Components) and expand the User Interface folder. Drag an instance of the TextArea component onto the Stage.**

3. **Using the Properties panel, change the TextArea component dimensions to 320 pixels wide by 40 pixels high. Center the component horizontally on the Stage, and position it directly below the FLVPlayback instance.**

4. **Type caption in the Instance Name field.**

   Like all other elements, a TextArea component must be named before you can address it in ActionScript.

Component instance names, dimensions, and positions can be defined in the Properties panel.

TextArea Component Parameters

A number of parameters are available for customizing TextArea components:

- **condenseWhite.** This option affects text areas set to export as HTML text. When this parameter is true, extra spaces and line breaks are removed from the text.

- **editable.** This option determines whether users can change the text in the area.

- **enabled.** This option sets a value that indicates whether the component can accept user interaction. A value of true indicates that the component can accept user interaction; a value of false indicates that it cannot. When the enabled property is set to false, the color of the container becomes dimmed and the user input is blocked (with the exception of the Label and ProgressBar components).

- **horizontalScrollPolicy.** This option can be set to true to allow horizontal scrolling.

- **htmlText.** If enabled, this option formats text in the area as HTML text.

- **maxChars.** This parameter limits the number of characters in the component.

- **restrict.** This option defines specific sets of characters that are allowed in the component (for example "0–9" allows only numerals).

- **text.** This field defines specific text that will appear in the component. (You can also use ActionScript to define and/or change the text content in a TextArea component.)

- **verticalScrollPolicy.** This option can be set to true to allow vertical scrolling.

- **visible.** This option can be set to true to allow the visibility of the text or caption added in the component.

- **wordWrap.** If this option is set to false, text in the text area does not automatically wrap, based on the component's defined width.

---

5. **In the Component Parameters section of the Properties panel, click the text field to place the insertion point.**

6. **Type** Click a thumbnail to see video clips of recent tours. **and press Return/Enter to finalize the text in the field.**

   This text will appear in the caption area when the module first opens (before a user clicks a specific thumbnail).

Click here and type the text that you want to appear in the component.

When you press Return/Enter after typing the caption, the text appears in the component.

7. **Save the file and continue to the next exercise.**

 ## ADD THUMBNAIL NAVIGATION OBJECTS

Flash components are prebuilt elements that make it easy to create and control the behavior of common interface objects that would otherwise require complex design and coding. When you imported the video file into Flash, the video was added inside a predefined playback module. This module is actually an instance of the FLVPlayback component, which is available in the Video folder of the Components panel.

Other common interface elements are also available in the Components panel, including a scrolling area for holding multiple thumbnail images. Rather than building your own scrolling area from scratch, you can use the built-in TileList component to hold the video thumbnails that will act as links to the various video files.

1. **With** travel_videos.fla **open, create a new layer named** Thumbnails **at the top of the layer stack.**

2. **Drag an instance of the TileList component from the Components panel to the Stage.**

3. **Change the component width to 320 pixels and height to 85 pixels. Align the TileList component horizontally on the Stage, below the TextArea component.**

4. In the Properties panel, type thumblist in the Instance Name field.

As with other types of instances, component instances must be named before they can be addressed by ActionScript.

Note:

The TileList component is actually a type of scrolling area, but it is specifically designed to create a grid of images in a scrollable area. The ScrollPane component, on the other hand, is primarily intended to hold text-based content; you can't define columns or rows in the parameters of a ScrollPane component.

5. In the Component Parameters, choose on from the scrollPolicy menu.

By default, the scrolling TileList component scrolls only when necessary. By setting the scrollPolicy to on, the scrollbar appears within the component, even if the included content does not require scrolling.

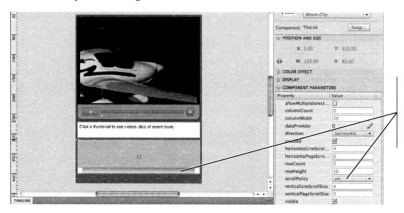

When the ScrollPolicy parameter is set to on, the scrollbar appears within the component on the Stage.

6. Save the file and continue to the next exercise.

ADD CONTENT TO THE TILELIST COMPONENT

If you use the dataProvider parameter to add content to the TileList component, each item will include a text label. You don't want labels on the thumbnails, and you will later add data to each item, so you are going to use ActionScript to manually define the items included in the TileList component.

The Flash file needs to be able to locate the thumbnail images you will script into the TileList component. The relative path that you define for the thumbnail images in the script must remain consistent when the exported SWF file is uploaded to a Web server.

1. With travel_videos.fla open, create a new layer named Actions at the top of the layer stack.

2. With Frame 1 of the Actions layer selected, open the Actions panel.

3. Click in the Script pane of the Actions panel to place the insertion point.

4. **On Line 1 of the Script pane, type:**

   thumblist.addItem({source:"Images/thumbnail1.jpg"});

   The first part of the script identifies the component (**thumblist**) where items will be added (using the **addItem** command). Inside the parentheses, you define the content that will be added to the TileList. Make sure you type the command exactly as we show here.

   - Capitalization counts; the folder containing the thumbnail images is named "Images" (capitalized).

   - The source statement must be enclosed within both parentheses and braces.

   - The location of the source parameter must be enclosed within quotation marks.

   - The statement must have a semicolon at the end of the line.

You are adding this statement to Frame 1 of the Actions layer.

5. **Press Return/Enter to move to Line 2 of the Script pane.**

6. **Beginning on Line 2, add seven more lines to the script that will add each thumbnail image in the Images folder into the TileList component:**

   thumblist.addItem({source:"Images/thumbnail2.jpg"});

   thumblist.addItem({source:"Images/thumbnail3.jpg"});

   thumblist.addItem({source:"Images/thumbnail4.jpg"});

   thumblist.addItem({source:"Images/thumbnail5.jpg"});

   thumblist.addItem({source:"Images/thumbnail6.jpg"});

   thumblist.addItem({source:"Images/thumbnail7.jpg"});

   thumblist.addItem({source:"Images/thumbnail8.jpg"});

   ```
   1  thumblist.addItem({source:"Images/thumbnail1.jpg"});
   2  thumblist.addItem({source:"Images/thumbnail2.jpg"});
   3  thumblist.addItem({source:"Images/thumbnail3.jpg"});
   4  thumblist.addItem({source:"Images/thumbnail4.jpg"});
   5  thumblist.addItem({source:"Images/thumbnail5.jpg"});
   6  thumblist.addItem({source:"Images/thumbnail6.jpg"});
   7  thumblist.addItem({source:"Images/thumbnail7.jpg"});
   8  thumblist.addItem({source:"Images/thumbnail8.jpg"});
   ```

   Note:

   If you copy and paste the first line of code, make sure you change the number for each thumbnail.

7. **Press Command-Return/Control-Enter to test the movie.**

   The TileList scroll panel includes all eight thumbnail images. The thumbnails are proportionally scaled to fit into the grid size, which is defined by the default columnWidth and rowHeight parameters of the TileList component.

8. **Close the Player window and return to Flash.**

9. **Save the file and continue to the next exercise.**

Adjust TileList Parameters

By default, a TileList component shows small thumbnails (50 × 50 pixels) within the defined dimensions of the component. You can customize many parameters in a TileList, including the component's scroll behavior and the size of items in the component.

1. **On your desktop, click one of the thumbnail images in the WIP>Tourism> Images folder. If your system does not automatically show the physical dimensions of the selected file, Control/right-click a thumbnail file and choose Get Info/Properties from the contextual menu.**

   On Macintosh, the file dimensions are listed in the More Info section of the Info dialog box.

   On Windows, the dimensions are listed in the Summary tab of the Properties dialog box.

Each thumbnail is 90 pixels wide by 61 pixels high.

2. **With travel_videos.fla open in Flash, select the TileList component instance on the Stage.**

3. **In the Properties panel, change the columnWidth parameter value to 90.**

4. **Change the rowHeight parameter value to 61.**

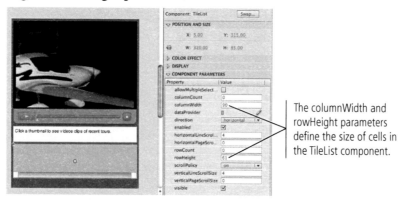

The columnWidth and rowHeight parameters define the size of cells in the TileList component.

5. **Press Command-Return/Control-Enter to test the movie. Click the scroll buttons in the TileList component to test their functionality.**

The default behavior for the scrollbar buttons moves the area very slowly (4 pixels at a time).

6. **Close the Player window and return to Flash.**

7. **In the Properties panel, change the component height to 77 pixels.**

To remove the large gap between the thumbnails and the scrollbar, you have to change the height of the actual instance. The thumbnails (and the row in which they are placed) are 61 pixels high, and the scrollbar occupies 15 pixels. You're changing the component height to the scrollbar height plus the thumbnail height, plus one pixel for white space between the scrollbar and thumbnail tiles.

Note:

If the component is high enough to accommodate more than one row using the defined height, multiple rows will appear unless you use the rowCount parameter to restrict the number of rows to 1.

8. **Change the horizontalLineScrollSize parameter value to 90.**

This value is the same as the columnWidth value, so clicking the scroll buttons will move to the next or previous tile in the component.

Use this option to change the component height.

Use this option to change the scrolling distance.

TileList Component Parameters

The TileList component is a versatile tool for showing multiple thumbnails in a scrolling area. You can customize this component using a variety of parameters:

FLASH FOUNDATIONS

- **allowMultipleSelection.** This parameter has two possible values: true or false. False is the default value. If you select true, a user can select multiple thumbnails in the component. (This parameter should remain at the default value if you are using a TileList component to change other areas of the movie.)

- **columnCount.** This parameter limits the number of columns to a specific number. By default, a TileList displays as many rows and columns as possible, based on the component size and the defined columnWidth and rowHeight parameters.

- **columnWidth.** This parameter defines the horizontal size of cells in the TileList grid.

- **dataProvider.** This parameter defines the label and source for items in the TileList.

- **direction.** This parameter determines whether the TileList scrolls horizontally or vertically.

- **enabled.** This option sets a value that indicates whether the component can accept user interaction. A value of true indicates that the component can accept user interaction; a value of false indicates that it cannot. When the enabled property is set to false, the color of the container becomes dimmed and the user input is blocked (with the exception of the Label and ProgressBar components).

- **horizontalLineScrollSize.** This parameter defines the scrolling increment for the Arrow button in a horizontal scrollbar.

- **horizontalPageScrollSize.** This parameter defines the scrolling increment when a user clicks the scrollbar track on a horizontal scrollbar.

- **rowCount.** This parameter limits the number of rows in the TileList grid.

- **rowHeight.** This parameter defines the vertical size of cells in the TileList grid.

- **scrollPolicy.** This parameter determines whether scrollbars are visible only when necessary (auto), always (on), or never (off).

- **verticalLineScrollSize.** This parameter defines the scrolling increment for the Arrow button in a vertical scrollbar.

- **verticalPageScrollSize.** This parameter defines the scrolling increment when a user clicks the scrollbar track on a vertical scrollbar.

- **visible.** This option can be set to true to allow the visibility of the text or caption added in the component.

9. **Press Command-Return/Control-Enter to test the movie. Click the scroll buttons in the TileList component to test their functionality.**

Clicking the scroll buttons moves the area by 90 pixels.

10. **Close the player window and return to Flash.**

11. **Save the file and continue to the next exercise.**

USE A CHANGE EVENT TO LINK IMAGES, MOVIES, AND CAPTIONS

Two things need to happen when a user clicks a thumbnail in the TileList component: first, the related video needs to appear in the FLVPlayback component; and second, the appropriate caption needs to appear in the caption dynamic text area.

To accomplish these goals, you first need to define the caption and video file related to each thumbnail. Then, you need to define an event listener and function to change the content in the video player and caption area.

1. **With travel_videos.fla open, select Frame 1 of the Actions layer.**

2. **Open the Actions panel Options menu and make sure the Word Wrap option is checked.**

   When this option is active (toggled on), each line of the script wraps to fit inside the Script pane.

3. **In Line 1 of the Actions panel Script pane, place the insertion point after the closing quote but before the closing brace.**

Place the insertion point here.

4. **Type the following:**

```
, data1:"F4V/video1.f4v", data2:"caption"
```

For each thumbnail, **data1** will contain the path to the related movie, and **data2** will contain the caption for that movie.

5. **For each line of the script, add the same statements, making sure to change the number of the video in each line of the script.**

Each line should refer to a different number video.

6. **From the WIP>Tourism folder, open the file** `captions.txt` **in a text editor.**

7. **Select the first caption (excluding the opening number and space) and copy it.**

Don't select the opening number and space.

8. **In Flash, select the word "caption" in Line 1 of the script and paste the copied caption.**

9. **For each line in the script, copy the appropriate caption from the text file and paste it in place of the word "caption" in the data2 value.**

Note:

Remember, when you work in the Actions panel Script pane, you have to use the keyboard shortcuts:

Copy (Command/Control-C)

Cut (Command/Control-X)

Paste (Command/Control-V)

10. **Click at the end of the existing script (in the Script pane), then press Return/Enter twice to move to Line 10 of the script.**

11. Type the following:

```
thumblist.addEventListener(Event.CHANGE, thumbclicked);
```

The images in the TileList component do not technically exist on the Stage, so you must add the event listener to the actual component (named **thumblist**).

In this case, you're going to change the contents of the FLVPlayback and TextArea components based on which thumbnail is clicked. The CHANGE event is used whenever you want to change something on the Stage.

12. Press Return/Enter twice, then type the following:

```
function thumbclicked(event:Event):void {
```

This creates the function that will be called by the event listener you just defined.

```
11    );
12    thumblist.addEventListener(Event.CHANGE, thumbclicked);
13
14    function thumbclicked(event:Event):void {
15
16    }
```

13. Press Return/Enter to move to the next line of the Script pane. On the empty line between the function braces, type the following line of code and then press Return/Enter.

```
player.source = event.target.selectedItem.data1;
```

This line of code says, "Change the source parameter of the player instance to the data1 value in the selected item (the clicked thumbnail)."

14. Inside the function body (on the emtpy line between the braces), type the following:

```
caption.text = event.target.selectedItem.data2;
```

This line of code says, "Change the text in the caption instance to the data2 value in the selected item (the clicked thumbnail)."

```
11    );
12    thumblist.addEventListener(Event.CHANGE, thumbclicked);
13
14    function thumbclicked(event:Event):void {
15        player.source = event.target.selectedItem.data1;
16        caption.text = event.target.selectedItem.data2;
17    }
```

15. Press Command-Return/Control-Enter to test the movie. Click the various thumbnails in the TileList component to test the link functionality.

16. Close the Player window and return to Flash.

17. Save the file and continue to the next exercise.

EDIT AN INTERFACE COMPONENT SKIN

As you might have noticed, each built-in component has a predefined default appearance; in most cases, this appearance is controlled by using skins. You can access and edit the pieces of skins by double-clicking a component instance on the Stage.

1. **With travel_videos.fla open, double-click the TileList component (the thumblist instance) on the Stage.**

   Double-clicking a component enters into the component. Unlike a standard symbol Stage, the component Stage shows the various elements that make up the overall component. You can double-click these elements to enter into and edit the appearance of those elements.

You are editing the TileList component.

Double-click any object to edit that part of the component.

2. **In the TileList component Stage, double-click the ScrollBar Skins instance to access that element on the Stage.**

You are editing the ScrollBar movie clip.

3. **In the Layers panel, click Frame 2 of the Assets layer.**

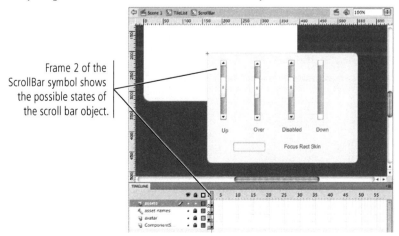

Frame 2 of the ScrollBar symbol shows the possible states of the scroll bar object.

4. Double-click the scrollbar track of the Down instance to edit that element.

You are editing the ScrollTrack_skin movie clip, which is used in each variation of the ScrollBar movie clip.

5. Double-click the only available object on the Stage to enter into the group, and then double-click again to access the drawing object — which is the scrollbar track.

When you edit component skins, you might need to double-click multiple times to access the element you want. In this case, you have drilled five steps away from the main Stage to access the gradient in the scrollbar track.

You are editing the drawing object that represents the gradient-filled scrollbar track.

Note:

When you edit the appearance of components, keep an eye on the Edit bar to see which element you are editing.

6. Click the scrollbar track with the Selection tool to select the object.

7. In the Color panel (Window>Color), double-click the left gradient stop to open the Color Picker for that stop. Choose #006666 as the new stop color.

All four variations use the ScrollTrack Skin movie clip.

Double-click the gradient stop to change the color of that stop.

8. **Click Scene 1 in the Edit bar to return to the main Stage.**

Unfortunately, the scroll track on the Stage does not show the modified color. This is a flaw — or at least, an oversight — in the application. Your changes will reflect in the exported file.

9. **Press Command-Return/Control-Enter to test the movie.**

The scroll track shows the modified gradient color.

10. **Close the Player window and return to Flash.**

11. **Save the file and continue to the next exercise.**

Although a number of component types include text, component skins do not include predefined text areas — which means you can't use the Properties panel to control the appearance of text in a component. To control text styles for these components, you need to use ActionScript.

1. **With travel_videos.fla open, add a new layer named Format Code at the top of the layer stack.**

2. **With Frame 1 of the new layer selected, click in the Script pane of the Actions panel to place the insertion point.**

3. **On Line 1 of the script pane, type the following:**

   ```
   import fl.managers.StyleManager;
   ```

   The first step to formatting text in a component instance is to import the StyleManager class of commands. In most keyframe scripts (such as the ones you have built in this book), you don't need to import classes. The StyleManager class is an exception; you have to manually import this class into the script so the script will execute properly when you use StyleManager to change the properties of a component.

4. **On Line 3 of the Script pane, define a variable that is a new TextFormat object:**

   ```
   var capstyle:TextFormat = new TextFormat();
   ```

   You must use the **new TextFormat()** syntax to create a TextFormat object before you can set its properties.

   When you define the TextFormat object in the script, Flash automatically adds the necessary import statement at the beginning of the script (after the existing import statement). This allows Flash to correctly interpret the code that you add in the rest of the script.

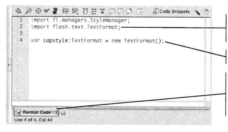

Flash added this line automatically.

You added this line manually.

You are adding this code to Frame 1 of the Format Code layer.

5. **Beginning on Line 5 of the Script pane, assign new property values to the capstyle variable:**

   ```
   capstyle.bold=true;
   capstyle.size=12;
   ```

   Each line defines a different text property of the capstyle TextFormat object.

6. **On Line 8 of the Script pane, use the StyleManager to set the style of text to the capstyle variable:**

   ```
   StyleManager.setStyle("textFormat", capstyle);
   ```

   The first parameter (**"textFormat"**) is the style you are setting; it refers to the overall text formatting of components. The second parameter (**capstyle**) is the specific object you are setting — in other words, the variable that contains the formatting instructions.

You can control formatting of specific types of components using a slight variation of the command you just typed:

> StyleManager.setComponentStyle(TextArea, "textFormat", capstyle);

You can also change the appearance of a specific instance (regardless of type) by using the name of the instance:

> instanceName.setStyle("textFormat", capstyle);

7. Press Command-Return/Control-Enter to test the movie.

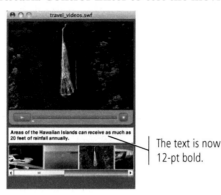

The text is now 12-pt bold.

8. Close the Player window and return to Flash.

9. Save the file and continue to the next exercise.

Text Properties in ActionScript 3

The TextFormat class of ActionScript 3 controls character formatting. Properties are defined by typing the property, then an equal sign, and then the value (in the appropriate format). The properties of the TextFormat class include:

- The **align** property defines paragraph alignment, using a string as the value (e.g., align = "left").
- The **blockIndent** property defines the indent value for all lines in a paragraph (e.g., blockIndent = 0).
- The **bold** property determines whether text is bold, using a true-or-false value (e.g., bold = false).
- The **color** property uses the hexadecimal color value; the "#" in the color name is replaced in code with the character "0x" (e.g., color = 0x000000).
- The **font** property defines the typeface to use as a string (e.g., font = "Times New Roman"). The font may be substituted if the defined font is unavailable on a user's computer.
- The **indent** property defines the first-line distance from the left margin (e.g., indent = 0).
- The **italic** property determines whether text is italic, using a true-or-false value (e.g., italic = false).

- The **kerning** property determines whether text kerning is enabled, using a true-or-false value (e.g., kerning = false).
- The **leading** property defines the space between lines of text (e.g., leading = 0).
- The **leftMargin** property defines the size of the paragraph left margin (e.g., leftMargin = 10).
- The **letterSpacing** property defines an amount of space that is distributed across all characters (e.g., letterSpacing = 0).
- The **rightMargin** property defines the size of the paragraph right margin (e.g., rightMargin = 12).
- The **size** property defines the size of text (e.g., size = 10).
- The **underline** property determines whether text is underlined, using a true-or-false value (e.g., underline = false).

1. With travel_videos.fla open, choose File>Publish Settings.

2. In the Formats tab of the Publish Settings dialog box, check only the Flash option.

3. Click Publish. When the process is complete, click OK to close the Publish Settings dialog box.

4. Close the Flash file, saving if prompted.

5. On your desktop, create a new folder named upload in your WIP>Tourism folder.

6. Move the following into the upload folder:

Images folder	F4V folder
SkinUnderPlaySeekStop.swf	travel_videos.fla
travel_videos.swf	

As we mentioned earlier, the relative path to the encoded movie files and thumbnail image files must remain constant when files are uploaded. You are also moving the working Flash file into the upload folder so you can reopen the file and make changes later (if necessary) without changing the paths from travel_videos.fla to the movie and image files.

Project Review

fill in the blank

1. The _____ application is used to convert video files into a format that can be imported into Flash.

2. When encoding video, the _____ option refers to the software method used to compress video data on video frames.

3. When encoding video, the _____ option specifies the number of frames per second in the exported video file.

4. Using _____ video, video content is placed on the Flash timeline and stored in the SWF file with other content.

5. Using _____ video, the video file remains separate from the primary Flash file. When the video file is called by the SWF file, the video downloads from its source location on the Web server.

6. Using _____ video, each user (client) opens a connection to the server, which sends the video bits to individual users; these bits are used by the client, and then immediately discarded.

7. The _____ component is used to deliver video in a Flash movie.

8. The _____ panel is used to define the parameters of a user interface component.

9. The _____ component can be used to present a series of thumbnail images in a scrollable window.

10. A(n) _____ event can be used to define different contents for an object depending on which object a user clicks.

short answer

1. Briefly explain the difference between lossy compression and lossless compression.

2. Briefly explain the three different ways to deliver video using the Flash Player.

3. Briefly explain the concept of a skin.

Portfolio Builder Project

Use what you learned in this project to complete the following freeform exercise.
Carefully read the art director and client comments, then create your own design to meet the needs of the project.
Use the space below to sketch ideas; when finished, write a brief explanation of your reasoning behind your final design.

art director comments

Your client hosts several tours a year for extreme sports enthusiasts, ranging from skydiving over the Grand Canyon to wind surfing in the Grand Banks. They hired you to build a separate video module to feature movies from those trips.

To complete this project, you should:

❏ Download the client's supplied files in the **FL5_PB_Project7.zip** archive on the Student Files Web page.

❏ Encode the client's video files as necessary for use in Flash. Crop the video files to be no longer than 10 seconds each.

❏ Create a thumbnail image from each video file to use as a link to the related movie.

❏ Develop a complete interface that shows the movie thumbnails, each linking to the appropriate movie in a FLVPlayback component.

client comments

Our extreme tourism business is very popular, so our site is going to include a whole different collection of related movies purely for those clients. We want you to create some kind of interface for that page to feature the movies.

This video module should be different than the one on our home page. We were thinking of an overall horizontal orientation, with a scrolling area on the left and the video on the right. We don't need to include captions, but there should be some kind of text that identifies the sport in each video.

The page title is 'Travel XTreme', which you can include in the module. We won't place it in the HTML page if it's already in the Flash file. We're open to any ideas you have for the page. Some kind of custom animation at the top or bottom might be a good addition.

Keep in mind the type of people who are interested in this kind of package: usually a younger demographic, people who like to be outdoors, and who look for an adrenaline rush.

project justification

_____
_____
_____
_____
_____
_____
_____
_____
_____
_____
_____
_____
_____
_____

Video is one type of multimedia file that adds depth and dimension to a Web page. Video provides the photographic realism that is not typically part of Flash animation. As an isolated task, importing video into Flash is not a particularly difficult process. You have to convert the video into the required format, but Flash walks you through this process and includes default settings that create acceptable quality for many applications.

To complete this project, you learned how to use several built-in components that simplify complex processes required for common interface tools. Rather than spending hours to manually build a scrolling area, for example, you learned how to use the TileList component to build a thumbnail navigation object. You also learned how to define parameters for, edit the visual appearance of, write ActionScript to interact with, and in general, customize built-in Flash components.

Define the skin that appears in the FLVPlayback component when you import video into Flash

Control FLVPlayback component parameters to customize the player module

Create a TextArea component to hold dynamic captions

Use ActionScript to format text in a component instance

Create and populate a TileList component to hold thumbnail navigation items

Seabreeze Web Site

Seabreeze is a family-oriented theme park in the southern United States. The owner wants to bring the company's Web site up to date by adding dynamic Flash content to the pages. Your agency was hired to build a Flash-based version of the existing site to accommodate the new content. Every page in the site should be designed separately and fed into a main container page, making it easy to change the content of individual pages as necessary without affecting the overall site.

This project incorporates the following skills:

❏ Creating a site navigation structure

❏ Controlling navigation and dynamic text with ActionScript

❏ Creating a dynamic date constructor

❏ Importing external images

❏ Adding objects to the display list

❏ Importing an external text file

❏ Creating custom scroll buttons

❏ Importing external SWF files

client comments

Our site is already popular with visitors to the Atlanta area who are looking for an aquatic theme park with safe and enjoyable activities for the whole family. We want to incorporate a lot of Flash-based content in our site in the near future, but we need to start with the overall site structure.

Until we decide exactly what we want in the new pages, we want the Flash-based site to look the same as the HTML version. Most of the pages have static content that doesn't change (at least, not very often). The Home and About the Park pages, however, have dynamic content that changes frequently.

The Home page is really just two static images, but the background image changes every time the page reloads. Although the overall page layout remains constant, the text on the About the Park page changes every week. We'd like to be able to change the text ourselves without redesigning the page every week.

art director comments

There are two stages to this project. First, you need to build the site navigation structure, and then you need to build the individual pages that will feed into the main site.

Each button on the left side of the site links to a different page. There are also five buttons along the bottom; three refer to their own pages, and the other two duplicate links on the left navigation bar.

Because there are so many pages to build, I'm going to have the junior designers create the static pages. After you've built the site navigation, I want you to take control of the two pages with dynamic content.

For the Home page, you need to build a script to randomly place one of several images into the page. You also need to place a second static image on top of the random image.

For the About the Park page, the easiest way to allow frequent text changes is to build an interface that reads in text from an external file. You should build a scrolling dynamic text area to hold whatever text the client writes.

project objectives

To complete this project, you will:

❏ Build site navigation using frame labels

❏ Create site navigation with a switch conditional statement

❏ Change dynamic text using a switch case

❏ Create a dynamic date constructor

❏ Define a Loader object to import external image files

❏ Use the addChild function to add objects to the display list

❏ Define a URLLoader object to import an external text file

❏ Create custom scroll buttons

❏ Use the UILoader component to import external SWF files

Stage 1 Building Site Navigation

Many users do not have the luxury of high-speed Internet access (cable, DSL, or satellite). Although high-speed access is certainly more common now than even a year ago, a large part of the world — including many areas of the United States — still relies on dial-up modem connections. And because Flash movies are typically much larger than HTML files, they require longer download times, which can keep users waiting for longer periods of time.

When you design Flash content for Internet distribution, use the following guidelines when evaluating the size of your files:

- If your audience is primarily business or professional users, you can assume they have high-speed Internet access; file size is still a concern, but not as much as when designing for the dial-up audience.

- If you are targeting a general-consumer audience, design for the lowest common denominator (dial-up modem); reduce file size as much as possible without sacrificing quality.

Having issued those warnings, the client in this project asked you to create a Flash version of their existing site. Their Web developer will later include a simple introduction page that will allow users to select which version they want to use — HTML or Flash.

Note:

When you build a Flash file for Web distribution, always keep your target audience in mind. Research has shown that if a Web page doesn't capture a user's attention within 10 to 15 seconds, the user will abandon the page and move on to another site.

ADD FRAME LABELS

There are many ways to create site navigation in Flash. One common method — especially for visually oriented designers — is to use a separate frame on the timeline to hold the content for each page of the site. With so many navigation buttons, it can be difficult to remember which frame contains which page. Fortunately, you can use ActionScript to define text-based frame labels to use in place of frame numbers.

1. **Download FL5_RF_Project8.zip from the Student Files Web page.**

2. **Expand the ZIP archive in your WIP folder (Macintosh) or copy the archive contents into your WIP folder (Windows).**

   This results in a folder named **Seabreeze**, which contains the files you need for this project. You should also use this folder to save the files you create in this project.

3. **Open the file seabreeze.fla from your WIP>Seabreeze folder.**

   The site graphics were created and arranged on a series of logically named layers. Each button in the site has an indicative instance name, so you can address these instances in ActionScript.

This area will show the accurate date whenever the page is opened.

This area will show the name of the active "page."

This area will show the content of the active "page."

Note:

This file uses Arial for the heading and date text. If you receive a warning about missing fonts, click the option to use the default substitute.

4. **Create a new layer named Navigation at the top of the layer stack.**

5. **Click Frame 1 of the Navigation layer to select the keyframe and deselect all objects on the Stage.**

6. **In the Properties panel, type home in the Label Name field. Press Return/ Enter to finalize the frame name.**

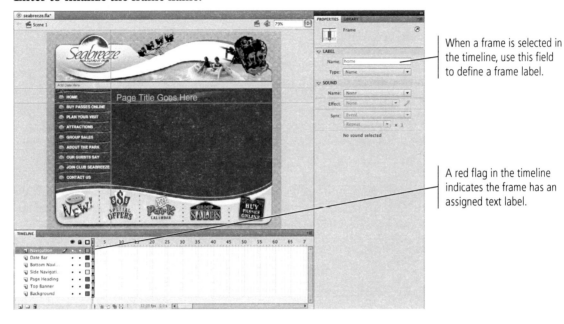

When a frame is selected in the timeline, use this field to define a frame label.

A red flag in the timeline indicates the frame has an assigned text label.

7. **Add a keyframe at Frame 5 of the Navigation layer.**

   Because the Navigation layer now has frames after Frame 1, the text label of Frame 1 is partially visible in the timeline.

8. **With the Frame 5 keyframe selected, type passes in the Frame Label field of the Properties panel.**

The red flag shows that the Frame 5 keyframe has a defined label.

The first letter of the Frame 1 label is now visible in the timeline.

9. **Repeat Steps 7–8 to add labeled keyframes (on the Navigation layer) for each page in the site, using the following information:**

Frame number	Label	Frame number	Label
Frame 10	plan	Frame 35	join
Frame 15	attractions	Frame 40	contact
Frame 20	group	Frame 45	calendar
Frame 25	about	Frame 50	specials
Frame 30	guests	Frame 55	new

The text label for Frame 55 is not visible because it is the final frame in the timeline.

10. **Insert a new regular frame at Frame 60 of all six layers.**

    Because the Navigation layer extends to 60 frames (to accommodate the necessary site navigation), the other layers must also extend to 60 frames.

11. **Select Frame 1 of the Navigation layer and open the Actions panel (Window>Actions).**

12. **On Line 1 of the Script pane, type stop();.**

    Because you are using keyframes for navigation purposes, you want the playhead to move only when a user clicks a button. This means you have to stop the timeline at Frame 1 to prevent the playhead from automatically moving forward when the movie first opens.

Frame 1 of the Navigation layer now includes the stop function.

13. **Save the file and continue to the next exercise.**

CREATE SWITCH CASE NAVIGATION

Each button in this site needs to be connected to the appropriate frame in the timeline. To accomplish this task, you need to define event listeners and functions for each of the 14 buttons. Rather than defining 14 separate functions that basically do the same thing, you can use a **switch conditional statement** to define a different action that will be called when each button is clicked.

- In Stage 2 of this project, you will add the UILoader component to import different SWF files on each labeled keyframe. Each button's action, then, needs to navigate to the appropriate labeled frame.

- The page title placeholder (on the Page Heading layer) is part of the main site structure. Rather than placing static text areas on each labeled keyframe — which will add to the file size — you will use dynamic text to change the page heading text, according to which button the user clicks.

1. **With seabreeze.fla open, select Frame 1 of the Navigation layer.**

2. **In the Actions panel, place the insertion point at the end of Line 1 in the Script pane, and then press Return/Enter twice.**

3. **Open the Actions panel Options menu and choose Import Script.**

   In many workflows, a code expert will write ActionScript in a separate file that the designer can add to the Flash file. This process is made easy by the ability to import an existing script file directly into the Script pane.

Click here to open the panel Options menu.

Frame 1 of the Navigation layer is selected.

4. **Navigate to listeners.as in the WIP>Seabreeze>Script folder and click Open.**

Note:

".as" is the extension for an ActionScript file.

This code adds event listeners to the buttons on the page, each one listening for the MOUSE_UP mouse event. Notice that each event listener calls the same function, named **browse**. You will create this function in the rest of this exercise.

Note:

You have already learned about defining event listeners, so we wrote the required code for you as an illustration of how to import existing code.

5. **With the insertion point at the end of Line 16, press Return/Enter twice to move to Line 18 of the Script pane.**

6. **Add a line to the script that defines the browse function, using the following code:**

   ```
   function browse(event:MouseEvent):void {
   ```

   The **browse** function is called by the **MOUSE_UP** mouse event, so the function parameter is **event:MouseEvent**.

7. **Press Return/Enter to start a new line.**

   Flash automatically adds the necessary import statement (at the beginning of the script), as well as the function's closing brace.

   ```
   1   import flash.events.MouseEvent;
   2
   3   stop();
   4
   5   home_btn.addEventListener(MouseEvent.MOUSE_UP, browse);
   6   passes_btn.addEventListener(MouseEvent.MOUSE_UP, browse);
   7   plan_btn.addEventListener(MouseEvent.MOUSE_UP, browse);
   8   attractions_btn.addEventListener(MouseEvent.MOUSE_UP, browse);
   9   group_btn.addEventListener(MouseEvent.MOUSE_UP, browse);
   10  about_btn.addEventListener(MouseEvent.MOUSE_UP, browse);
   11  guests_btn.addEventListener(MouseEvent.MOUSE_UP, browse);
   12  join_btn.addEventListener(MouseEvent.MOUSE_UP, browse);
   13  contact_btn.addEventListener(MouseEvent.MOUSE_UP, browse);
   14  new_btn.addEventListener(MouseEvent.MOUSE_UP, browse);
   15  specials_btn.addEventListener(MouseEvent.MOUSE_UP, browse);
   16  calendar_btn.addEventListener(MouseEvent.MOUSE_UP, browse);
   17  group2_btn.addEventListener(MouseEvent.MOUSE_UP, browse);
   18  passes2_btn.addEventListener(MouseEvent.MOUSE_UP, browse);
   19
   20  function browse(event:MouseEventMouseEvent):void {
   21      |
   22  }
   ```

8. **On the empty Line 21 between the opening and closing function braces, add the switch conditional statement using the following code:**

   ```
   switch (event.target.name) {
   ```

   The switch conditional statement allows you to define different actions within a single function. The condition, **event.target.name**, refers to the name property of the target instance that triggered the function (in other words, the specific instance the user clicked to call the function). If a user clicks the passes_btn instance, for example, the switch parameter is passes_btn.

9. **Press Return/Enter to start a new line.**

   Again, Flash adds the closing brace for you — this time for the switch statement.

   ```
   18  passes2_btn.addEventListener(MouseEvent.MOUSE_UP, browse);
   19
   20  function browse(event:MouseEvent):void {
   21      switch (event.target.name) {
   22          |
   23      }
   24  }
   ```

Type the following code between the switch statement braces:

```
case "home_btn" : gotoAndStop("home");
```

In plain English, this line of code says, "If the switch condition is home_btn, move the playhead to the frame labeled 'home' and then stop."

Note:

In the gotoAndStop function, the frame label must be enclosed within quotation marks.

```
18  passes2_btn.addEventListener(MouseEvent.MOUSE_UP, browse);
19
20  function browse(event:MouseEvent):void {
21      switch (event.target.name) {
22          case "home_btn" : gotoAndStop("home");
23      }
24  }
```

11. **Press Return/Enter and type break; on the next line of the Script pane.**

The break statement simply tells the function to stop processing once the appropriate case has been identified.

```
19
20  function browse(event:MouseEvent):void {
21      switch (event.target.name) {
22          case "home_btn" : gotoAndStop("home");
23          break;
24      }
25  }
```

12. **Press Return/Enter after the break statement.**

13. **Define a new case for the Buy Passes Online button, using the following code:**

```
case "passes_btn" : gotoAndStop("passes");
break;
```

```
18  passes2_btn.addEventListener(MouseEvent.MOUSE_UP, browse);
19
20  function browse(event:MouseEvent):void {
21      switch (event.target.name) {
22          case "home_btn" : gotoAndStop("home");
23          break;
24          case "passes_btn" : gotoAndStop("passes");
25          break;
26      }
27  }
```

14. **Add cases for the remaining buttons, using the appropriate instance names and frame labels (as assigned in the previous exercise) for each.**

The passes2_btn and group2_btn instances at the bottom of the page are alternate navigation tools; they link to the same pages as the left-side navigation buttons. These buttons navigate to the passes and group frames, respectively.

Note:

You can copy and paste the entire browse function from the browse1.txt file in the WIP>Seabreeze>Code Text folder. This file includes the entire function, including the lines you already typed. If you copy and paste the function from the text file, select and delete the existing lines of function code in the Script pane before you paste.

```
18  passes2_btn.addEventListener(MouseEvent.MOUSE_UP, browse);
19
20  function browse(event:MouseEvent):void {
21      switch (event.target.name) {
22          case "home_btn" : gotoAndStop("home");
23          break;
24          case "passes_btn" : gotoAndStop("passes");
25          break;
26          case "plan_btn" : gotoAndStop("plan");
27          break;
28          case "attractions_btn" : gotoAndStop("attractions");
29          break;
30          case "group_btn" : gotoAndStop("group");
31          break;
32          case "about_btn" : gotoAndStop("about");
33          break;
34          case "guests_btn" : gotoAndStop("guests");
35          break;
36          case "join_btn" : gotoAndStop("join");
37          break;
38          case "contact_btn" : gotoAndStop("contact");
39          break;
40          case "new_btn" : gotoAndStop("new");
41          break;
42          case "specials_btn" : gotoAndStop("specials");
43          break;
44          case "calendar_btn" : gotoAndStop("calendar");
45          break;
46          case "group2_btn" : gotoAndStop("group");
47          break;
48          case "passes2_btn" : gotoAndStop("passes");
49          break;
50      }
51  }
```

Navigation : 1

15. **Save the file and continue to the next exercise.**

CHANGE DYNAMIC TEXT USING SWITCH CASES

In the previous exercise, you created code that navigates to the appropriate frame, based on which button the user clicks. The page title, which is included in the primary site structure, also needs to change, based on the currently active frame. Although you could create static text objects with the correct headings on each labeled frame, it is easier to use a dynamic text area that changes according to which button the user clicks.

1. **With seabreeze.fla open, select the Text tool in the Tools panel.**

2. **Select and delete the words "Page Title Goes Here" from the text area in the center of the Stage.**

3. **In the Properties panel, change the text area type to Dynamic Text.**

4. **In the Instance Name field, type PageHead.**

   Remember, a dynamic text area must be named before you can address it in ActionScript.

Change the text area type to Dynamic Text...

...and then define "PageHead" as the instance name.

5. **Click Frame 1 in the Navigation layer to select it.**

6. **In the Actions panel, place the insertion point at the end of the passes_btn case (Line 24) and press Return/Enter.**

   You are adding title text for the different cases in the switch condition, beginning with the passes_btn instance. (The Home page will fill the available space with images; it will not include title text.)

You are adding to the passes_btn case, so you need to add the new code before the related break statement.

7. **Add a statement that changes the contents of the PageHead dynamic text instance, using the following code:**

   PageHead.text = "Buy Passes Online";

   The right side of this statement defines the string that will be used in the text property of the PageHead instance. In other words, you're telling ActionScript what to show as the page title when the user clicks the passes_btn instance.

Add the statement to the passes_btn case.

8. **Place the insertion point after the plan_btn case statement and press Return/Enter.**

9. **Define the PageHead text for this case, using the following code:**

   PageHead.text = "Plan Your Visit";

Add the statement to the plan_btn case.

10. **Using the same technique from Steps 8–9, define the page headings for each case in the switch condition.**

```
19
20    function browse(event:MouseEvent):void {
21        switch (event.target.name) {
22            case "home_btn" : gotoAndStop("home");
23            break;
24            case "passes_btn" : gotoAndStop("passes");
25            PageHead.text = "Buy Passes Online";
26            break;
27            case "plan_btn" : gotoAndStop("plan");
28            PageHead.text = "Plan Your Visit";
29            break;
30            case "attractions_btn" : gotoAndStop("attractions");
31            PageHead.text = "Attractions";
32            break;
33            case "group_btn" : gotoAndStop("group");
34            PageHead.text = "Group Sales";
35            break;
36            case "about_btn" : gotoAndStop("about");
37            PageHead.text = "About the Park";
38            break;
39            case "guests_btn" : gotoAndStop("guests");
40            PageHead.text = "Our Guests Say";
41            break;
42            case "join_btn" : gotoAndStop("join");
43            PageHead.text = "Join Club Seabreeze";
44            break;
45            case "contact_btn" : gotoAndStop("contact");
46            PageHead.text = "Contact Us";
47            break;
48            case "new_btn" : gotoAndStop("new");
49            PageHead.text = "What's New";
50            break;
51            case "specials_btn" : gotoAndStop("specials");
52            PageHead.text = "Special Offers";
53            break;
54            case "calendar_btn" : gotoAndStop("calendar");
55            PageHead.text = "Park Calendar";
56            break;
57            case "group2_btn" : gotoAndStop("group");
58            PageHead.text = "Group Sales";
59            break;
60            case "passes2_btn" : gotoAndStop("passes");
61            PageHead.text = "Buy Passes Online";
62            break;
63        }
64    }
```

Note:

You can copy and paste the entire browse function (including the PageHead.text statements) from the browse2.txt file in the WIP>Seabreeze>Code Text folder. The text file contains the entire browse function; if you copy and paste the function from the text file, select and delete the existing lines of function code in the Script pane before you paste.

11. **Press Command-Return/Control-Enter to test the movie. Click the various buttons to test their functionality.**

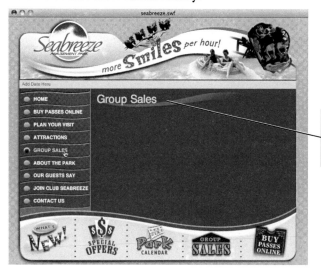

Clicking a button should show the appropriate text string in the PageHead text area.

12. **Close the Player window and return to Flash.**

13. **Save the file and continue to the next exercise.**

CREATE A DYNAMIC DATE OBJECT

The yellow bar between the top banner and the main site area needs to include the current date. Obviously, you aren't going to republish this file every day, so you need to use a dynamic text area and ActionScript to place the date text, based on the user's system information. Although there is no one-step method for adding a dynamic date to a Flash movie, you can accomplish the task using an established procedure that requires only a few lines of ActionScript.

1. **With seabreeze.fla open, use the Text tool to select and delete the words "Add Date Here" from the Stage.**

2. **In the Properties panel, change the text area type to Dynamic Text.**

3. **In the Instance Name field, type PageDate.**

Select and delete the text in this area.

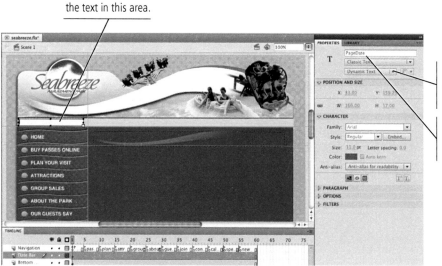

Change the text area type to Dynamic Text...

...and then define "PageDate" as the instance name.

4. **Select Frame 1 of the Date Bar layer. Place the insertion point on Line 1 of the Actions panel Script pane.**

5. **Define a new variable, using the following code:**

   ```
   var myDate = new Date();
   ```

Frame 1 of the Date Bar layer is selected.

In ActionScript 3, the Date class is an object class that includes very specific methods for retrieving and storing date elements (day, date, month, and year).

- getDate() is a number that represents the day of the month.
- getDay() is a number from 0 to 6 that represents the day of the week, beginning with Sunday (Sunday = 0, Monday = 1, etc.).
- getMonth() is a number from 0 to 11 that represents the month, beginning with January (January = 0, February = 1, March = 2, etc.).
- getFullYear() is a number that represents the four-digit year (such as 2009).

Note:

The Date object uses the date information retrieved from the user's computer.

6. **On Line 3 in the Script pane, define an array variable named "weekday" that stores text strings of the weekday names:**

   ```
   var weekday = new Array("Sunday", "Monday", "Tuesday", "Wednesday", "Thursday", "Friday", "Saturday");
   ```

   ```
   1  var myDate = new Date();
   2
   3  var weekday = new Array("Sunday", "Monday", "Tuesday", "Wednesday", "Thursday", "Friday", "Saturday");
   ```

The getDay() function returns a number from 0 to 6, which corresponds to the positions in the array you just defined.

Note:

Recall from Project 5, you can access the different array positions using the syntax "array[N]", where "array" is the name of the variable and "N" is a specific index value in the array.

7. **On Line 4, define an array variable named "month" that stores text strings of the month names:**

   ```
   var month = new Array("January", "February", "March", "April", "May", "June", "July", "August", "September", "October", "November", "December");
   ```

   ```
   1  var myDate = new Date();
   2
   3  var weekday = new Array("Sunday", "Monday", "Tuesday", "Wednesday", "Thursday", "Friday", "Saturday");
   4  var month = new Array("January", "February", "March", "April", "May", "June", "July", "August", "September", "October", "November", "December");
   ```

The getMonth() function returns a number from 0 to 11, which corresponds to the positions in this second array.

8. **On Line 6 of the Script pane, add a line of code to define the text in the PageDate dynamic text area:**

```
PageDate.text = (weekday[myDate.getDay()] + month[myDate.
getMonth()] + myDate.getDate() + myDate.getFullYear());
```

```
1  var myDate = new Date();
2
3  var weekday = new Array("Sunday", "Monday", "Tuesday", "Wednesday", "Thursday", "Friday", "Saturday");
4  var month = new Array("January", "February", "March", "April", "May", "June", "July", "August", "September", "October", "November", "December");
5
6  PageDate.text = (weekday[myDate.getDay()] + month[myDate.getMonth()] + myDate.getDate() + myDate.getFullYear());
```

As explained in Step 5, the methods of the date class retrieve specific parts of the date.

For example, the syntax **myDate.getDay()** retrieves a value representing the day that is stored in the myDate variable.

Using the statement **weekday[myDate.getDay()]**, that value is treated as the array index value of the month array. If the getDay value is 3, for example, this statement returns the value at index position 3 of the weekday array (in other words, Tuesday).

9. **Press Command-Return/Control-Enter to test the movie.**

The PageDate text area shows the correct bits of information (based on your system's clock), but the necessary punctuation and spacing are missing. You need to add these characters as strings in the script.

The date is correct, but the conventional spacing and punctuation are missing.

Note:

Because the getDate and getFullYear functions retrieve actual numbers for the date and year, those functions do not need to be treated as array index values.

10. **Close the Player window and return to Flash.**

11. **With Frame 1 of the Date Bar layer selected, add the red code shown here (framed in red in the screen capture) to Line 6 of the script:**

```
PageDate.text = (weekday[myDate.getDay()] + ", " +
month[myDate.getMonth()] + " " + myDate.getDate() + ", " +
myDate.getFullYear());
```

```
1  var myDate = new Date();
2
3  var weekday = new Array("Sunday", "Monday", "Tuesday", "Wednesday", "Thursday", "Friday", "Saturday");
4  var month = new Array("January", "February", "March", "April", "May", "June", "July", "August", "September", "October", "November", "December");
5
6  PageDate.text = (weekday[myDate.getDay()] + ", " + month[myDate.getMonth()] + " " + myDate.getDate() + ", " + myDate.getFullYear());
```

Note:

The date text does not apear on the Flash Stage. It only appears in the FlashPlayer window.

12. **Press Command-Return/Control-Enter to test the movie again.**

The necessary spacing and punctuation are now included in the PageDate text area.

Note:

You can copy and paste the necessary date code from the file date.txt in the WIP>Seabreeze> Code Text folder.

13. **Close the Player window and return to Flash.**

14. **Save the file and continue to the next stage of the project.**

Stage 2 Loading External Content

Flash movies often require external content. In Project 5, you loaded audio files into the Library panel, and then used a variety of methods to incorporate the sounds into your Flash movie. In Project 7, you imported video files into the Flash file library, and then used ActionScript to deploy video inside an FLVPlayback component. To complete this project, you need to import a variety of files, including images, text, and other Flash movies.

One important difference exists between this project and the others you already completed — the files you load in this project will not be imported into the Flash Library panel. Instead, you will use ActionScript 3 to dynamically import external files into the movie. Using this method, you can update your movie by simply changing the linked content; there is no need to open, edit, and republish the Flash movie that relies on external content.

DEFINE A LOADER OBJECT FOR IMAGE FILES

The Seabreeze Home page looks very simple on the surface — a single image in the background with a second composite image on top. Based on the project specifications, however, the background image should not be a single static image. Instead, it needs to randomly change each time a user navigates back to the Home page.

Because the background image for the Seabreeze Home page needs to dynamically change, you need to create a mechanism that loads only one of a variety of images when a user views the page. In ActionScript 3, the Loader object class is perfectly suited to this task.

Note:

The Loader object class allows you to load JPEG, PNG, GIF, and SWF files into a Flash movie.

1. **Open the file child_layout.fla from the WIP>Seabreeze>Children folder.**

   The site designer created this file using dimensions that fill the variable area in the main site structure.

2. **Save the file as a Flash file named home.fla in your WIP>Seabreeze> Children folder.**

   The location of this file is very important. It must be saved in the same folder that contains the Images folder.

The vertical guide indicates the left edge of the PageHead text area.

The child_layout file has guides to indicate the top edges of the bottom navigation banner.

3. **Select Frame 1 of the Content layer. Place the insertion point in Line 1 of the Script pane.**

4. On Line 1 of the Script pane, type:

```
var getImage:URLRequest = new URLRequest("Images/home1.jpg");
```

In ActionScript 3, the URLRequest object identifies the path to a specific image file. This line creates a new URLRequest object named **getImage** with the value **Images/home1.jpg**.

The necessary import statement for the URLRequest class is automatically added at the beginning of the script as soon as you define the variable of the URLRequest type (var getImage:URLRequest).

The images for the Home page are in the Images folder, which is in the same Children folder where you saved the file you're building now. The path from the home.fla Flash file to the image must include the name of the folder that contains the image.

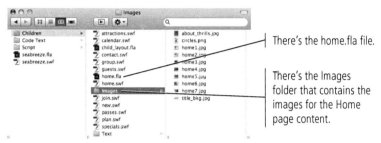

There's the home.fla file.

There's the Images folder that contains the images for the Home page content.

5. On the next line of the Script pane, type `var loadImage:Loader = new Loader();`

The Loader class is a partner of the URLRequest object. The URLRequest object simply makes a file available to Flash; the Loader object actually brings the file into the Flash movie.

The necessary import statement for the Loader class is automatically added at the beginning of the script, after the existing import statement, as soon as you define the variable of the Loader type (var loadImage:Loader).

6. On the next line of the Script pane, type `loadImage.load(getImage);`

The load function of the Loader object is the third required step to loading an external file into a Flash file. This statement loads the URLRequest object (**getImage**, which has a value of **Images/home1.jpg**) into the Loader object (**loadImage**).

7. On the next line of the Script pane, type `addChild(loadImage);`

The addChild method places the defined Loader object (the external file) in the movie (technically called "adding to the display list").

Line 4 identifies the file to import.

Line 5 brings the external file into Flash.

Line 6 loads the file into the movie by connecting the URL Request object and the Loader object.

Line 7 places the file into the movie ("in the display list").

Objects added to the display list using ActionScript do not appear on the development Stage.

8. **Press Return/Enter twice to move to Line 9 of the Script pane.**

9. **Using the same process as in Steps 4–7, add code that places the external file circles.png (in the Images folder) on the Stage:**

```
var getImage2:URLRequest = new URLRequest("Images/circles.png");
var loadImage2:Loader = new Loader();
loadImage2.load(getImage2);
addChild(loadImage2);
```

10. **Press Command-Return/Control-Enter to test the movie.**

The two images appear in the movie, stacked according to the order they were added by the script. When you use the addChild method, new objects are added by default at X:0, Y:0 (in the top-left corner of the movie).

11. **Close the Player window and return to Flash.**

12. **Save the file and continue to the next exercise.**

USE THE addCHILD FUNCTION TO ADD TO THE DISPLAY LIST

The home.fla file now has two static images that both load at the top-left corner of the movie. For the background image, you need to create a mechanism that loads the home images randomly each time the file loads. You can accomplish this task by using a random math variable, similar to the technique you used to move random characters when you completed Projects 5 and 6.

The second image is a static image, but it needs to appear on the right side of the window instead of the default X:0, Y:0 position. To complete this task, you need to change the display properties of the Loader object that contains the circles image.

1. **With home.fla open, make sure the Content layer is selected, and then place the insertion point at the beginning of Line 4 in the Script pane.**

2. **Press Return/Enter twice to move the existing code down.**

3. Place the insertion point on Line 4 and declare a number-type variable named "num". Initialize the num variable to a random number, multiplied by 7:

> **var num:Number = Math.random()*7;**

If you recall from Project 5, the Math.random function generates a number from 0 to 1. The Images folder contains 7 images, so you need to multiply the random number by 7.

```
 2   import flash.display.Loader;
 3
 4   var num:Number = Math.random()*7;
 5
 6   var getImage:URLRequest = new URLRequest("Images/home1.jpg");
 7   var loadImage:Loader = new Loader();
 8   loadImage.load(getImage);
 9   addChild(loadImage);
10
11   var getImage2:URLRequest = new URLRequest("Images/circles.png");
```

You are adding these variable declarations above the existing functions on Frame 1.

4. On the next line of the Script pane, declare a second number-type variable named "imageNum" that ceils the num variable:

> **var imageNum:Number = Math.ceil(num);**

```
 3
 4   var num:Number = Math.random()*7;
 5   var imageNum:Number = Math.ceil(num);
 6
 7   var getImage:URLRequest = new URLRequest("Images/home1.jpg");
```

Note:

Remember, the Math.ceil function rounds the number up to the next whole number.

5. On the next line of the Script pane, define a string-type variable named "image" using the following code:

> **var image:String = "Images/home" + imageNum + ".jpg";**

The right side of the image variable statement appends strings to the imageNum variable, resulting in the full path to one of the seven home images in the Images folder.

```
 2   import flash.display.Loader;
 3
 4   var num:Number = Math.random()*7;
 5   var imageNum:Number = Math.ceil(num);
 6   var image:String = "Images/home" + imageNum + ".jpg";
 7
 8   var getImage:URLRequest = new URLRequest("Images/home1.jpg");
```

The following table explains what happens in these three lines of code:

Random number	*7	Ceiled	Identifies file
.1	0.7	1	Images/home1.jpg
.2	1.4	2	Images/home2.jpg
.3	2.1	3	Images/home3.jpg
.4	2.8	3	Images/home3.jpg
.5	3.5	4	Images/home4.jpg
.6	4.2	5	Images/home5.jpg
.7	4.9	5	Images/home5.jpg
.8	5.6	6	Images/home6.jpg
.9	6.3	7	Images/home7.jpg

The final step to randomizing the background image is to replace the URLRequest parameter with the image variable you just defined.

6. In Line 8 of the script, change the URLRequest object parameter from the specific path name to the image variable (as shown below in red):

> **var getImage:URLRequest = new URLRequest(image);**

```
 3
 4   var num:Number = Math.random()*7;
 5   var imageNum:Number = Math.ceil(num);
 6   var image:String = "Images/home" + imageNum + ".jpg";
 7
 8   var getImage:URLRequest = new URLRequest(image);
 9   var loadImage:Loader = new Loader();
10   loadImage.load(getImage);
11   addChild(loadImage);
```

Change this parameter to the image variable.

7. **Place the insertion point at the beginning of the second addChild statement (on Line 16 of the Script pane) and press Return/Enter to move the statement to Line 17.**

8. **On the empty Line 16, type:**

```
loadImage2.x = 225;
```

If you add this statement after the addChild statement, the image will load first, and then move to the new X position. By changing the x property of the loadImage2 object before it's added, the image appears in the correct position as soon as it's visible.

```
 2   import flash.display.Loader;
 3
 4   var num:Number = Math.random()*7;
 5   var imageNum:Number = Math.ceil(num);
 6   var image:String = "Images/home" + imageNum + ".jpg";
 7
 8   var getImage:URLRequest = new URLRequest(image);
 9   var loadImage:Loader = new Loader();
10   loadImage.load(getImage);
11   addChild(loadImage);
12
13   var getImage2:URLRequest = new URLRequest("Images/circles.png");
14   var loadImage2:Loader = new Loader();
15   loadImage2.load(getImage2);
16   loadImage2.x = 225;
17   addChild(loadImage2);
```

Add this statement to define the X position of the added display object.

Changing Object Properties in ActionScript

ActionScript 3 allows you to modify a number of properties for objects in the movie (display objects):

alpha	instance.alpha = 0.5;	The object's transparency from 0 (fully transparent) to 1 (fully opaque).
height	instance.height = 250;	The object's height in pixels.
rotation	instance.rotation = 30;	The object's rotation (in degrees) from its original orientation. Positive values (0 to 180) indicate clockwise rotation; negative values (0 to −180) indicate counterclockwise rotation.
scaleX	instance.scaleX = 1.30;	The object's horizontal scale percentage (applied from the object's registration point); 1 equals 100%.
scaleY	instance.scaleY = 1.30;	The object's vertical scale percentage; 1 equals 100%.
visible	instance.visible = true;	Whether the object is visible (true) or not (false).
width	instance.width = 250;	The object's width in pixels.
x	instance.x = 5;	The object's x position relative to the parent object.
y	instance.y = 26;	The object's y position relative to the parent object.

Additional properties can be modified for dynamic text fields, including:

background	instance.background = true;	Whether the text field has a background fill.
backgroundColor	instance.backgroundColor = 0xCC0066;	The text field's background color (defined using hexadecimal values, preceded by "0x").
border	instance.border = true;	Whether the text field has a border.
borderColor	instance.borderColor = 0xFF9966;	The text field's border color (in hexadecimal format).
scrollH	instance.scrollH = 0;	The horizontal scrolling position of text in the field (measured in pixels); 0 represents the left side of the field (no scrolling).
scrollV	instance.scrollV = 1;	The vertical position of text in the field (measured in lines); 1 represents the first line of text at the top of the field.
selectable	instance.selectable = true;	Whether the text field is selectable by the user.
text	instance.text = "This text appears.";	The text that will appear in the field.
textColor	instance.textColor = 0x443724;	The color of text in the field (in hexadecimal format).
wordWrap	instance.wordWrap = true;	Whether the text field has word wrap.

9. **Press Command-Return/Control-Enter to test the movie.**

10. **Return to Flash, and then press Command-Return/Control-Enter to test the movie again.**

    A different image might appear in the movie background. If the same image appears, return to Flash and continue testing the movie until you see a different background image. (Because the process is random, the same image might appear two or more times in a row.)

11. **Close the Player window and return to Flash.**

    When you test a movie in Flash, a SWF file is generated using the default publish settings in the same location as the original Flash file. Because you are testing the final FLA file, you do not need to separately republish the home.fla file (or the about.fla file that you will create in the following exercises). You will use the SWF files in the Children folder later, when you load them into the primary site structure.

There's the home.swf file that was generated when you last tested the home.fla file.

12. **Save the file, close it, and continue to the next exercise.**

 ## DEFINE A URLLOADER OBJECT FOR AN EXTERNAL TEXT FILE

Displaying an external text file allows you to create an environment where your client can edit the textual content without touching the Flash files — basically, building an interface that allows easy and frequent updates without editing or republishing the Flash movie file.

The URLLoader object class is basically the same as the Loader class, except the URLLoader object brings external text or XML files into a Flash movie. You will use this type of object to import the client's text file into the Seabreeze About Us page.

1. **Open the file child_layout.fla from the WIP>Seabreeze>Children folder.**

2. **Save the file as a Flash file named about.fla in your WIP>Seabreeze>Children folder.**

3. **Select the Content layer. Using the Text tool, create a classic dynamic text area with the following dimensions:**

> X: 20   Y: 15
> W: 240   H: 180

4. **With the text area selected, choose a sans-serif font such as Arial or Helvetica. Set the type size to 10 and the color to white.**

5. **Choose Use Device Fonts in the Anti-Alias menu.**

This option allows the user's system to display the text in whatever font the user defined as the default font for sans-serif text.

6. **In the Paragraph area of the Properties panel, change the area Behavior type to Multiline.**

7. **In the Instance Name field of the Properties panel, type** contents.

8. **In the Library panel, expand the For About Page folder.**

9. **Drag instances of the Thrills, Grilling, and Smoking symbols onto the Stage. Position each instance as follows:**

Thrills	X: 330	Y: 5
Smoking	X: 55	Y: 220
Grilling	X: 315	Y: 220

These objects are static images that won't change, so they can be placed as library items instead of dynamically loading items.

10. Click Frame 1 of the Content layer to select that frame.

11. Place the insertion point on Line 1 of the Actions panel Script pane. Type:

```
var externalReq:URLRequest = new URLRequest("Text/aboutus.txt");
var externalLoad:URLLoader = new URLLoader();
externalLoad.load(externalReq);
```

These three lines perform essentially the same function as the URLRequest/Loader object statements you used in the previous exercise. In this case, you use the URLLoader object instead of the Loader object because you are loading an external text file instead of an image file. (Two required import statements are automatically added to the beginning of the script.)

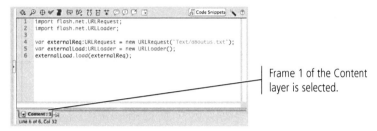

Frame 1 of the Content layer is selected.

12. On Line 8 of the Script pane, type:

```
externalLoad.addEventListener(Event.COMPLETE, textReady);
```

Like the Loader object class, the URLLoader object brings the text file into Flash. For external text files, however, you must use a custom function that triggers only when the external file is completely loaded.

This line of code adds an event listener to the external load object that you created in Line 3. The COMPLETE event triggers the custom function (textReady) when the external text file is completely loaded.

```
1  import flash.net.URLRequest;
2  import flash.net.URLLoader;
3
4  var externalReq:URLRequest = new URLRequest("Text/aboutus.txt");
5  var externalLoad:URLLoader = new URLLoader();
6  externalLoad.load(externalReq);
7
8  externalLoad.addEventListener(Event.COMPLETE, textReady);
```

13. Beginning on Line 10 of the Script pane, type the following code to define the custom textReady function:

```
function textReady(event:Event):void {
    contents.text = event.target.data;
}
```

The function body defines the text property of the dynamic text field named "contents." The right half of the statement (**event.target.data**) calls the target of the COMPLETE event (**externalLoad**) as the data of the defined text area.

```
1  import flash.net.URLRequest;
2  import flash.net.URLLoader;
3  import flash.events.Event;
4
5  var externalReq:URLRequest = new URLRequest("Text/aboutus.txt");
6  var externalLoad:URLLoader = new URLLoader();
7  externalLoad.load(externalReq);
8
9  externalLoad.addEventListener(Event.COMPLETE, textReady);
10
11 function textReady(event:Event):void {
12     contents.text = event.target.data;
13 }
```

14. Press Command-Return/Control-Enter to test the movie.

The external text file loads into the contents text area.

15. Close the Player window and return to Flash.

16. Save the file and continue to the next exercise.

 ## CREATE CUSTOM SCROLL BUTTONS

If your client had requested a simple scrollbar attached to the dynamic text field, you could have used the TextArea component or attached the UIScrollBar component to the dynamic text field. In this case, however, the client wants custom scroll buttons — triangles pointing up and down, but disconnected from the actual text area. To accomplish this task, you need to attach event listeners and custom functions to movie clip instances that serve as the Scroll Up and Scroll Down buttons.

1. With **about.fla** open and the Content layer active, drag an instance of the Arrow button symbol onto the Stage from the For About Page folder in the Library panel.

2. Using the Selection tool, position the instance to the right of the dynamic text area, aligned to the top edge of the text area.

3. In the Properties panel, type **up_btn** in the Instance Name field.

4. Drag a second instance of the Arrow button onto the Stage. Align the second instance to the bottom edge of the text area.

5. Using the Free Transform tool, rotate the second instance 180 degrees.

6. Use the Selection tool to select the second instance, and then name the rotated arrow instance **down_btn** (in the Instance Name field of the Properties panel).

7. **Click Frame 1 of the Contents layer to select it, and then place the insertion point at the end of the script in the Actions panel.**

8. **Press Return/Enter twice to move to Line 15 of the script.**

9. **Add event listeners for each arrow button instance, using the following code:**

```
up_btn.addEventListener(MouseEvent.CLICK, scrollUp);
down_btn.addEventListener(MouseEvent.CLICK, scrollDown);
```

```
12   contents.text = event.target.data;
13 }
14
15   up_btn.addEventListener(MouseEvent.CLICK, scrollUp);
16   down_btn.addEventListener(MouseEvent.CLICK, scrollDown);
```

10. **Beginning on Line 18 of the script, define the custom scrollUp function, using the following code:**

```
function scrollUp(event:MouseEvent):void {
    contents.scrollV--;
}
```

```
1    import flash.net.URLRequest;
2    import flash.net.URLLoader;
3    import flash.events.Event;
4    import flash.events.MouseEvent;
5
6    var externalReq:URLRequest = new URLRequest("text/aboutus.txt");
7    var externalLoad:URLLoader = new URLLoader();
8    externalLoad.load(externalReq);
9
10   externalLoad.addEventListener(Event.COMPLETE, textReady);
11
12   function textReady(event:Event):void {
13       contents.text = event.target.data;
14   }
15
16   up_btn.addEventListener(MouseEvent.CLICK, scrollUp);
17   down_btn.addEventListener(MouseEvent.CLICK, scrollDown);
18
19   function scrollUp(event:MouseEvent):void {
20       contents.scrollV--;
21   }
```

The import statement for the MouseEvent class is automatically added at the beginning of the script.

The scrollV property of a text field controls the vertical scrolling behavior of the text field. Using the decrement operator (--), clicking the up_btn instance moves the text up one line in the frame.

11. **Beginning on Line 23 of the script, define the custom scrollDown function, using the following code:**

```
function scrollDown(event:MouseEvent):void {
    contents.scrollV++;
}
```

```
1    import flash.net.URLRequest;
2    import flash.net.URLLoader;
3    import flash.events.Event;
4    import flash.events.MouseEvent;
5
6    var externalReq:URLRequest = new URLRequest("text/aboutus.txt");
7    var externalLoad:URLLoader = new URLLoader();
8    externalLoad.load(externalReq);
9
10   externalLoad.addEventListener(Event.COMPLETE, textReady);
11
12   function textReady(event:Event):void {
13       contents.text = event.target.data;
14   }
15
16   up_btn.addEventListener(MouseEvent.CLICK, scrollUp);
17   down_btn.addEventListener(MouseEvent.CLICK, scrollDown);
18
19   function scrollUp(event:MouseEvent):void {
20       contents.scrollV--;
21   }
22
23   function scrollDown(event:MouseEvent):void {
24       contents.scrollV++;
25   }
```

Using the increment operator (++) with the scrollV property, clicking the down_btn instance moves the text down one line in the frame.

Note:

The scrollV property essentially defines which line appears at the top of the area.

If the scrollV property equals 4, for example, the fourth line of text appears at the top of the area.

Incrementing the scrollV property adds 1, so the next line moves to the top of the area — effectively scrolling down: 4 + 1 = 5, so Line 5 would appear at the top of the area.

Decrementing the scrollV property subtracts 1, so the previous line appears at the top of the area — effectively scrolling up: 4 − 1 = 3, so Line 3 would appear at the top of the area.

12. **Press Command-Return/Control-Enter to test the movie. Click the up-arrow and down-arrow buttons to test the scrolling functionality.**

13. **Close the Player window and return to Flash.**

14. **Save the file, close it, and continue to the next exercise.**

Use the UILoader Component for External SWF Files

In this final exercise, you bring the necessary pages into the primary Seabreeze site structure. To accomplish this task, you use the built-in UILoader component, which simplifies the loading process to a single entry in the Component Parameters section of the Properties panel.

When you created the Seabreeze Home page, you manually created the necessary code to bring external images — both random and specific — into a Flash movie. We already showed you how to write this kind of code manually; now that you understand the underlying mechanism, you can better understand what happens when you use the built-in component as a shortcut.

1. **If it is not already open, open seabreeze.fla from your WIP>Seabreeze folder.**

2. **Create a new layer named Page Contents. Place the Page Contents layer between the Page Heading and Side Navigation layers in the layer stack.**

3. **Select Frame 1 of the Page Contents layer.**

4. **Open the Components panel (Window>Components), and then drag an instance of the UILoader component onto the Stage.**

5. **With the UILoader instance selected, use the Properties panel to define the loader dimensions and position as follows:**

    X: 210   Y: 175
    W: 530   H: 350

6. **Type homeContent in the Instance Name field of the Properties panel.**

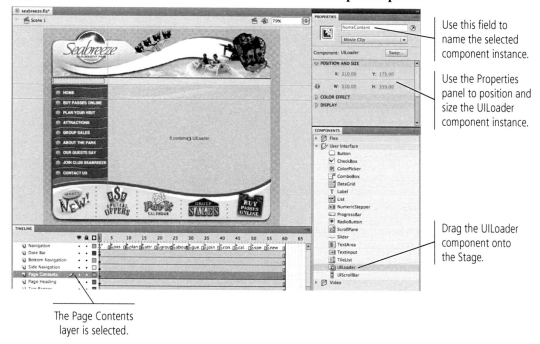

Use this field to name the selected component instance.

Use the Properties panel to position and size the UILoader component instance.

Drag the UILoader component onto the Stage.

The Page Contents layer is selected.

7. **With the UILoader instance on Frame 1 selected, uncheck the scaleContent parameter in the Properties panel.**

This parameter loads the external files at their exact sizes, instead of scaling the files to fit the defined component size.

8. **Click the source parameter field and type Children/home.swf. Press Return/Enter to finalize the entry.**

When you created the Home and About Us pages, you published the SWF files into the Children folder. We also included placeholder SWF files in this folder for the other site pages.

Uncheck this parameter.

Type in this field to define the location of the component content.

9. **Add a keyframe to Frame 5 of the Page Contents layer.**

10. **With the Frame 5 keyframe selected, select the UILoader instance on the Stage.**

11. In the Properties panel, change the instance name to pageContent, and then change the Y position of the UILoader component to 230.

For the Home page, the external SWF file fills the entire central area, including the space used for the page title on other pages. To show the page title (and background graphic) for all pages but the Home page, you are simply moving the UILoader instance down far enough so it doesn't obscure the dynamic text area where the page title is placed.

You are also assigning a separate name to the UILoader instance on Frame 5 because Flash has a difficult time managing multiple unnamed UILoaders on the same Stage. If you don't change the instance name for the Frame 5 instance, the UILoader on Frame 5 will not reflect the new Y position in the final SWF movie.

12. With the UILoader instance on Frame 5 selected, change the source parameter to Children/passes.swf.

Because you added the Frame 5 keyframe after defining the UILoader scaleContent parameter, that parameter is maintained in the new keyframe on Frame 5. You only need to change the source path for the component instance on each new keyframe of the Page Contents layer.

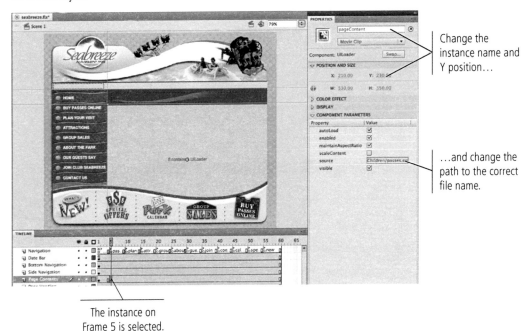

Change the instance name and Y position...

...and change the path to the correct file name.

The instance on Frame 5 is selected.

13. **Add keyframes to the Page Contents layer for each page of the site, select the UILoader instance on the Stage, and then change the source parameter of the UILoader component to the appropriate SWF file:**

When you select the instance for each keyframe, click near the top of the instance to select it. If you click near the bottom, you might select the bottom graphic instead of the component instance.

In this case, you don't need to change the UILoader instance name for these frames because you haven't changed the physical properties of the UILoader.

Frame Number	Source Parameter
Frame 10	Children/plan.swf
Frame 15	Children/attractions.swf
Frame 20	Children/group.swf
Frame 25	Children/about.swf
Frame 30	Children/guests.swf
Frame 35	Children/join.swf
Frame 40	Children/contact.swf
Frame 45	Children/calendar.swf
Frame 50	Children/specials.swf
Frame 55	Children/new.swf

Each keyframe on the Page Contents layer defines a different source parameter for the UILoader component.

14. **Press Command-Return/Control-Enter to test the movie.**

The Output panel appears, indicating that I/O errors have occurred (URL not found).

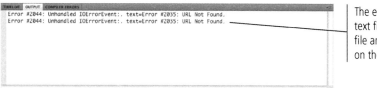

The external image and text files in the home.swf file are not available based on the defined paths.

You loaded an external SWF file into the primary site structure, and that file (home.swf on Frame 1) calls for other external files. When you built and tested the home.fla file, the external images loaded properly because they were in the correct position relative to the file that called them:

seabreeze.fla	calls home.swf	which calls homeN.jpg and circles.png from the Images folder

When home.swf loads into the primary site structure, the relative image paths in the home.swf file map from the primary site instead of the location of the child pages. In other words, you need to move the Images and Text folders to the same location as the seabreeze.fla file.

15. **On your desktop, open the WIP>Seabreeze>Children folder. Copy the Images and Text folders from the Children folder and paste them into the primary Seabreeze folder.**

If you simply move the Images and Text folders, you will receive error messages when you open and test the home.fla and about.fla files. The Images and Text folders need to be in both locations for development and test purposes (although you do not need to upload the Children/Images and Children/Text folders onto the Web server).

The Images and Text folders should appear in the primary Seabreeze folder and in the Children folder.

16. **In Flash, press Command-Return/Control-Enter to test the movie again. Click the Home and About the Park buttons to test the UILoader functionality.**

17. **Close the Player window and return to Flash.**

18. **Save the Flash file and close it.**

1. A(n) _____ in the timeline indicates that a frame has a defined text label.

2. A(n) _____ conditional statement can be used to define different actions for a single event within the same function.

3. The _____ function returns a number from 0 to 6, which corresponds to the days of the week.

4. The _____ function returns a number from 0 to 11, which corresponds to the 12 months of the year.

5. When creating a loader, the _____ object identifies the path to a specific image file.

6. The _____ method places the defined Loader object (the external file) in the movie (technically called "adding to the display list").

7. The _____ object class is used to bring external text or XML files into a Flash movie.

8. The _____ event triggers a function when the external file is completely loaded.

9. The _____ property of a text field controls the vertical scrolling behavior of the field.

10. The _____ component can be used to import external content based on parameters defined in the Properties panel.

1. Briefly explain the process of using frames to build site navigation.

2. Briefly explain how arrays are used to create a dynamic date in a Flash movie.

3. Briefly explain two different methods for adding external images to a Flash movie.

Portfolio Builder Project

Use what you learned in this project to complete the following freeform exercise.
Carefully read the art director and client comments, then create your own design to meet the needs of the project.
Use the space below to sketch ideas; when finished, write a brief explanation of your reasoning behind your final design.

art director comments

Every professional Flash designer or developer needs a portfolio to display their work to prospective clients. If you have completed the projects in this book, you now have a number of different examples to show off your skills using Flash CS5.

The eight projects in this book were specifically designed to include a wide variety of skills and techniques, as well as different types of movies for different types of clients. Your portfolio should follow the same basic principle, offering a variety of samples of both creative and technical skills.

client comments

For this project, you are your own client. Using the following suggestions, gather your work and create your own portfolio.

❏ If possible, get your own domain name to host your portfolio site. If you can't get a personal domain name, use a free subdomain name from an established server company. (If you use a subdomain or a free host, look for one where external ads are not added to your pages.)

❏ Include sample movies that you have created, including those that you completed for this book or for other clients.

❏ If you can't include links to certain files, take screen shots and post those on your own site.

❏ For each sample you include, add a brief description or explanation of your role in the job. (Did you design it? What techniques were used to build the movie?)

❏ Be sure to include full contact information in a prominent location on your site.

project justification

_____
_____
_____
_____
_____
_____
_____
_____
_____
_____
_____
_____
_____
_____
_____

Project Summary

To complete this project, you used named frames to establish the framework of the site navigation, where each button on the page links to a specific frame using the gotoAndStop function. This type of navigation is common for complex files; by naming the individual frames, you don't need to remember which frame number goes with which site page.

This project incorporated a number of techniques for importing external files — images, text, and entire Flash movies — into a Flash file. You should now understand how to use ActionScript to incorporate external objects, as well as how to use built-in Flash components that simplify the import process.

Create a date object to read a user's system information

Define frames and labels to represent each page in the site

Use a conditional statement to link buttons to representative frames

Load a random image onto the Stage

Add an object to the display list

Change properties of a specific display object

Load external SWF files into a Flash file

Change page titles based on the active switch case

Load an external text file into a Flash movie

Create custom scroll buttons for a dynamic text field

--. *See* decrement operator
++. *See* increment operator
==. *See* equality operator
3D animation   205–207
3D Rotation tool   205

A

absolute path   244
Actions panel   218, 242–247, 352, 356
Actions toolbox   243, 245, 246, 248
ActionScript   151, 155, 160, 216–218, 233–253, 263, 302, 346, 347, 350
Add Anchor Point tool   32, 38
Add Classic Motion Guide   135, 142
addChild   383–387
addEventListener   255
addItem   353
addition operator   262
Adobe Bridge   160
Adobe Illustrator   20, 76–80, 169, 291
Adobe Media Encoder   335–341
Adobe Photoshop   20, 167–169, 177
ADPCM compression   112
AIFF format   94
Align panel   23, 91, 173
align property   349, 363
align to stage   23, 91, 172
allowMultipleSelection parameter   355
alpha value   58–59, 122, 125, 202, 203, 338, 386
anchor points   37–45, 189, 191
anti-aliasing   147
Application bar   9
Application frame   16
apply block comment   243
apply line comment   243
arguments   242
armature   209–212
array   264–267–270, 380
artboard   79–81, 291
assignment operator   259
audio (AU) format   94
audio event   160
audio stream   160
auto-collapse icon panels   3
auto format   243, 273
auto kern   147
autoPlay parameter   348, 349
AVI format   158, 335
axis overlay   205

B

background color   120, 341
background property   386
backgroundColor property   386
Behaviors panel   155–158
Bézier curves   47, 191
bit rate   112, 339
bitmap   21
bitrate encoding   338
blank keyframe   293, 295, 305
blend   133
block comment   316
blockIndent property   363
blur   204
bold property   363
Bone tool   207–209
boolean value   252, 259
border property   386
borderColor property   386
bounding box   26, 46, 50
braces   242, 257, 258, 312
break apart   40, 51, 129, 154
bring to front   321
Brush tool   61–62
Button component   347
button symbols   85–88, 151–154, 292, 300–309
buttonMode   278

C

case sensitivity   249, 255, 328, 353
CHANGE event   358
channels   99
check syntax   243
CheckBox component   347
classes   241, 243
classic motion guide   135, 142
classic text   144, 156
classic tween   138
classic tweening   130
clear guides   50
clear keyframe   299
click accuracy   25
CLICK event   255, 274, 312, 323
cloning   58
close path   45
code hints   243, 256, 260
Code Snippets panel   217–226
codec   335, 338
collapse between braces   243

collapse selection   243
color effects   202
Color panel   64, 122
color property   363
ColorPicker component   347
columnCount parameter   355
columnWidth parameter   354, 355
ComboBox component   347
comments   243, 316
common libraries   152
Compiler Errors panel   328
COMPLETE event   389
component parameters   348–352, 355
Components panel   350
compress movie   160
compression   94, 335
condenseWhite parameter   350
conditional statement   269, 270, 313, 327, 375
connect lines   25
constant bitrate   338
constraining   178
contextual menu   3
Controller panel   16
Convert Anchor Point tool   32, 38
convert layers to   78, 290
convert lines to fills   60
convert to symbol   82–85, 124, 126, 131, 173–177, 185, 291, 292
copy frames   193, 212
corner point   32, 35
corner radius   45
create classic tween   138
create motion tween   186, 197, 202, 236, 304
create movie clip   80
crop options   340
cuePoints parameter   349
curve point   32
customize Tools panel   8

D

data types   259, 260, 268
DataGrid component   347
dataProvider parameter   352, 355
date object   379–382
debug options   243
decrement operator   266, 391
Delete Anchor Point tool   32, 38
delete envelope   175
destructive editing   27, 39–42, 128, 134
detect Flash version   161

device font   161
direction parameter   355
display list   384–387
display menu   161
distort   175
do while loop   266
dock   3–6
Document Settings dialog box   22, 120, 341
document tab   12, 16
dot syntax   241
down frame/state   85, 101
Drawing preferences   25
drop zone   6
duplicate selection and transform   175
dynamic text   144, 301–303, 324, 377, 379, 388

E

easing   133, 190
Edit bar   27, 88, 89, 177, 178, 184, 201, 207, 208, 211, 237, 300, 301, 309
edit envelope   98–99, 102–104
edit in new window   89
edit in place   86, 89, 208
Edit mode   27, 40, 51
edit multiple frames   188
editable parameter   350
editable paths   80
editable text   80
effects   201–204
embed FLV in SWF and play in timeline   343
embedded video   342
embedding fonts   149–150
enable JPEG deblocking   160
enable simple buttons   87, 88, 92, 100
enabled parameter   350, 355
encoding passes   339
end angle   45
envelope   175
EPS format   20
equality operator   272
event handler   221–226, 256
event listener   221, 241, 312, 321, 327, 356, 389, 391
event sounds   96–98, 100, 101
EventDispatcher   255, 322
events   241
exclude objects outside artboard   80
expand all   243
expand fill   129
export device sounds   160
export for ActionScript   280
export image   69, 159
export movie   158, 159
Export Settings dialog box   337–341
export SWC   160

F

F4V format   338, 339
field order   338
file weight   75
fill color   26, 28, 53, 59, 63, 121
filters   201–204
finish video import   345
fit in window   13, 120, 234
FLA format   16, 20, 159
Flash alignment   161
Flash Player   16, 20, 97, 105, 138, 159–161, 328, 339
flip horizontal   175, 195
flip vertical   175
floating panel   4
FLV format   338, 339
FLVPlayback component   343–349, 356, 358, 382
font property   363
fonts   147, 149
for each...in loop   267
for...in loop   267–270
for loop   266, 271–273
FPS. *See* frame rate
frame animation   182–184
frame labels   371–373, 376
frame rate   104, 119, 120, 289, 338, 341
frame width   340
frames   13, 139, 141, 142, 186, 236, 237, 305, 342
frames per second. *See* frame rate
Free Transform mode   45, 46, 125, 174–177, 197, 320, 390
function body   221
function name   221
functions   241–246, 312, 321

G

General preferences   2, 8, 43
generate size report   160
getDate   380
getDay   380
getFullYear   380
getMonth   380
GIF format   20, 158, 159, 382
goto and stop at frame or label   156, 157
gotoAndPlay   248–250, 313
Gradient Transform tool   65–67
gradients   63–67, 121–122
graphic symbol   200
grids   43
groups   26, 50–53, 80, 180
guide layer   135–139, 142
guides   43, 50, 307–308

H

Hand tool   14
handles   37–45, 189
hardware acceleration   161
height property   386
hiding layers   39
hinting   29, 194
hit frame   85, 87–88
horizontalLineScrollSize parameter   355
horizontalPageScrollSize parameter   355
horizontalScrollPolicy parameter   350
hot spot   85
HTML   159–161, 371
HTML alignment   161
htmlText parameter   350

I

if   269–270
if else   271–273, 314, 327
IK nodes   208
import   257
import as bitmap   80
import as mobile device video bundled in SWF   343
import hidden layers   80
import image layers as   168
import paths as   80
import shape layers as   168
import text as   80
import text layers as   168
import to library   20, 81, 123
import to Stage   20, 76–80, 95, 168–169, 290
import video   20, 343–347
include hidden layers   160
include XMP metadata   160
increment operator   266, 314, 391
indent property   363
index   246
index value   264–270
Info dialog box   354
initializing   268
Ink Bottle tool   56–58
inner radius   45
input text   144
insert blank keyframe   106, 305
insert frame   196
insert keyframe   86, 87, 137, 183, 300
insert target path   222, 243, 244, 251, 324
instance names   151–152, 216, 235, 258, 292, 302, 304, 309, 346
instances   75, 174, 185, 216
integer   259
inverse kinematics   207
isLive parameter   349
italic property   363
iteration   266, 269

J

JavaScript   159
JPEG format   20, 158, 159, 382
JPEG quality   160

K

kerning property   363
keyboard shortcuts   8, 11, 14
KeyEvent   255
keyframes   13, 78, 86, 104, 110, 137, 143, 183, 185, 186, 191, 236, 237, 262, 297, 299

L

Label component   347
language elements   252, 256
Layer Properties dialog box   108
layers   13, 24, 27, 39, 68, 78, 80, 134, 169, 242, 245
   folders   68
   groups   168
   locking   20
leading property   363
leftMargin property   363
letter spacing   147
letterSpacing property   363
Library panel   12, 75, 76, 80–88, 92–95, 140–141, 152, 170–171, 176, 180–182, 185, 216, 234, 279
line comment   316
Line tool   28–30
linkage   280
lip syncing   107–116
List component   347
load external video with Playback component   343, 344
Loader object   382–384, 389
local playback security   161
lock fill   67
looping   98, 104, 107, 161, 247–250, 266–278, 310

M

masks   123–129, 306–310
match movie   161
Math.ceil   261, 313, 385
Math.random   261, 313, 385
maxChars parameter   350
Menu bar   9
menus   11
merged bitmaps   168
methods   241
modify onion markers   188
Motion Editor panel   135, 196–207

motion guide layer   135
motion presets   192
motion tweens   130–143, 138, 197–208, 242
Mouse.hide   319
Mouse.show   319
MOUSE_DOWN event   322
MOUSE_UP event   322, 375
MouseEvent   255, 257
MOV format   158
movie clip   124, 126, 141–144, 182–185, 200, 201, 236, 244, 292, 293
movie clip registration   80
MovieClip(parent)   325
Moving Pictures Experts Group   335
MP3 compression   112
MP3 format   94, 335

N

named instances. *See* instance names
nested tools   8
new document   19
new symbol   207, 303
new workspace   9
non-roving keyframe   191
not_yet_set   246, 322
null   259
number   259, 260
NumericStepper component   347

O

object-drawing mode   27, 31, 40, 50, 125
omit trace options   160
On Press event   157
On Release event   157
onion skinning   188
open   12
open external library   20, 171
orient to path   133
Output panel   315, 316, 395
Oval tool   43–47, 121, 131
over frame   85, 86, 91, 101, 300, 301
override sound settings   160
overset text icon   145

P

packages   241
paint behind   61
Paint Bucket tool   54–55
paint fills   61
paint inside   61
paint selection   61
panel dock. *See* dock
panel groups   4, 7
panel tabs   5

panels
   Align   23, 91, 173
   Code Snippets   217–226
   Color   64, 122
   Compiler Errors   328
   Components   350
   Controller   16
   Library   12, 75, 76, 80–88, 92–95, 140–141, 152, 170–171, 176, 180–182, 185, 216, 234, 279
   Motion Editor   135, 196–207
   Output   315, 316, 395
   Properties   12, 15, 21, 28, 45, 83, 91, 96, 98, 100, 120, 121, 131, 133, 142, 145, 147–148, 151, 154, 174, 179, 192, 202, 216, 235, 276, 289, 345, 350, 355, 372, 388, 392
   Timeline   13, 24–28, 68
   Tools   8, 11, 26, 27
   Transform   175, 176, 211
paragraph alignment   147
parameters   242
parent timeline   130
password   161
paste frames   193, 213
paste in place   42, 45, 49, 62, 135, 142, 295
paused at start   161
Pen tool   25, 32–38, 47
Pencil tool   47–50
permit debugging   161
place objects at original position   81, 290
playhead   13, 15, 104–106, 108, 110, 111, 184, 282
PNG format   158, 382
preferences   2, 11
   Drawing   25
   General   2, 8, 43
   User Interface   3
preview   349
ProgressBar component   347, 355
progressive download   104, 342
Properties dialog box   354
Properties panel   12, 15, 21, 28, 45, 83, 91, 96, 98, 100, 120, 121, 131, 133, 142, 145, 147–148, 151, 154, 174, 179, 192, 202, 216, 235, 276, 289, 345, 350, 355, 372, 388, 392
protect from import   160
PSD File Importer preferences   167, 168
publish   159
publish settings   155, 159–161, 168, 364

Q

quality   161, 339
QuickTime (MOV) format   94, 159, 335

R

RadioButton component   347
random numbers   260–263, 313, 385
raw sound   112
Real Media Players   335
RealVideo   335
recognize lines   25
recognize shapes   25
Rectangle tool   45, 88
registration   80, 83
relative path   244
remove comment   243
remove frames   215, 299
remove transform   175
remove tween   214
removeEventListener function   322
repeat   96
restrict parameter   350
return type   242, 257, 275
reverse keyframes   195
rightMargin property   363
RM format   335
rotate and skew   175
rotation   133
rotation property   386
roving keyframes   191
rowCount parameter   355
rowHeight parameter   354, 355
rulers   43, 306

S

sample rate   112, 113
save as   20
saved workspaces   2, 9–11
scale   133, 161, 175
scale and rotate   175
scaleContent parameter   393, 394
scaleMode parameter   348, 349
scaleX property   386
scaleY property   386
scene   89
scientific data   119
script   160
Script navigator   243
Script pane   272
script time limit   161
scrollH property   386
ScrollPane component   347, 352
scrollPolicy parameter   352, 355
scrollV property   386, 391
scrubbing   15, 108, 184
select all   209
selectable property   386

Selection tool   15, 26, 27, 31, 37, 40, 41, 50, 51, 129, 135, 147, 189
semicolon   255
send to back   128, 151
sequences   158
set key frame distance   339
set Stage size to same size as Illustrator artboard   81, 290
set Stage size to same size as Photoshop canvas   169
shape hinting   194
shape layers   168
shape tween   133, 194
show all   233
show code hint   243
show import dialog box   80
show pen preview   25
show precise colors   25
show solid points   25
show warning messages   161
simple profile   339
size property   363
skinAutoHide parameter   349
skinBackgroundAlpha parameter   348, 349
skinBackgroundColor parameter   348, 349
skins   344, 348, 349, 359–361
Slider component   347
smooth curves   25
snap to objects   29, 30, 136
snapping   29, 43, 125, 133, 136
soften fill edges   60
sound   94–103, 279–284
sound compression   111–113
sound properties   112–113, 279
source parameter   349, 395
spatial compression   335
speech compression   112, 113
Spray Brush tool   178–180
stacking order   24, 54, 321
Stage   16, 19, 22, 27, 79, 81, 82, 89, 95, 106, 119, 120, 124, 176, 177, 183, 187, 234, 291
standard-drawing mode   26, 40
start angle   45
start sync option   101
startDrag function   318
states   85
static text   144–148
stop function   245, 311
stop sync option   101
stopDrag function   319
stream sounds   104, 282
stream sync option   105
streaming video   343
strings   259, 262, 272, 385
stroke   26
stroke color   28, 53

stroke weight   29
StyleManager class   362
Subselection tool   32, 37–39, 41, 80, 189
swap symbol   109, 110
Swatches palette   28, 122
SWF format   16, 20, 144, 158, 159, 161, 342, 343, 352, 382, 387, 393, 395
switch case   374–379
switch keyframes to roving   191
symbol editing mode   89, 176
symbol properties   88–90
symbol registration point   83, 84, 90–92, 127, 131, 176, 177, 202, 207, 213, 217, 293, 303, 320
symbol Stage   134, 176
symbols   75–94
symmetrical point   35
sync option   133
syntax   241, 244, 273
syntax errors   273

T

templates   161
temporal compression   335
test movie   16
text   144–150, 387–390
text layout framework (TLF) text   144, 156
text parameter   350
text properties   362–363, 386
Text tool   80, 144–148, 153, 301, 377, 379, 388
TextArea component   347, 350–351, 358
textColor property   386
TextInput component   347
TIF format   20
TileList component   347, 351–357
time in control bar   102, 103
time out control bar   103
timeline   24, 81, 86, 89, 105-106, 125, 130, 134, 139, 151, 180, 183, 184, 187, 218, 220, 234, 238, 242, 245, 294, 305, 342, 343
Timeline panel   13, 24–28, 68
tool tip   8
tools
    3D Rotation   205
    Add Anchor Point   32, 38
    Bone   207–209
    Convert Anchor Point   32, 38
    Delete Anchor Point   32, 38
    Gradient Transform   65–67
    Hand   14
    Ink Bottle   56–58
    Line   28–30
    Oval   43–47, 121, 131

Paint Bucket   *54–55*

Pen   *25, 32–38, 47*

Pencil   *47–50*

Rectangle   *45, 88*

Selection   *15, 26, 27, 31, 37, 40, 41, 50, 51, 129, 135, 147, 189*

Spray Brush   *178–180*

Subselection   *32, 37–39, 41, 80, 189*

Text   *80, 144–148, 153, 301, 377, 379, 388*

Zoom   *14*

Tools panel   8, 11, 26, 27

trace   160, 315–317

transformation registration point   45, 47, 49, 174, 320

transform options   175

Transform panel   175, 176, 211

transparency   58, 121–122, 348

tweening   130, 138, 185–187

U

UILoader component   347, 392–399

UIScrollBar component   347

underline property   363

undershoot   339

ungroup   51

unsigned integer   259

up state   85

URLLoader   387–390

URLRequest   383, 385

user interface   1–16

User Interface components   347

User Interface preferences   3

V

variable bitrate   338

variables   259–265, 268, 313, 323

vector art   21

vector outlines   80

verticalLineScrollSize parameter   355

verticalPageScrollSize parameter   355

verticalScrollPolicy parameter   350

video   335–346

View menu   14

view percentage   13, 14

visible parameter   350, 355

visible property   251–252, 275, 386

void   242, 257, 259, 275

volume parameter   349

W

waveform   99, 108

WAV format   94, 158

welcome screen   2

while loop   266

width property   386

Window menu   6, 23

window mode   161

Windows Media Player   335

WMV format   335

word wrap   356

wordWrap property   350, 386

Workspace switcher   2, 9, 10

workspaces   2

X

x axis   205

x position   92, 177

x property   386

XML   387

Y

y axis   205

y position   92

y property   386

Z

z axis   205

Zoom tool   14

Use our portfolio to build yours.

The Against The Clock Professional Portfolio Series walks you step-by-step through the tools and techniques of graphic design professionals.

Order online at www.againsttheclock.com
Use code **PFS710** for a 10% discount

Go to **www.againsttheclock.com** to enter our monthly drawing for a free book of your choice.